Intelligent Cybersecurity and Resilience for Critical Industries: Challenges and Applications

RIVER PUBLISHERS SERIES IN DIGITAL SECURITY AND FORENSICS

Series Editors:

ANAND R. PRASAD
Deloitte Tohmatsu Cyber LLC , Japan

R. CHANDRAMOULI
Stevens Institute of Technology, USA

ABDERRAHIM BENSLIMANE
University of Avignon, France

PETER LANGENDÖRFER
IHP, Germany

The "River Publishers Series in Security and Digital Forensics" is a series of comprehensive academic and professional books which focus on the theory and applications of Cyber Security, including Data Security, Mobile and Network Security, Cryptography and Digital Forensics. Topics in Prevention and Threat Management are also included in the scope of the book series, as are general business Standards in this domain.

Books published in the series include research monographs, edited volumes, handbooks and textbooks. The books provide professionals, researchers, educators, and advanced students in the field with an invaluable insight into the latest research and developments.

Topics covered in the series include-

- Blockchain for secure transactions
- Cryptography
- Cyber Security
- Data and App Security
- Digital Forensics
- Hardware Security
- IoT Security
- Mobile Security
- Network Security
- Privacy
- Software Security
- Standardization
- Threat Management

For a list of other books in this series, visit www.riverpublishers.com

Intelligent Cybersecurity and Resilience for Critical Industries: Challenges and Applications

Editors

Mounia Zaydi
ICL, Junia, Université catholique de Lille, LITL (Lille Interdisciplinary Transitions Laboratory), 59000, France

Yassine Maleh
Sultan Moulay Slimane University, Beni Mellal, Morocco

Gabriel Chênevert
ICL, Junia, Université catholique de Lille, LITL (Lille Interdisciplinary Transitions Laboratory), 59000, France

Hayat Zaydi
National Superior School of Mines (ENSMR), Rabat, Morocco

Amina El Yaagoubi
ICL, Junia, Université catholique de Lille, LITL (Lille Interdisciplinary Transitions Laboratory), 59000, France

NEW YORK AND LONDON

Published 2025 by River Publishers
River Publishers
Alsbjergvej 10, 9260 Gistrup, Denmark
www.riverpublishers.com

Distributed exclusively by Routledge
605 Third Avenue, New York, NY 10017, USA
4 Park Square, Milton Park, Abingdon, Oxon OX14 4RN

Intelligent Cybersecurity and Resilience for Critical Industries: Challenges and Applications / by Mounia Zaydi, Yassine Maleh, Gabriel Chênevert, Hayat Zaydi, Amina El Yaagoubi.

© 2025 River Publishers. All rights reserved. No part of this publication may be reproduced, stored in a retrieval systems, or transmitted in any form or by any means, mechanical, photocopying, recording or otherwise, without prior written permission of the publishers.

Routledge is an imprint of the Taylor & Francis Group, an informa business

ISBN 978-87-7004-226-0 (hardback)
ISBN 978-87-7004-783-8 (paperback)
ISBN 978-87-7004-775-3 (online)
ISBN 978-87-7004-774-6 (master ebook)
DOI 10.1201/9788770047746

While every effort is made to provide dependable information, the publisher, authors, and editors cannot be held responsible for any errors or omissions.

Contents

Preface   xv

List of Figures   xix

List of Tables   xxiii

List of Contributors   xxv

List of Abbreviations   xxix

Introduction   1

Part I: Intelligent Cybersecurity and Resilience: Challenges and Applications   5

1 AI-driven Threat Management in Healthcare Systems   7
Ismaila S. Y., Birahime Diouf, Abdou Khadre Diop, Cyril Drocourt, and David Durand

1.1 Introduction 8
1.2 The Internet of Medical Things (IoMT) 10
     1.2.1 IoMT applications 11
     1.2.2 IoMT challenges 13
     1.2.3 Critical implications of attacks on connected medical devices 14
1.3 Securing Healthcare Systems: Ensuring Patient Safety and Data Integrity 15
1.4 Exploring Existing Insights: Navigating the Landscape of Security in IoMT 16
     1.4.1 Deep learning approaches 16
     1.4.2 Security threat identification 17
     1.4.3 Transfer learning for IoT attacks detection 17

		1.4.4	Generative adversarial networks (GANs) for cyber threats	17
		1.4.5	Deep belief networks (DBNs) for anomaly detection	17
	1.5	Methodological Framework for Securing IoT in Healthcare Systems		18
		1.5.1	Dataset selection and characteristics	18
		1.5.2	Deep learning-based attack detection solution	20
		1.5.3	Unveiling insights: Results and discussions	22
			1.5.3.1 Binary classification	22
			1.5.3.2 Multi-class classification	24
	1.6	Conclusion		29

2 Practical Use of AI for Cyber Risk Management in Critical Infrastructures: A Review — 33

Jean Bertholat, Myriam Merad, Johann Barbier, and Jules Clerc

	2.1	Introduction		34
	2.2	Tackling Cybersecurity Problems Based on Risk Problems Approaches		36
		2.2.1	Motivations	36
		2.2.2	Definitions analysis	36
		2.2.3	Bibliometric analysis	40
		2.2.4	Main Conclusions at this stage	49
	2.3	Review of How AI Is used and Mobilized in Risk Management Processes		50
		2.3.1	Methodology	51
		2.3.2	Documents selection	52
		2.3.3	Results	54
			2.3.3.1 Scope, context, and criteria	56
			2.3.3.2 Risk identifications	57
			2.3.3.3 Risk analysis and risk evaluation	57
			2.3.3.4 Risk treatment	57
	2.4	Discussion		58
		2.4.1	Potential analysis bias and limitations	59
	2.5	Conclusion and Perspectives		59

3 Fraud Detection in Decentralized Autonomous Organization (DAO) with Machine Learning — 69

Aderonke Favour-Betty Thompson, Bukola Abimbola Onyekwelu, and Samson Nsikan Obong

	3.1	Introduction		70

3.2	Related Works		72
3.3	Methodology		78
	3.3.1	Data collection	78
	3.3.2	Data preprocessing	79
		3.3.2.1 Class imbalance	79
		3.3.2.2 Feature scaling	81
	3.3.3	Data Modeling	81
		3.3.3.1 Training data and fitting the model/ algorithm	85
	3.3.4	Improving the models (hyperparameter tuning)	85
	3.3.5	Evaluating the models	86
	3.3.6	Model deployment	89
3.4	Results and Discussions		89
	3.4.1	Results	89
		3.4.1.1 Fitting and evaluating selected models	89
		3.4.1.2 Improving the models by hyperparameter tuning	90
		3.4.1.3 Making predictions with the tuned models	90
		3.4.1.4 Model evaluation	92
	3.4.2	Discussions	96
3.5	Conclusion		97

4 Improving Machine Learning Performance using Sampling Techniques for COVID-19 Imbalanced Data — 103
Sokaina El Khamlichi and Loubna Taidi

4.1	Introduction		104
4.2	Related Work		105
4.3	Background		107
	4.3.1	Oversampling and undersampling techniques	107
		4.3.1.1 Oversampling techniques	107
		4.3.1.2 Undersampling approaches	108
4.4	Machine Learning Models		109
	4.4.1	k-nearest neighbors algorithm	109
	4.4.2	Decision tree	109
	4.4.3	Logistic regression	110
	4.4.4	Gradient naïve Bayes	110
	4.4.5	Random forest	110
4.5	Evaluation Metrics		110
	4.5.1	Accuracy	111

viii *Contents*

        4.5.2   Precision 111
        4.5.3   Recall 111
        4.5.4   F1-score 112
        4.5.5   ROC_AUC 112
        4.5.6   Average precision 112
  4.6   Data and Methods 113
        4.6.1   Data description 113
        4.6.2   Proposed solution 113
  4.7   Results 115
        4.7.1   Balancing data with ADASYN 115
        4.7.2   Balancing data with SMOTE technique 116
        4.7.3   Balancing data with RUS technique 116
  4.8   Discussion 116
  4.9   Conclusion 118

Part II: Cybersecurity Challenges and Resilience in Healthcare and Industrial Domains   123

5 Penetration Testing in Operations Technology and SCADA Environments   125
Yassine Maleh and Mounia Zaydi

  5.1   Introduction 126
  5.2   Methodology 127
  5.3   Implementation and Experiments 128
        5.3.1   Implementation of the test environment 128
                5.3.1.1   Installation of OpenPLC and ScadaBR . . 130
                5.3.1.2   Installation of OpenPLC in VM2 130
                5.3.1.3   Installation of ScadaBR in MV3 131
                5.3.1.4   Downloading and installing FactoryIO . . 133
                5.3.1.5   Physical process simulation – scene 134
                5.3.1.6   Simulation RTU – driver 135
                5.3.1.7   Integrating OpenPLC with FactoryIO . . . 137
                5.3.1.8   Programming control logic 138
  5.4   Pentesting OT 141
        5.4.1   Information gathering 141
                5.4.1.1   Assessment of the Shodan public subnet . 141
  5.5   Discovering Vulnerabilities 144
        5.5.1   Dissection of OpenPLC communications 144

	5.5.2	Traffic capture	145
	5.5.3	Network traffic capture with Wireshark	146
		5.5.3.1 Analysis of captures	146
		5.5.3.2 Communication loop analysis	146
	5.5.4	Analysis of Modbus TCP requests and responses	147
		5.5.4.1 Reading inputs	147
		5.5.4.2 Writing coils	148
		5.5.4.3 Network mapping of Grassmarlin	149
5.6	Modbus TCP Packet Injection with Scapy		151
	5.6.1	Configuring the IP and TCP layers	153
	5.6.2	Implementation and configuration of Modbus and Modbus TCP layers	155
	5.6.3	Packet injection	156
5.7	Results		156
5.8	Conclusion		158

6 Cyberattacks in Healthcare: Analyzing Recent Trends and Preventive Measures — 161
Seidi Sanae, Jabari Khawla, Moussaid Hind, and Abdellaoui Abderrahim

6.1	Introduction		161
6.2	Security Issues in Healthcare		162
6.3	Types of Cyberattacks in Healthcare		163
	6.3.1	Malware	163
	6.3.2	Ransomware	164
		6.3.2.1 General ransomware attack operation	165
		6.3.2.2 Common methods of ransomware infection in the healthcare sector	166
		6.3.2.3 Case studies of ransomware attacks in the healthcare sector	168
	6.3.3	Phishing	169
		6.3.3.1 Phishing simulation in healthcare: A case study	170
	6.3.4	Distributed Denial of Service (DDoS)	171
		6.3.4.1 DOS/DDOS attacks	171
		6.3.4.2 Methods of Distributed Denial of Service attacks	172
		6.3.4.3 DDoS attacks in eHealth concept	173
		6.3.4.4 DDoS attack for COVID-19 pandemic	174

x *Contents*

6.4	Prevention of Cyberattacks in Healthcare		175
6.5	The Consequences of Cyberattacks in the Healthcare Sector		176
	6.5.1	Loss or alteration of medical data	176
	6.5.2	Consequences of phishing attacks	177
	6.5.3	Examination of the different forms of cyberattacks that can disrupt operations and health services	178
	6.5.4	Consequences of Distributed Denial of Service (DDoS) attacks	179
	6.5.5	Impacts of cyberattacks in the healthcare sector on reputation and financial costs	179
6.6	Conclusion		181

7 Enhancing Cyber Resilience: A Study of Red Teaming within Operational Technology Domains — **187**
Mounia Zaydi and Yassine Maleh

7.1	Introduction		188
7.2	Background and Related Works		189
7.3	Methodology		191
	7.3.1	Adversary-centric security testing preparation	191
	7.3.2	Frameworks for adversary-centric security testing	192
	7.3.3	Technical depth in adversary-centric testing	192
	7.3.4	Considerations for IT and OT systems	193
7.4	Experiments		193
	7.4.1	Setting up the virtual architecture	193
		7.4.1.1 Integration of OpenPLC with FactoryIO	195
		7.4.1.2 Programming the control logic	196
	7.4.2	Launching a red team campaign for ICS/OIT environment	197
		7.4.2.1 Essential elements and technologies in red teaming	198
	7.4.3	Threat intelligence platforms	198
		7.4.3.1 Red team engagements	199
	7.4.4	Engagement documentation	199
	7.4.5	Operation OT down	199
		7.4.5.1 Caldera	200
		7.4.5.2 Unpacking Caldera	200
		7.4.5.3 Tactics and techniques used in operation OT Down	203
		7.4.5.4 Initial access	203
		7.4.5.5 Command and control establishment	204

		7.4.5.6	Operation guidelines	204
		7.4.5.7	Operation guidelines	205
7.5	Discussion			206
7.6	Conclusion			207

8 Demystifying the Role of Publicly Available Up-to-Date Benchmark Intrusion Datasets: A Case Study of Web Security 211
Oumaima Chakir and Yassine Sadqi

8.1	Introduction		212
8.2	Web Application Security		213
	8.2.1	Broken access control (A01)	214
	8.2.2	Cryptographic failures (A02)	214
	8.2.3	Injection (A03)	215
	8.2.4	Insecure design (A04)	215
	8.2.5	Security misconfiguration (A05)	215
	8.2.6	Vulnerable and outdated components (A06)	215
	8.2.7	Identification and authentication failures (A07) . . .	216
	8.2.8	Software and data integrity failures (A08)	216
	8.2.9	Security logging and monitoring failures (A09) . . .	216
	8.2.10	Server-side request forgery (SSRF) (A10)	217
8.3	Related Work		217
8.4	Benchmark Datasets and ML-based WAF's Effectiveness . .		218
8.5	Evaluation Metrics		220
	8.5.1	System's overall performance evaluation	220
	8.5.2	System's detection ability evaluation	221
		8.5.2.1 Attack detection ability evaluation	221
		8.5.2.2 Normal detection ability evaluation	222
	8.5.3	System's availability evaluation	222
8.6	Publicly Available Benchmarking Datasets and Web Security		222
	8.6.1	ECML/PKDD 2007	222
	8.6.2	HTTP CSIC 2010	223
	8.6.3	CIC-IDS 2017	224
	8.6.4	CIC DoS 2017	225
	8.6.5	CSE-CIC-IDS 2018	225
	8.6.6	CIC-DDoS 2019	226
8.7	Limitations of Current Web-based Attack Datasets		226
8.8	Toward Novel Up-to-Date Benchmark Datasets		229
8.9	Conclusion		230

Part III: Advanced Technologies for Cybersecurity and Privacy — 237

9 Advancing Blockchain Privacy: The Role of Homomorphic Encryption — 239
Yulliwas Ameur, Idriss Taberkane, and Samia Bouzefrane
- 9.1 Blockchain 240
  - 9.1.1 Introduction to blockchain 240
    - 9.1.1.1 Blockchain technology and privacy protection 242
    - 9.1.1.2 Assymetric encryption intro 245
    - 9.1.1.3 Symmetric encryption intro 246
    - 9.1.1.4 Comparison 247
  - 9.1.2 Hash functions 247
    - 9.1.2.0.1 SHA-256 247
    - 9.1.2.1 Digital signature 248
- 9.2 Enhancing Privacy 251
  - 9.2.1 Enhancing privacy protection with homomorphic cryptography 251
    - 9.2.1.0.1 SHE encryption 252
    - 9.2.1.0.2 FHE encryption 253
    - 9.2.1.0.3 FHE and smart contracts 254
    - 9.2.1.0.4 Limitations and challenges 255
  - 9.2.2 Application of homomorphic encryption in blockchain 257
  - 9.2.3 IoT application 259
  - 9.2.4 Future 260
    - 9.2.4.1 Conclusion 265

10 Developing a Big Data Infrastructure: Integral Modules and Best Procedures for Alleviating Security and Privacy Challenges — 269
Danish Bilal Ansari
- 10.1 Introduction 269
- 10.2 Literature Review 271
- 10.3 Attributes Of Big Data 272
  - 10.3.1 Volume 272
  - 10.3.2 Velocity 272
  - 10.3.3 Variety 272
  - 10.3.4 Veracity 273

		10.3.5	Variability	273
		10.3.6	Visualization	273
		10.3.7	Value	274
		10.3.8	Validity	274
	10.4	Security and Privacy Challenges in Big Data	274
		10.4.1	Big Data Security	276
			10.4.1.1 Inadequate Standard Solutions	276
			10.4.1.2 Primitive Security Applications	277
			10.4.1.3 Data Secrecy	277
			10.4.1.4 Data Reliability	277
			10.4.1.5 Data Accessibility	278
		10.4.2	Big Data Privacy	278
			10.4.2.1 Data Acquisition/Generation Phase	278
			10.4.2.2 Data Sharing/Storage Phase	279
			10.4.2.3 Data Processing Phase	280
		10.4.3	Security and Privacy Comparison in Big Data	280
	10.5	Infrastructure for alleviating Security and Privacy in Big Data	280
		10.5.1	Data Management	283
			10.5.1.1 Data Classification	283
			10.5.1.2 Data Tagging	285
			10.5.1.3 De-personalization Data	286
			10.5.1.4 Data Identification/Categorization	286
		10.5.2	IAM	287
			10.5.2.1 Authentication	287
			10.5.2.2 Authorization	288
			10.5.2.3 Server and DB Authorization	288
			10.5.2.4 Central User Repository	289
		10.5.3	Data Safety and Privacy	289
			10.5.3.1 Data Masking and Encryption	289
			10.5.3.2 Data Loss Prevention	290
			10.5.3.3 Disk Level Encryption	291
			10.5.3.4 File/Folder Encryption	292
			10.5.3.5 Tokenization	292
		10.5.4	Network and Transport Security	293
			10.5.4.1 Packet Encryption	293
			10.5.4.2 Zone Filtering Policies	294
		10.5.5	Structural Security	294
			10.5.5.1 Auditing/Logging	294
			10.5.5.2 GRSecurity	295

xiv *Contents*

              10.5.5.3 File Integrity Monitoring 296
              10.5.5.4 User Activity Monitoring and User Behavior Analytics 296
    10.6 Research Methodology 297
        10.6.1 Methodology 298
            10.6.1.1 Homomorphic Encryption Implementation 298
            10.6.1.2 Data Storage Separation 298
            10.6.1.3 Performance Metrics 298
    10.7 Conclusion 299

11 Evaluation of the Performance of Pattern Search and Genetic Algorithms for Enhancing the Lifetime of WSNs   305
Ibtissam Larhlimi, Maryem Lachgar, Hicham Ouchitachen, Anouar Darif, and Hicham Mouncif
    11.1 Introduction 306
    11.2 Wireless Sensor Network 307
    11.3 Related Work 308
    11.4 Modeling and Problem Formulation 309
        11.4.1 Energy consumption in wireless sensor networks (WSNs) 309
            11.4.1.1 Sensing energy 309
            11.4.1.2 Energy processing 310
            11.4.1.3 Communication energy 310
        11.4.2 Mathematical model 310
    11.5 Proposed Approaches 311
        11.5.1 Genetic algorithm approach 311
            11.5.1.1 Initialization 311
            11.5.1.2 Fitness 312
            11.5.1.3 Selection 312
            11.5.1.4 Crossover 312
            11.5.1.5 Mutation 312
            11.5.1.6 Fitness assessment of offspring 312
        11.5.2 Pattern search algorithm approach 312
    11.6 Simulation and Results 314
    11.7 Conclusion 317

Index   **321**

About the Editors   **325**

Preface

The emergence of Industry X.0 and the Internet of Things (IoT) has enabled the connection of billions of devices and objects, leading to significant improvements in the operational efficiency of critical industries such as energy networks, intelligent transport systems, healthcare, medical systems care, and industrial control systems. However, this increased connectivity has also expanded the attack surface for cybercriminals, posing a threat to the security of critical operations and infrastructure. For instance, the nature of data generated by both Health Information Systems (HIS) and the Internet of Medical Things (IoMT) raises concerns about the privacy of patients. To address these threats, technologies such as artificial intelligence (AI), cryptography, and mathematical optimization have become essential in ensuring the digital security and resilience of critical industries. In addition, the integration of mathematical optimization techniques can further enhance the effectiveness of these technologies in mitigating cyber threats and ensuring the optimal allocation of security resources. The purpose of this book is to provide an in-depth analysis of the latest trends, challenges, and best practices in cybersecurity for critical industries. The book will focus specifically on the applications of AI, optimization and cryptography in cybersecurity to ensure resilience.

As societies increasingly rely on interconnected and complex infrastructures, ensuring the security and resilience of critical infrastructure systems has become a major concern. Critical sectors such as energy, transportation, logistics, healthcare, and finance are increasingly vulnerable to cyberattacks that can cause significant disruptions and damage. To address these challenges, a range of technologies and strategies have been developed, including advanced cybersecurity measures, network segmentation, and secure communication protocols. Resilience concepts have also been developed to ensure that critical systems can continue to operate even in the face of cyberattacks, natural disasters, and other disruptions. The need to secure these systems has become more urgent than ever before. Unfortunately, these industries are gradually vulnerable to sophisticated cyberattacks that can cause major disruptions and significant damage. The current state of cybersecurity in these industries is alarming, with attacks becoming more frequent and complex. Therefore, it is crucial to develop more robust and intelligent innovative approaches to protect these critical infrastructures. The defense mechanisms deployed should be capable of making real-time decisions to efficiently counteract sophisticated attacks.

Ensuring the resilience of industrial systems has become a crucial concern for critical industries, as they need to maintain continuous operations in the event of disruptions such as cyberattacks and natural disasters. Industrial systems must be capable of quickly recovering after incidents and continuing to function reliably to ensure that critical activities are not affected. One way to improve this resilience is by modern technologies such as AI, cryptography, and optimization. In fact, these latter are three powerful tools that have a wide range of applications in various fields, including cybersecurity. AI is a prominent subfield of computer science that extensively deals with the creation and implementation of intelligent agents capable of executing tasks typically associated with human intelligence. Its application in cybersecurity has gained momentum due to its potential for developing advanced systems capable of detecting, mitigating, and preventing cyberattacks by identifying anomalies while ensuring maximum security measures are always maintained. Cryptography is another highly effective technique that plays a vital role in protecting data from malicious attacks and unauthorized access. By employing robust encryption algorithms and digital signature protocols, modern cryptography can ensure the confidentiality, integrity, and authenticity of sensitive information. Furthermore, it offers enhanced security to industrial networks by providing secure communication protocols for safeguarding data during transmission. For instance, using encryption keys, secure communication protocols prevent unauthorized access to critical data while also guarding against any attempts at modification or tampering. Additionally, these same cryptographic protocols allow for verifying the source of trusted information using digital signatures. Overall, effective use of modern cryptography techniques can offer greater protection for valuable assets and reduce vulnerabilities associated with cyberattacks on confidential data, thus promoting safe online interactions across different domains. Optimization, on the other hand, is a critical process that involves finding the most effective solution to a specific problem from various possible solutions while using sophisticated models and algorithms. In cybersecurity, optimization plays an essential role in efficiently allocating resources, designing secure systems, and minimizing risks associated with potential cyberattacks. For example, by utilizing optimization models and algorithms effectively, security experts can ensure that network infrastructure is adequately protected by allocating resources based on potential risks and designing cryptographic systems that are highly resistant to attacks. Together, AI, optimization, and cryptography can help to enhance the security of digital systems and protect sensitive data from cyber threats.

This book aims to tackle the complex challenges that critical industries face when it comes to safeguarding their infrastructure against cyber threats. One of the biggest obstacles is the overwhelming amount of data generated by these systems, which can make it difficult for human analysts to effectively analyze and respond to potential threats. To address this issue, the book will explore multidisciplinary approaches that utilize advanced mathematical and statistical techniques to process and analyze large datasets. These methods can provide actionable insights and improve cybersecurity in critical industries, all while driving innovation forward. However, it is crucial to balance the benefits of data analysis with the need to protect sensitive information from potential exposure during the analysis process. The book will delve into secure and robust systems that can mitigate these risks while still making the most of the analytical capabilities at hand.

Intelligent Cybersecurity and Resilience: Challenges and Applications comprises many state-of-the-art contributions from scientists and practitioners working in cyber resilience for critical industries. It aspires to provide a relevant reference for students, researchers, engineers, and professionals working in this area or those interested in grasping its diverse facets and exploring the latest advances in intelligent systems and data analytics for cyber-threat prevention and detection. More specifically, the book contains 11 chapters. The accepted chapters of this book navigate the cutting-edge intersections of technology and security, offering insights into operational technologies, the healthcare sector's cyber challenges, and the protective layers of red teaming. It evaluates algorithmic advances, scrutinizes fraud detection in decentralized systems, and enhances machine learning for pandemic-related datasets. Further, it dissects web security through benchmark datasets, explores blockchain through the lens of privacy encryption, and reviews AI's critical role in infrastructural risk management. It concludes by laying a blueprint for big data infrastructure, emphasizing security and privacy in the digital age. Each chapter serves as a critical piece in the puzzle of building a resilient cyber future.

We want to take this opportunity to express our thanks to the contributors of this volume and the editorial board for their tremendous efforts by reviewing and providing interesting feedback. The editors would like to thank Rajeev Prasad, Junko Nakajima, and Nicki Dennis from River Publisher for the editorial assistance and support to produce this important scientific work. Without this collective effort, this book would not have been possible to be completed.

Lille, France   *Assistant Professor Mounia ZAYDI*
Khouribga, Morocco   *Professor Yassine MALEH*
Lille, France   *Assistant Professor Gabriel CHÊNEVERT*
Rabat, Morocco   *Professor Hayat ZAYDI*
Lille, France   *Assistant Professor Amina EL YAAGOUBI*

List of Figures

Figure 1.1	IoMT applications.	11
Figure 1.1	Anomaly detection process	21
Figure 1.2	Model's performances.	23
Figure 1.3	Six classes categorization confusion matrix.	27
Figure 2.1	Percentage of definitions with each component (n = 167 definitions) [5].	37
Figure 2.2	WoS Bibliographic coupling output.	44
Figure 2.3	Scopus keywords co-occurrences.	46
Figure 2.4	ISO Risk Model Associated to NIST CSF 2.0 - 2023	52
Figure 3.1	System flowchart of DAO threat detection.	78
Figure 3.2	Cleaned dataset uploaded in Jupyter notebook.	79
Figure 3.3	Diagram of logistic function (sigmoid function).	83
Figure 3.4	Diagram of a random forest.	84
Figure 3.5	Schematic representation of the extreme gradient boosting algorithm.	84
Figure 3.6	Importing classifiers into Jupyter notebook.	85
Figure 3.7	Image of a confusion matrix.	86
Figure 3.8	Image of an AUC-ROC curve.	88
Figure 3.9	Score accuracy on the three (3) models and comparison with a bar chart.	90
Figure 3.10	Accuracy scores on the tuned models and comparison with a bar chart.	91
Figure 3.11	Accuracy comparison of the three models after prediction on the test data.	91
Figure 3.12	ROC_AUC curve on the predictions.	92
Figure 3.13	Confusion matrix for logistic regression.	92
Figure 3.14	Confusion matrix for random forest.	93
Figure 3.15	Confusion matrix for XGBoost.	93
Figure 3.16	Classification for logistic regression.	94
Figure 3.17	Classification report for random forest.	94
Figure 3.18	Classification report for XGBoost.	94

Figure 3.19	Model comparison on their accuracy, f1, recall and precision score.	95
Figure 3.20	Feature importance on random forest.	96
Figure 3.21	Feature importance on XGBoost.	96
Figure 5.1	Virtual industrial cybersecurity laboratory – physical diagram.	129
Figure 5.2	Virtual industrial cybersecurity laboratory – logical diagram.	129
Figure 5.3	OpenPLC interface.	131
Figure 5.4	ScadaBR web administration portal.	132
Figure 5.5	Automatic startup of ScadaBR.	132
Figure 5.6	Factory IO scene and driver simulating the physical process and RTU respectively.	133
Figure 5.7	Placement of elements in the FactoryIO scene.	135
Figure 5.8	Configuration of the driver as Modbus TCP server.	136
Figure 5.9	Configuration of Modbus TCP server values in FactoryIO.	136
Figure 5.10	Assigning different sensors and actuators from the scene to the inputs and outputs of the driver.	137
Figure 5.11	Left: driver configured in FactoryIO; Right: configuration of the slave device in OpenPLC.	138
Figure 5.12	Top: variable range of the slave device in OpenPLC; Bottom: variables declared in the OpenPLC editor within the range of the slave device.	139
Figure 5.13	Process ladder diagram.	139
Figure 5.14	Compilation completed.	140
Figure 5.15	OpenPLC monitoring interface.	140
Figure 5.16	Process in FactoryIO controlled from OpenPLC.	141
Figure 5.17	Search for a public IP on IPinfo.io.	141
Figure 5.18	Public IP subnet range.	142
Figure 5.19	Search for an IP address range on Shodan.	143
Figure 5.20	Search for exposed Siemens Systems.	143
Figure 5.21	Search for exposed Rockwell Systems.	144
Figure 5.22	Exposed Rockwell System – details.	144
Figure 5.23	Filtering in Wireshark to Observe Only Modbus TCP Traffic.	145
Figure 5.24	Wireshark filtering results.	145
Figure 5.25	Analysis of the OpenPLC communication loop.	146

List of Figures xxi

Figure 5.26	Request (left) and response (right) of the "Read Inputs" function.	147
Figure 5.27	Request (left) and response (right) of the "Write Coils" function.	148
Figure 5.28	Examples of data in the "Write Coils" requests.	149
Figure 5.29	Grassmarlin - Import PCAP.	150
Figure 5.30	Grassmarlin - Logical graph view.	151
Figure 5.31	Packet injection attack design.	152
Figure 5.32	Importing from Scapy.	153
Figure 5.33	Red: Time between messages during a single iteration of the OpenPLC communication loop; Green: Time between OpenPLC communication loops.	153
Figure 5.34	Top: ModbusTCP packet captured with Wireshark // Bottom left: ModbusTCP packet sniffed with Scapy // Bottom right: Non-ModbusTCP packet sniffed with Scapy;	154
Figure 5.35	Packet sniffing with Scapy.	155
Figure 5.36	Configuration of TCP and IP layers with Scapy.	155
Figure 5.37	Dark background: Implementation of ModbusTCP and Modbus layer with Scapy // Light background: Example Modbus packet extracted from Wireshark.	156
Figure 5.38	Identification of Short Field (2-byte integer) and Byte Field (1-byte integer) parameters using Wireshark.	157
Figure 5.39	Adding Modbus TCP and Modbus layers, and packet injection.	157
Figure 5.40	Script execution and verification of attack results.	158
Figure 6.1	Personal health information (PHI) reporting during ransomware attacks [10]	164
Figure 6.2	Number of ransomware attacks on US hospitals, clinics, and other healthcare service delivery organizations, 2016-2021[12].	165
Figure 6.3	Estimated ransom demanded from U.S. healthcare organizations 2019-2023 YTD Statista Published by Ani Petrosyan, Nov 7, 2023.	167
Figure 6.4	eHealthcare system [41].	174
Figure 6.5	DDoS scenario [42].	174
Figure 7.1	The proposed architecture.	194
Figure 7.2	The formulated design.	195

Figure 7.3	The coding of the model.	196
Figure 7.4	Block diagram.	203
Figure 7.5	The proposed Laboratory Architecture.	204
Figure 7.6	Phishing mail.	205
Figure 7.7	Deployed agents.	205
Figure 7.8	Adversary Profiles.	206
Figure 7.9	Operation results.	206
Figure 8.1	Benchmark dataset and ML-based WAF construction.	219
Figure 9.1	Blockchain.	243
Figure 9.2	Comparaison.	247
Figure 9.3	Merkle Tree.	250
Figure 9.4	PHE.	252
Figure 9.5	FHE.	254
Figure 9.6	Homomorphic encryption enhancing IoT.	263
Figure 9.7	Homomorphic encryption market size.	264
Figure 10.1	Big Data Structure.	270
Figure 10.2	Amazon Revenue.	274
Figure 10.3	V's of Big Data.	275
Figure 10.4	Infrastructure for Alleviating Security and Privacy Challenges in Big Data.	284
Figure 10.5	File/Folder Encryption.	292
Figure 10.6	Big Data Research Methodology.	297
Figure 11.1	WSN architecture.	308
Figure 11.2	Pattern search algorithm.	313
Figure 11.3	Network lifetime by the active time slots.	315
Figure 11.4	Network lifetime by the number of sensors.	316

List of Tables

Table 1.1	Number of records per traffic category in UNSW-NB15 dataset.	19
Table 1.2	Edge-IIoTset dataset traffic categories.	19
Table 1.3	Binary classification performances.	22
Table 1.4	Fifteen-class model classification performances.	25
Table 1.5	Six class classification performances.	26
Table 2.1	General statistics about research DB where **NR**: number of results, **PC**: proportion of the sample in each DB, **BY**: year with bigger number of publications, **MS**: major source.	42
Table 2.2	Research keywords.	47
Table 2.3	Comparison of this review with existing studies.	53
Table 2.4	Sample of references	55
Table 2.5	Bibliometric literature review	56
Table 3.1	Results of the four (4) major evaluation metrics on the three (3) models.	95
Table 3.2	The evaluation metrics of each classifier in columns.	95
Table 3.3	Five (5) most important features for each model.	97
Table 4.1	Final list of the variables employed in this research.	114
Table 4.2	Algorithms comparison after balancing data with ADASYN.	115
Table 4.3	Algorithms comparison after balancing data with SMOTE.	116
Table 4.4	Algorithms comparison after balancing data with RUS.	116
Table 4.5	Results comparison.	117
Table 5.1	Translation of the data in the "Write Coils" request to RTU outputs.	149
Table 6.1	Phishing simulation tools	171
Table 8.1	Characteristics of the most widely used publically available benchmark datasets.	227

xxiii

Table 10.1	Comparison of Security Challenges and Privacy Concerns in Big Data.	281
Table 10.2	Performance Metrics.	298
Table 11.1	Parameters of simulations.	315

List of Contributors

Abderrahim, Abdellaoui, *Engineering Sciences Lab, ENSA, University Ibn Tofail, Morocc; E-mail: abderrahim@uit.ac.ma*

Ameur, Yullivas, *CEDRIC Lab, Cnam, 292 rue Saint Martin, France*

Ansari, Danish Bilal, *Department of Computer Science and Information Technology, Virtual University of Pakistan; E-mail: danishbilalansari@gmail.com*

Barbier, Johann, *PhD in Cybersecurity, previously worked at the Ministry of the Armed Forces as technical expert. Has taught for 15 years at various prestigious institutions. Currently in charge of innovation projects management; E-mail: johann.barbier@abh-technologies.com*

Bertholat, Jean, *Cyber Security CIFRE PhD Student - Laboratoire d'Analyse et de Modélisation de Systémes d'Aide à la Décision (LAMSADE - Paris Dauphine PSL), Direction de l'Innovation ALTEN SA; E-mail: jean.bertholat@dauphine.eu*

Bouzefrane, Samia, *CEDRIC Lab, Cnam, 292 rue Saint Martin, France*

Chakir, Oumaima, *Laboratory LIMIATI FPBM, USMS University, Morocco; E-mail: oumaima.chakirfpb@usms.ac.ma*

Clerc, Jules, *AI-LLMs CIFRE PhD Student - Laboratoire Heuristique et Diagnostic des Systèmes Complexes (Heudiasyc - UTC Compiègne), Direction de l'Innovation ALTEN SA; E-mail: jules.clerc.pro@gmail.com*

Darif, Anouar, *Laboratory of Innovation in Mathematics, Applications and Information Technology, Polydisciplinary Faculty, Sultan Moulay Slimane University, Morocco; E-mail: a.darif@usms.ma*

Diop, Abdou Khadre, *UADB, Université Alioune Diop de Bambey, Senegal; E-mail: abdoukhadre.diop@uadb.edu.sn*

Diouf, Birahime, *UADB, Université Alioune Diop de Bambey, Senegal; E-mail: birahime.diouf@uadb.edu.sn*

Drocourt, Cyril, *MIS, Modélisation, Information et Systèmes, UR UPJV 4290, France; E-mail: cyril.drocourt@u-picardie.fr*

Durand, David, *MIS, Modélisation, Information et Systèmes, UR UPJV 4290, France; E-mail: david.durand@u-picardie.fr*

El Khamlichi, Sokaina, *LyRICA – Laboratory of Research in Computer Science, Data Sciences and Knowledge Engineering, School of Information Sciences, Morocco; E-mail: sokaina.elkhamlichi@gmail.com*

Hind, Moussaid, *Engineering Sciences Lab, ENSA, University Ibn Tofail, Morocc; E-mail: hind.moussaid@uit.ac.ma*

Khawla, Jabari, *Engineering Sciences Lab, ENSA, University Ibn Tofail, Morocc; E-mail: khawla.jabari@uit.ac.ma*

Lachgar, Maryem, *Laboratory of Innovation in Mathematics, Applications and Information Technology, Polydisciplinary Faculty, Sultan Moulay Slimane University, Morocco*

Larhlimi, Ibtissam, *Laboratory of Innovation in Mathematics, Applications and Information Technology, Polydisciplinary Faculty, Sultan Moulay Slimane University, Morocco; E-mail: ibtissam.larhlimifpb@usms.ac.ma*

Maleh, Yassine, *LaSTI Laboratory, Sultan Moulay Slimane University, Morocco; E-mail: y.maleh@usms.ma*

Merad, Myriam, *Research Director at CNRS (LAMSADE - Paris Dauphine PSL) and international expert in risk management and decision-making support. Member of EU organizations such as IMdR, UNDRR, and COPRNM; E-mail: myriam.merad@lamsade.dauphine.fr*

Mouncif, Hicham, *Laboratory of Innovation in Mathematics, Applications and Information Technology, Polydisciplinary Faculty, Sultan Moulay Slimane University, Morocco; E-mail: h.mouncif@usms.ma*

Obong, Samson Nsikan, *Department of Cyber Security, Federal University of Technology, Nigeria; E-mail: obongsamson00@gmail.com*

Onyekwelu, Bukola Abimbola, *Department of Mathematics and Computer Science, Elizade University, Nigeria;*
E-mail: bukola.onyekwelu@elizadeuniversity.edu.ng

Ouchitachen, Hicham, *Laboratory of Innovation in Mathematics, Applications and Information Technology, Polydisciplinary Faculty, Sultan Moulay Slimane University, Morocco*

Sadqi, Yassine, *Laboratory LIMIATI FPBM, USMS University, Morocco; E-mail: y.sadqi@usms.ma*

Sanae, Seidi, *Engineering Sciences Lab, ENSA, University Ibn Tofail, Morocc; E-mail: sanae.seidi@uit.ac.ma*

S. Y., Ismaila, *UADB, Université Alioune Diop de Bambey, Senegal; E-mail: ismaila.sy@uadb.edu.sn*

Taberkane, Idriss, *CEDRIC Lab, Cnam, 292 rue Saint Martin, France*

Taidi, Loubna, *Laboratory of Innovative Technology, Faculty of Sciences and Technologies / Abdelmalek Essaadi University, Morocco; E-mail: taidiloubna_91@hotmail.fr*

Thompson, Aderonke Favour-Betty, *VTT Technical Research Institute of Finland; E-mail: ext-aderonke.thompson@vtt.fi*

Zaydi, Mounia, *ICL, Junia, Université catholique Lille, LITL (Lille Interdisciplinary Transitions Laboratory), France; E-mail: mounia.zaydi@junia.com*

List of Abbreviations

ABAC	Attribute-based access control
ACL	Access control list
AD	Active directory
ADASYN	Adaptive synthetic sampling
ANND	Anomaly-based network intrusion detection
AP	Average precision
APT	Advanced persistent threat
AST	Abstract syntax tree
AUC	Area under the curve
AWS	Amazon web services
BAS	Building automation system
CBDC	Central bank digital currency
CI	Critical infrastructure
CIA	Confidentiality, integrity, and availability
CIC	Canadian institute of cybersecurity
CKC	Cyber kill chain
CLI	Command line interface
CNI	Critical national infrastructure
CNN	Convolutional neural network
CP-ABE	Ciphertext-policy attribute-based encryption
CPS	Cyber–physical system
CSE	Communications security establishment
CTI	Cyber threat intelligence
CVE	Common vulnerabilities and exposure
DAO	Decentralized autonomous organization
DBMS	Database management systems
DBN	Deep belief network
DDOS	Distributed denial of service
DeFi	Decentralized finance
DES	Dynamic ensemble selection
DLP	Data loss prevention

DMZ	Demilitarized zone
DNN	Deep neural network
DoS	Denial-of-Service
DTL	Deep transfer learning
ECDSA	Elliptic curve digital signature algorithm
ENISA	European union agency for cybersecurity
EoT	Edge of things
FBE	File-based encryption
FDE	Full disk encryption
FFN	Feedforward neural network
FHE	Fully homomorphic encryption
FIM	File integrity monitoring
FPR	False-positive rate
GAN	Generative adversarial network
GBDT	Gradient-boosted decision tree
GFS	Google file system
GNB	Gradient naïve Bayes
GPL	General public license
HDFS	Hadoop distributed file system
HEED	Hybrid energy-efficient distributing
HER	Electronic health record
HMCBCG	Hybrid multiple clustering and bagging classifier generation
HMI	Human–machine interface
IAM	Identity and access management
ICMP	Internet control message protocol
ICS	Industrial control systems
IDE	Integrated development environment
IDS	Intrusion detection systems
IIoT	Industrial internet of things
ILP	Integer linear programming
IoMT	Internet of medical things
IoT	Internet of things
ISP	Internet service provider
KNN	k-nearest neighbor
LDAP	Lightweight directory access protocol
LEACH	Low-energy adaptive clustering hierarchy
LGBM	Light gradient boosting machine
LLM	Large language model

LR	Logistic regression
LR-RUS	Logistic regression-random undersampling
LSTM	Long short-term memory
MAC	Mandatory access control
MCE	Misclassification error
MCSS	Maximum coverage set scheduling
MIS	Medical information system
MITM	Man-in-the-middle
MLCP	Maximum lifetime coverage problem
MLP	Multilayer perceptron
NEDA	Neighborhood-based estimation of distribution algorithm
NHS	National health service
NIS	Network and information security
NLP	Natural language processing
NVD	National vulnerability database
PASH	Privacy-Aware S-Health
PB-DID	Protocol-based intrusion detection
PCAP	Packet capture
PHA	Partially homomorphic encryption
PII	Personally identifiable information
PLC	Programmable logic controller
PrivDA	Privacy preserving IoT data aggregation
PSA	Pattern search algorithm
RBAC	Role-based access control
RDP	Remote desktop protocol
RF	Random forest
RLWE	Ring-learning with error
RNN	Recurrent neural network
ROC	Receiver operator characteristic
RTU	Remote terminal unit
RUS	Random undersampling
SHAP	SHapley Additive explanation
SHE	Somewhat homomorphic encryption
SHR	Shared health records
SMOTE	Synthetic minority oversampling technique
SMOTE-ENN	Synthetic minority oversampling technique with edited nearest neighbor
SSL	Secure socket layer

SSO	Single-Sign-On
SVC	Support vector classification
SVM	Support vector machine
TCP	Transmission control protocol
TDCSS	Topology-driven cooperative self-scheduling
TLS	Transport layer security
TPR	True-positive rate
TTP	Tactics, techniques, and procedure
UBA	User behavior analytics
UDP	User datagram protocol
UML	Unified modeling language
VOS	Visualization of similarities
VRF	Verifiable random function
WAF	Web application firewall
WDLSTM	Weight-dropped long short-term memory
WoS	Web of science
WSN	Wireless sensor network

Introduction

In an era where the fabric of our society is increasingly woven through digital threads, the importance of cybersecurity and resilience cannot be overstated. A new era of connectedness has been ushered in with the introduction of Industry X.0 and the ubiquitous growth of the Internet of Things (IoT), which has connected billions of devices in the fields of healthcare, energy, transportation, and industrial control systems. As connectivity fosters innovation and operational efficiencies, it has also expanded the opportunities for cybercriminals and created difficult obstacles in the way of protecting vital infrastructure from ever changing cyber threats. This book uses a multidisciplinary lens that includes artificial intelligence (AI), cryptography, and mathematical optimization to forge pathways toward robust cybersecurity measures and resilient systems. Through its carefully chosen chapters, it embarks on a thorough exploration of these challenges.

The book is structured into three cohesive parts, each addressing a distinct facet of cybersecurity and resilience within critical industries.

Part I: Intelligent Cybersecurity and Resilience: Challenges and Applications

Part I sets the stage by exploring the burgeoning role of artificial intelligence (AI) in safeguarding critical industries. The section commences with a focus on healthcare systems, where AI-driven threat management holds immense potential to mitigate vulnerabilities and guarantee the privacy and security of sensitive patient data. This initial exploration is then broadened to encompass the practical application of AI in cyber risk management for critical infrastructures, emphasising the essential role it plays in protecting the bedrock of our society's operational capabilities. Moving beyond centralized systems, chapter 3 explores the world of digital autonomous organizations (DAOs), examining how AI-powered fraud detection can combat financial irregularities within these emerging blockchain-based structures. Finally, the section concludes by addressing a pertinent challenge in machine learning – imbalanced datasets. Drawing on the example of COVID-19 data, chapter 4 showcases how innovative sampling techniques can enhance the performance of machine learning algorithms in situations where data distribution is uneven.

Part II: Cybersecurity Challenges and Resilience in Healthcare and Industrial Domains

Part II immerses us in the heart of critical infrastructure, shifting the spotlight to the operational technologies (OT) and supervisory control and data acquisition (SCADA) systems that form the lifeblood of industrial operations. This crucial section unravels the intricacies of safeguarding these environments through meticulous penetration testing methodologies, as outlined in chapter 5. Chapter 6 then takes aim at the evolving cyber threat landscape targeting healthcare institutions, offering valuable insights and preventive measures to ensure the continuous operation of critical medical services and the protection of sensitive patient data. Moving beyond traditional defence strategies, chapter 7 delves into the strategic implementation of red teaming exercises within OT domains, highlighting their effectiveness in bolstering cyber resilience and exposing vulnerabilities before adversaries can exploit them. Finally, chapter 8 sheds light on the invaluable role of up-to-date benchmark intrusion datasets in enhancing web security. By emphasising the continuous need for adaptive and proactive cybersecurity strategies, this chapter underscores the importance of staying ahead of the ever-evolving threat landscape.

Part III: Advanced Technologies for Cybersecurity and Privacy

Part III acts as a springboard, propelling the reader into the dynamic future of cybersecurity. This section unveils groundbreaking advancements in blockchain privacy through the lens of homomorphic encryption. This promising technology holds immense potential to ensure data integrity and confidentiality, even while computations are performed on encrypted data. Chapter 9 delves into the intricate details of this revolutionary approach, offering a glimpse into a future where secure and confidential transactions within blockchain systems become a reality. Next, chapter 10 tackles the complex task of constructing big data infrastructures. It meticulously outlines the integral modules and best practices designed to navigate the security and privacy challenges inherent in managing massive datasets. By providing a roadmap for robust and secure big data infrastructure development, this chapter empowers organizations to leverage the power of data analytics without compromising security or privacy. Finally, chapter 11 serves as a fitting culmination of the book's forward-thinking approach. It delves into the evaluation of pattern search and genetic algorithms for enhancing the lifetime of wireless sensor networks (WSNs). This exploration epitomizes the book's commitment to not only addressing current security concerns but also anticipating and proactively mitigating future challenges in resource-constrained environments.

This book serves as more than an academic treatise; it's a resounding call to action for students, researchers, engineers, and professionals invested in the cybersecurity and resilience of critical infrastructure. By illuminating the multifaceted challenges at hand and navigating the intricate intersections of technology and security, it aims to cultivate a deeper understanding of these issues and inspire the development of innovative, intelligent solutions.

The meticulous review process undertaken by the editorial board and the collaborative efforts of all contributors solidify the book's position as a cornerstone reference for anyone dedicated to advancing cybersecurity in our increasingly digital world. This collective effort ultimately aspires to contribute to the creation of more robust, resilient infrastructure systems, safeguarding the integrity and continuity of vital services in the face of ever-evolving cyber threats.

Part I

Intelligent Cybersecurity and Resilience: Challenges and Applications

1
AI-driven Threat Management in Healthcare Systems

Ismaila S. Y.[1], Birahime Diouf[1], Abdou Khadre Diop[1], Cyril Drocourt[2], and David Durand[2]

[1]UADB, Université Alioune Diop de Bambey, Senegal
[2]MIS, Modélisation, Information et Systèmes, UR UPJV 4290, France
E-mail: ismaila.sy@uadb.edu.sn; birahime.diouf@uadb.edu.sn; abdoukhadre.diop@uadb.edu.sn; cyril.drocourt@u-picardie.fr; david.durand@u-picardie.fr

Abstract

This chapter delves into the critical realm of securing interconnected medical Internet of Things (IoMT) networks by employing a sophisticated deep learning-based anomaly detection approach. The research utilizes datasets such as UNSW-NB15 and the IoT-specific EdgeIIoT dataset, employing a range of deep learning models including the multilayer perceptron (MLP), convolutional neural network (CNN), long short-term memory (LSTM), and the amalgamation of CNN-LSTM. The primary focus is on achieving precision in detecting security threats and minimizing false positives. Through extensive experiments on real-world medical IoT network data, the approach demonstrates exceptional precision rates, emphasizing its efficacy in accurately identifying anomalies within the complex network fabric. Additionally, the chapter addresses the consequences of cyberattacks in the healthcare domain, highlighting the imperative of robust security measures in the ever-evolving digital healthcare landscape. The findings contribute to ongoing efforts to strengthen security measures, providing an innovative solution to mitigate security risks in IoMT environments and improve the overall quality of healthcare delivery.

Keywords: Internet of Things (IoT), cybersecurity, data collection, privacy, artificial intelligence (AI).

1.1 Introduction

The expansion of connected devices is experiencing a staggering surge, with 127 new devices connected to the Internet for the first time every second (McKinsey Computerization). The coming of 5G remote innovation, explicitly intended for the Internet of Things (IoT) and empowering arrangement in confidential organizations additionally advances this outstanding development, projected to arrive at 75 billion associated gadgets by 2025.

While different business areas embrace IoT, the medical services industry is quickly developing, representing 6% of IoT usage in 2018 (iot-analytics.com). By 2019, a faltering 86% of medical organizations were utilizing associated objects, and Forbes extended the sending of 646 million IoT gadgets in emergency clinics, facilities, and specialists' medical procedures by 2020.

IoT improvement has achieved a transformation in medical care frameworks, especially in the clinical IoT space, where associated networks work with continuous patient checking, consistent information assortment, and upgraded medical care conveyance. Be that as it may, this incorporation additionally presents critical security gambles, compromising patient classification, information honesty, and generally speaking organization security. Thusly, executing hearty IoT safety efforts and finding appropriate capacity arrangements are becoming main concerns in the medical services area.

Inside the initial 5 minutes of interfacing with the Web, an IoT gadget is powerless to assaults by bots or other vindictive specialists, a basic concern given that around half of all organizations stay ignorant about digital assaults focusing on them. This issue is especially intense in the medical services area, underscoring the requirement for hearty safety efforts, with irregularity location assuming an urgent part in distinguishing and moderating potential security weaknesses.

Conventional IDS techniques, for example, rule-based and signature-based frameworks, uncover constraints in successfully recognizing and adjusting to new dangers in unique IoT conditions. To address these difficulties, more complicated and versatile arrangements, like profound learning, have exhibited exceptional abilities in design acknowledgment and irregularity discovery undertakings.

At the core of this section, our process includes an extensive investigation committed to building up safety efforts inside the interconnected organizations of the Internet of Things (IoT) in clinical settings. Our focal center rotates around the execution of a modern irregularity discovery framework, controlled by profound learning philosophies. To support our exploration, we influence datasets, for example, UNSW-NB15 and the IoT-explicit Edge IIoT dataset. Our tool compartment incorporates a scope of profound learning models, including the multilayer perceptron (MLP), convolutional neural network (CNN), long short-time memory (LSTM), and the blend of CNN-LSTM.

Our essential goal is to achieve the apex of accuracy in identifying security dangers while at the same time relieving the effect of bogus upsides. Through a progression of inside and out tests utilizing valid information from clinical IoT organizations, our methodology emerges with remarkable accuracy rates – 99.8% and 99.9% for various models. These outcomes highlight the momentous viability of our procedure in precisely recognizing peculiarities inside the perplexing organization texture.

Besides, we dive into the basic domain of limiting misleading positive rates, perceiving its critical job in keeping up with framework dependability. This nuanced approach diminishes superfluous disturbances as well as fills in as a hindrance against ready weariness among medical services experts. In this unique situation, our part unfurls as a story of development, featuring the outcome of our profound learning-based irregularity discovery approach in bracing the security foundation of interconnected clinical IoT organizations.

Besides, we address an urgent feature connected with the outcomes of digital assaults in the medical services space. The repercussions of these assaults convert into significant dangers for patient classification, information uprightness, and generally speaking organization security. These challenges emphasize the critical need to enhance security measures in the rapidly evolving field of medical services. It is essential to adopt innovative strategies that effectively mitigate these risks and elevate the overall quality of healthcare delivery.

The discoveries of this exploration fundamentally add to progressing endeavors to fortify safety efforts in associated clinical IoT organizations. The execution of our creative assault identification arrangement, engaged by profound learning, remains as a proactive measure to relieve security takes a chance in the Internet of Medical Things (IoMT) conditions. This effectively defends patient information as well as endeavors to improve the general nature of medical care conveyance inside the powerfully developing advanced scene.

The resulting segments of this section unfurl with a top to bottom investigation, beginning with a broad writing audit tending to security challenges in associated clinical IoT organizations. We then, at that point, dive into existing methodologies for peculiarity discovery, giving an exhaustive comprehension of the ongoing scene. Following this, we expand on the procedure utilized in our examination, revealing insight into the complexities of our profound learning-based approach.

Pushing ahead, we present the outcomes got from our examinations and give a careful examination, offering bits of knowledge into the exhibition of different profound learning models in recognizing oddities inside genuine clinical IoT network information. Finally, we close this section by summing up the key discoveries got from our examination and illustrating potential future exploration bearings. This comprehensive methodology means to direct and rouse further drives in improving the security of associated IoT clinical organizations.

1.2 The Internet of Medical Things (IoMT)

The IoMT, known as healthcare IoT is a set of medical tools and applications that connect IT networks to the healthcare sector. The IoMT involves the use of medical tools with an Internet connection for machine-to-machine interaction, and this technology is powerful because it allows interacting devices to communicate directly without human intervention. For managing or preventing a number of chronic diseases, healthcare professionals use several instruments. It includes monitoring tools that monitor health values/signs continuously, automatic treatment kit-management tools, and real-time information trackers when a patient manages their own treatments [1]. As the IoMT is connected to the Internet, many patients use mobile applications for Mobile Health Monitoring (MHM). Some examples of IoMT applications (Figure 1.1) are wearable devices that send the patient data to doctors, tracking instructions (patient treatment orders, remote monitoring on persons with chronic conditions). IoMT has become a more significant consideration over the past 10 years. This concept involves using electronic instruments that are linked to a public or private cloud in managing patient information.

1.2 The Internet of Medical Things (IoMT) 11

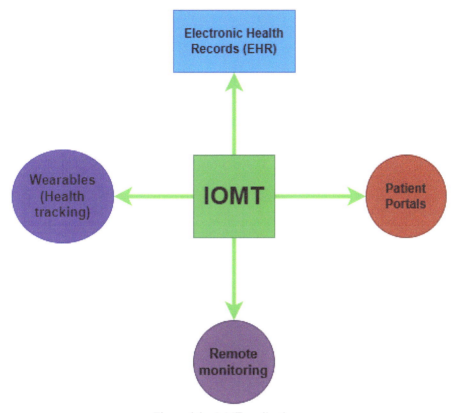

Figure 1.1 IoMT applications.

1.2.1 IoMT applications

With the evolution of technology and networks, using and accessing patient data (vitals information's, body temperature, medical records, etc.) digitally and in real time has become a necessity for healthcare staff, but also for monitoring certain chronic diseases.

○ **Body temperature monitoring**

Body temperature monitoring system is one of the most widely used e-health systems to monitor health parameters related in patients' level concerning their temperatures. This kind of system can identify temperature anomalies that should be recorded or need medical response. In extreme cases, the system notifies a physician if he detects an increase in temperature far beyond some range.

To obtain a complete body temperature monitoring function, certain requirements must be met such as:

- collect temperature data several times a day (e.g., every two hours) using a suitable sensor;
- detection of any abnormal body temperature in relation to normal temperature and other parameters;
- storage of data recorded in the healthcare monitoring database system at the periphery;
- the application of appropriate artificial intelligence techniques to extract and predict useful knowledge;
- in the event of a serious situation, inform the patient and the person in charge.

◦ **Heart rate monitoring**

The main objective of heart rate monitoring system is to gather information about people's heartbeat usually with raw data based on pulse measurements. The system is used in the process of identifying any unusual changes to heart rate as well as classification of a patient's condition. It can be classified as normal resting condition when the rate falls between 60 and 110 bpm; while if a patient is at rest with a heart rate greater than six score, then such position cannot be considered quite standard. This system will store and relay health data in the cloud and can send SMS messages or notifications to a specific person selected by the patient, such as their doctor, nurse, or a family member. It will also send alerts in case of detected anomalies in the patient's health data. This system must meet certain requirements:

- The system must monitor a patient's heart rate (BPM).
- The system needs to display a digital result of heart rate.
- The system needs to send the recorded normal and abnormal BPM rate from periphery to a healthcare database.
- In severe cases with a pathological rate of BPM, the system should notify the patient and third party involved in caring for this case (doctor, nurse, or parents).

◦ **Blood glucose monitoring**

This type of system is aimed at assisting in better self-control and management of diabetic patients' chronic disease. It helps to develop optimal treatment strategies by examining the influence of various external factors on diabetic patients like diet, medication, and daily activity. It can help you learn how blood glucose, insulin, food, and exercise relate to one another. Besides, blood glucose monitoring systems can be used for the benefit of non-diabetic patients to alert them on unordinary changes in their levels during sporting or activity and relay those results.

- **Monitoring elderly's health**

The elderly health monitoring system aims to provide emergency medical assistance within a few hours of the event. Today, it is widely recognized that elderly health monitoring and an emergency alert system are one of the main application areas for IoT and cloud computing and biomedical applications [1]. In other moderate cases, the system can offer computerized decision support for doctors, nurses, and community clinicians by monitoring and analyzing all the activities of the elderly using comfortable, wearable all-in-one monitoring devices. The data collected from these devices can also be used to inform the hospital, nurse, or even just a relative of an elderly person of abnormal situations. In the long term, the data can be used to build a personalized model that helps predict the state of well-being of the elderly using appropriate AI techniques.

1.2.2 IoMT challenges

Though the IoMT is an undoubtful beneficial development, it has faced a number of major challenges demanding special attention. Many of these issues are related to data protection, patient confidentiality breaches as well as not being able to standardize communication protocols and efficiently maintaining huge amounts of generated data.

- **Personal data security**

Although various healthcare-related tools use proven communication techniques to transfer information to the cloud, they can still be susceptible to hackers. In addition to the misuse of personal information, IoMT tools can be used for destructive purposes. For example, the 2012 episode of a TV series, Homeland, established a hacked pacemaker causing a heart attack. Consequently, the security of IoMT tools is essential.

- **Patient confidentiality**

According to the HIMSS 2019 survey, 82% of medical staff faced major privacy issues in 2019. The use of legacy technologies by hospitals is the main cause behind these incidents. For instance, MRI machines are only 11 years old while some hospitals use them for more than over 22 years in service. In addition, a third of IoMT tools are obsolete and not maintained by their manufacturer; this can cause vulnerabilities to IoMT systems.

- **Maintaining connectivity**

Full connectivity is inevitable in the IoMT, where doctors, nurses, and patients need to be connected all the time. Internet connectivity fluctuates or disrupts for a number of reasons; for example, limited network bandwidth, experienced network/web administrators, or any other physical obstacle that disrupts Wi-Fi signals. The aforementioned probabilities are intolerable in IoMT-deployed sanatoriums. Therefore, the question arises as to how bandwidth can be sufficiently utilized to provide uninterrupted connectivity in the IoMT environment. The answer is to foster a secure network structure where Internet professionals are allowed to distribute bandwidth according to the needs of functional IoMT equipment [2].

1.2.3 Critical implications of attacks on connected medical devices

Cyberattacks on connected medical devices can have several detrimental effects on interconnected healthcare structures:

Data theft: With data growing in value with the Big Data era, and sensitive information like medical reports or patients' social security numbers being vulnerable targets for an attacker. This stolen information can then be resold on the dark web to organizations such as insurance companies and pharmaceutical conglomerates.

Healthcare system paralysis: DDoS attacks and malware can result in a full blockage of services such as remote consultations or bookings for appointments. In extreme cases, such attacks can even stop the entire system thereby jeopardizing critical healthcare services.

Physical integrity of patients: As wearables that monitor patients' vital signs in real time find their way into common use, code injection attacks can cause manipulation of the information gathered by these sensors. This compromises the integrity of critical medical information; as a result, it might lead to incorrect decision-making regarding very serious health issues and illustrates why connected medical devices need their security enhanced is necessary.

In conclusion, the implications of attacks on medical devices go beyond service interruptions as they affect data integrity and healthcare continuity or even patient safety. To protect against these evolving vulnerabilities, an effective and broad strategy is necessary for building confidence in the rising popularity of connected medical technology.

1.3 Securing Healthcare Systems: Ensuring Patient Safety and Data Integrity

The Internet of Medical Things (IoMT) is an evolving domain that holds immense promise for revolutionizing healthcare, patient monitoring, and disease management. Through the integration of interconnected medical devices and systems, IoMT has the potential to significantly improve patient outcomes and healthcare efficiency. However, this rapid growth and interconnectivity also expose IoMT to a myriad of security and privacy challenges.

Cyberattacks on connected medical devices can have severe consequences for healthcare facilities. Firstly, the theft of sensitive data, including medical records and social security numbers, poses a significant risk as attackers can exploit this information for illicit purposes, such as selling it on the dark web to insurance companies and pharmaceutical giants. Secondly, cyber threats like DDoS attacks and malware can lead to a complete disruption of remote healthcare services, appointment bookings, and even halt essential medical operations. Moreover, the increasing use of wearables that monitor patients' vital signs makes them vulnerable to code injection attacks, potentially compromising the accuracy and integrity of the collected data. Securing medical devices and systems is crucial to safeguarding patient privacy, ensuring uninterrupted healthcare services, and maintaining the integrity of medical data [6].

Ensuring the security of IoMT is of paramount importance to protect patients' sensitive medical data and maintain the integrity of healthcare systems. With cyber threats, becoming increasingly sophisticated, inadequate security measures could lead to disastrous consequences. Patient confidentiality may be compromised and unauthorized access to medical devices or networks could put patients' lives at risk.

Numerous researchers and experts have recognized the gravity of the situation and are actively studying the security aspects of IoMT. Johnson [7] emphasized the need to address security concerns in the context of the Internet of Things in healthcare. Uslu [8] delved into the specific security and privacy implications of the Internet of Medical Things, underscoring the urgency of robust protection measures. Zeadally et al. [9] provided an extensive survey on IoT security, encompassing IoMT as a critical domain. Additionally, Kocabas et al. [10] conducted a comprehensive review of recent advancements and future directions in IoMT, with a particular focus on security implications.

As IoMT continues to expand and integrate into healthcare practices, it is vital for stakeholders to collaborate and implement stringent security protocols. Healthcare providers, device manufacturers, and policymakers must work in unison to mitigate potential threats and safeguard patient well-being. Emphasizing security measures right from the design and development stages will be pivotal in building a resilient IoMT ecosystem that engenders trust among both medical professionals and patients.

1.4 Exploring Existing Insights: Navigating the Landscape of Security in IoMT

The surge in data transmission via various IoT devices has led to increased security concerns, necessitating effective intrusion detection systems (IDS) with a focus on artificial intelligence (AI)-based approaches [6]. Researchers have explored diverse methods to enhance intrusion detection capabilities, addressing security challenges in IoT networks, and safeguarding against various cyber threats.

1.4.1 Deep learning approaches

Ferrag et al. [11] conducted an in-depth investigation into intrusion detection using deep learning. They compared seven models across well-known datasets, with convolutional neural networks (CNNs) outperforming feedforward neural networks (FFNs) and recurrent neural networks (RNNs) in tasks like target tracking and image processing. The study highlights the efficacy of deep learning in handling diverse attack scenarios.

Odetola et al. [12] extended deep learning to edge IoT devices, implementing a multi-label classification method with a convolutional neural network. Their framework achieved low latency and efficient operations, demonstrating the applicability of deep learning in resource-constrained environments.

Hassan et al. [15] proposed a hybrid approach combining weight-dropped long short-term memory (WDLSTM) and CNN models for intrusion detection. This innovative approach displayed the adaptability of deep learning techniques to optimize detection accuracy and mitigate computation overhead.

Priya et al. [16] introduced a deep neural network (DNN) for cyberattack recognition in Internet of Medical Things (IoMT) networks. The DNN exhibited improved accuracy and reduced computation time, emphasizing its potential in securing healthcare IoT ecosystems.

1.4.2 Security threat identification

Idrissi et al. [13] conducted a comprehensive study to identify vulnerabilities and security threats in IoT environments. Their work contributes to understanding real-world threats and proposes strategies to fortify security measures against emerging risks.

Tian et al. [14] presented a distributed approach using deep learning algorithms to identify network threats via URLs. This framework, designed for Edge of Things (EoT) environments, highlights the versatility of deep learning in distributed settings, ensuring the protection of web applications.

1.4.3 Transfer learning for IoT attacks detection

In [17], the authors proposed a deep transfer learning (DTL) approach for IoT attacks detection. Using auto encoders trained in supervised and unsupervised modes, the DTL model demonstrated enhanced accuracy compared to traditional intrusion detection methods.

1.4.4 Generative adversarial networks (GANs) for cyber threats

Kandro et al. [18] leveraged generative adversarial networks (GANs) to detect cyber threats in Industrial Internet of Things (IIoT) networks. Their approach highlighted superior performance, emphasizing the role of generative models in enhancing efficiency and accuracy.

1.4.5 Deep belief networks (DBNs) for anomaly detection

In [19], the authors utilized deep belief networks (DBNs) for implementing IDS in IoT systems. The DBN's ability to perform unsupervised learning contributed to robust execution in anomaly detection, highlighting its effectiveness against various types of attacks.

These studies collectively demonstrate the versatility and efficacy of AI-driven intrusion detection methods in addressing evolving cybersecurity challenges in IoT environments. The integration of deep learning, transfer learning, and generative models enhances the adaptability and robustness of intrusion detection systems, contributing to the security and integrity of IoT ecosystems [11–19].

1.5 Methodological Framework for Securing IoT in Healthcare Systems

Throughout this chapter, our exploration delves into the extensive evaluation of our proposed methodologies, drawing insights from the analysis of two pivotal datasets. The primary dataset under scrutiny is the UNSW-NB15 dataset, a hybrid compilation encompassing a diverse array of Internet of Things (IoT) traffic intricately interwoven with traditional network traffic. Additionally, our study incorporates the Edge-IIoTset dataset, meticulously crafted for IoT applications, offering a rich repository of records pertinent to IoT technology and its intricate protocols.

In our endeavor to assess the effectiveness of the proposed methodologies, we employ a comprehensive set of evaluation metrics commonly employed in the scrutiny of deep learning algorithms. These metrics, including recall, accuracy, F1 -score, detection rate, and false alarm rate, serve as the quantitative yardstick for our analysis. The intricacies of these metrics' computation unfold through the strategic utilization of a confusion matrix, enhancing the robustness and precision of our evaluation framework. Through this methodical approach, we aim to provide a nuanced understanding of the methodologies' performance in the dynamic context of IoT datasets.

1.5.1 Dataset selection and characteristics

In carefully selecting our research approach, we opted to integrate the UNSW-NB15 and Edge-IIoTset datasets, a decision motivated by the desire to capture the diversity of scenarios and combine the respective strengths of these two distinct sets.

Integrating the UNSW-NB15 and Edge-IIoTset datasets, a complex process including the need to incorporate different scenarios, while considering their differences, is very important in research process. The UNSW-NB15 dataset gives a general overview of common IoT threats.In contrast, the Edge-IIoTset dataset focuses on industrial IoT applications, offering more detailed

1.5 Methodological Framework for Securing IoT in Healthcare Systems

Table 1.1 Number of records per traffic category in UNSW-NB15 dataset.

Categories	Number of samples
Normal	93,000
Generic	58,871
Exploits	44,525
Fuzzers	24,246
DoS	16,353
Recognition	13,987
Analysis	2677
Backdoor	2329
Shellcode	1511
Worms	174

Table 1.2 Edge-IIoTset dataset traffic categories.

Categories	Number of samples
Normal	1,615,643
DDoS_UDP	121,568
DDoS_ICMP	116,436
SQL_injection	51,203
Password	50,153
Vulnerability_scanner	50,110
DDoS_TCP	50,062
DDoS_HTTP	49,911
Uploading	37,634
Backdoor	24,862
Port_Scanning	22,564
XSS	15,915
Ransomware	10,925
MITM	1214
Fingerprinting	1001

and specific informations on targeted threats suited for complex industrial IoT environments. Combining these two datasets synergizes their strengths, creating a more robust detection model capable of recognize potential attacks on IoT devices in a variety of industries including healthcare. The analysis of Table 1.1 (UNSW-NB15) and Table 1.2 (Edge-IIoTset) shows that combining these datasets improves threat detection by integrating general IoT threats with specific industrial IoT details. This approach enhances the identification of threats in medical IoT applications

1.5.2 Deep learning-based attack detection solution

Our anomaly detection solution employs a multi-tier approach with models like multilayer perceptron (MLP), convolutional neural network (CNN), and long short-term memory (LSTM), as well as the hybrid setup of an interlinked structure between CNNs and LSTMs. Data preprocessing is the initial step; it involves data cleaning, missing values handling, and normalizing of features if required. Following that, domain-based knowledge and feature selection algorithms occur in the subprocess of feature extraction (Algorithm 1.1).

The model-training phase has several stages, where each step is related to one or another type of the model. Different training sets are used for MLP, CNN, LSTM, and the hybrid CNN-LSTM model. Evaluation of each model's performance after using a validation set follows, and then we choose the most efficient one according to prescribed evaluation metrics. We will use these metrics' aggressiveness accuracy, validation accuracy, loss, recall, and false-positive rate. Accuracy is a measure of the proportion of instances that were correctly classified, while validation accuracy measures performance with respect to the set for which it was validated; loss indicates modeling errors using mean squared error function; and recall calculates anomaly detection capabilities. While false-positive rate describes how many normal cases are disposed as abnormal when being evaluated against this threshold criterion among those the respective formulas for these metrics are ((1.1)–(1.4)):

$$\text{Accuracy} = \frac{TP + TN}{TP + TN + FP + FN}, \tag{1.1}$$

$$\text{Validation Accuracy} = \frac{\text{Number of correct predictions}}{\text{Total number of predictions on the validation set}}, \tag{1.2}$$

$$\text{Loss} = \frac{\text{Sum of errors for all instances}}{\text{Total number of instances}}, \tag{1.3}$$

$$\text{False positive rate} = \frac{FP}{FP + TN}, \tag{1.4}$$

where TP represents true positive, TN represents true negative, FP represents false positive, and FN represents false negative. These metrics enable a comprehensive assessment of the performance of our anomaly detection solution.

1.5 Methodological Framework for Securing IoT in Healthcare Systems

Algorithm 1.1 Anomaly detection process

Algorithm anomaly detection architecture with MLP, CNN, LSTM, and CNN-LSTM

1: **Input:** Dataset with features
2: **Output:** Detected anomalies
3: **Step 1:** Data preprocessing
4: Perform data cleaning, handle missing values, and normalize features if necessary
5: **Step 2:** Feature selection
6: Select relevant features based on domain knowledge or using feature selection algorithms
7: **Step 3:** Model training
8: Split the dataset into training and validation sets
9: **Step 3a:** MLP
10: Train a multilayer perceptron (MLP) model on the training set
11: **Step 3b:** CNN
12: Reshape the data to be compatible with CNN input requirements
13: Train a convolutional neural network (CNN) model on the training set
14: **Step 3c:** LSTM
15: Transform the data into sequential format for LSTM input
16: Train a long short-term memory (LSTM) model on the training set
17: **Step 3d:** CNN-LSTM
18: Train a combined CNN-LSTM model on the training set
19: **Step 4:** Model evaluation
20: Evaluate the performance of each model on the validation set
21: Select the best-performing model based on evaluation metrics
22: **Step 5:** Anomaly detection
23: Apply the selected model on unseen data to detect anomalies
24: **Step 6:** Post-processing
25: Analyze detected anomalies and interpret results
26: Take appropriate actions based on the severity of the anomalies
27: **Step 7:** Iteration and improvement
28: Renew the models, feature selection, or preprocessing techniques based on feedback

1.5.3 Unveiling insights: Results and discussions

We split the dataset into training and test sets in a ratio of 70:30. The training set is used to train the classification model, while the test set is used to evaluate its performance. We used four classification models: multilayer perceptron (MLP), long short-term memory (LSTM), convolutional neural network (CNN), and hybrid CNN-LSTM architecture. Each model is implemented using standard deep learning libraries and optimized with appropriate hyper parameters.

1.5.3.1 Binary classification

During the binary classification phase of our study, we focused on distinguishing between normal and malicious network traffic. This process includes training our chosen classification model, namely multilayer perceptron (MLP), long short-term memory (LSTM), convolutional neural network (CNN), and hybrid CNN-LSTM architecture.

The performance results of each model on the test dataset are summarized as follows:

In Table 1.3, each row represents a different model for binary classification, and the columns show the accuracy, validation accuracy, and loss achieved by each model during training and evaluation. Accuracy represents the proportion of correctly classified instances to the total number of instances, while validation accuracy is the accuracy achieved in the validation dataset. Loss represents the error of the model during the training process. The lower the value, the better the performance.

Based on our experience, we evaluate several classification models for binary network traffic analysis. The LSTM_UNSW-NB15 model performed well, achieving an accuracy of 93.98% on the test dataset, and an even higher accuracy of 94.99% during the validation process. The relatively low loss value of 0.13 indicates that the model's predictions are generally close to the actual labels. The MLP_Edge-IIoTset model demonstrated excellent accuracy, achieving perfect accuracy of 99.99% on the test dataset and

Table 1.3 Binary classification performances.

Model	Accuracy	Validation accuracy	Loss
LSTM_UNSW-NB15	93,98	94,99	0.13
MLP_Edge-IIoTset	99,99	99,80	2.67e-04
LSTM_Edge-IIoTset	99,99	99,99	9.98e-05
CNN_Edge-IIoTset	99,99	99,87	0.16
CNN-LSTM_Edge-IIoTset	99,98	99,97	1.13e-04

1.5 Methodological Framework for Securing IoT in Healthcare Systems 23

maintaining an extremely high accuracy of 99.98% during the validation process. The model achieved an extremely low loss value of 2.67e-04, which demonstrates its successful ability to differentiate between normal and malicious network traffic.

Additionally, we observed excellent performance of the LSTM_Edge-IIoTset model, achieving perfect accuracy of 99.99% both on the test dataset and during validation. The extremely low loss value of 9.98e-05 indicates that network traffic classification is accurate and reliable. For the CNN_Edge-IIoTset model, the accuracy of the test dataset reaches 99.98%, the verification accuracy reaches 99.97%, and the loss value is relatively small at 0.16, showing strong performance in classifying normal traffic and malicious traffic.

Finally, the CNN_LSTM_Edge-IIoTset model achieved a perfect accuracy of 99.99% on both the test dataset and the validation process. The model's low loss value of 1.13e-04 further confirms its effectiveness in accurately classifying network traffic. Overall, these results demonstrate the powerful ability of LSTM and CNN-based models in distinguishing between normal and malicious network traffic, and the hybrid CNN-LSTM architecture performs exceptionally well on this binary classification task (Figure 1.2).

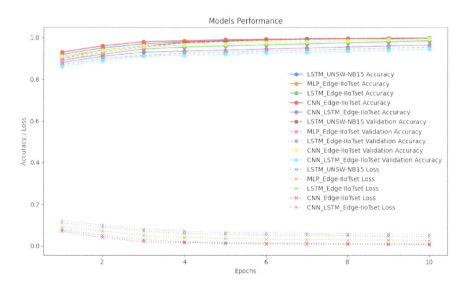

Figure 1.2 Model's performances.

1.5.3.2 Multi-class classification

In the multi-class classification stage, we focus on the challenging task of classifying network traffic into multiple classes. We used two different classification scenarios: one with 15 categories and another with 6 categories, both extracted from the Edge IIoTset dataset.

The 15-category classification is designed to identify different types of network traffic, including normal traffic and various attack categories. A six-category classification, on the other hand, should provide a broader overview by grouping similar types of traffic into broader categories. This approach allows us to simplify the classification task and capture key differences between network behaviors.

○ Categorization across fifteen (15) classes

In this multi-class classification, we focus on classifying network traffic into 15 classes of the Edge IIoTset dataset using LSTM models. LSTM (long short-term memory) is a powerful recurrent neural network that is ideal for sorting data such as network traffic.

We designed a multilayer LSTM model consisting of a series of LSTM layers followed by dense layers with activation functions (e.g., relu) to introduce nonlinearity. The output layer has 15 neurons, representing the 15 categories in the dataset, and uses a "softmax" activation function to generate probability values for each category.

The model is trained using the Adam optimizer and categorical cross-entropy loss function and is suitable for multi-class classification problems. We also evaluate the model's performance using various metrics, including accuracy, precision, recall, F1-score, and support, to evaluate its ability to correctly classify network traffic into different categories.

The accuracy metric signifies the ratio of correct positive predictions to all positive predictions within each category. Recall, or sensitivity, indicates the ratio of correct positive predictions to all actual positive cases for each class. The F1- score, representing the harmonic mean of precision and recall, offers a gauge of the equilibrium between these two metrics [20]. The support value indicates the frequency of each class's occurrence in the dataset.

The outcomes (Table 1.4) show that a few classes, like Typical, DDoS_UDP, DDoS_ICMP, and MITM, accomplished wonderful accuracy, review, and F1- scores, demonstrating that the model performed particularly well in accurately grouping occasions of these classes. Nonetheless, different classes, similar to SQL_injection, Secret phrase, XSS, and Fingerprinting,

1.5 Methodological Framework for Securing IoT in Healthcare Systems

Table 1.4 Fifteen-class model classification performances.

	Precision	Recall	F1-score	Support
Normal	1.0	1.0	1.0	545,600
DDoS_UDP	1.0	1.0	1.0	48,627
DDoS_ICMP	1.0	1.0	1.0	27,176
SQL_injection	0.47	0.76	0.58	20,330
Password	0.58	0.34	0.43	19,973
Vulnerability_scan	0.98	0.85	0.91	20,010
DDoS_TCP	0.82	1.00	0.90	20,025
DDoS_HTTP	0.75	0.93	0.83	19,418
Uploading	0.67	0.48	0.56	14,723
Backdoor	0.97	0.96	0.97	9610
Port_Scanning	1.00	0.50	0.66	7991
XSS	0.58	0.38	0.45	6026
Ransomware	0.93	0.92	0.92	3876
MITM	1.00	1.00	1.00	143
Fingerprinting	0.72	0.40	0.52	341

have lower F1-scores, proposing that the model might experience challenges in precisely recognizing cases of these classes. Working on the model's presentation on these classes might require further tuning and information augmentation methods.

○ Categorization across six (06) Classes

Subsequent to leading a top to bottom investigation of various assault classes in light of organization information and existing security assaults, we have renamed the information into six categories:

- Ordinary: Addresses traffic with no assault.
- Man-in-the-middle (MITM) assault: Includes an assailant capturing and controlling correspondence between two gatherings.
- Code injection attacks: Incorporates XSS (Cross-Site Prearranging), SQL infusion, and transferring assaults, where vindictive code is infused into a framework to exploit weaknesses.
- Malware assaults: Including secondary passage, ransomware, and secret phrase assaults, which include malevolent programming intended to acquire unapproved access or truly hurt.
- Distributed denial of service (DDoS) assaults: Includes DDoS UDP, DDoS TCP, DDoS ICMP, and DDoS HTTP assaults, which overpower an objective framework with a high volume of traffic, delivering it distant to real users.

- Information theft: Comprising of port checking, weakness scanner, and fingerprinting assaults, which plan to assemble delicate data about an objective framework.

By categorizing the data, we may acquire a better understanding of the many sorts of assaults contained in the dataset and design more targeted and effective security solutions to prevent these risks. This reclassification gives a clearer and succinct depiction of the varied spectrum of assaults experienced in real-world network data, allowing us to improve cyber threat detection and prevention.

These measurements (Table 1.5) give significant experiences into the presentation of the classification model for each class. Accuracy addresses the extent of genuine positive expectations among all certain expectations for a particular class. Review, otherwise called responsiveness, gauges the extent of genuine positive expectations among all genuine positive occasions of a class. The F1-score is the consonant mean of precision and review and gives a decent measure between the two. The help shows the quantity of tests in each class.

Upon closer assessment of the arrangement report, we can see that the model precisely identifies the "Typical" and "MITM" classes with next to no blunders. We likewise note that no pernicious traffic class is misclassified as typical, showing that the LSTM_6_Class model performs extraordinarily well for DDoS and MITM assaults, as well concerning infusion-related assaults. It is worth focusing on that specific assaults might share normal attributes, for example, a similar assault port or protocol.

The model exhibits strong performance for the "DDoS" class, achieving high precision of 0.91 and recall of 0.99, implying that most instances of DDoS attacks are correctly identified while minimizing false positives.

However, the model's performance is slightly lower for the code injection class, with a precision of 0.68 and a recall of 0.89. This might be attributed to

Table 1.5 Six class classification performances.

	Precision	Recall	F1-score	Support
Normal	1.00	1.00	1.00	409,200
DDoS	0.91	0.99	0.95	86,434
Code injection	0.66	0.87	0.75	30,810
Malware	0.94	0.49	0.65	25,094
Information theft	0.95	0.74	0.83	21,257
MITM	1.00	1.00	1.00	107

1.5 Methodological Framework for Securing IoT in Healthcare Systems 27

the diverse nature of code injection attacks, making them more challenging to detect accurately (Figure 1.3).

For the "Malware" class, the model achieves high precision of 0.94, indicating that the majority of instances predicted as malware are correct. However, the recall is relatively lower at 0.50, suggesting that the model struggles to identify all true instances of malware. This could be attributed to the constantly evolving and diverse nature of malware.

Based on Table 1.5, we can observe that the models trained on the Edge-IIoTset dataset outperform the model based on the UNSW-NB15 dataset.

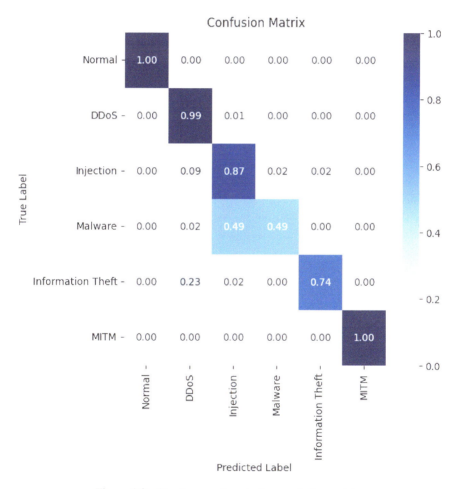

Figure 1.3 Six classes categorization confusion matrix.

This difference in performance can be attributed to the fact that the Edge-IIoTset dataset is larger and provides more data for model training. As a result, models trained on Edge-IIoTset have a richer and more diverse set of samples, leading to improved performance. It is evident that the availability of more training data positively influences the model's ability to make accurate predictions, making Edge-IIoTset the preferred choice for training our models.

Lower loss values indicate better model performance in binary classification. A loss near 0 suggests high prediction accuracy. Thus, models with the lowest loss are preferred for accurately detecting normal traffic.

The presented multi-class classification results serve as valuable indicators of the model's performance in accurately classifying different types of network traffic. Notably, the model demonstrates exceptional precision, recall, and F1-score for the "Normal" and "MITM" classes. This signifies that the model successfully identifies normal traffic with high accuracy and effectively detects instances of Man-in-the-Middle attacks.

However, the results also shed light on certain challenges faced by the model in classifying classes that are more complex. For instance, the "Code Injection" class exhibits a relatively low precision, indicating the model's tendency to misclassify some normal traffic as code injections. Additionally, the "Malware" class displays a significant discrepancy between precision and recall, implying that while the model accurately identifies numerous malware instances, it also misclassifies certain normal traffic as malware, leading to some false positives. Similarly, the "Information Theft" class demonstrates a trade-off between precision and recall.

Our methods show promising results in accurately identifying most attacks linked on medical gadgets. This proves how useful and significant our approach is in important situations, like healthcare. With accuracy and validation accuracy rates over 98%, our models show an outstanding skill. Our models can detect and classify attacks by distinguishing between typical actions and potential security threats. This distinction considerably reduces the risk of false alarms, demonstrating that the models are capable of accurately identifying and classifying various types of attack.

The model's performance is of considerable importance in securing connected medical devices. Medical devices are potential targets of attack like DDoS, information theft. The accuracy of our models in identifying and classifying threats such as DDoS attacks, data theft, or code injection must be taken into account to preserve the integrity of medical information and the availability of services. These results reinforce the relevance of our approach to the security of connected medical devices. The ability of our models to detect attacks with low false-positive rates suggests that our system is trustworthy in critical environments. Consequently, the proposed detection approach is highly effective and reliable for securing connected medical devices, which has a positive influence on maintaining the integrity of medical data confidentiality and increasing confidence in new technologies among healthcare professionals.

1.6 Conclusion

This study presents a profound learning-based way to deal with IoT attacks identification and classification. The review researches the use of profound learning models for both binary and multi-class classification, meaning to recognize normal and abnormal traffic while distinguishing explicit attack category.

The evaluation metrics of the approach include accuracy, validation accuracy loss, and false positive and negative rates (false alarm). In binary classification, our models demonstrated high accuracy ranging from 96% to 99%. For multi-class classification, we achieved good results with 94.0% and 96.1%, classifying data into fifteen (15) classes or six (06) classes respectively. Based on the results of the six (06) class classification (Figure 1.3), our models were able to accurately identify different categories of attacks such as DDoS, code injection, information theft, and Man-in-the-Middle (MITM). The results show the power of our approach for capturing threats that occurred in IoT environments.

The promising results of our approach in recognizing attacks such as DDoS, malware, and code injection suggest that our approach can be effectively deployed to defend IoMT environments against potential threats, as the medical field is often the victim of DDoS attacks causing service interruptions, as well as code injection and information theft attacks.

The ability of our approach to categorize data further enhances its relevance in the context of medical devices. Through the identification of distinct categories of attack, such as information theft and man-in-the middle (MITM) attacks our model gives a thorough view on what threats might undermine security or confidentiality for medical data.

In conclusion, our deep learning-based approach is positioned as a robust solution for the defense of connected medical objects, offering an exceptional ability to identify and classify various attacks. These encouraging results boost confidence in the security of IoT environments in general, paving the way for more widespread and secure use of connected medical objects in healthcare.

References

[1] I. Ud Din, A. Almogren, M. Guizani and M. Zuair, "A Decade of Internet of Things: Analysis in the Light of Healthcare Applications," in IEEE Access, vol. 7, pp. 89967-89979, 2019, doi:10.1109/ACCESS.2019.2927082.

[2] T. Ahmed Alhaj et al., "A Survey: To Govern, Protect, and Detect Security Principles on Internet of Medical Things (IoMT)," in IEEE Access, vol. 10, pp. 124777-124791, 2022, doi:10.1109/ACCESS.2022.3225038.

[3] M. Wazid, A. K. Das, J. J. P. C. Rodrigues, S. Shetty and Y. Park, "IoMT Malware Detection Approaches: Analysis and Research Challenges," in IEEE Access, vol. 7, pp. 182459-182476, 2019, doi:10.1109/ACCESS.2019.2960412.

[4] V.-T. Tran, C. Riveros and P. Ravaud, "Patients' views of wearable devices and AI in healthcare: Findings from the compare E-cohort", Npj Digit. Med., vol. 2, no. 1, pp. 1-8, Jun. 2019.

[5] S.-R. Oh, Y.-D. Seo, E. Lee and Y.-G. Kim, "A comprehensive survey on security and privacy for electronic health data", Int. J. Environ. Res. Public Health, vol. 18, no. 18, pp. 9668, Sep. 2021.

[6] B. K. Tripathy and J. Anuradha, Eds., Internet of Things (IoT): Technologies, Applications, Challenges and Solutions, 1st ed. CRC Press, Boca Raton, FL, USA, 2017.

[7] M. E. Johnson, "The Internet of Things in healthcare: Prospects for the future," Journal of Law and Medicine, vol. 23, no. 4, pp. 923-927, 2016.

[8] B. Uslu, İ. Akkaya, and E. G. Sirer, "Security and privacy aspects of the Internet of Medical Things (IoMT)," Current Medical Research and Opinion, vol. 36, no. 5, pp. 805-808, 2020.

[9] S. Zeadally, M. A. Tounsi, M. S. Obaidat, and M. E. Hassan, "Security of the Internet of Things: A review of the state of the art," ACM Computing Surveys (CSUR), vol. 47, no. 2, pp. 1-54, 2014.

[10] O. E. Kocabas, M. Gumussoy, M. Cetinkaya, and S. Yildirim, "Internet of Medical Things (IoMT): A comprehensive survey on recent advancements and future directions," Journal of Medical Systems, vol. 42, no. 11, pp. 1-20, 2018.

[11] M. A. Ferrag, O. Friha, L. Maglaras, H. Janicke, and L. Shu, "Federated deep learning for cybersecurity in the internet of things: Concepts, applications, and experimental analysis," IEEE Access, vol. 9, pp. 138509-138542, 2021.

[12] T. A. Odetola, O. Oderhohwo, and S. R. Hasan, "A scalable multi-label classification to deploy deep learning architectures for edge devices," arXiv preprint arXiv:1911.02098, 2019.

[13] I. Idrissi, M. Azizi, and O. Moussaoui, "IoT security with deep learning-based intrusion detection systems: A systematic literature review," in 2020 Fourth International Conference on Intelligent Computing in Data Sciences (ICDS), pp. 1-10, IEEE, 2020.

[14] Z. Tian, C. Luo, J. Qiu, X. Du, and M. Guizani, "A distributed deep learning system for web attack detection on edge devices," IEEE Transactions on Industrial Informatics, vol. 16, no. 3, pp. 1963-1971, 2019.

[15] M. M. Hassan, M. A. Hossain, M. S. Uddin, and M. R. Islam, "A hybrid deep learning model for efficient intrusion detection in big data environment," Computers & Security, vol. 87, 101681, 2019.

[16] L. Liu, P. Wang, W. Wang, H. Li, and R. Wang, "Intrusion detection of imbalanced network traffic based on machine learning and deep learning," IEEE Access, vol. 9, pp. 7550-7563, 2021.

[17] L. Vu, Q. U. Nguyen, D. N. Nguyen, D. T. Hoang, and E. Dutkiewicz, "Deep transfer learning for IoT attack detection," IEEE Access, vol. 8, pp. 107335-107344, 2020.

[18] I. A. Kandhro, S. M. Alanazi, F. Ali, A. Kehar, K. Fatima, M. Uddin, and S. Karuppayah, "Detection of real-time malicious intrusions and attacks in IoT empowered cybersecurity infrastructures," IEEE Access, vol. 11, pp. 9136-9148, 2023.

[19] W. Wang et al., "Anomaly detection of industrial control systems based on transfer learning," in Tsinghua Science and Technology, vol. 26, no. 6, pp. 821-832, Dec. 2021, doi:10.26599/TST.2020.9010041.

[20] Evaluation Metrics for Classification Model. 2023, www.analyticsvidhya.com accessed 10 Nov. 2023.

2

Practical Use of AI for Cyber Risk Management in Critical Infrastructures: A Review

Jean Bertholat[1], Myriam Merad[2], Johann Barbier[3], and Jules Clerc[4]

[1]Cyber Security CIFRE PhD Student - Laboratoire d'Analyse et de Modélisation de Systémes d'Aide à la Décision (LAMSADE - Paris Dauphine PSL), Direction de l'Innovation ALTEN SA
[2]Research Director at CNRS (LAMSADE - Paris Dauphine PSL) and international expert in risk management and decision-making support. Member of EU organizations such as IMdR, UNDRR, and COPRNM
[3]PhD in Cybersecurity, previously worked at the Ministry of the Armed Forces as technical expert. Has taught for 15 years at various prestigious institutions. Currently in charge of innovation projects management
[4]AI-LLMs CIFRE PhD Student - Laboratoire Heuristique et Diagnostic des Systèmes Complexes (Heudiasyc - UTC Compiègne), Direction de l'Innovation ALTEN SA
E-mail: jean.bertholat@dauphine.eu; myriam.merad@lamsade.dauphine.fr; johann.barbier@abh-technologies.com; jules.clerc.pro@gmail.com

Abstract

The use of AI in cybersecurity has been mainly mobilized through the prism of enhancing existing technologies such as IDS, cryptographic algorithms, or malware analysis. These technologies, initially developed for IT infrastructures, are increasingly being deployed within Industry 4.0 without fundamental changes to cater to OT/IoT systems, which share similarities with pure IT systems.

To date, the use of AI technologies within the risk management global process has been sparse. In the realm of cybersecurity, many research that purports enhancing the decision-making through AI, for tasks ranging from risk assessment to incident response, often tends to veer toward refining previous technological components. However, the emergence of generative AI and advances in NLP that could improve and foster reflexional processes, focusing on strategic decision support rather than simple phenomena classification, seems not to be sufficiently mobilized in practice.

This review addresses the diverse implementations of AI technologies in enhancing the risk prevention for cybersecurity purposes on CIs, particularly through the risk management prism.

An overview of the trends within cybersecurity domains and a focus on where AI applications and research are mobilized will be provided. The discussion then pivots to the critical review of the integration of AI in the cyber risk management process. Exploring how AI can be incorporated into decision-making processes to support comprehensive risk study methodologies that traditionally require expert intervention. Also, evaluating the maturity of AI technologies to address global issues like cyber risk management.

Keywords: Artificial intelligence, cybersecurity, critical infrastructures, risk management, review, definition.

2.1 Introduction

Since the end of 2022, there has been a noticeable global and multi-sectoral surge and enthusiasm for the use and the implementation of artificial intelligence (AI), spanning both industrial and personal realms thanks to the broad adoption and use of generative AI technologies. This rapid and widespread acclaim of AI as a solution for a myriad of today's industrial and personal challenges sparks a curiosity to critically evaluate where AI practically stands and how.

Over the last decade [1], AI's footprint has expanded significantly across various sectors. In the primary production sector, such as agriculture, AI has been utilized for enhancing efficiencies and yield. The service-oriented tertiary sector has seen AI's implementation for optimization and management purposes. Moreover, the secondary sector, which encompasses a broad spectrum of production activities, has specific needs in terms of security and resilience where AI's role has become significant.

The diverse challenges presented across these sectors are increasingly met with AI-based solutions, as evidenced by the growing body of research demonstrating AI's capability to practically address these specific sectoral challenges [2]. The prioritization of these challenges often depends on the critical importance of the system within its ecosystem. Especially for critical production infrastructures where security is paramount, the

2.2 Tackling Cybersecurity Problems Based on Risk Problems Approaches 35

implementation of the most effective defense mechanisms against external threats is necessary.

The types of threats faced by these infrastructures are diverse, ranging from physical to cyber and even cyber–physical threats. While AI has long been a cornerstone in bolstering the safety and security of infrastructures, it paradoxically has also played a role in advancing the sophistication of malicious cyberattack [4 p.157]. Its application mostly spans the improvement of detection technologies, analytical processes, and surveillance activities in cyberspace. A notable example is AI's role in enhancing intrusion detection systems (IDS) and predictive maintenance in these infrastructures.

With the advent of Industry 4.0, the increasing interconnectedness of systems has made the need for effective cybersecurity measures more pressing [4]. As anticipated, the sudden extensive promotion of AI-based solutions has significantly influenced the cybersecurity market, showcasing a broad promotion of these technologies to response to evolving threats.

Considering this trend, it is pertinent to question whether there is a genuine acceleration in research and implementation of these technologies to address cybersecurity threats menacing critical infrastructures (CIs); or if the ubiquitous promotion of AI in cybersecurity solutions/products is more of a prevailing trend to boost their visibility.

The aim of this research contribution is thus to provide empirical evidence demonstrating that cybersecurity challenges are inherently linked to the risks associated with digital technology use, illustrating that risk management is a fundamental aspect across cybersecurity applications (RQ1). Building on this premise, this chapter focuses on exploring the circumstances, extent, and methods of AI application in addressing cybersecurity risk issues, particularly within the realm of CIs (RQ2). Additionally, it offers food for thought about AI application for cyber risk management problems that have been inadequately addressed or not yet tackled.

The first section of this chapter presents empirical arguments suggesting that cybersecurity practice is part of a broader scope of cyber risk management. To structure the review of AI's practical use at each stage of the risk management process a comprehensive framing of risk management will be mentioned.

In the second section, the chapter delves into the current use of AI at each stage of the previously defined risk management framing, drawing upon literature reviews. Furthermore, the work offers a contribution to explore potential applications of AI in areas not uncovered by the systematic review, offering new avenues for consideration and development in the field.

An identification of the main contributions and limits of AI in practice will be discussed in section 2.3 and research and operational challenges will be discussed.

2.2 Tackling Cybersecurity Problems Based on Risk Problems Approaches

2.2.1 Motivations

In our pursuit of a comprehensive understanding of cybersecurity practices, it's essential to delve into the underlying reasons for cybersecurity needs, the paradigms under which it operates, and the objectives it aims to achieve. This deep dive lays the groundwork for insightful analyses of the evolving trends in cybersecurity. It also substantiates the coherence of a risk-centered approach to tackle cybersecurity challenges.

Our journey firstly leads us to a taxonomic study of cybersecurity. Here, we propose that addressing cybersecurity issues inherently involves tackling risks associated with our reliance on digital technologies. This section will start with an analysis of various definitions of cybersecurity and what they collectively signify.

Subsequently, we will conduct an empirical examination of the primary issues addressed by the cybersecurity discipline through a bibliometric analysis of relevant literature. This study aims to provide a comprehensive overview of cybersecurity applications, assessing their performance and attempting to structure the existing literature. This study also aims to gain an overarching understanding and outline of the various communities within cybersecurity.

Through these studies, we aim to demonstrate that approaching cybersecurity from a risk perspective is intrinsically aligned with the essence of the field. Once this foundation is established, we can then explore how cyber risk management is effectively putted in place with the use of AI in CIs.

2.2.2 Definitions analysis

When tackling to the term "cybersecurity," we encounter a multitude of definitions and scholarly efforts aimed at forging a common understanding among them [5–7].

To explore our study's goals (RQ1), we would ideally analyze the cybersecurity literature, focusing on its definitions. Such a methodology would entail:

1. **Collecting definitions**: Gathering diverse definitions from academic, industry, and organizational sources.
2. **Analyzing definitions**: Extracting key themes and principles from these definitions.

2.2 Tackling Cybersecurity Problems Based on Risk Problems Approaches 37

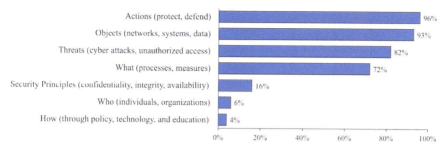

Figure 2.1 Percentage of definitions with each component ($n = 167$ definitions) [5].

3. **Synthesizing core elements**: Identifying consistent components across definitions to understand cybersecurity's concerns.

However, this methodology has already been meticulously followed by National Institute of Standards and Technology (NIST) researchers [5], who conducted a novel analysis of commonly used components in defining cybersecurity. Therefore, our initial step will be to review this existing analysis and to discuss their results.

This review [5] provides valuable statistic insights about the frequency of usage of identified thematic components to define cybersecurity (Figure 2.1). These sources encompass academic literature but also mainly institutional and industrial references, including government documents, standards, and industry publications.

The study addresses two research questions focused on data-driven analysis. However, it doesn't delve into the reasons why cybersecurity definitions are composed of the specific thematic components identified.

In analyzing the diverse landscape of cybersecurity definitions, this study offers a compelling framework for understanding the field. The research identifies several core themes that consistently emerge in definitions[1], painting a comprehensive picture of cybersecurity's essence.

Firstly, the operational aspect of cybersecurity is highlighted (*What*), with a significant majority of definitions portraying it as a practical, action-oriented discipline primarily aimed at protection. This operational focus underscores the active role of cybersecurity in defending against various threats.

Secondly, the intent of cybersecurity (*Action*), predominantly identified as "protection," emphasizes the proactive nature of this field. This protective

---
[1]Definition source list available at: https://bit.ly/42HGWLI

action is intrinsically linked to the concept of *Threats*, which are directly correlated with risks. The study aligns with standards such as ISO 27032:2023 [8, p. 31], which encapsulate threats under the broader notion of cyber risk in their definition, including non-malicious incidents like software bugs.

The third essential element of the definitions is the notion of entities potentially vulnerable to cyber incidents (*Objects*), which is used to establish the scope and applications of cybersecurity measures.

While the above elements form the core of cybersecurity definitions, the study also noted additional operational themes that, although less frequently mentioned, contribute to refining the definition in specific domain contexts. These themes, found in less than 20% of definitions, reflect characteristics unique to particular application domains.

This study shows that definitions of cybersecurity tend to be aligned with the key concepts behind the practice. That the measures taken to foster cybersecurity are primarily in response to risks, arising from the potential interaction between entities identified as *Threats* and *Objects*/systems to protect. The coherence between these operational definitions and a risk-based approach not only validates the relevance and applicability of viewing cybersecurity through the lens of risk management but also highlights that every cybersecurity framework aims to enhance the defense mechanisms within this overarching risk process. This alignment underscores the intrinsic connection between cybersecurity practices and risk management strategies.

The previous study aims to provide simple, universally understandable results, distinguishing itself from prior research that often analyzes themes or relied on expert elicitation. This approach is highly beneficial, particularly considering that decision-makers tasked with protecting systems are not always experts in cybersecurity. However, for the purpose of our study, we take a brief look at how experts define cybersecurity. Concurrently, through the review of [6], we will examine how experts define cybersecurity and cybersecurity risk. Regarding the established link between these two concepts, this exploration evaluates whether experts come to a conclusion similar to ours, or whether it aligns more closely with a significant corpus of scientific research – that the definitions of these concepts are complex to establish due to the protean nature of this practice.

In the definitions gathered by [6], there's an immediate shift toward technical terminology, focusing primarily on the "How" [5] of cybersecurity. This emphasis on implementation and manifestation drives the evocation of measures to ensure the integrity of the CIA triad (confidentiality, integrity, availability) inside the cybersecurity definition. As previously mentioned,

2.2 Tackling Cybersecurity Problems Based on Risk Problems Approaches 39

this indicates a specialization of these definitions tailored to the specific application domain of cybersecurity practice.

When it comes to defining cyber risks, experts seem to focus on a descriptive approach. Referring to a non-exhaustive list of risk factors, most notably human elements. While recognizing the important role of human factors as a source of risk, this approach may overlook other major factors. In reality, human involvement often exacerbates existing vulnerabilities rather than being the only origin of risk. Despite the fact that experts in this study hail from the same laboratory, their approach of crafting complex and specialized definitions for cyber concepts is reflective of a broader trend observed in numerous other research studies.

The study also touches upon the concept of ontology, which is crucial for defining such complex concepts. However, it is observed that there is no affirmed consensus on a cybersecurity ontology, even though some are beginning to emerge [9]. Numerous studies offer their propositions, varying in complexity, attempting to provide a comprehensive meaning applicable across all cybersecurity domains. Given the wide range of applications in cybersecurity, a more effective methodology might involve defining these concepts incrementally for specific use cases. This approach would contribute to the development of a "cyber ontology lifecycle," enriched through practical experience. However, this modeling work is the foundation of comprehensive and efficient result, the detailed formulation of this taxonomy, for cyber risk management, is a topic for future research.

Reflecting on this review of expert definitions, we are reminded of the challenge in defining complex concepts of cybersecurity. However, considering that cybersecurity affects everyone, both experts and non-experts, an effective approach would be to adopt simple, abstract concepts that are easily understandable by all. This is similar to an expert conveying these concepts to a non-expert.

Therefore, a taxonomy that encompasses the ontological concepts identified in [5] would be adequate for defining cybersecurity in its most general paradigm.

Moving forward, to tackle cybersecurity in a cross-disciplinary manner and within specific fields of expertise, these foundational elements of the definition could be further specified. This would allow for the integration of a domain-specific taxonomy, catering to the unique requirements of each professional field of application.

The analysis of cybersecurity definitions reveals a lack of a widely adopted risk-based approach. However, examined definitions align with a more holistic perspective of cybersecurity, emphasizing cyber as an interactive system rather than disparate tasks to achieve. A discernible trend shows a shift toward viewing cyber conceptually, and not just an operational one, signaling an evolving awareness across domains. This transition addresses the first research question (RQ1), indicating an emerging consensus on embracing a global vision of cybersecurity.

Having established this foundation, we now have a starting point to address cybersecurity practice within CIs. In this context, cybersecurity is engaged to mitigate the effects of uncertainties on CIs goals.

Various methods are use in cybersecurity practice to address risk related to CIs. In this chapter, we focus specifically on methods that are enhanced or powered by AI technologies (RQ2). This approach aims to understand how AI is leveraged to bolster cybersecurity measures, particularly in scenarios where the stakes are high and the need for robust security is paramount.

2.2.3 Bibliometric analysis

Our bibliometric analysis will delve into the existing body of cybersecurity literature. This exercise aims to draw out overarching trends and patterns, offering insights into the current and evolving landscape of cybersecurity research. Specifically, we will focus on two key areas:

1. **General trends in cybersecurity research**: The analysis concentrates on identifying the broad themes and directions within the global field of cybersecurity. This includes understanding the major areas of focus, prevalent communities, and evolving paradigms. We aim to chart the trajectory of cybersecurity research, understanding how it has developed and where it might be heading.
2. **The role of AI in cybersecurity, especially in critical infrastructures**: A significant portion of our analysis is dedicated to explore how AI is being integrated into cybersecurity practices. This involves investigating the specific applications and effectiveness of AI technologies in enhancing cybersecurity measures. We pay particular attention to the utilization of AI in safeguarding CIs, understanding how AI is leveraged to mitigate risks in these highly sensitive and vital systems.

The outcomes of this analysis paint a comprehensive picture of the intellectual structure and emerging trends within the field of cybersecurity research.

Regarding existing bibliometric studies, Table 2.5, this section takes a broader perspective on the practice of cybersecurity across various

2.2 Tackling Cybersecurity Problems Based on Risk Problems Approaches

application domains. It aims to explore thematic trends in cybersecurity, distinct from studies focusing on "performances" (author affiliations, country affiliations, or collaborations). Existing works, predominantly delve into specific applications of cybersecurity, such as maritime security, Industry 4.0, cybercrime, or 5G. Notably, there is a gap in comprehensive studies examining cybersecurity practices globally. While other studies acknowledge the significance of AI in cybersecurity, they often lack in-depth analyses. This document seeks to consolidate a bibliometric analysis to substantiate the presence of AI in cybersecurity and provide a more nuanced understanding of its practical applications. Furthermore, our analysis is distinctive in its exploration of how the concept of risk is addressed within the realm of cybersecurity.

For the methodology of our bibliometric analysis, we use a comprehensive approach, drawing inspiration from established practices in the field [9, 10]. Our methodology is tailored to first provide an in-depth and wide-ranging exploration of the cybersecurity literature. Then, focus on the incorporation of AI, especially in the context of CIs. Here's how we have structured our approach:

1. **Data source selection**: To ensure a thorough and representative analysis, we have chosen to utilize both Scopus and Web of Science (WoS) as our primary data sources. These platforms are particularly relevant due to their extensive coverage of diverse sources and the complementarity of the materials they aggregate [11]. By leveraging these two databases, we aim to capture a broad spectrum of research.
2. **Performance analysis**: In our initial stage of analysis, we will execute a succinct performance analysis to grasp the influence and contributions of different entities within the cybersecurity realm. This will encompass a high-level assessment of key performance indicators, enabling us to compare and contrast the samples from both Scopus and Web of Science databases. Our focus is firstly to be on the broader field of cybersecurity research, before delving into specific concerns about the integration of AI and its application within CIs contexts.
3. **Mapping and visualization technique**: To visualize the landscape of cybersecurity research, we will employ the VOS (visualization of similarities) mapping technique [12]. VOS allows for the construction of detailed and insightful bibliometric maps, enabling us to identify and illustrate the relationships and clusters within the cybersecurity literature thanks to the VosViewer software. Using this technique, we aim to uncover the intellectual structure and emerging trends in a way that is both comprehensive and easily interpretable.

Table 2.1 General statistics about research DB where **NR**: number of results, **PC**: proportion of the sample in each DB, **BY**: year with bigger number of publications, **MS**: major source.

Databases	NR	PC	BY: NR	MS: NR
Scopus	59,825	0.22%	2022: 9,373	IEEE Access: 2052
WoS	32,039	0.14%	2022: 4,713	IEEE Access: 981

To initiate our bibliometric analysis, we employ a funnel approach, starting with the broadest possible perspective. In this initial phase, our focus will be on articles that respond to the search query "*cybersecurity OR cyber-security OR cyber security*" across both databases[2]. The search encompasses titles, abstracts, and keywords. This comprehensive approach is designed to capture the full spectrum of research within the domain of cybersecurity.

Our initial analysis revealed several performance indicators, as detailed in Table 2.1. These metrics not only enable a comparative analysis of the two databases but also shed light on the positioning of cybersecurity within the wider spectrum of research disciplines. It appears that cybersecurity, while experiencing an exponential increase in research interest since the early 21st century, still occupies a relatively marginal space compared to dominant fields like health research (which accounts for 22% of Scopus database publications under the keyword "Health"). Interestingly, the year 2023 shows a slight dip in productivity compared to 2022, raising questions about whether this is a temporary fluctuation, an indicator of a new trend in the domain's evolution or a specialization of the cybersecurity research around a specific topic. For instance, the number of research combining cybersecurity AI and CIs continued its exponential growth in 2023.

Further investigation into document types, research areas, and the geographic origins of publications has confirmed the widespread nature of cybersecurity research, demonstrating its expanding role across various disciplines and regions globally (USA – China). While there are some differences in proportions concerning document types and research areas, both databases predominantly feature publications in computer science and engineering, presented mainly through articles and conference proceedings. These results are presented in our Github repository.

This analysis offers an initial glimpse into the diverse ways cybersecurity is tackled within the research community. However, no substantial differences are observed between the two databases in terms of their content proportions.

---

[2] Performance graphics: Github

2.2 Tackling Cybersecurity Problems Based on Risk Problems Approaches

The primary variance lies in the volume of cybersecurity-related research, with Scopus housing a bigger volume. This is partly attributed to contributions from sources like the ACM International Conference Proceeding series that is not well represented in WoS, which is a notable distinction between the two databases.

A significant distinction between the two databases emerges from the additional analytical capabilities offered by Web of Science (WoS). These capabilities enable us to identify some specific subjects within the realm of cybersecurity (Security Systems, AI, Intrusion Detection, etc.).

At this stage, while both databases approach cybersecurity in a similar manner, further network analysis reveals emerging clusters, particularly in the fields of AI and natural language processing (NLP). This development indicates a nuanced expansion of focus within the cybersecurity domain, highlighting the incorporation of advanced computational techniques.

Our first network analysis delves into a subset of the 20,000 most-cited documents from each database, as identified earlier. We calculated a 51% similarity between the two databases (WoS and Scopus) by comparing identical Digital Object Identifier (DOI) within each dataset. While merging the two datasets could have eliminated duplicates, our aim was also to discern how cybersecurity as a research theme is approached through different communication channels.

The initial step of our network analysis, focused on cybersecurity, was to identify the various themes addressed in this corpus. For this purpose, we applied bibliographic coupling analysis: this method helps reveal the themes emerging within the dataset. It creates links between documents that cite the same references, thus connecting those based on similar foundational knowledge.

The analysis shows no significant differences between the two databases, with the exception of WoS, which shows slightly more documents in cluster 5. This cluster appears to be the least represented in our various analyses, suggesting either a lack of interest or a considerable challenge in conducting research on regulations and more reflective studies on the nature of cybersecurity. Addressing these topics is crucial for better implementation, as starting with comprehensive studies in these areas can pave the way for building models and algorithms that closely align with the practical challenges faced by security teams in the field.

From this visualization, Figure 2.2, we observed the emergence of five thematic clusters:

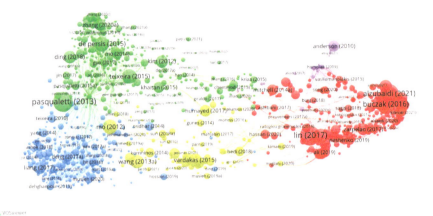

Figure 2.2 WoS Bibliographic coupling output.

1. **Green**: Concentrating on cyber–physical systems (CPS)
2. **Blue**: Focusing on cyberattacks (mostly false data injection)
3. **Yellow**: Covering smart grid/industrial control systems (ICS)
4. **Red**: Merging IoT and AI
5. **Purple**: Emphasizing regulation studies and taxonomy studies

It is noteworthy that while each theme has been consistently addressed over time, cluster 4, focusing on IoT (Internet of Things) and AI, exhibits a particularly high density. This observation implies that among the most-cited documents today, topics related to IoT and AI are frequently encountered. This trend suggests a growing interest and recognition of the importance of these areas within the cybersecurity research community. Such a concentration indicates not only the evolving nature of cybersecurity challenges but also points to the increasing relevance of advanced technologies in addressing these challenges. Surprisingly, this analysis predominantly reveals themes related to the industry, indicating that this sector mostly drives big research in cybersecurity. Innovations in this field often stem from challenges encountered, yet paradoxically, these infrastructures remain among the most vulnerable (highlighted in annual cybersecurity reports – Orange CD or IBM Threat Intelligence). Within these clusters, it's challenging to gauge the extent of works aiming to evaluate and enhance specific protocols, formal methods for security, and best practices for cybersecurity. Thus, we can't status about trends of technical optimizations in this analysis.

2.2 Tackling Cybersecurity Problems Based on Risk Problems Approaches 45

- **Inter-cluster relationships**: Notably, references [13] and [14] illustrate the interplay between studies on cyberattacks and the systems vulnerable to that threat. These studies stand out prominently in the graph. They establish a connection between clusters 1 and 2, hinting at the logical rationale to consider "Threat" and "Object" to defend as an integral whole from the inception of a security project. Effective threat mitigation requires a comprehensive understanding of business requirements, emphasizing that these needs cannot be ignored.
- **The concept of risk**: This notion predominantly appears at the intersections of clusters 1, 3, and 4. This highlights that, in current discourse, "Risk" is more directly connected to systems rather than to attacks as such. However, for a comprehensive understanding of cybersecurity risks associated with these systems, it's crucial to consider past incidents, offering a more nuanced understanding of these risks.

The second analysis, focusing on the co-occurrence of keywords within the same sample, reveals new insights (Figure 2.3). Again, we observe five clusters, but the themes identified within each are not exactly the same as those in the first analysis:

1. **Green**: Cyber–physical systems (CPS) and cyberattacks
2. **Blue**: Internet of Things (IoT)
3. **Yellow**: Industrial control systems (ICS), CIs, and Industry 4.0
4. **Red**: AI and data-driven approaches
5. **Beige**: Macro themes in cybersecurity taxonomy

We notice firstly that the green and blue clusters from the first analysis have merged into the green cluster in the second analysis. This is not surprising given the close proximity of these themes previously observed. The potential amalgamation of these two clusters is associated with the surge in research on Industry 4.0. This sector, driven by increasing digitization and the adoption of technologies like Industrial Internet of Things (IIoT), has led researchers to employ new terms (CPs) when referring to industrial systems composed of these emerging objects.

The red cluster has split into two (blue and red), distinctly highlighting the challenges associated with IoT on one side and the one of AI on the other. The yellow cluster remains unchanged, discussing the challenges cybersecurity aims to address in the fields mentioned, including safety, resilience, and automation. The purple cluster from the first analysis has evolved into a beige cluster that encapsulates broader taxonomic terms in cybersecurity (risk management, information security, model, threat, impact).

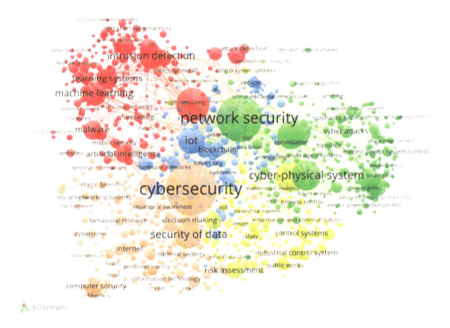

Figure 2.3 Scopus keywords co-occurrences.

This analysis reveals more about our sample, particularly how cybersecurity intersects with AI technologies. Although the keywords appearance related to AI are relatively recent, the substantial size of this cluster indicates that AI has been utilized for several years in addressing cybersecurity challenges. This suggests that the integration of AI into cybersecurity solutions is not merely a result of the recent global surge in AI interest. However, it's notable that the focus is primarily on intrusion detection with classification-based and anomaly detection methods, with minimal or no mention of emerging AI technologies like generative AI.

Once again, the results derived from both databases exhibit a general similarity, although with differing distributions. However, a distinctive feature in Scopus is the focus on human factors and health within the cybersecurity context, particularly highlighted in the beige cluster. This theme has only emerged in recent years, indicating the influence of the COVID-19 pandemic on certain aspects of cybersecurity research.

In the context of our research on developing a methodology for managing cyber risks in CIs, we will narrow our focus to AI-based methods that enhance

2.2 Tackling Cybersecurity Problems Based on Risk Problems Approaches 47

the resilience of these infrastructures against specific types of cyber threats. This involves conducting an analysis alike to the previous one, but with a specific emphasis on the use of AI for cybersecurity within the realm of CIs.

By focusing on this aspect, we aim to glean more nuanced insights into how AI is leveraged to fortify CIs against evolving cyber threats. Thereby identify future research directions and potential gaps in the existing body of knowledge.

To refine our analysis, we will concentrate on a subset of the previously examined dataset. Building on the prior research, we incorporate additional keywords from Table 2.2, forming a query that combines cybersecurity, artificial intelligence, and CIs keywords ({cyber security Keywords} AND {AI keywords} AND {CIs Keywords}).

This refined query reveals a significant difference in the results yielded by Scopus and Web of Science. Specifically, Scopus provides a much more concentrated sample (870 documents), while WoS only reduces the sample by about a third (23,042 documents). This discrepancy highlights a difference in how the two databases interpret and respond to the same query. A closer examination of the WoS results indicates that most of the documents meet only two out of the three criteria, meaning many are not strictly within our defined scope. Consequently, we will focus our analysis on the Scopus sample.

By conducting a new keyword co-occurrence analysis on this Scopus subset, we aim to discern the emerging trends and patterns specifically related to the use of AI in cybersecurity within the context of CIs. This targeted approach should allow us to gain a more nuanced understanding of how AI is being applied to enhance cybersecurity measures in CIs settings.

In our focused research on cybersecurity and AI within CIs, we observe trends that align with those identified in our broader initial study. Particularly, components of CI, previously highlighted in the blue and yellow clusters, remain prominent. The observed reduction in the size of "network security" indicates that this term is primarily employed to address issues outside the

Table 2.2 Research keywords.

AI keywords	Critical infrastructure keywords	
Artificial intelligence	Cyber–physical	Industry 4.0
AI	Cyber–physical	Industrial
Learning	CPS	ICS
Machine learning	Infrastructure	Grids
Deep learning Network	Critical infrastructure	System

operational technology (OT)/Internet of Things (IoT) domain and should be leaning more toward traditional information technology (IT) environments. Elements that we filtered out with our scope.

At the core of this study's network graph, we observe a strong correlation between intrusion detection and "Machine Learning." This trend, already noted in our initial study, is their further associated with classification and clustering methods like k-nearest neighbors (KNN), decision trees, random forests, and k-means. These AI methods are thus being employed to enhance the monitoring of the cyberattack risk.

The observation regarding the treatment of risk in the cybersecurity research literature is indeed insightful. While IDS, broadly detection and response platforms, are frequently presented as a solution to cybersecurity threats, the broader concept of risk management is notably underrepresented. When the notion of risk is addressed, it is often in the context of proposing new frameworks or specializing methods for risk evaluation using techniques like Bayesian analysis, Markov models, fault-tree analysis, and threat modeling. However, these approaches do not typically encompass a comprehensive methodological approach to managing cyber risks from personalized identification through to the evaluation of mitigation strategies.

Regarding this analysis, other phases of risk management process [15], do not seem to be significantly addressed using AI technologies. Nonetheless, in our network graph, there is a spatial proximity between mentions of risk and technologies like NLP, text processing, and long short-term memory (LSTM) networks. These technologies are suited to more reflective and analytical processes, suggesting potential avenues for future application in cyber risk management for CIs. This analysis shows that this evolution in AI has the potential to change the way risks are studied today (RQ2).

From this network, it becomes clear that research cybersecurity for CIs predominantly concentrated on tangible assets and the technologies employed for their safeguarding. This focus reflects an operational perspective, where these elements are critical points susceptible to hazards that could disrupt service continuity or affect the operational environment.

Thus, the analysis far provides an insightful perspective on the current application of AI and machine learning in the field of cybersecurity for CIs. This investigation highlights a pronounced emphasis on detection and response mechanisms. However, it also brings to light a significant underrepresentation in the literature regarding comprehensive cyber risk management strategies that effectively integrate AI technologies.

2.2 Tackling Cybersecurity Problems Based on Risk Problems Approaches

While this method offers a broad overview, it falls short in detailing the specific AI methodologies employed and their intended purposes within the cybersecurity domain. To address the objectives outlined in (RQ2), a more in-depth analysis is required. This subsequent phase of the study will focus on discerning the various AI methods used in cybersecurity, particularly how they are applied across different phases of the risk management process. Going deeper, we aim to uncover a more detailed understanding of AI's role in not just detecting and responding to cyber threats but also in proactively managing and mitigating cyber risks in a comprehensive and holistic manner.

2.2.4 Main Conclusions at this stage

Based on our analysis, the conclusion for this section on cybersecurity in CIs, with an emphasis on the role of AI, can be distilled as follows:

Our exploration of cybersecurity in the realm of CIs, driven by RQ1, revealed a multifaceted and evolving landscape. Initially, we addressed the challenge of defining cybersecurity in a manner that resonates across various domains, particularly in CIs. We recognized the need for a simplified, yet comprehensive taxonomy to make the concept accessible to a broad audience, encompassing both experts and non-experts. This approach serves as a foundation for understanding the specific nuances and requirements of cybersecurity in different CIs contexts.

In delving into the practices of cybersecurity within CIs, we observed a significant reliance on AI technologies that led us to tackle RQ2. AI's role, particularly in intrusion detection and response, is pronounced. However, our analysis also uncovered the underrepresentation of holistic cyber risk management strategies that effectively integrate AI. This suggests that while AI has been instrumental in enhancing certain aspects of cybersecurity, its potential in comprehensive risk management remains underexploited.

Our comparative study of the Web of Science and Scopus databases provided insights into the trends and focus areas within the cybersecurity research communities. We noted a general alignment in the themes explored across both databases.

The analysis points out that the integration of AI into cybersecurity predates the recent widespread hype around AI. The predominant focus has been on intrusion detection using AI-driven classification and anomaly detection methods. However, there is a noticeable lack of exploration into emerging AI technologies, such as generative AI, within this domain.

In conclusion, our investigation underscores the need for future research to extend beyond the current focus on detection and response. There is a crucial requirement for more in-depth studies that examine the diverse possible applications of AI across the entire spectrum of cybersecurity risk management in CIs. Such research would contribute significantly to developing more effective, proactive, and comprehensive cybersecurity strategies, ensuring the resilience and safety of CIs in an increasingly digital and interconnected world.

2.3 Review of How AI Is used and Mobilized in Risk Management Processes

It appears that some research communities directly address cybersecurity from a risk perspective, while others approach it implicitly. This is particularly evident in studies focused on intrusion detection. Such research addresses the monitoring aspects of cyberattack risks and aids in risk analysis, as these systems enhance our understanding of incident behaviors. Building upon the analysis from the first part of our study, we now focus onto the risks of cyber incidents that threaten the resilience, safety, and security of systems. This exploration led us to consider the strategies for cybersecurity and risk management that are employed to counter these threats.

To address our research question on the evaluation of AI use in cybersecurity, we will adopt a risk-focused perspective, particularly with regard to the cyber risks posed by digital technologies usage. As noted at the conclusion of our previous analysis, a more in-depth exploration is required to understand the circumstances, extent, and methods of AI application in addressing cybersecurity risks, particularly within CIs (RQ2).

Our approach will involve classifying AI methods according to the cyber risk phase they address [15, p. 31]. For instance, risk identification can be achieved using convolutional neural networks (CNNs) [16]. To ensure a comprehensive and structured analysis, we will align our exploration with the framework provided by the ISO 31k standard, which offers a well-defined structure for addressing cyber risk issues.

This structured approach allows us to systematically explore, inside our corpus, the various AI methods used in cybersecurity, specifically focusing on how these methods align with different stages of risk management as defined by the ISO 31k standard. By doing so, we aim to provide a clear and thorough understanding of the role of AI in cyber risk management within CIs.

2.3 Review of How AI Is used and Mobilized in Risk Management Processes

For each phase of the risk management process, we will review the current AI techniques being utilized. Additionally, we offer our insights on how AI can potentially contribute to enhancing the effectiveness and relevance of each stage of the cyber risk management process. Our goal is to not only depict the current state of AI in cyber risk management but also to identify opportunities where AI can further advance the field. This approach will allow us to propose innovative and tailored AI solutions that can improve the overall cybersecurity posture of CIs.

2.3.1 Methodology

In our review, we acknowledge the significant contributions of previous studies [17–20] that have meticulously compiled, following similar methodologies, various references that address AI for cybersecurity issues. They have classified their findings based on criteria fine-tuned to their respective research projects. In a similar vein, we propose to categorize these sources through the lens of risk-based cybersecurity approach.

Among these studies, the study in [17] aligns the most closely with our perspective. It adopts a classification based on the description of the cybersecurity enhancement process provided by the NIST [21] in 2018. Notably, this framework has been revised since 2023, introducing a new category of governance that precedes other phases.

By aligning our risk-based approach with the NIST framework, we can affiliate its categories with the risk management description outlined by ISO [16], which serves as the framework for our study (Figure 2.4). This alignment allows us to systematically organize and analyze the AI methods within the context of both cybersecurity and risk management, providing a comprehensive high-level overview of cybersecurity.

Our initial analysis has effectively exposed the relevance of a risk-based approach in the implementation of cybersecurity practices. This methodology comprehensively considers the entire chain of actors and their interactions.

By embracing this global approach, we are able to reuse a wide range of cybersecurity research bricks, emphasizing the critical need for defining a tailored context and framework. This includes the personalized identification of unique hazards that pose risks to each system and their unique characteristics.

Integrating this approach with technologies that are adaptable to the nuances of each system leads, by design, to the implementation of customized, efficient, and effective defense solutions. This strategy not only addresses the multi-faceted nature of cybersecurity challenges but also

52 *Practical Use of AI for Cyber Risk Management in Critical Infrastructures*

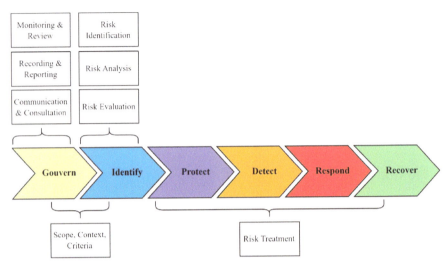

Figure 2.4 ISO Risk Model Associated to NIST CSF 2.0 - 2023

ensures that the solutions are highly relevant and specifically attuned to the distinct requirements of each system.

2.3.2 Documents selection

In our research, we will concentrate on documents previously identified as relevant in other studies, recognizing that all documents dealing with cybersecurity inherently address risk-related problems. This approach allows us to utilize the selection work already done in these studies, ensuring that we focus on sources that are pertinent to our investigation.

After identifying their references under study, we elaborate a condensed[3] dataset that encompasses all the references from the four identified reviews. An interesting first result is the low overlap in the sources used by these reviews. Based on the references DOIs, we found that there is less than 1% similarity among the documents across the four studies. Indeed, the four studies, Table 2.3, share very similar selection criteria but manage to select literature studies that are almost entirely distinct. The work in [18] and [19] is mostly descriptive and, in contrast to the others, serves as a valuable source of information on the machine learning algorithms used in cybersecurity and the contexts in which they can be applied. The study in [18] focuses on

---
[3] Dataset available at : Github

2.3 Review of How AI Is used and Mobilized in Risk Management Processes

Table 2.3 Comparison of this review with existing studies.

	AI classification	Systematic review	Risk approach	Guidance to foster cyber sec	Date
Kaur et al. [17]	Domains [22]	Yes	No	Yes	2023
De Azambuja et al. [19]	Methods	Yes	No	No	2023
Abdullahi et al. [18]	Methods	Yes	No	No	2022
Peres et al. [20]	Domains	Yes	No	Yes	2020
Proposed study	Methods	Yes	Yes	Yes	2023

detection, while the study in [19] conducts an analysis to determine whether AI is beneficial or not for cybersecurity by examining its advantages and disadvantages. They investigate how AI can be utilized by both attackers and defenders. This approach is highly relevant as these two aspects should always be correlated when striving for greater cyber resilience.

In this context, the authors in [17] introduce data representation as a gap in the literature. Addressing this gap is particularly challenging, requiring a comprehensive view of cybersecurity practices and collaboration with industrial partners to build models tailored to their specific business needs. Our work to develop a methodological approach for managing industrial cyber risks aligns with the overarching goal of decision support in the field of cyber risks, whether in prevention or response during crisis management events. The foundation of this methodology relies on knowledge management within the industrial cyber ecosystem and the cyber threats it may face, with a focus on studying factual data from past cyber incidents to construct specialized conceptual decision support models.

The study in [20] takes a broader perspective on AI for industry, considering cybersecurity as one of its components. Unlike other studies, it adopts a proactive stance, providing recommendations based on its literature analysis regarding best practices to maximize the benefits of AI while mitigating negative aspects described in [19]. The study addresses issues such as data availability and quality in the industrial environment, emphasizing that knowledge remains central to all innovations in this sector.

The primary objective of our analysis is not to delve into the metadata of the sources, such as document types or subject areas, but rather to focus on associating AI methods with specific stages of the risk management process. For this chapter, we will examine a representative sample from this condensed dataset, specifically selecting sources from [17]. This is the closest work to our study as it tries to provide a practical methodology for implementing cybersecurity practice (Table 2.3). Additionally, we will augment this corpus with few recent literatures that has been published after the time frame of the previous study, ensuring our analysis remains current and comprehensive.

As part of our broader research project, we plan to explore the remaining sources in this dataset in future work. This will provide an opportunity to conduct statistical analyses on the corpus, categorizing the documents based on various criteria such as AI methods used, stages of risk management addressed, mention of specific technologies, and documents presenting use cases.

2.3.3 Results

Our analysis, as outlined in Annex, Table 2.4, offers a first overview of AI methods in the context of cybersecurity, particularly through the lens of risk management. This classification aligns AI techniques with the various stages of the risk management process, providing a clear perspective on how these technologies are applied in practice. In the following sections, we delve into the specifics of each phase, highlighting notable trends and observations that emerge from our dataset. The full review is available on Github.

It is observed that most AI technology applications are related to cyber risk treatment (RT), a trend previously identified in the bibliometric study with the emergence of the red and green clusters (AI and cyber incidents). Additionally, comparing the ISO 31k standard on generic risks to the NIST CSF or MITRE D3FEND frameworks (Figure 2.4), more than half of the action phases are dedicated to cyber risk treatment rather than than Risk Identification (RI), Risk Assessment (RA) or even Risk Evaluation (RE). This is understandable as these preliminary phases are currently the most subjective and least concrete. They represent the most challenging aspects to address and evaluate concretely. Nevertheless, it is crucial to emphasize that these initial phases, which group together the majority of actions in a risk-based approach, are just as important as the concrete action/deployment phases.

The MITRE Framework alone is challenging to utilize in its current state, but it shows promise in attempting to link the actions of an attacker with those that a defender should take to counter them. Detailed refinement of these preliminary phases is essential for enhancing cybersecurity, making them less subjective and more accessible for frontline security operators today. In the following studies, we will explore that, currently, there is no substantial effort leveraging AI for this specific purpose.

2.3 Review of How AI Is used and Mobilized in Risk Management Processes

Table 2.4 Sample of references

References	AI methods/domain	Refers to dataset	Risk management stage	Date
Promyslov et al. [23]	K-means clustering	no	RI	2019
Millar et al. [24]	Random forest	no	Scope – context	2020
Cam [25]	Logistic regression	no	RT	2017
Tozer et al. [26]	Reinforcement learning	no	RI	2015
Huff et al. [27]	NLP	yes	RI	2021
Valero et al. [28]	k-nearest neighbors, Bayes net, decision tree, SVM	no	RT	2018
Baldini et al. [29]	SVM, K-NN, decision tree, CNN	yes	RT	2021
Cui et al. [30]	Random forest classification	no	RT	2021
Le et al. [31]	Unsupervised learning	no	RT	2021
Gualberto et al. [32]	XGBoost, Random forest	yes	RT	2020
Li et al. [33]	RNN	yes	RT	2021
Kumar et al. [34]	ANN	no	RT	2021
Wu et al. [35]	Auto-encoder	yes	RT	2021
Abdulhammed et al. [36]	Random forest, naive Bayes	yes	RT	2018
Huang & Lei [37]	Deep learning, CNN, generative adversarial network	yes	RT	2020
Shah et al. [38]	Reinforcement learning	no	RA	2018
Decastro-Garcia et al. [39].	Machine learning	no	RE	2020
Sakhnini et al. [40]	Machine learning	yes	RI	2021
Piplai et al. [41]	Deep learning	no	RI	2020
Meyers and Meneely [42]	NLP	no	RI	2021
Carriegos et al. [43]	Machine learning	no	RI – RA – RE	2021
Ragab et al. [44]	Deep learning	no	RT	2023
Perales Gómez et al. [45]	Decision trees, random forest, deep learning	no	Scope – RI	2023
Singh Sangher et al. [46]	Random forest, XGBoost algorithm	no	RI – RA	2024

Table 2.5 Bibliometric literature review

References	Cybersecurity general analysis	Performances focus	Trends focus	Cyber risk mentions	AI mentions	Industrial topic mentions	Sample size
[18]		x			x	x	80
[47]	x	x	x		x	x	1133
[48]		x		x			749
[49]		x	x		x		820
[50]		x	x		x		1068
[51]		x	x	x			417
[52]		x	x			x	1500
[53]		x	x				715
[54]		x					10 607
[19]		x			x	x	138
Proposed Study	x	x	x	x	x	x	20 000

The use of AI capable of explaining its decisions, coupled with factual data, would significantly contribute to informed strategic decision-making and optimize the implementation of relevant security measures. Today, as observed in the following study, the majority of data used in training datasets are simulated or based on expert judgment. While more accessible, this type of data unfortunately does not reflect reality as well as factual data on real cyber incidents. In our future research, we will focus on developing a knowledge base of detailed and factual data on past incidents to enhance the relevance of results derived from risk assessment techniques. This approach aims to address emerging trends in the use of new AI technologies to tackle the aforementioned challenges.

2.3.3.1 Scope, context, and criteria

The initial stage of risk assessment is pivotal, as it involves understanding the client's specific needs and requirements. This step is essential for determining the appropriate taxonomy and approach to address the identified issues effectively. Our literature review reveals that the practical application of AI in this phase is relatively limited. This is primarily due to the necessity for advanced natural language understanding and processing capabilities.

However, the potential use of finely-tuned large language models (LLMs) in this context is promising. These models could be employed to analyze organizational documents such as statutes, policies, and strategic objectives. By doing so, they can assist in identifying areas that are most relevant for the application of risk management strategies, thereby providing a tailored and efficient approach to addressing the unique challenges faced by each organization.

2.3.3.2 Risk identifications

In the NIST framework, Figure 2.4, the identification phase is associated with the entire risk management process. However, when adopting a risk-based approach, this phase aims to accurately depict the threats that could interact with the system's vulnerabilities, potentially compromising it in various ways, such as through espionage, destruction, or motivated by economic gain.

In terms of identification, there are more studies addressing this topic. This includes research focusing on cyberattacks and their consequences on systems, as well as studies on cyber threat intelligence. However, the number of these studies is relatively limited compared to those illustrating risk treatment. This observation suggests a potential gap in the literature, highlighting the need for more focused research on the initial stages of risk management, particularly in the context of identifying and understanding the nature of cyber threats.

2.3.3.3 Risk analysis and risk evaluation

The concepts of risk assessment and risk evaluation typically go hand in hand and are often discussed in studies addressing risk-related topics. These concepts are crucial in determining, based on the context, which risks should be prioritized. This vital step is not commonly addressed in practice through AI methods. Instead, statistical mathematical methods or expert judgments are often used to classify risks.

However, there is potential for AI, particularly LLMs, to play a role in this process. LLMs could be employed to model the likelihood of specific events occurring based on structured modeling of historical data or contextual information. Furthermore, they can assist in analyzing various scenarios and estimating the potential impact of a risk on the business. This approach to risk evaluation using AI could provide a more nuanced and data-driven understanding of risks, enhancing the traditional methods of risk assessment and evaluation.

2.3.3.4 Risk treatment

The concept of risk treatment is prominently featured in our study, echoing the conclusions drawn in Section 2.1. Indeed, all solutions – whether software, hardware, organizational, or human – aimed at protection are essentially responses to identified or unidentified risks.

In this context, LLMs have the potential to offer customized risk management strategies based on the information available and their specific training.

For instance, if an LLM is knowledgeable about best practice frameworks, it could suggest appropriate measures to address the specific risks identified for a client.

2.4 Discussion

This study, as an initial version, highlights the need for a more specific taxonomy tailored to cyber risk management. For instance, in the identification phase, a detailed description of potential consequences on CIs due to cyberattacks, such as system failure risks, would enhance the relevance of the analysis.

A notable limitation in the documents reviewed was the often unclear distinction of the specific AI methods used. In many cases, we could only ascertain the high-level domain of AI application, which does not provide detailed insights into the actual methods employed for addressing these risks.

Despite these limitations, our analysis demonstrates the applicability of our methodology, which aims for a more holistic approach to cybersecurity risk studies. This approach goes beyond "simple" detection and response to threats; it systematically manages the entire spectrum of cybersecurity risks. It encompasses the identification of potential risks, assessment of their impact, development of mitigation strategies, and continuous monitoring and adjustment of these strategies. This comprehensive approach ensures effective and dynamic management of cybersecurity risks, adapting to evolving threats and organizational needs.

Indeed, the current focus on specific techniques and tools, while important, does not fully address the need for an overarching methodology that integrates these elements into a cohesive risk management process. The development of such a comprehensive framework would be a significant contribution to the field, ensuring that cybersecurity measures are not only reactive but also proactive in identifying and mitigating potential threats before they materialize.

However, employing AI to address these issues is not a panacea, as this technology brings its own set of challenges. The need for high-quality data, the demand for explainability in AI, and ethical considerations are significant hurdles. Moreover, LLMs still exhibit a degree of hallucinatory behavior, which can be detrimental to our studies. Further research is necessary for future LLMs to effectively follow complete scenarios or methodologies. This highlights the importance of a balanced and cautious approach in integrating

AI into cyber risk management, ensuring that the technology's limitations are understood and addressed.

2.4.1 Potential analysis bias and limitations

Our study on cybersecurity in CIs, particularly regarding AI applications, has inherent methodological biases that need consideration for accurate interpretation. Key bias includes firstly a language bias, potentially missing non-English research. A publication bias, where studies with positive results are more frequently published. Additionally, the subjective nature of data interpretation and the challenge of contextualizing findings within a rapidly evolving field are significant. To address these biases, employing varied sources and methodologies, and regularly updating our analysis to include the latest research is also crucial for maintaining relevance and accuracy.

Our study on cybersecurity in CIs, with a focus on AI applications, faces limitations in its scope and findings due to several factors. The reliance on Web of Science and Scopus databases, while comprehensive, means we might have overlooked relevant studies published in less-known sources. Additionally, our methodology's heavy dependence on specific keywords could have limited the research scope, potentially missing significant studies that use different terminologies or focus on less common aspects of cybersecurity. Furthermore, the analysis excludes publications after April 2023, leaving out the most recent studies and developments in the field, which could provide fresh insights or emerging trends in cybersecurity and AI applications in CIs.

2.5 Conclusion and Perspectives

In this chapter, we undertook a detailed examination of the concept of cybersecurity, demonstrating that it is a practice aimed at implementing solutions to protect systems from potential hazards they may encounter. We focused on the field of CIs to discern how research in this domain addresses the use of AI in cybersecurity.

In our review, we scrutinized the various AI methods employed to address different phases of the risk management process for underlying cyber risks. This examination was guided by an understanding of cybersecurity in CIs, where the stakes are exceptionally high, and the need for robust and effective risk management strategies is paramount.

Our analysis highlighted that AI technologies are predominantly applied in the risk treatment stage of cyber risk management and that the other phases of the process are not yet tackled with these technologies (from RQ2 study). This includes the use of machine learning algorithms for intrusion detection, neural networks for anomaly detection, and NLP for threat intelligence. These AI-driven methods have shown effectiveness in identifying potential cyber threats and understanding the paths of incidents, thus contributing to a more informed risk analysis phase.

However, our review also revealed a gap in the application of AI in other phases of the risk management process, particularly in the identification of risks. While AI has made strides in enhancing the capabilities of cybersecurity systems in terms of detection and response, its integration into a holistic risk management framework is still in its nascent stages.

In addressing the initial question regarding the potential overemphasis of AI in the tech market, our analysis reveals an interesting trend. New technologies indeed promise significant advancements, but the portrayal of AI in the market often leans toward marketing strategies. Vendors are capitalizing on the widespread enthusiasm for a particular AI technique, leveraging this interest to emphasize their use of AI in marketing their products. However, behind this facade, many solutions rely on classical and well-established machine learning (ML) techniques that have been around for years.

Moreover, our findings emphasize that AI, as potent as it is, does not operate in isolation. It achieves its best when integrated with other technologies and methodologies, especially in the context of cybersecurity for CIs. This integration ensures that AI is not just a buzzword but a key component of a comprehensive and effective cybersecurity solution. A global approach, which is becoming increasingly popular, and which is part of the overall vision that a risk approach can offer (RQ1).

This finding underscores the need for a more comprehensive approach to AI application in cybersecurity, one that extends beyond detection and analysis to encompass the entire spectrum of risk management activities. Such an approach would not only improve the resilience and safety of CIs but would also contribute to the development of more robust and adaptive cybersecurity strategies that can anticipate, evaluate, and mitigate risks more effectively. For this purpose, the use of new AI technologies has to be studied.

Thus, this review is part of a broader effort to develop a cyber risk management methodology specifically tailored for CIs sectors. It represents an initial step toward creating customized frameworks designed to meet the unique needs of these industries, as depicted in section 2.1. The aim of our contribution is to support professionals that are responsible for managing cybersecurity, enabling them to adapt to specific business context and systems. This approach offers an input, complementing more generalized frameworks like EBIOS (Expression des besoins et identification des objectifs de sécurité) from French National Agency for Information Systems Security or CSF (Cybersecurity Framework) from the NIST, which are designed to address a wide range of business domains. A forthcoming step in this project involves *identifying* typologies of *risks* posed by cyber threats to CIs, to refine our understanding and approach to managing these risks in a targeted and effective manner.

Acknowledgment

This work has been founded by ALTEN SA. We extend our gratitude to some interns at Sophia DIN Lab, for their efforts in gathering and organizing the myriad references from various studies. their meticulous work has been instrumental in enabling the comparative analysis that forms the backbone of our research.

References

[1] "A Brief History of Neural Nets and Deep Learning," Skynet Today. Accessed: Nov. 15, 2023. [Online]. Available: https://www.skynettoday.com/overviews/neural-net-history

[2] S. Das, A. Dey, A. Pal, and N. Roy, "Applications of Artificial Intelligence in Machine Learning: Review and Prospect," IJCA, vol. 115, no. 9, pp. 31–41, Apr. 2015, doi:10.5120/20182-2402.

[3] M. Christen, B. Gordijn, and M. Loi, Eds., The Ethics of Cybersecurity, vol. 21. in The International Library of Ethics, Law and Technology, vol. 21. Cham: Springer International Publishing, 2020. doi:10.1007/978-3-030-29053-5.

[4] S. M. Khalil, H. Bahsi, and T. Korõtko, "Threat modeling of industrial control systems: A systematic literature review," Computers & Security, vol. 136, p. 103543, Jan. 2024, doi:10.1016/j.cose.2023.103543.

[5] L. Neil, J. M. Haney, K. Buchanan, and C. Healy, "Analyzing Cybersecurity Definitions for Non-experts," IFIP Advances in Information and Communication Technology, vol. 674, pp. 391–404, 2023, doi: 10.1007/978-3-031-38530-8_31.

[6] M. G. Cains, L. Flora, D. Taber, Z. King, and D. S. Henshel, "Defining Cyber Security and Cyber Security Risk within a Multidisciplinary

Context using Expert Elicitation," Risk Analysis, vol. 42, no. 8, pp. 1643–1669, 2022, doi:10.1111/risa.13687.

[7] H. Taherdoost, "Cybersecurity vs. Information Security," Procedia Computer Science, vol. 215, pp. 483–487, Jan. 2022, doi:10.1016/j.procs.2022.12.050.

[8] "ISO/IEC 27032:2023(en), Cybersecurity — Guidelines for Internet security." Accessed: Nov. 14, 2023. [Online]. Available: https://www.iso.org/obp/ui/#iso:std:iso-iec:27032:ed-2:v1:en

[9] N. Donthu, S. Kumar, D. Mukherjee, N. Pandey, and W. M. Lim, "How to conduct a bibliometric analysis: An overview and guidelines," Journal of Business Research, vol. 133, pp. 285–296, 2021, doi:10.1016/j.jbusres.2021.04.070.

[10] T. Venturini, M. Jacomy, and P. Jensen, "What do we see when we look at networks: Visual network analysis, relational ambiguity, and force-directed layouts," Big Data & Society, vol. 8, no. 1, p. 205395172110184, Jan. 2021, doi:10.1177/20539517211018488.

[11] M. Visser, N. J. Van Eck, and L. Waltman, "Large-scale comparison of bibliographic data sources: Scopus, Web of Science, Dimensions, Crossref, and Microsoft Academic," Quantitative Science Studies, vol. 2, no. 1, pp. 20–41, Apr. 2021, doi:10.1162/qss_a_00112.

[12] N. J. van Eck, L. Waltman, R. Dekker, and J. van den Berg, "A comparison of two techniques for bibliometric mapping: Multidimensional scaling and VOS," Journal of the American Society for Information Science and Technology, vol. 61, no. 12, pp. 2405–2416, 2010, doi:10.1002/asi.21421.

[13] Y. Zacchia Lun, A. D'Innocenzo, F. Smarra, I. Malavolta, and M. D. Di Benedetto, "State of the art of cyber-physical systems security: An automatic control perspective," Journal of Systems and Software, vol. 149, pp. 174–216, Mar. 2019, doi:10.1016/j.jss.2018.12.006.

[14] H. S. Sánchez, D. Rotondo, T. Escobet, V. Puig, and J. Quevedo, "Bibliographical review on cyber attacks from a control oriented perspective," Annual Reviews in Control, vol. 48, pp. 103–128, Jan. 2019, doi:10.1016/j.arcontrol.2019.08.002.

[15] "ISO 31000:2018(en), Risk management — Guidelines." Accessed: Nov. 30, 2023. [Online]. Available: https://www.iso.org/obp/ui/#iso:std:iso:31000:ed-2:v1:en

[16] F. Sufi, "A global cyber-threat intelligence system with artificial intelligence and convolutional neural network," Decision Analytics Journal, vol. 9, p. 100364, Dec. 2023, doi:10.1016/j.dajour.2023.100364.

[17] R. Kaur, D. Gabrijelčič, and T. Klobučar, "Artificial intelligence for cybersecurity: Literature review and future research directions," Information Fusion, vol. 97, p. 101804, Sep. 2023, doi:10.1016/j.inffus.2023.101804.

[18] M. Abdullahi et al., "Detecting Cybersecurity Attacks in Internet of Things Using Artificial Intelligence Methods: A Systematic Literature Review," Electronics, vol. 11, no. 2, Art. no. 2, Jan. 2022, doi:10.3390/electronics11020198.

[19] A. J. G. de Azambuja, C. Plesker, K. Schützer, R. Anderl, B. Schleich, and V. R. Almeida, "Artificial Intelligence-Based Cyber Security in the Context of Industry 4.0—A Survey," Electronics, vol. 12, no. 8, Art. no. 8, Jan. 2023, doi:10.3390/electronics12081920.

[20] R. Peres, X. Jia, J. Lee, K. Sun, A. Colombo, and J. Barata, "Industrial Artificial Intelligence in Industry 4.0 - Systematic Review, Challenges and Outlook," IEEE Access, vol. 8, pp. 220121–220139, Dec. 2020, doi: 10.1109/ACCESS.2020.3042874.

[21] National Institute of Standards and Technology, "Framework for Improving Critical Infrastructure Cybersecurity, Version 1.1," National Institute of Standards and Technology, Gaithersburg, MD, NIST CSWP 04162018, Apr. 2018. doi:10.6028/NIST.CSWP.04162018.

[22] S. Samoili, C. M. Lopez, G. E. Gomez, P. G. De, F. Martinez-Plumed, and B. Delipetrev, "AI WATCH. Defining Artificial Intelligence," JRC Publications Repository. Accessed: Nov. 30, 2023. [Online]. Available: https://publications.jrc.ec.europa.eu/repository/handle/JRC118163

[23] y"A Clustering Method of Asset Cybersecurity Classification - ScienceDirect." Accessed: Nov. 30, 2023. [Online]. Available: https://www-sciencedirect-com.proxy.bu.dauphine.fr/science/article/pii/S2405896319312881

[24] K. MILLAR, A. CHENG, H. G. CHEW, and C.-C. LIM, "Operating System Classification: A Minimalist Approach," in 2020 International Conference on Machine Learning and Cybernetics (ICMLC), Dec. 2020, pp. 143–150. doi:10.1109/ICMLC51923.2020.9469571.

[25] H. Cam, "Online detection and control of malware infected assets," in MILCOM 2017 - 2017 IEEE Military Communications Conference (MILCOM), Oct. 2017, pp. 701–706. doi: 10.1109/MILCOM.2017.8170869.

[26] "Optimizing Attack Surface and Configuration Diversity Using Multi-objective Reinforcement Learning | IEEE Conference Publication | IEEE Xplore." Accessed: Nov. 30, 2023. [Online]. Available: https://ieeexplore.ieee.org/document/7424300

[27] P. Huff, K. McClanahan, T. Le, and Q. Li, "A Recommender System for Tracking Vulnerabilities," in Proceedings of the 16th International Conference on Availability, Reliability and Security, in ARES '21. New York, NY, USA: Association for Computing Machinery, août 2021, pp. 1–7. doi: 10.1145/3465481.3470039.

[28] "Sensors | Free Full-Text | Improving the Security and QoE in Mobile Devices through an Intelligent and Adaptive Continuous Authentication System." Accessed: Nov. 30, 2023. [Online]. Available: https://www.mdpi.com/1424-8220/18/11/3769

[29] G. Baldini, R. Giuliani, M. Gemo, and F. Dimc, "On the application of sensor authentication with intrinsic physical features to vehicle security," Computers & Electrical Engineering, vol. 91, p. 107053, May 2021, doi:10.1016/j.compeleceng.2021.107053.

[30] Y. Cui, F. Bai, R. Yan, T. Saha, R. K. L. Ko, and Y. Liu, "Source Authentication of Distribution Synchrophasors for Cybersecurity of Microgrids," IEEE Transactions on Smart Grid, vol. 12, no. 5, pp. 4577–4580, Sep. 2021, doi:10.1109/TSG.2021.3089041.

[31] D. C. Le and N. Zincir-Heywood, "Anomaly Detection for Insider Threats Using Unsupervised Ensembles," IEEE Transactions on Network and Service Management, vol. 18, no. 2, pp. 1152–1164, Jun. 2021, doi:10.1109/TNSM.2021.3071928.

[32] E. S. Gualberto, R. T. De Sousa, T. P. De Brito Vieira, J. P. C. L. Da Costa, and C. G. Duque, "The Answer is in the Text: Multi-Stage Methods for Phishing Detection Based on Feature Engineering," IEEE Access, vol. 8, pp. 223529–223547, 2020, doi:10.1109/ACCESS.2020.3043396.

[33] Z. Li, A. L. G. Rios, and L. Trajković, "Machine Learning for Detecting Anomalies and Intrusions in Communication Networks," IEEE Journal on Selected Areas in Communications, vol. 39, no. 7, pp. 2254–2264, Jul. 2021, doi:10.1109/JSAC.2021.3078497.

[34] K. P. S. Kumar, S. A. H. Nair, D. Guha Roy, B. Rajalingam, and R. S. Kumar, "Security and privacy-aware Artificial Intrusion Detection System using Federated Machine Learning," Computers & Electrical Engineering, vol. 96, p. 107440, Dec. 2021, doi:10.1016/j.compeleceng.2021.107440.

[35] J.-C. Wu, S. Lu, C.-S. Fuh, and T.-L. Liu, "One-class anomaly detection via novelty normalization," Computer Vision and Image Understanding, vol. 210, p. 103226, Sep. 2021, doi:10.1016/j.cviu.2021.103226.

[36] "Enhancing Wireless Intrusion Detection Using Machine Learning Classification with Reduced Attribute Sets | IEEE Conference Publication IEEE Xplore." Accessed: Nov. 30, 2023. [Online]. Available: https://ieeexplore.ieee.org/document/8450479

[37] S. Huang and K. Lei, "IGAN-IDS: An imbalanced generative adversarial network towards intrusion detection system in ad-hoc networks," Ad Hoc Networks, vol. 105, p. 102177, Aug. 2020, doi:10.1016/j.adhoc.2020.102177.

[38] A. Shah, R. Ganesan, S. Jajodia, and H. Cam, "Dynamic Optimization of the Level of Operational Effectiveness of a CSOC Under Adverse Conditions," ACM Trans. Intell. Syst. Technol., vol. 9, no. 5, p. 51:1-51:20, avril 2018, doi: 10.1145/3173457.

[39] N. DeCastro-García, Á. L. Muñoz Castañeda, and M. Fernández-Rodríguez, "Machine learning for automatic assignment of the severity of cybersecurity events," Computational and Mathematical Methods, vol. 2, no. 1, p. e1072, 2020, doi:10.1002/cmm4.1072.

[40] J. Sakhnini, H. Karimipour, A. Dehghantanha, and R. M. Parizi, "Physical layer attack identification and localization in cyber–physical grid: An ensemble deep learning based approach," Physical Communication, vol. 47, p. 101394, Aug. 2021, doi:10.1016/j.phycom.2021.101394.

[41] "Creating Cybersecurity Knowledge Graphs From Malware After Action Reports | IEEE Journals & Magazine | IEEE Xplore." Accessed: Nov. 30, 2023. [Online]. Available: https://ieeexplore.ieee.org/document/9264152

[42] B. S. Meyers and A. Meneely, "An Automated Post-Mortem Analysis of Vulnerability Relationships using Natural Language Word Embeddings," Procedia Computer Science, vol. 184, pp. 953–958, Jan. 2021, doi:10.1016/j.procs.2021.04.018.

[43] M. V. Carriegos, Á. L. M. Castañeda, M. T. Trobajo, and D. A. De Zaballa, "On Aggregation and Prediction of Cybersecurity Incident Reports," IEEE Access, vol. 9, pp. 102636–102648, 2021, doi:10.1109/ACCESS.2021.3097834.

[44] "Mathematics | Free Full-Text | Robust DDoS Attack Detection Using Piecewise Harris Hawks Optimizer with Deep Learning for a Secure Internet of Things Environment." Accessed: Jan. 09, 2024. [Online]. Available: https://www.mdpi.com/2227-7390/11/21/4448

[45] A. L. Perales Gómez, L. Fernández Maimó, A. Huertas Celdrán, and F. J. García Clemente, "VAASI: Crafting valid and abnormal adversarial samples for anomaly detection systems in industrial scenarios," Journal of Information Security and Applications, vol. 79, p. 103647, Dec. 2023, doi:10.1016/j.jisa.2023.103647.

[46] "Holistic Cyber Threat Hunting Using Network Traffic Intrusion Detection Analysis for Ransomware Attacks," springerprofessional.de. Accessed: Jan. 09, 2024. [Online]. Available: https://www.springerprofessional.de/en/holistic-cyber-threat-hunting-using-network-traffic-intrusion-de/26253044

[47] Y. Cao, A. Yang, H. Li, Q. Zeng, and J. Gao, "A comprehensive knowledge map for AI improving security management of cyber-physical system enabled smart manufacturing," Computers & Security, vol. 137, p. 103650, Feb. 2024, doi:10.1016/j.cose.2023.103650.

[48] H. Nobanee, A. Alodat, R. Bajodah, M. Al-Ali, and A. Al Darmaki, "Bibliometric analysis of cybercrime and cybersecurity risks literature," Journal of Financial Crime, vol. 30, no. 6, pp. 1736–1754, 2023, doi: 10.1108/JFC-11-2022-0287.

[49] M. O. Enebechi, C. N. Enebechi, and V. G. Duffy, "A Bibliometric Analysis on Cybercrime in Nigeria," Lecture Notes in Computer Science (including subseries Lecture Notes in Artificial Intelligence and Lecture Notes in Bioinformatics), vol. 13094 LNCS, pp. 249–269, 2021, doi: 10.1007/978-3-030-90238-4_18.

[50] R. Raman, V. K. Nair, P. Nedungadi, I. Ray, and K. Achuthan, "Darkweb research: Past, present, and future trends and mapping to sustainable development goals," Heliyon, vol. 9, no. 11, Nov. 2023, doi:10.1016/j.heliyon.2023.e22269.

[51] M. Chaal et al., "Research on risk, safety, and reliability of autonomous ships: A bibliometric review," Safety Science, vol. 167, p. 106256, Nov. 2023, doi:10.1016/j.ssci.2023.106256.

[52] C.-H. Lin and V. G. Duffy, "Safety Management and Challenges Associated with Industry 4.0 on Transportation and Logistics: A Systematic Literature Review," in HCI International 2021 - Late Breaking Papers: HCI Applications in Health, Transport, and Industry, C. Stephanidis, V. G. Duffy, H. Krömker, F. Fui-Hoon Nah, K. Siau, G. Salvendy, and J. Wei, Eds., in Lecture Notes in Computer Science. Cham: Springer International Publishing, 2021, pp. 562–575. doi:10.1007/978-3-030-90966-6_38.

[53] M. N. I. Farooqui, J. Arshad, and M. M. Khan, "A bibliometric approach to quantitatively assess current research trends in 5G security," Library Hi Tech, vol. 39, no. 4, pp. 1097–1120, Jan. 2021, doi:10.1108/LHT-04-2021-0133.

[54] S. M. Dhawan, B. M. Gupta, and B. Elango, "Global Cyber Security Research Output (1998–2019): A Scientometric Analysis," Science & Technology Libraries, vol. 40, no. 2, pp. 172–189, Apr. 2021, doi:10.1080/0194262X.2020.1840487.

3
Fraud Detection in Decentralized Autonomous Organization (DAO) with Machine Learning

Aderonke Favour-Betty Thompson[1], Bukola Abimbola Onyekwelu[2], and Samson Nsikan Obong[3]

[1]VTT Technical Research Institute of Finland
[2]Department of Mathematics and Computer Science, Elizade University, Nigeria
[3]Department of Cyber Security, Federal University of Technology, Nigeria
E-mail: ext-aderonke.thompson@vtt.fi;
bukola.onyekwelu@elizadeuniversity.edu.ng; obongsamson00@gmail.com

Abstract

A decentralized autonomous organization (DAO) is a type of enterprise that operates on a decentralized structure where all members have equal contribution, right, and decision-making in the organization. This organization makes use of smart contracts, a software where the rules and policies of the organization are embedded. They are susceptible to threats and fraudulent activities which compromise their security. A flaw in the DAO's smart contract could lead to exploitation by hackers. This research is aimed at developing a fraud detection system using machine learning models and evaluating the performance of the system using standard performance metrics. Machine learning algorithms were employed to detect frauds in the DAO platform built under the Ethereum blockchain using a dataset of transactions, consisting of fraudulent and non-fraudulent transactions. Algorithms employed were the logistic regression, XGBoost, and random forest. These models were built and trained, and hyper parameter tuning was carried out on them. The results obtained from the evaluation metrics show that random forest and XGBoost give better results when compared to logistic regression. Logistic regression had accuracy and precision of 82.07% and 55.53%. Random forest had accuracy and precision of 98.52% and 96.49%. For XGBoost, its accuracy and precision are 98.12% are 93.33%. Other evaluation metrics were used in carrying out analysis, showing the best performing models, the random forest and the XGBoost. At the end of this research, a model for predicting threats in DAO was developed for the ecosystem. The developed system could be utilized in making predictions from past information like patterns of transactions and other available features, to ascertain if the account is fraudulent or not, that account can be terminated.

Keywords: Decentralized autonomous organization, logistic regression, random forest, extreme gradient boosting, Ethereum.

3.1 Introduction

A decentralized autonomous organization (DAO) is a form of bottom-up enterprise having no central authority. It is organized, managed, and facilitated by members or groups of members driven by goals of equal similarities. Members of a DAO have tokens of the DAO, and can vote on initiatives for the entity. Smart contracts are implemented for the DAO, and the code governing the DAO's operations is publicly disclosed [1]. DAO appears to be one of the most pertinent applications of Ethereum in the world of digital currencies, blockchain, and crypto blockchain. As opposed to traditional organizations whose management and governance are performed by central authorities like the Board of Directors, DAOs' governance is coordinated by computer programs. This makes the organization accessible and transparent, making it easy for all members to participate. DAOs also differ from traditional organizations in the sense that the principals all have equal voting power on projects in the firm and they all can partake in decision-making process based of the number of tokens they each have. Unlike the traditional organizations where only the board of directors is involved in the structuring and modification of the system, DAOs governance is carried out by stakeholders who all have their tokens in the system. DAOs make use of "Smart contracts" which is a coded computer software containing the rules, regulations, and policies of the organization. It is immutable and decisions done in it cannot be changed unless there is a voting of equal number by members of that community [2]. MakerDAO is a major example of a DAO which is progressing rapidly in the ecosystem. Other examples are pleasrDAO, HerstoryDAO, and MetacartelDAO.

Decentralized autonomous organization (DAO) began through a crowdfunding campaign that was done as crypto tokens were sold to the general public for members to acquire. An excess amount of these tokens was sold to the large public making it one the largest crowd-funding in history, which led to the launching of DAO on the 30th of April, 2016 on the Ethereum blockchain with its source code being an open source. DAO's code was first published into Github for other developers to work on and to modify. The establishment and governance of these decentralized autonomous organizations is performed based on regulations embedded in smart contract software executed alongside the blockchain technology. With blockchain, the provision of a well-fortified "peer-to-peer distributed trustless ledger of transaction" is made available, making it differ from centralized ledgers in which both the maintenance of the ledger and transaction processes is carried out by a centralized authority [3]. Smart contracts give members the privilege to vote based on the amount of investment they have in the community. Therefore, both blockchain and smart contracts serve as major foundations for a lot of DAOs in that it solely relies on these applications for its day-to-day documentation and transaction of funds, maintenance, and also activities performed [3].

While we have seen the upsides of this decentralized autonomous system, there are also a few downsides as well as risks and threats that could wreak havoc in this transparent organization. As much as the DAO system is a good-proof-concept, it fails because of the vulnerabilities in its code. Due to its transparency and open-source system; it has exposed DAO to cyberattacks.

Although we have seen the upsides of this decentralized autonomous system, there are also a few downsides as well as risks and threats that could wreak havoc in a transparent organization. This has led and exposed DAO to attacks by hackers. When a smart contract has been deployed live on the Ethereum blockchain by developers for a DAO, a bugged system can no longer be changed, modified, or upgraded unless it undergoes severe and thorough measures. A flaw in the DAO's smart contract led exploitation by hackers, who are very hell-bent on taking advantage of the bugs present on DAOs and smart contracts. The aim of this research is to proffer a solution through artificial intelligence and machine learning that would help curb threats and illicit behaviors that occur and affect the security and integrity of DAO. It aims to solve the problem of little data used in previous work by retaining as much features as possible in order to have a vast amount of data to train our models to give accurate and better results. The objectives are to develop a fraud detection system using machine learning models and evaluate the performance of this system using standard performance metrics.

At the end of this research, a model for predicting threats in DAO was developed for the ecosystem. The developed system could be utilized in making predictions from past information like patterns of transactions carried out and other available features, to ascertain if the account is a fraudulent account or not, or if it is simply going to carry out malicious practice in the organization and that account can be terminated before it imposes more malicious acts in the system.

3.2 Related Works

Several traditional vulnerability tools such as static analysis, dynamic analysis tools, and other machine learning algorithms as well have been used in the detection vulnerabilities present in smart contracts. However, a lot of these tools have their accuracy levels, some depending on the smart contracts it's used on and some of these researchers have limitations in their work.

In their research, the authors in [4] proposed ContractFuzzer, a special fuzzing framework helpful for the detection of precisely seven (7) vulnerabilities out of a total of 6991 vulnerabilities of smart contracts. The infamous "TheDAO" re-entrancy vulnerability was among the 459 smart contract vulnerabilities that this detection tool in their experiment was able to find. Further testing revealed that ContractFuzzer outperformed ONYENTE (a security verification tool) not only by being able to identify more vulnerability but also by having low false-positive rates. The tool's limitations include a review of how to reduce the number of false negatives it encounters by looking for patterns left behind by the bugs that plague the smart contract. Additionally, their suggested methodologies were unable to identify additional EVM vulnerabilities in the blockchain.

In their research, the authors in [5] used supervised learning to identify fake accounts on the Ethereum blockchain. Based on information from the Etherscan.io website, one of the most well-known Ethereum blockchain browsers, three classification methods – random forests, support vector machines, and XGBoost – were compared to determine which accounts were suspicious. With a recall of 84.92%, random forest outperformed the other three classifiers. Sensitivity testing was done, and the results demonstrated that the suggested models are not very sensitive to specific explanatory variables.

In their survey, the authors in [6] provided a number of analytical procedures that have been used to verify the accuracy and lack of vulnerable patterns in smart contracts. In their survey, the security analysis techniques were divided into three categories – static, dynamic, and formal verification. They provide a number of symbolic execution tools, including

ONYENTE, MAIAN, ZEUS, and GASPER, SECURIFY, MYTHRIL, and SMARTCHEK, to uncover flaws in smart contracts' code. They contrasted the three (3) in terms of detecting vulnerabilities' accuracy, effectiveness, and coverage. The static and dynamic analysis techniques used automation and tools that are highly practical to utilize and assess weak points in smart contracts. The limitation of these tools is that they can only identify a limited set of vulnerabilities, whereas the formal verification method makes use of theorem provers to verify the accuracy properties of smart contracts by interpreting their interpreted proofs.

In their work, the authors in [7] tried to detect fraudulent accounts based on their transaction history using the XGBoost classifier utilizing 2179 accounts identified by the Ethereum community for their criminal activities together with 2502 regular accounts. In their experiment, XGBoost obtained an average accuracy of 0.963 (0.006) and an average AUC of 0.994 (0.0 0.07) using 10-fold cross-validation. And finally, they drew the conclusion that the recommended approach is relatively effective at identifying unauthorized accounts on the Ethereum network based on the results.

In their work, the authors in [8] illustrated how traditional machine learning-based algorithms, such as one-class support vector machine and isolation forest, are inefficient in recognizing anomalies in Ethereum transactions due to their shortcomings in capturing the inter node or account relationship information in the transactions. However, they proposed using a methodology for detecting abnormalities in the Ethereum blockchain network that is based on one-class graph neural networks. The suggested approach outperforms conventional non-graph-based machine learning algorithms in terms of anomaly detection accuracy, according to empirical evaluation. It has been demonstrated that the framework can learn from and detect anomalies accurately with minimal amounts of data. For their limitations, they are unable to solve the problem of real-time identification of emerging aberrant behaviors in the Ethereum network. Consequently, for the purpose of anomaly discovery in the future, incremental, multi-stage graph embedding procedures can be examined in addition to one-class approaches.

In their study, the authors in [9] used supervised machine learning-based anomaly detection in the transactional behavior of the accounts to find malicious nodes. They gather the features from the addresses' transactions and chose them, then train various machine learning models, such as random forest, decision tree, XGBoost, and K-NN, for externally owned account (EOA) and smart contract account analysis and they attained the maximum accuracy, 96.54% and 96.82%, respectively for both the EOA and the smart contract account analysis. For future works, they hope to look into ways to lessen false positives and false negatives.

In their paper, the authors in [10] proposed ways in discovering accounts in the Ethereum blockchain that performs phishing scam. A technique called graph-based cascade feature extraction was implemented and also LGBM-based dual sampling ensemble classifiers were used to create the models used for identification. The models were evaluated from different perspectives and the outputs of the evaluation depict proper performance of the model. For futuristic works, they aim to put into consideration other cybercrimes and also develop a website for identifying scams relating to blockchain. This site would provide services in form of an API that detects phishing.

The authors in [11], using three different machine learning algorithms – decision tree, random forest, and K-nearest neighbors – illicit accounts were studied on the Ethereum blockchain and a fraud detection approach (KNN) was suggested. These methods were carried out on a dataset with 42 features, downloaded from Kaggle.com. To build a new dataset with just six features, a correlation coefficient was used to determine which features were the most useful. The three algorithms used in their research significantly improve time measurements, and the random forest approach also significantly improves the F measure.

The authors in [12] developed a model for analyzing smart contract vulnerabilities using machine learning. In this model, feature vectors were first collected from an abstract syntax tree (AST), which is an abstract representation of the source code syntax structure. After that, shared child nodes from two ASTs were obtained. Finally, the feature vector was used to train machine learning models and create a model that can identify the various types of Solidity-written smart contract vulnerabilities in Ethereum with 90% accuracy, recall, and precision. They assessed the accuracy of their work against some tools, like Onyente and smartChek, and found that it was more accurate. However, in order to make the model simple for experts to use, they also require ASTs of the examined smart contracts in order to uncover vulnerabilities without creating complex patterns or requiring executing them in Ethereum. Another limitation of their research was that they could only identify the types of vulnerabilities that a smart contract has; they were unable to identify specific issues or pinpoint the line of code in the smart contract where the vulnerability exists. The model could only identify smart contracts written in Solidity, which was another drawback. Additionally, the insufficient amount of fraudulent smart contracts employed in their research could have affected how accurate their method was. Additionally, they don't create a tool to identify smart contracts using their approach.

The authors in [13] introduced ESCORT, the first deep learning-based automated framework that supports simultaneous detection of several vulnerability classes and light weight transfer learning. They separated these two subtasks – feature extraction of general smart contracts and each specific vulnerability class – which they identified as two essential elements of vulnerability detection. According to empirical findings, ESCORT can swiftly adapt to the new vulnerability data and obtains an average detection accuracy of 95% in terms of f1-score across a variety of vulnerability classes. In 0.02 seconds, ESCORT provides a parallel identification of eight vulnerabilities. Additionally, they developed a tool-chain called ContractScraper based on the bytecode of smart contracts downloaded from the Ethereum blockchain and an already-existing vulnerability identification tool for dataset generation and labeling.

The authors in [14] suggested Dynamit as a framework for monitoring smart contracts to find re-entrancy problems. Their solution doesn't need unique execution environments, code instrumentation, or domain expertise because it depends on transaction meta-data from the blockchain. Dynamit employs machine learning to classify transactions as harmful or malicious by extracting attributes from transaction data. Along with discovering contracts that are susceptible to re-entrancy assaults, Dynamit also obtained an execution trail that replicates the attack. Additionally, their model achieves greater than 90% accuracy on 105 transactions using a random forest classifier, demonstrating the viability of their approach. Their research has certain limitations, including the need to identify new features to improve detection accuracy. They are also looking into automatic test-case generation technologies like vultron as they seek to improve Dynamit. Finally, they take into account applying various sorts of machine learning to the data to enhance the detector's capabilities and to examine more types of vulnerabilities.

The authors in [15] presented contractward, a technique for quickly and accurately identifying six types of smart contract vulnerabilities based on extracted static characteristics. They conducted comparative experiments using three supervised ensemble classification algorithms XGBoost, ADABoost, and random forest – along with two simple classification algorithms SVM and KNN and two sampling methods SMOTEomek and SMOTE. They also used two straightforward classification algorithms SVM and KNN, along with two sampling techniques. And lastly, a model using SMOTEomek as the sampling method and XGBoost as a multi-label classifier was chosen. A smart contract may be detected by contractward in an average of 4 seconds, which is faster than onyente and securify. It is suitable for rapid batch detection of vulnerabilities in smart contracts. Because high-level languages like Solidity, Serpent, and lisp like language (LLL) can all be turned into opcodes, contractward is dependable with the predicted Micro-f1 and Macro-f1 above 96% and it can be used to find flaws in smart contracts written in these high-level languages. A limitation is that contractward cannot be expanded to include new exploitation attacks. Lastly, contractward cannot handle lengthy contracts. This means that contractward cannot capture long-term dependency in the code and is not scalable to long contracts. The smart contract source code is required by contractward, and this method investigates smart contracts using opcodes. Decompiling the source code and then turning it to opcodes makes this possible. And as a result, information loss during decompilation is possible.

The authors in [16] proposed SCSGuard, a deep learning framework for scam detection, takes advantage of smart contracts' automatically extractable bytecodes as one of its new features. They created a GRU network with attention mechanisms to understand the Ngram bytecode patterns, and it assesses whether or not a smart contract is genuine. By offering a consistent response to many scam genres, SCSGuard eliminates the requirement for code analysis expertise. Second, SCSGuard's inference is several orders of magnitude quicker than code analysis. Thirdly, experimental results show that SCSGuard performs well in detecting new phishing smart contracts with good accuracy (0.92~0.94), precision (0.94~0.96%), and recall (0.97~0.98) for both Ponzi and Honeypot schemes in similar situations.

The authors in [17] sought to identify Ethereum fraud transactions through the use of the LGBM technique. As part of their research, they also compared the suggested strategy to other classifier models. The accuracy of eight (8) machine learning techniques, such as logistic regression, the random forest classifier, and the MLP classifier, was given primary attention. Following an experiment, LGBM and XGBoost had the highest accuracy, outperforming cutting-edge machine learning techniques. This method's downside was that for the LGBM to function successfully, the dataset needed to be incredibly vast.

The authors in [17] built a model based on the light gradient boosting machine (LGBM) approach. Using the Euclidean distant structured estimation approach, the improved LGBM model optimized the LGBM's parameters. Their study also assesses the performance of various well-known models with limited features, including random forest (RF), multi-layer perceptron (MLP), logistic regression, k-nearest neighbors (KNNs), XGBoost, support vector classification (SVC), and ADAboost, and likens their performance metrics with the suggested model for classifying fraudulent Ethereum activity. Comparative performance evaluation matrices scores between the proposed model and other widely used models showed the usefulness of the suggested strategy. When contrasted with other models with the highest accuracies, the modified LGBM algorithms and RF models perform the best, with the modified LGBM algorithm marginally outperforming the RF model (99.17% vs. 98.26%).

The authors in [18] proposed the use of homogenous and heterogeneous GNN models to detect accounts in the Ethereum network of trading that carries out fraudulent acts of phishing fraud. However, more data will be needed to conduct detection of phishing fraud in an already existing Ethereum blockchain that carries out transaction. For futuristic improvements, they plan on carrying out more evaluations on how the model performs and also enhance it utilizing GNN model to integrate the information.

The authors in [19] proposed a message passing-based graph convolution network, a phishing identification technique. A transaction network was first created using data of transaction in Ethereum where information details the nodes were extracted using the message passing. In addition, a graph convolution network was utilized in classifying normal nodes and nodes that perform phishing. The performance of their model was validated by a comparison with the outputs derived from other recorded test data. Their proposed method is said to outperform other conventional techniques which have been proposed to detect phishing in the Ethereum network.

The authors in [20] proposed a genetic algorithm (GA), which is applied in the exploration phase in order to solve a weakness in the Cuckoo search (CS) technique. They carried out an in-depth experiment to assess the effectiveness and performance of the suggested approaches in comparison to a number of well-known methods, including k-nearest neighbors (KNN), logistic regression (LR), multi-layer perceptron (MLP), XGBoost, light gradient boosting machine (LGBM), random forest (RF), and support vector classification (SVC). While deep learning with the suggested optimization method surpasses the RF model, with slightly higher performance of 99.71% vs. 98.33%, the recommended technique and SVC models outperform the rest of the models, with the highest accuracy. The limitation in their work was that although the proposed model yielded trustworthy results, it had one drawback: for LGBM to be successful, the dataset must be excessively huge.

3.3 Methodology

Machine learning algorithms, as well as the Python programming language are used to create the tools used in detecting threats that decentralized autonomous organizations (DAOs) faced by evaluating the precedent threats on some datasets of attributes, predicting the probability of the vulnerability being exploited, and evaluating the prediction accuracy. The system flow chart was created using the unified modeling language (UML), and is shown in Figure 3.1.

3.3.1 Data collection

In this study, the dataset was obtained from www.kaggle.com, a website that serves as a community for data scientists and machine learning practitioners.

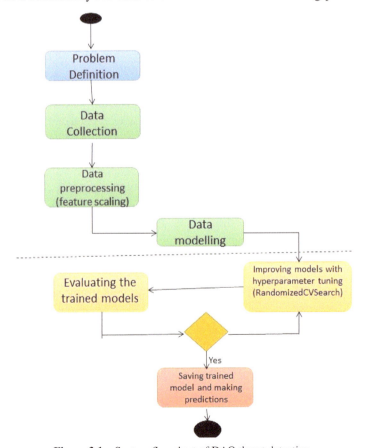

Figure 3.1 System flowchart of DAO threat detection.

3.3 Methodology   79

There are 9841 rows in this dataset, representing accounts, documented scams, and legitimate Ethereum transactions. The dataset was downloaded in CSV format, cleaned and uploaded on Jupyter notebook. A screenshot of the cleaned dataset is shown in Figure 3.2.

	Address	FLAG	Avg min between sent tnx	Avg min between received tnx	Time Diff between first and last (Mins)	Sent tnx	Received Tnx	Number of Created Contracts	Unique Received From Addresses	Unique Sent To Addresses	...	ERC20 min val sent
0	0x00009277775ac7d0d59eaad8fee3d10ac6c805e8	0	844.26	1093.71	704785.63	721	89	0	40	118	...	0.000000
1	0x0002b44ddb1476db43c868bd494422ee4c136fed	0	12709.07	2958.44	1218216.73	94	8	0	5	14	...	2.260809
2	0x0002bda54cb772d040f779e88eb453cac0dea244	0	246194.54	2434.02	516729.30	2	10	0	10	2	...	0.000000
3	0x00038e6ba2fd5c09aedb96697c8d7b8fa6632e5e	0	10219.60	15785.09	397555.90	25	9	0	7	13	...	100.000000
4	0x00062d1dd1afb6fb02540ddad9cdebfe568e0d89	0	36.61	10707.77	382472.42	4598	20	1	7	19	...	0.000000
...												
9836	0xff481ca14e6c16b79fc8ab299b4d2387ec8ecdd2	1	12635.10	631.39	58748.48	4	13	0	11	4	...	0.000000
9837	0xff718805b09199ebf024ab6acd333e603ad77c85	1	0.00	0.00	0.00	0	0	0	0	0	...	0.000000
9838	0xff8e6af02d41a576a0c82f7835535193e1a6bccc	1	2499.44	2189.29	261601.88	67	43	0	31	44	...	0.000000
9839	0xffde23396d57e10abf58bd929bb1e856c7718218	1	0.00	0.00	0.00	0	1	0	1	0	...	NaN
9840	0xd624d046edbdef805c5e4140dce5fb5ec1b39a3c	1	37242.70	149.56	670817.33	18	3	0	1	5	...	0.000000

9841 rows × 49 columns

Figure 3.2   Cleaned dataset uploaded in Jupyter notebook.

Jupyter notebook was used because it offers an intuitive interactive data science environment usable for presentations or educational purposes, and also serves as an integrated development environment (IDE). Due in large part to its versatility, Jupyter provides a means to work with Python inside of a virtual "notebook," and allows the combination of photos, programs, comments, graphs, and other elements that concur with the data science method phase.

3.3.2 Data preprocessing

The dataset contains 9841 rows of known fraud and valid transactions made over the Ethereum and the dataset is split into features and labels which would be denoted as X and Y.

3.3.2.1 Class imbalance

It was observed that this particular dataset is imbalanced and this can hamper the model accuracy in a major way. Class imbalance is a common problem in machine learning because when the dataset is imbalanced; a high accuracy would be obtained just by predicting the majority class but failing to capture the minority class. Working with imbalanced datasets is a challenge since machine learning methods frequently overlook them, which ultimately results in poor performance in the minority class – a result that should, in theory, be the most relevant one. Class imbalance can lead to biased models that are ineffective in predicting minority class [21], thereby rendering the fraud detection process ineffective. To solve this problem, two techniques are employed, namely resampling technique and balancing with Imbalanced_Learn Python module. Our trained model may be impacted by training the machine learning model on unbalanced datasets; there is a chance that it may overfit the dominant class and ignore all other minor classes with small numbers.

a. *Resampling technique:* This is used in dealing with the highly unbalanced datasets. This involves eliminating samples from the majority class (under sampling) or simply injecting more examples from the minority class, i.e., oversampling. The minor drawbacks in balancing classes despite its advantages are:

   i. In the oversampling, reproducing random records from the minority class can cause overfitting.
   ii. In the under sampling, removing arbitrary records from the majority class can lead to loss of information.

b. *Balancing the data with Imbalanced_Learn Python module: SMOTE (synthetic minority oversampling technique):* This method generates synthetic data for the minority class. It involves duplicating values in the minority class instead of simply removing values in the dataset that are in abundance. SMOTE was chosen over the resampling technique in this research in order to avoid the mentioned drawbacks of oversampling or undersampling in the use of the resampling technique which could have led to overfitting or loss of information from the dataset respectively. In order for it to function, instances that are near to one another in the feature space are first selected at random from the minority class. Next, k (usually $k = 5$) of the closest neighbors from that example are located. Every k neighbor of the chosen example is connected by a synthetic example that is generated at a randomly determined position on the line. Because fresh synthetic instances from the minority class are generated relatively close to existing examples in feature space, this strategy is effective. Tackling the class imbalance of the dataset using SMOTE would drastically improve the accuracy of our models in training. The imbalance in our dataset may be easily fixed with SMOTE thanks to Imbalanced-Learn, a Python tool that offers several resampling methods, including SMOTE.

3.3.2.2 Feature scaling

Feature scaling technique is employed to scale homogeneously, the independent features that are included in the data. This is carried out during the preprocessing of the data, to handle greatly variable magnitudes, units, or values. If feature scaling is not carried out, a machine learning algorithm tends to give preference to larger values over smaller ones, irrespective of the units of measurement. There are two important types of feature scaling in machine learning which are:

i. *Min-Max normalization:* An observation or feature value having a distribution value between 0 and 1 is rescaled using this method, as shown in eqn (3.1).

$$X_{new} = \frac{X_i - \min(X)}{\max(x) - \min(X)}. \quad (3.1)$$

ii. *Standardization:* It is said to be an extremely efficient technique that rescales the value of a feature so that its distribution has a mean of 0 and a variance of 1. This is shown in eqn (3.2).

$$X_{new} = \frac{X_i - X_{mean}}{\text{Standard Deviation}}. \quad (3.2)$$

Standardization is used for the feature scaling because of its level of efficiency in data preprocessing, being applied to features of data or independent variables. It standardizes the data within a particular range and also re-scales a feature value so that it has distribution with 0 mean values and variance equals 1. It also helps in fast-tracking the calculations in an algorithm. This is shown in eqn (3.3).

$$Z = \frac{x - \mu}{\sigma}, \quad (3.3)$$

where x = score, μ = mean, and σ = standard deviation.

3.3.3 Data Modeling

Here, the available datasets are taken and machine learning algorithms are applied to find insights on that dataset. Supervised learning approach is employed. Supervised learning involves the use of labeled datasets to train algorithms to classify data or predict outcomes accurately. It can be categorized into two major problems, which are;

a) **Classification problems:** These machine learning algorithms are utilized when an output variable has two classes for example, Yes-No, Male-Female, True-False, etc.

b) **Regression problems:** If there is a correlation between the input and output variables, these algorithms are applied. It is used to predict continuous variables like market trends, weather, and so on.

Based on the dataset being worked on and for the purpose of this research, the problem is classification problem. This type of learning requires the algorithm to map the newly acquired data to either of the two classes already in the datasets. The classes must be mapped to either one or zero, which corresponds to yes or no in real life. A classification model attempts to deduce some meaning from the observed values. A categorization model attempts to predict the value of one or more outputs, given one or more inputs. A few of these algorithms are:

i. Logical regression
ii. Random forest
iii. Naive–Bayes classifier
iv. Support vector machine (SVM)
v. Gradient-boosted tree

Three (3) classifiers are compared to see which one performs better. For the anomaly detection, three (3) supervised learning algorithms are randomly selected, concentrated on, namely:

- Random forest (RF),
- Logistic regression, and
- Extreme gradient boosting (XGBoost)

When making a categorical judgment, supervised learning methods like the selected logistic regression, random forest, and XGBoost can be employed. It implies that if a transaction takes place in DAO, the outcome will be flagged either "fraud" or "non-fraud." For instance, a combination of decision trees is used by random forest to enhance the outcomes. Different conditions are checked by each decision tree. Each decision tree provides the likelihood that a transaction is "fraudulent" or "non-fraudulent," based on the training of the trees using random datasets. The model then makes the appropriate result prediction. And as for techniques such as the XGBoost, it employs ensemble techniques to enhance performance for techniques. To manage imbalanced class distributions, existing classification models are modified using ensemble approaches of the XGBoost. Multiple learners are trained to answer categorization issues in ensemble learning. The main idea behind it is to blend many inexperienced learners with enthusiastic learners in order to improve the classifier's performance.

a. **Logistic regression**: This type of supervised learning model is famous among other machine learning algorithms. In a categorical dependent variable, the output is forecasted through logistic regression. Because of this, the result must be a categorical or discrete value. Instead of providing the exact values of 0 and 1, it provides the probabilistic values that fall between 0 and 1. In other words, it can be Yes or No, true or false, 0 or 1, etc. The logistic regression is shown in eqn (3.4).

$$\log\left[\frac{y}{1-y}\right] = b_0 + b_1x_1 + b_2x_2 + b_3x_3 + \cdots + b_nx_n. \quad (3.4)$$

In classifying observations using several data sources, logistic regression can be employed to quickly identify the factors that will be effective. The logistic function is displayed in Figure 3.3.

b. **Random forest (RF)**: This is a common machine learning algorithm that is a part of the supervised learning method. It can be applied to machine learning problems involving both regression and classification. Random forest is preferred sometimes based on the fact that, when compared to other machine learning models, it requires less training time. Even with the enormous dataset, it operates efficiently and predicts the outcome with a high degree of accuracy, and when a significant amount of data is absent, accuracy can still be retained. However, while random forest can be utilized for both classification and regression problems, it is not better suited for applications requiring regression. This is illustrated in Figure 3.4.

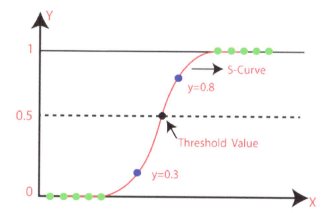

Figure 3.3 Diagram of logistic function (sigmoid function).

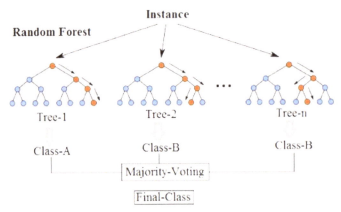

Figure 3.4 Diagram of a random forest.

c. **Extreme gradient boosting (XGBoost)**: This is a distributed, scalable gradient-boosted decision tree (GBDT) machine learning framework. It is the leading machine learning library for classification, regression, and ranking issues, and it offers parallel tree boosting. It is comparable to random forest. By consecutively building decision trees, XGBoost aims to learn from incorrectly classified observations by giving them more weight in the following trees. A schematic representation of the XGBoost is shown in Figure 3.5.

The three (3) classifiers were imported into the workspace using sci-kit learn function. This is shown in Figure 3.6.

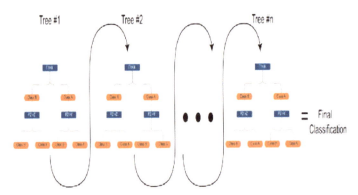

Figure 3.5 Schematic representation of the extreme gradient boosting algorithm.

Building machine learning model

- trying out 3 different models

1. Logistic Regression
2. Random Forest
3. XGBoost

```
#importing models
from sklearn.linear_model import LogisticRegression
from sklearn.ensemble import RandomForestClassifier
from xgboost import XGBClassifier
```

Figure 3.6 Importing classifiers into Jupyter notebook.

3.3.3.1 Training data and fitting the model/algorithm

Splitting the dataset into training and testing, the datasets are divided into parts of ratio 4:1 in which 80% are used for training and 20% for testing. The training data are then fitted into the trained model and evaluation is carried out to see what the model has learned on test data which it has never seen before.

3.3.4 Improving the models (hyperparameter tuning)

Optimizing a model's performance by selecting the finest mix of hyperparameters is known as hyperparameter tuning (or hyperparameter optimization). Multiple trials are conducted within a single training phase to make it work. Each trial involves the full execution of the training application with the values of the carefully chosen hyperparameters set within the designated boundaries. A grid of probable hyperparameter values was constructed for the random search approach. Each repetition tries a different arbitrary combination of these hyperparameters, assesses the results, and returns the set of hyperparameters that produced the best results.

  i **RandomizedCVSearch**: Further optimization with Randomized-CVSearch is carried out on the models to give better accuracy with the help of hyperparameter tuning. A grid of potential hyperparameter values for the random search approach was constructed. This optimization controls several aspects of the model such as overfitting and underfitting of data. Therefore, different numbers of $n\_estimators$ and randomized hyperparameters were applied.

3.3.5 Evaluating the models

This defines the success of the system and how well machine learning can predict the future. Here, the models are evaluated using the validated dataset. With the model trained, it needs to be tested to see how well the machine learning classifiers has done learning on the training data. Classification report, confusion matrix, accuracy score and others are performed on the test data to give a report of accuracies. Real-world data is inherently unbalanced, as seen in our dataset on fraud detection in DAO. Hence, other measures like recall and precision need to be taken into account, to obtain a complete view of the model evaluation.

a) **Confusion matrix:** This matrix is used for evaluating the performance of the classification models for a certain set of test data. Only after the true values of the test data are known can it be determined. It is useful in assessing how well classification models perform when they make predictions based on test data and indicates how effective the classification algorithm is and also various model parameters can be computed, such as accuracy, precision, etc., using the confusion matrix. Precision and recall evaluation metric become more important when the classes are imbalanced. An image of the confusion matrix is shown in Figure 3.7.

   i. **Accuracy:** Accuracy is obtained by dividing the total number of forecasts by the proportion of true predictions. This echoes how frequently the classifier predicts correctly. The accuracy is usually in decimal form and a 1.0 denotes a perfect accuracy. It is a very useful measure if classes are all balanced, as shown in eqn (3.5).

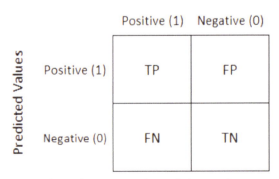

Figure 3.7 Image of a confusion matrix.

$$\text{Accuracy} = \frac{\text{True positive (TP)} + \text{True negactive (TN)}}{\text{True positive (TP)} + \text{True negative (TN)} \\ + \text{False positive (FP)} + \text{False negative (FN)}} \quad (3.5)$$

ii. **Precision:** Precision shows how many of the situations that were predicted with accuracy ended up being positive. Precision is helpful when false positives are more challenging than false negatives. A model that does not produce any false positives (FN) would have a precision of 1.0. The formula for precision is shown in eqn (3.6).

$$\text{Precision} = \frac{\text{True positive (TP)}}{\text{True positive (TP)} + \text{False positive(FP)}}. \quad (3.6)$$

iii. **Recall:** This defines how many of the actual positive cases our model was able to properly predict. When false negative is more significant than false positive, it is a valuable metric. Therefore, a model that does not output any false negatives has a recall of 1.0. The formula for calculating recall is shown in eqn (3.7).

$$\text{Recall} = \frac{\text{True positive (TP)}}{\text{True positive(TP)} + \text{False negative(FN)}}. \quad (3.7)$$

iv. **f1-score:** It offers a synthesis of the precision and recall measurements. When precision and recall are equal, f1-score reaches its optimum. The harmonic mean of recall and precision is the f1-score. Perfect model has a f1-score of 1.0. The formula for calculating the f1-score is shown in eqn (3.8).

$$f1 = 2 \times \frac{\text{precision} \times \text{recall}}{\text{precision} + \text{recall}}. \quad (3.8)$$

v. **AUC-ROC:** A probability curve called the receiver operator characteristic (ROC) separates the "signal" from the "noise" by plotting the TPR (true positive rate) vs. the FPR (false positive rate) at different threshold values. A classifier's capacity to distinguish between classes is measured by the area under the curve (AUC). The *X* and *Y* axes, as well as the area of the curve ABDE can be easily identified from the graph. AUC does a better job at telling you how well your model is at choosing between classes. A perfect model has an AUC score of 1.0. Figure 3.8 shows that the higher the AUC, the better the performance of the model at various threshold points between positive and negative classifications.

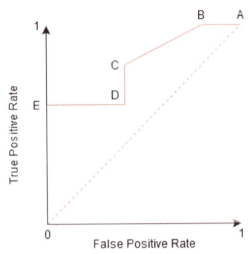

Figure 3.8 Image of an AUC-ROC curve.

vi. **Log_loss:** How well the projected probability matches the actual label is indicated by log loss. Log loss ranges from 0 to infinity. A better model is one with a lower log loss. The formula for finding the log_loss is shown in eqn (3.9).

$$\text{logloss}_{(N=1)} = y \log(p) + (1 - y) \log(1 - p) \qquad (3.9)$$

vii. **Mathew correlation coefficient:** The phi coefficient is another name for the Matthews correlation coefficient. It serves as a bench mark for binary and multi-class classification quality in machine learning. It considers the true positive and the false positive, and also the true negative and false negatives as well, and it is typically seen as a measurement that is applicable even when the classes have significantly varied sizes. A correlation coefficient value between −1 and +1 is essentially what the Matthews correlation coefficient is. A coefficient of 1 indicates an accurate prediction; a coefficient of 0 indicates an average random prediction while a coefficient of −1 indicates an inverse prediction. The formula for calculating this is shown in eqn (3.10).

$$\text{MCC} = \frac{(TP * TN - FP * FN)}{\sqrt{(TP + FP)(TP + FN)(TN + FP)(TN + FN)}} \qquad (3.10)$$

b) **Classification report:** Sklearn has a built-in function known as *classification-report()* which explains everything about the classification. This is the summary of the quality of classification made by the constructed machine learning algorithms. It generally consists of ($N + 3$) rows and 5 columns. The name of the class label appears in the first column, and is followed by precision, recall, f1-score, and support. N rows are for the number of class labels, while the remaining three rows are for accuracy, the macro-average, and the weighted-average.

c) **Cross-validation:** Cross-validation is a method used in evaluating the performance of machine learning models by dividing the available data into two parts: training and validation. The idea is to train the model on the training data and then assess its performance on the validation data. *cross_val_score* is a function in the scikit-learn library that implements this technique in a convenient manner. The function performs k-fold cross-validation, where k is a specified number of folds (the default being 5). During the process, the data is split into k subsets and the model is trained on $k-1$ subsets and evaluated on the remaining subset. This process is repeated k times, with each subset serving as the validation set once. The result of using *cross_val_score* is an array of k scores, one for each fold, which represent the performance of the model on iterations of cross-validation. These scores can then be aggregated to give an overall understanding of the model's performance.

3.3.6 Model deployment

It is important to save the trained model into a file so it can be restored, loaded, and used in the future to test new data. There are several ways of saving the model after training, which are;

i. With *Joblib module*
ii. With *Python's pickle module*

For this research work, Python's Pickle module is used.

3.4 Results and Discussions

3.4.1 Results

3.4.1.1 Fitting and evaluating selected models

The training data were fitted into all three (3) classifiers accordingly and their score accuracy were also evaluated when used on the test data and

```
Out[48]: {'Logistic Regression': 0.7546978161503302,
          'Random Forest': 0.9822244794311833,
          'xgboost': 0.9710512950736414}

In [49]: model_compare = pd.DataFrame(model_scores, index=["accuracy"])
         model_compare.plot(kind="bar", figsize=(10,4), color=['blue', 'green', "orange"]);
```

Figure 3.9 Score accuracy on the three (3) models and comparison with a bar chart.

compared among themselves. It was observed that logistic regression, random forest, and XGBoost all came out with an accuracy score of 75.46%, 98.22%, and 97.11% (in two decimal places). Figure 3.9 gives a snippet of these evaluated score accuracies on fitted training data on each model and shows the comparison of the three (3) models.

3.4.1.2 Improving the models by hyperparameter tuning

To further improve the scores of the three (3) models, *RandomizedSearchCV* was used in carrying out hyperparameter tuning on all models (i.e., logistic regression, random forest, and XGBoost) and their scores were compared. It was observed that logistic regression, random forest, and XGBoost each came out with an improved accuracy score of 82.07%, 98.52%, and 99.87% respectively (in two decimal places). Figure 3.10 gives a snippet of the tuned accuracy scores on each model and also shows the comparison of the three (3) models after hyperparameter tuning.

3.4.1.3 Making predictions with the tuned models

After tuning with *RandomizedSearchCV*, the tuned models were each used to carry out predictions on the test data and their accuracy scores on the prediction on the test data was compared on a bar chart, as shown in Figure 3.11. On further evaluation of the model, an ROC_AUV curve was plotted using *scikit*

3.4 Results and Discussions   91

```
Out[61]: {'Logistic Regression': 0.8207211782630777,
          'Random Forest': 0.9852717115286947,
          'xgboost': 0.9987485457919851}

In [62]: rs_model_compare = pd.DataFrame(rs_model_scores, index=["ACCURACY"])
         rs_model_compare.plot(kind="bar", figsize=(10,4), color=['blue', 'green', "orange"]);
         # rs_model_compare.T.plot.bar();
```

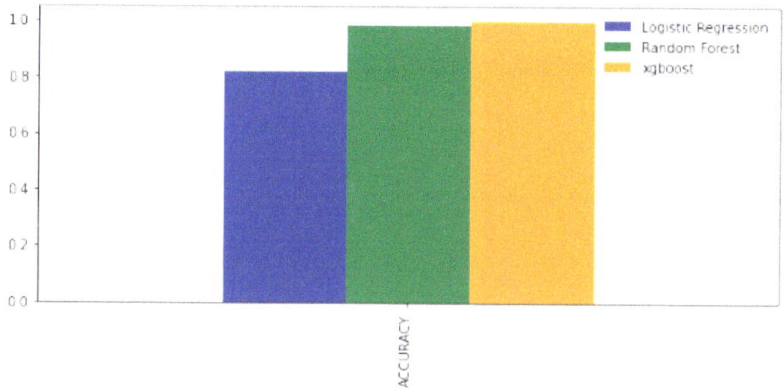

Figure 3.10 Accuracy scores on the tuned models and comparison with a bar chart.

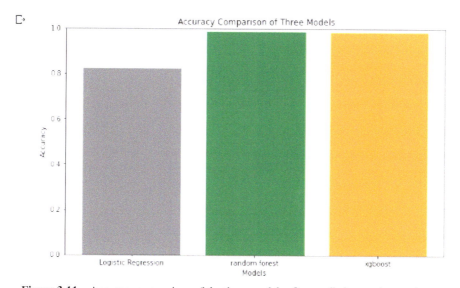

Figure 3.11 Accuracy comparison of the three models after prediction on the test data.

learn's seaborn. Figure 3.12 is a chart of the ROC_AUC curve comparing the three (3) models.

92 *Fraud Detection in Decentralized Autonomous Organization (DAO)*

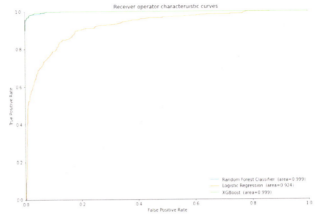

Figure 3.12 ROC_AUC curve on the predictions.

3.4.1.4 Model evaluation

A. **Confusion matrix:** In addition to the other evaluation metrics, a confusion matrix display (gives a heatmap of the trained model) and a classification report was imported from Sci-kit learn function to give a heat map and a report on the test set prediction. These are shown in Figures 3.13, 3.14, and 3.15.

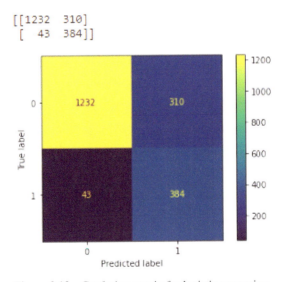

Figure 3.13 Confusion matrix for logistic regression.

3.4 Results and Discussions 93

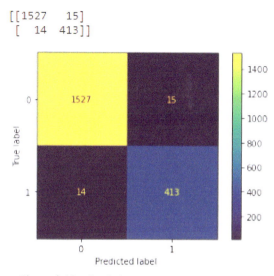

Figure 3.14 Confusion matrix for random forest.

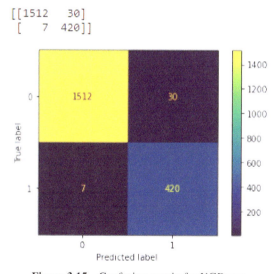

Figure 3.15 Confusion matrix for XGBoost.

B. **Classification report:** Also, a classification report containing an explicit information of the various metrics of the trained model given in a matrix format was imported into the work space and implemented on each classifiers as seen in Figures 3.16, 3.17, and 3.18.

```
: from sklearn.metrics import classification_report
  print(classification_report(y_test, y_preds_lr))
                precision    recall  f1-score   support

             0     0.97      0.80      0.87      1542
             1     0.55      0.90      0.69       427

      accuracy                         0.82      1969
     macro avg     0.76      0.85      0.78      1969
  weighted avg     0.88      0.82      0.83      1969
```

Figure 3.16 Classification for logistic regression.

```
: from sklearn.metrics import classification_report
  print(classification_report(y_test, y_preds_rf))
                precision    recall  f1-score   support

             0     0.99      0.99      0.99      1542
             1     0.96      0.97      0.97       427

      accuracy                         0.99      1969
     macro avg     0.98      0.98      0.98      1969
  weighted avg     0.99      0.99      0.99      1969
```

Figure 3.17 Classification report for random forest.

```
: from sklearn.metrics import classification_report
  print(classification_report(y_test, y_preds_xgb))
                precision    recall  f1-score   support

             0     1.00      0.98      0.99      1542
             1     0.93      0.98      0.96       427

      accuracy                         0.98      1969
     macro avg     0.96      0.98      0.97      1969
  weighted avg     0.98      0.98      0.98      1969
```

Figure 3.18 Classification report for XGBoost.

C. **Accuracy, precision, recall, and f1-score evaluation metric:** For better evaluations, some evaluation metrics like the accuracy, precision, f1 and recall score as well as ROC, log_loss, and Mathew_corrcoef were imported into the work space from sci-kit learn to give more information on the model's accuracy. This is shown in Figure 3.19. Table 3.1 gives

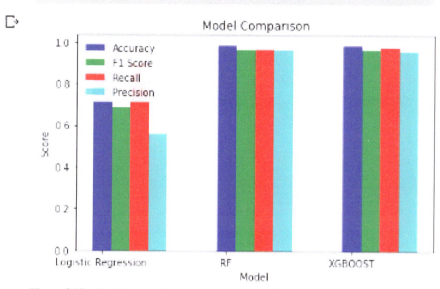

Figure 3.19 Model comparison on their accuracy, f1, recall and precision score.

Table 3.1 Results of the four (4) major evaluation metrics on the three (3) models.

	Accuracy	Precision	Recall	f1
Logistic regression	82.07%	55.53%	89.92%	68.51%
Random forest	98.52%	96.49%	96.72%	96.60%
XGBoost	98.12%	93.33%	98.53%	95.78%

Table 3.2 The evaluation metrics of each classifier in columns.

	model	Accuracy	Precision	Recall	Specificity	F1 Score	ROC	Log_Loss	mathew_corrcoef
0	xgboost	0.981209	0.933333	0.983607	0.980545	0.957811	0.982076	0.649039	0.946272
1	LogressionRegression	0.820721	0.553314	0.899297	0.798962	0.685103	0.849130	6.192197	0.602335
2	RandomForest	0.985272	0.964953	0.967213	0.990272	0.966082	0.978743	0.508703	0.956677

a tabular representation of the top four (4) various evaluation metrics used in evaluating the models that the data has been trained on. Other evaluation metrics like log_loss, AUC and ROC, specificity, and Mathew correlation coefficient are shown in Table 3.2.

D. **Feature importance:** Feature importance is employed to determine the various features in the dataset which majorly contributed the outcome of each of our model. Observing how logistic regression evaluation metrics has been giving rather low scores on every evaluation metric, this model

96 *Fraud Detection in Decentralized Autonomous Organization (DAO)*

was dropped and feature importance was done on just the random forest classifier and the XGBoost due to their better performance based on their evaluation metrics scores. Figures 3.20 and 3.21 depict the feature importance chart of the two classifiers.

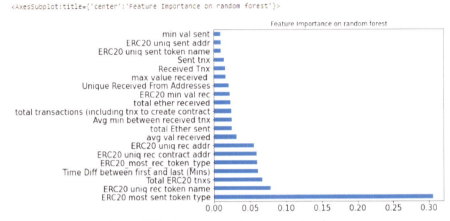

Figure 3.20 Feature importance on random forest.

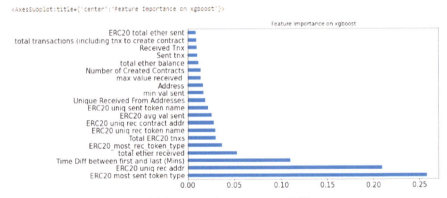

Figure 3.21 Feature importance on XGBoost.

3.4.2 Discussions

There are a lot of threats and fraud that occurs on decentralized autonomous organizations built on Ethereum blockchain all over the world and with its increase, there is a massive demand for systems and new approaches that can improve the analysis of threats detection and better protect customers and member funds with provision of safe transaction as well. The development of a fraud detection system using logistic regression, random forest, and XGBoost has been carried out in this work. The created system combines past transaction records on Ethereum and models them with the aid of feature scaling methods like standardization and machine learning models like the random forest classifier to make predictions on frauds. This approach was implemented in Jupyter notebook with the help of packages from miniconda and performance of the models are evaluated using the accuracy_score, precision_score, recall_score, and f1-score metrics from sci-kit learn function. The three (3) models are then compared together after carrying out hyperparameter tuning on them and the results gotten from score of the evaluation metrics show that random forest and XGBoost give better results when compared to logistic regression. Logistic regression had an accuracy, precision, recall, and f1-score of 82.07%, 55.53%, 89.92%, and 68.51% respectively. Random forest had its accuracy, precision, recall, and f1-score as 98.52%, 96.49%, 96.72%, and 96.60% respectively. Lastly, XGBoost, had its accuracy, precision, recall, and f1-score as 98.12%, 93.33%, 98.53%, and 95.78% respectively. The best performing models which were the random forest and the XGBoost were then saved using Python's pickle module. For each of the best trained model, the five (5) most important features which contributed to the accuracy of the models are summarized in Table 3.3.

Table 3.3 Five (5) most important features for each model.

Random forest	XGBoost
• the ERC20 most sent token type	• the ERC20 most sent token type
• ERC2O uniq rec token name	• ERC20 uniq rec addr
• Total ERC20 tokens	• Time diff between first and last (Mins)
• Time diff between first and last (Mins)	• Total ether received
• ERC20 most_rec_token_type.	• ERC20 most_rec_token_type

3.5 Conclusion

Machine learning algorithms were proposed to detect threats and frauds in the decentralized autonomous organization (DAO) platform built under the Ethereum blockchain using a dataset of transactions carried out on the Ethereum blockchain. This dataset contains both fraud and non-fraudulent transactions. Algorithms used were the logistic regression, random forest, and the XGBoost. After these models were built and trained, hyperparameter tuning was carried out on them and the results obtained from the scores of the evaluation metrics showed that random forest and XGBoost give better results than logistic regressions. Other evaluation metrics were used in carrying out analysis and they include the confusion matrix, ROC curve, classification report, log_loss, and Mathew correlation coefficient. Cross-validation analysis was also carried out to give comparable scores on the results. All these still show the best performing models as the random forest and the XGBoost.

With the knowledge of the trained random forest model and the extra gradient boost model (XGBoost) giving the best accuracies, we recommend a means of integrating these two (2) best performing models into a system so that can both work hand in proffering solution and curbing the events and occurrences of frauds and threats in the decentralized autonomous organization. In a situation where there is a suspicious transaction or a registered account on a blockchain that conducts fraudulent actions in DAO ecosystem and in the Ethereum blockchain system, the developed system can be utilized in making predictions from past information and other available features, to ascertain if the account is a fraudulent account or not, if there is threat of malicious practice in the organization and that account can be terminated before it imposes more malicious acts in the system.

In conclusion, the major contribution of this research is the development and introduction of trained models for the sole purpose of anticipating vulnerabilities in DAO. The trained model can be used to predict, based on historical data such as patterns of completed transactions and other available features, whether an account is fraudulent or not, or if it is simply going to carry out malicious practices within the organization. Also, if there is a suspicious transaction or a registered account on a blockchain that conducts fraudulent actions in the DAO ecosystem and in the Ethereum blockchain system, the account can be terminated before it imposes more malicious acts in the system. For future research purposes and with the knowledge of the trained random forest model and the XGBoost model giving the best accuracies and also with the anticipation of a larger dataset the models can be well trained on, a means of integrating these two (2)l best performing models into a system could be further researched and worked upon so that both can work hand in hand in proffering solution and curbing the events and occurrences of frauds and threats in the decentralized autonomous organization.

References

[1] Reiff, N. (2023). Decentralized Autonomous Organization (DAO): Definition, Purpose, and Example, CRYPTOCURRENCY, Investopedia.https://www.investopedia.com/tech/what-dao/#:~:text=A%20DAO%20is%20a%20decentralized,DAO's%20operations%20is%20publicly%20disclosed.

[2] Locke, T. (2021). What are DAOs? Here's what to know about the "next big trend" in crypto. Retrieved December 5, 2021, from CNBC website:h://www.cnbc.com/2021/10/25/what-are-daos-what-to-know-about-the-next-big-trend-in-crypto.html.

[3] Morrison, R., Mazey, N. C. H. L., & Wingreen, S. C. (2020). The DAO Controversy: The Case for a New Species of Corporate Governance? *Frontiers in Blockchain*, *3*.h://doi.org/10.3389/fbloc.2020.00025

[4] Jiang, B., Liu, Y., & Chan, W. K. (2018)."ContractFuzzer: Fuzzing Smart Contracts for Vulnerability Detection," 2018 33rd IEEE/ACM International Conference on Automated Software Engineering (ASE), Montpellier, France, 2018, pp. 259-269, doi: 10.1145/3238147.3238177.

[5] Ostapowicz, M., & Żbikowski, K. (2019). Detecting Fraudulent Accounts on Blockchain: A Supervised Approach. In *Web Information Systems Engineering – WISE 2019* (pp. 18–31). Springer International Publishing.

[6] Praitheeshan, P., Pan, L., Yu, J., Liu, J.K., & Doss, R.R. (2019). Security Analysis Methods on Ethereum Smart Contract Vulnerabilities: A Survey. *ArXiv, abs/1908.08605*.h://www.semanticscholar.org/paper/Security-Analysis-Methods-on-Ethereum-Smart-A-Praitheeshan-Pan/a5039e4371358f64e3ca6108c8b2dcf50efa9a31

[7] Farrugia, S., Ellul, J., & Azzopardi, G. (2020). Detection of illicit accounts over the Ethereum blockchain. *Expert Systems with Applications*, *150*, 113318, ISSN 0957-4174,https://doi.org/10.1016/j.eswa.2020.113318.

[8] Patel, V., Pan, L., & Rajasegarar, S. (2020). Graph Deep Learning Based Anomaly Detection in Ethereum Blockchain Network. In *Network and System Security* (pp. 132–148). Springer International Publishing.

[9] Kumar, N., Singh, A., Handa, A., & K, S. S. (2020). Detecting Malicious Accounts on the Ethereum Blockchain with Supervised Learning. In *Lecture Notes in Computer Science* (pp. 94–109). Springer International Publishing.

[10] Chen, L., Peng, J., Liu, Y., Li, J., Xie, F., & Zheng, Z. (2020). Phishing Scams Detection in Ethereum Transaction Network. *ACM Transactions on Internet Technology*, *21*, 1–16.

[11] Ibrahim, R. F., Mohammad Elian, A., & Ababneh, M. (2021). Illicit Account Detection in the Ethereum Blockchain Using Machine Learning. *2021 International Conference on Information Technology (ICIT)*.https://doi.org/10.1109/icit52682.2021.9491653

[12] Xu, Y., Hu, G., You, L., & Cao, C. (2021). A Novel Machine Learning-Based Analysis Model for Smart Contract Vulnerability. *Security and Communication Networks*, *2021*, 1–12.https://doi.org/10.1155/2021/5798033

[13] Lutz, O., Chen, H., Fereidooni, H., Sendner, C., Dmitrienko, A., Sadeghi, A., & Koushanfar, F. (2021). ESCORT: Ethereum Smart COntRaCTs Vulnerability Detection using Deep Neural Network and Transfer Learning. *ArXiv, abs/2103.12607*.

[14] Eshghie, M., Artho, C., & Gurov, D. (2021). Dynamic Vulnerability Detection on Smart Contracts Using Machine Learning. In *Evaluation and Assessment in Software Engineering*. ACM.

[15] Wang, W., Song, J., Xu, G., Li, Y., Wang, H., & Su, C. (2021). ContractWard: Automated Vulnerability Detection Models for Ethereum Smart Contracts. *IEEE Transactions on Network Science and Engineering*, *8*, 1133–1144.

[16] Hu, H., Bai, Q., & Xu, Y. (2022). SCSGuard: Deep Scam Detection for Ethereum Smart Contracts. In *IEEE INFOCOM 2022 - IEEE Conference on Computer Communications Workshops (INFOCOM WKSHPS)*. IEEE.

[17] Aziz, R. M., Baluch, M. F., Patel, S., & Kumar, P. (2022). A Machine Learning based Approach to Detect the Ethereum Fraud Transactions with Limited Attributes. *Karbala International Journal of Modern Science*, *8*(2), 139–151.https://doi.org/10.33640/2405-609x.3229

[18] Kanezashi, H., Suzumura, T., Liu, X., & Hirofuchi, T. (2022). *Ethereum Fraud Detection with Heterogeneous Graph Neural Networks*.

[19] Yu, T., Chen, X., Xu, Z., & Xu, J. (2022). MP-GCN: A Phishing Nodes Detection Approach via Graph Convolution Network for Ethereum. *Applied Sciences*, *12*, 7294.

[20] Aziz, R. M., Mahto, R., Goel, K., Das, A., Kumar, P., & Saxena, A. (2023). Modified Genetic Algorithm with Deep Learning for Fraud Transactions of Ethereum Smart Contract. *Applied Sciences*, *13*(2), 697.https://doi.org/10.3390/app13020697

[21] Yenigun, O. (2023). Handling Class Imbalance in Machine Learning: Techniques and Strategies for Improving Model Performance on Imbalanced Datasets. *MLearning.ai*.h://medium.com/mlearning-ai/handling-class-imbalance-in-machine-learning-

4
Improving Machine Learning Performance using Sampling Techniques for COVID-19 Imbalanced Data

Sokaina El Khamlichi[1] and Loubna Taidi[2]

[1]LyRICA – Laboratory of Research in Computer Science, Data Sciences and Knowledge Engineering, School of Information Sciences, Morocco
[2]Laboratory of Innovative Technology, Faculty of Sciences and Technologies / Abdelmalek Essaadi University, Morocco
E-mail: sokaina.elkhamlichi@gmail.com; taidiloubna_91@hotmail.fr

Abstract

Identifying COVID-19 infected individuals who are at an elevated risk of death may have a great interest for the front-line health professionals to ensure resilience in healthcare industry and empower threat management in healthcare systems. However, COVID-19 collected datasets are often imbalanced, with a significantly lower proportion of deaths, making it more difficult to build a high performing machine learning model. The present work intends to create an accurate machine learning classifier for predicting COVID-19 severity based on an epidemiological dataset of patients from Mexico using different approaches of balancing data, namely SMOTE, ADASYN, and RUS as well as various machine learning models: Gradient naïve Bayes, logistic regression, decision tree, random forest, and K-nearest neighbors. The outcome of this analysis demonstrates that logistic regression applied to balanced data with RUS approach (LR-RUS) achieved the best results with 87.54% accuracy and 88.63% ROC_AUC.

Keywords: COVID-19, epidemiology, machine learning, threat management, imbalanced dataset, RUS, SMOTE, ADASYN.

4.1 Introduction

The novel coronavirus (COVID-19) infection has recently become a worldwide pandemic, and all countries across the world are striving to curb it effectively [1]. This illness presents a range of symptoms encompassing sore throats, coughs, headaches, fever, and respiratory problems, which, can sometimes result in fatality [2, 3]. Furthermore, numerous risk factors contribute to the severity of this ailment. Advanced age stands out as the most frequently cited risk factor, while male gender serves as a demographic factor influencing COVID-19 fatality. Additionally, prevalent prior health conditions including diabetes, hypertension, as well as coronary heart disease are commonly associated with increased risk [4]. Nevertheless, these factors exhibit variations across different countries. Previous research delved into disparities in case mortality rates across 93 countries, considering population risk factors like advanced age, comorbidities, and social factors such as poverty and overcrowding. Interestingly, countries with higher levels of social overcrowding and lower socioeconomic development demonstrated lower mortality rates [5]. Another study focused on the COVID-19 status among lower middle-income nations in the eastern Mediterranean part, revealing that Egypt, Tunisia, Sudan, and Djibouti exhibited the utmost case fatality rates compared to their regional counterparts. This discrepancy could be ascribed to the coexisting illnesses in Egypt, the relatively aged population in Tunisia compared to other nations in the region, and the inefficacy of medical care in Sudan and Djibouti [6].

Given the shortage of medical supplies like ventilators and hospital beds, healthcare professionals find themselves grappling with challenging decisions on resource allocation among patients, often entailing ethical considerations [7–9]. Taking advantage of powerful artificial intelligence algorithms, healthcare systems can analyze huge datasets to predict COVID-19 severity. These insights enable clinicians to allocate resources efficiently and implement targeted interventions for high-risk patients along with providing personalized treatments for the most vulnerable patients. AI-driven threat management acts as a proactive tool, assisting healthcare industries in anticipating and mitigating virus-related challenges. The integration of predictive modeling and AI-driven threat management not only optimize patient care but also strengthens the overall resilience of healthcare industries to face the dynamic and the complexity of this pandemic. Particularly, machine learning models play a crucial role in minimizing uncertainty and ambiguity, providing evidence-based techniques for risk analysis and prediction. They encourage accurate medical threat management and aim to enhance patient outcomes and boost the resilience of healthcare industries.

In the current investigation, we suggest a data-driven machine learning predictive technique for predicting the fatality risk among COVID-19 hospitalized individuals. The suggested approach can support medical industries to optimize the allocation of resources and prioritize patients for hospitalization, as well as avoiding delays in delivering necessary care, especially when the system is overloaded with patients. Thereby, it may boost the resilience of healthcare industries and empower the AI-driven threat management to tackle this health crisis. Because of the prevalent imbalance within COVID-19 data, where the number of deaths is significantly lower, the development of a high-performing machine learning model becomes more arduous. The scarcity of studies addressing this specific issue further accentuates the challenge. For this reason, our research aims to develop an accurate machine learning classifier that predicts COVID-19 fatality using different approaches for balancing data to achieve better results and make meticulous predictions of fatality among hospitalized infected patients.

The remainder of this research is structured in the following manner: Section 4.2 exhibits the related work; Section 4.3 deals with the background of this investigation; Section 4.4 illustrates the data and methods utilized in this work; Section 4.5 explains the results of this study; Section 4.6 presents the discussion; and Section 4.7 sums up this work with a conclusion.

4.2 Related Work

Due to the scarcity of medical supplies in contrast to the rapidly increasing number of COVID-19 instances. Predicting COVID-19 mortality plays a pivotal role to ensure resilience in healthcare industry, optimize the allocation of medical resources, and provide a personalized treatment to hospitalized patients. Accordingly, several machine learning models have been employed to predict COVID-19 risk of mortality. Iwendi *et al.* [10] built several machine learning classifiers for predicting COVID-19 mortality utilizing Mexican and Brazilian datasets. For Mexico dataset, the best result was obtained by logistic regression, which attained 0.92272 accuracy, 0.62169 precision, 0.46516 recall, and 0.53215 F1-score. However, for Brazil dataset, decision tree surpassed the other classifiers with 0.69158 accuracy, 0.74276 precision, 0.38502 recall, and 0.50715 F1-score. Wollenstein-Betech *et al.* [11] used XGBoost, logistic regression, support vector machine, and random forest for predicting COVID-19 mortality in two scenarios: one before and another one after visiting a healthcare center. The first scenario addresses situations in which only the basic features of an infected individual are known. The classification yielded an accuracy of 73% and an AUC of 69%. In the second scenario, details about the hospitalization such as the patient's ventilator, pneumonia, and ICU are taken into account. In this case, the classification's performance attained 76% accuracy, and 74% AUC. Additionally, Bolourani *et al.* [12] created machine learning classifiers that predict breathing difficulties in COVID-19 infected individuals within 48 hours of admission. Three models were assessed: logistic regression, XGBoost, and XGBoost combined with SMOTEENN (XGBoost+SMOTEENN). Consequently, XGBoost classifier attained the best outcome with 0.919 mean accuracy and 0.77 AUC.

On the other hand, other studies have been applied to address the issue of imbalanced datasets for COVID-19 detection. For instance, Mohammedqasem *et al.* [13] developed a deep learning optimization approach capable of handling imbalanced data to enhance the classification of infected individuals. They balanced the data using synthetic minority oversampling technique and they identified the most important features through recursive feature elimination method. Experimental prediction results showed that the model and data were compatible and stable, with 98% maximum accuracy and 97% precision. In another study, Wu *et al.* [14] proposed a new composite dynamic ensemble selection (DES) technique to identify COVID-19 from whole blood counts in imbalanced data. This approach merges improved DES and data preprocessing. The combination of synthetic minority oversampling technique with edited nearest neighbor (SMOTE-ENN) were used for balancing the dataset and eliminating the noise. Then, to increase DES performance, a new hybrid multiple clustering and bagging classifier generation (HMCBCG) algorithm was presented to enhance the variety and the local regional capacity of potential classifiers. The best results for COVID-19 detection were obtained by HMCBCG + k-nearest oracles eliminate, with an accuracy of 99.81%, an F1-score of 99.86%, a G-mean of 99.78%, and an AUC of 99.81%. Moreover, AlJame *et al.* [15] suggested a model combining the predictions of three popular diversified classifiers with various first-level learning characteristics and architectures: logistic regression, random forest, and additional trees. The algorithm employed extreme gradient boosting (XGBoost) classifier in the second stage. The suggested methodology uses isolation forest (iForest) for eliminating aberrant data, a synthetic minority oversampling technique (SMOTE) for balancing data distribution, and the KNNImputer algorithm for handling missing values for data preparation. Furthermore, feature importance is presented utilizing SHapley

Additive exPlanations (SHAP) approach to assure model understanding. The ensemble model performed outstandingly well with 99.88% overall accuracy, 99.38% AUC, 98.72% sensitivity, and 99.99% specificity.

4.3 Background

4.3.1 Oversampling and undersampling techniques

Recently, there has been a lot of attention to imbalanced class. Many scholars believe that this is a difficult problem requiring further investigation to be solved [16]. Prior to using a dataset for developing a model, sampling is a preprocessing procedure aimed at correcting the imbalance of a given dataset by adding or removing samples (modules) [17]. Oversampling and undersampling are two methods for correcting the imbalance among majority and minority instances and may be incorporated into general model [18]. Undersampling methods take away some of the majority instances, whereas oversampling techniques produce more minority samples found on the available instances [19].

4.3.1.1 Oversampling techniques

An oversampling method is employed to add new instances to the minority class for balancing the dataset [20]. These techniques may be classified into random and synthetic oversampling. The random oversampling approach repeats available minority instances to expand the minority class. The synthetic oversampling method creates synthetic observations for minority class instances. These novel observations provide valuable information to the minority class and prevent misclassification [21].

- **SMOTE technique**

  A smart approach of oversampling is to synthetically generate new observations of the minority group. The SMOTE approach has proven to be very successful in various application areas [22]. SMOTE was proposed to extend the range of minority classes by generating synthetic instances in the feature space [23]. This can be achieved by determining each minority observation's nearest neighbors and randomly picking one of them to generate a new synthetic observation. The novel observation is a randomly chosen set of the attributes of its closest neighbors [24]. The method can be described as follows [20]:

  1. Upload the data.
  2. Set K to the desired neighbors' number.

3. For every instance in the dataset:
   a. Compute the distance separating the query instance and the present instance from the dataset.
   b. Add the instance's distance and index to a sorted list.
4. Order the sorted list of indices and distances in increasing order by the distances.
5. Select the first K elements from the ordered list.
6. Take the labels for the chosen K elements.
7. In case of regression, give the K labels' mean.
8. In case of classification, give the K label's mode.

- **ADASYN technique**

  ADASYN is another key oversampling method that efficiently enhances learning concerning sample distributions [25]. In the process of creating synthetic samples, it is not necessary to analyze all sub-samples because there may be compatibility problems [21]. ADASYN uses a smaller sample size distribution minority sample. It allocates weight to the minority instance according to its importance. Instances that are not easily classified received greater weight than the other instances. Additional observations are created for a higher weight instance.

  The algorithm can be described as follows [26]:

  1. Start by a dataset D that comprises N instances.
  2. Determine the class distribution of the dataset D.
  3. Determine the count of minority observations E and the count of majority observations for every minority class.
  4. Generate a novel dataset D' through taking M instances from the majority group and E instances from the minority group at random.
  5. For every observation in the minority class, choose arbitrary a majority class instance and perform synthetic oversampling
  6. Continue with procedures 4 and 5 till every class has equal number of observations. Then give D' the novel dataset as the algorithm's output.

4.3.1.2 Undersampling approaches

Undersampling is a technique for balancing heterogeneous datasets by maintaining all the observations of the minority group and decreasing the number of instances in the majority group [27]. In this way, undersampling with an unbalanced dataset can be considered as a prototype selection method aimed to balance the dataset to achieve high classification rates and avoid bias toward examples of a large number of classes [28]. This method is useful when the data are enough for thorough investigation [29].

The algorithm for random undersampling functions as follows [33]:

1. Start by randomly selecting a set of data from the majority class (The class that has the most data points is known as the majority class).
2. Eliminate data points from the minority class to restore balance to the dataset.
3. Perform again steps 1 and 2 until the minority and the majority classes are balanced.
4. Instruct the model on the balanced dataset and assess the model's performance.

4.4 Machine Learning Models

4.4.1 k-nearest neighbors algorithm

K-nearest neighbors (KNN) is a straightforward and successful machine learning model that is suitable for problems involving regression and classification as well. The fundamental concept of this theory is very easy. Basically, it determines the distance separating a new instance and each observation in the train dataset. All types of distance can be employed, including Hamming distances, Manhattan, and Euclidean distances. The K-nearest observations are subsequently selected, with K being an integer. Lastly, the instance is assigned to the class comprising the major part of the K instances.

4.4.2 Decision tree

Decision tree technique is data mining method commonly used to build classification systems based on multiple covariates or to develop predictive algorithms for target variables. It is a directional tree made up of multiple nodes. With no inputs, the root node is the first node in the tree. Other nodes have inputs and outputs, called internal nodes. Other nodes can also have only one input, called leaf nodes or decision nodes. The aim is the generation of a model that uses several input variables to predict the value of a target variable. Decision tree techniques have several advantages compared to other data mining techniques. Easy to understand and interpret, the graph representation is simple, can handle both numeric and categorical data, little data preparation is required, and works well even with large datasets.

4.4.3 Logistic regression

Logistic regression method is the most commonly prevalent modeling technique employed for binary outcomes in epidemiology and medicine. It calculates the probability that a realization of an output variable belongs to the corresponding category. By using descriptive models that might be used to forecast risk, researchers were able to assess the relationship between several risk variables and a certain outcome through the use of traditional logistic regression procedures. Clinicians were able to measure the strength of the correlations between the risk variables and outcome by looking at the coefficients produced by the model.

4.4.4 Gradient naïve Bayes

Gradient naïve Bayes (NB) is an easy and well-known probabilistic classifier depending on Bayesian decision theory. It is "naïve" because it assumes that the attribute values of a particular class are independent of the values of other attributes. NB infers the possibility that one new example associated with some class depend on the assumption that all attributes are apart from one another given the class. This supposition is activated by the need to evaluate multivariate probabilities from training data.

4.4.5 Random forest

Random forest (RF) is a ML technique utilized for both classification and regression tasks. It employs ensemble learning, which combines various kinds of models or the identical model several times to create additional accurate prediction algorithm. Decision trees are generated by random forest using arbitrary selected instances. It evaluates each tree's prediction and uses voting to determine which one is the best.

4.5 Evaluation Metrics

A confusion matrix, in statistics, summarizes the prediction outcomes of a classification. From this matrix, we obtain the evaluation metrics below utilizing these terms: true negative (TN), false positive (FP), true positive (TP), and false negative (FN). The metrics listed below are employed to assess and compare different trained models:

4.5.1 Accuracy

Accuracy measures the percentage of the data points correctly predicted by ML technique. The accuracy is stated in eqn (4.1) below:

$$\text{Accuracy} = \frac{TP + TN}{TP + TN + FP + FN}. \quad (4.1)$$

As class imbalance goes up, the accuracy metric produces misleadingly high results. Because accuracy weights percentage of correct predictions per-class according to its size, it generally ignores the minority class's performance. Instead of producing a true, broadly applicable capacity to discriminate between the two classes, a binary classification algorithm, which acquires the ability to vote regularly for the majority class will cause an erroneously high decoding accuracy, which reveal the imbalance between them.

4.5.2 Precision

The precision of a model is its ability not to categorize negative instances as positive. The precision is defined as follows (eqn (4.2)):

$$\text{Precision} = \frac{TP}{TP + FP}. \quad (4.2)$$

Precision only considers the relevant samples among the predicted positive samples. It ignores false negatives. When false negatives are important, precision alone cannot offer a comprehensive view of the performance of the model. In our study, it is critical to correctly predict patients as positive and not make mistakes in predicting negative individuals as positive, because the resources are scarce, and it is interesting to predict correctly patients at high risk of mortality. Additionally, in imbalanced datasets, precision could not be the most appropriate metric.

4.5.3 Recall

Recall measures the capacity of the model to identify every positive samples. It is described by the following formula (eqn (4.3)):

$$\text{Recall} = \frac{TP}{TP + FN}. \quad (4.3)$$

Recall does not consider the number of false positives. When the false positives have significant impact, recall alone cannot reflect the model's performance. For instance, in this study, a high recall can result in false alarms since the model can predict erroneously patients as having high risk of mortality. Thus, this can hamper the optimal allocation of resources. Especially, when there is a limited number of medical supplies. Moreover, in case of imbalanced datasets, recall does not perform well.

4.5.4 F1-score

F1-score introduces the harmonic mean of the recall and precision. Precision and recall both contribute equally to the F1-score in terms of relative importance. The F1-score can be computed from eqn (4.4) given below:

$$f1_{score} = 2 * \frac{\text{precision} * \text{recall}}{\text{precision} + \text{recall}}. \quad (4.4)$$

A high F1-score often denotes a balanced performance, indicating that high precision and high recall can be achieved by the model at the same time. On the other hand, low F1-score generally demonstrates that the sample struggles to discover that equilibrium between the precision and recall.

Similarly to recall and precision, F1-score cannot be a suitable metric when there is an imbalance in classes.

4.5.5 ROC_AUC

Area under ROC curve score (ROC_AUC) computes the region under the operating characteristic curve of the receiver. It indicates the ability of the model to make distinctions between different classes. True-positive rate is plotted versus false-positive rate on the ROC curve.

It is noteworthy that the region within the curve (AUC) of the ROC curve computes the integral of the true-positive rate against the false-positive rate over decision threshold. This suggests that altering the decision threshold, which is frequently done to lessen the consequences of class imbalance, has no influence on AUC.

4.5.6 Average precision

Average precision (AP) recapitulates the precision–recall curve. It is the weighted average of the precision metrics obtained at every PR curve threshold, with the augmentation in recall from the preceding threshold serving as the weight. The AP metric can be computed from eqn (4.5) given below:

$$AP = \sum_n (R_n - R_{n-1}) P_n. \quad (4.5)$$

where R_n and P_n denote the recall and the precision at the nth threshold.

This statistic considers the precision–recall trade-off and evaluates the algorithm's performance at different recall levels. It prioritizes precision at different recall levels. In our study, this complies with our objective of reducing false positives and consequently minimizing false alerts. Thereby, this metric is crucial in our study.

4.6 Data and Methods

4.6.1 Data description

The data employed in the present work was supplied by Iwendi et al. [10]. It contains data of 1,129,258 COVID-19-infected individuals from Mexico. We selected 19 variables for our investigation, comprising 18 demographic and clinical features, in addition to the target variable: death. In the initial encoding of the dataset, the "Sex" attribute was originally represented by the values 1 for "female" and 2 for "male." Similarly, the "Type of patient" feature was encoded as 1 for "in transit" and 2 for "in hospital." Regarding other categorical variables, the encoding utilized 1 for "positive" and 2 for "negative." However, in this investigation, a modified coding scheme was employed. Specifically, the "Sex" variable was recoded as 0 for males and 1 for females. The "Type of patient" attribute was represented by 0 for "in transit" patients and 1 for those "in hospital." For the remaining categorical variables, they were represented by 0 for "negative" and 1 for "positive," as outlined in Table 4.1.

4.6.2 Proposed solution

The accurate prediction of COVID-19 fatality within infected individuals plays a crucial role in assisting healthcare industries to rationalize the allocation of resources, prioritize cases at high risk of mortality to benefit from a special attention, and minimize delays in providing essential medical treatments, particularly when the system is overfilled with patients. Consequently, this empowers the resilience of medical industries and fosters the AI-driven threat management to face this challenging health crisis. Nevertheless, the issue of COVID-19 imbalanced datasets makes the creation of an effective machine learning classifier more difficult. Accordingly, this research aims to

Table 4.1 Final list of the variables employed in this research.

Column	Variable	Description	Encoding (for categorical variables)	Data type
1	Sex	Patient's gender	0-male, 1-female	Categorical
2	Type of patient	Type of healthcare attention	0-in transit, 1-in hospital	Categorical
3	Intubated	Determine whether the patient needed intubation.	0-no, 1-yes	Categorical
4	Pneumonia	Illness observed by the infected individuals	0-no, 1-yes	Categorical
5	Pregnancy	Condition observed by the infected individuals	0-no, 1-yes	Categorical
6	Diabetes	Illness observed by the infected individuals	0-no, 1-yes	Categorical
7	Epoc	Illness observed by the infected individuals (Excess post exercise oxygen consumption)	0-no, 1-yes	Categorical
8	Asthma	Illness observed by the infected individuals	0-no, 1-yes	Categorical
9	Immunosuppression	Illness observed by the infected individuals	0-no, 1-yes	Categorical
10	Hypertension	Illness observed by the infected individuals	0-no, 1-yes	Categorical
11	Another complication	Another illness observed by the infected individuals	0-no, 1-yes	Categorical
12	Cardiovascular	Illness observed by the infected individuals	0-no, 1-yes	Categorical
13	Obesity	Illness observed by the infected individuals	0-no, 1-yes	Categorical
14	Renal failure	Illness observed by the infected individuals	0-no, 1-yes	Categorical
15	Smoking	Identifies if the infected individual is smoking or not	0-no, 1-yes	Categorical
16	ICU	Identifies whether the infected individual needed intensive care unit	0-no, 1-yes	Categorical
17	Age	Patient's age	NA	Numeric
18	Other_Case	Identifies whether the infected individual had contact with any other COVID-19 infected patient	0-no, 1-yes	Categorical
19	Death	Identifies if the infected individual died or recovered because of COVID-19	0-survived, 1-dead	Categorical

build an effective data-driven machine learning classifier to predict the risk of mortality in COVID-19 infected cases through leveraging various techniques for balancing data.

Initially, we started with pre-processing data. Aside from the attribute "Age," all features range between 0 and 1. To eliminate the effect of attributes with different scale, the variable "Age" was standardized through Z-score normalization. Then, the dataset was split into 75% for the train set and 25% for the test set. The train set was employed to create different machine learning algorithms, namely, decision tree, logistic regression, Gaussian naïve Bayes, random forest, and K-nearest neighbors. We selected these algorithms since they are some of the widely popular models utilized for COVID-19 prediction and they cover a wide range of techniques. Logistic regression and decision tree are characterized by their effectiveness and interpretability for binary classification. Gaussian naïve Bayes can be useful in estimating the likelihood of mortality based on related features. KNN might be suitable for mortality prediction based on the similarity of patient attributes. Besides, random forest was of a particular interest since it is an ensemble approach based on tree. It is supposed to perform better than the other techniques in dealing with class imbalance. The performance of these algorithms has been improved using various balancing data approaches, namely, SMOTE, ADASYN, and RUS.

4.7 Results

We compared different machine learning classifiers, namely decision tree (DT), gradient naïve Bayes (GNB), random forest (RF), K-nearest neighbor (KNN), and logistic regression (LR).

4.7.1 Balancing data with ADASYN

The application of ADASYN method shows that logistic regression outperformed the other models with 86.59% accuracy, 56.24% F1-score, 92% recall, 40.5% precision, 89.01% ROC_AUC, and 38% average precision. Followed by RF, KNN, GNB, and DT (Table 4.2).

Table 4.2 Algorithms comparison after balancing data with ADASYN.

Model	Train_score (%)	Test_accuracy (%)	F1-score (%)	Recall (%)	Precision (%)	ROC_AUC (%)	AP (%)
GNB	84.88	85.75	53.97	89.18	38.69	87.29	35.52
DT	93.39	88.15	54.76	76.55	42.63	82.95	34.83
RF	93.38	88.05	56.32	82.24	42.83	85.44	36.88
LR	86.37	86.59	56.24	92	40.5	89.01	38
KNN	76.73	91.27	56.60	60.77	52.96	77.59	35.86

Table 4.3 Algorithms comparison after balancing data with SMOTE.

Model	Train_score (%)	Test_accuracy (%)	F1-score (%)	Recall (%)	Precision (%)	ROC_AUC (%)	AP (%)
GNB	87.28	85.82	54.07	89.09	38.81	87.29	35.60
DT	94.24	88.96	56.02	75.02	44.70	82.71	35.87
RF	94.24	88.87	57.55	80.54	44.77	85.13	37.88
LR	88.68	87.53	57.46	89.90	42.22	88.59	38.91
KNN	83.44	91.45	56.88	60.23	53.88	77.45	36.18

4.7.2 Balancing data with SMOTE technique

Balancing data with SMOTE approach has generally improved the performance of all classifiers. Logistic regression remains the best algorithm in this comparison with 87.53% accuracy, 57.46% F1-score, 89.90% recall, 42.22% precision, and 38.91% average precision. Followed by RF, KNN, DT, and GNB (Table 4.3).

4.7.3 Balancing data with RUS technique

The comparison of the above-mentioned algorithms while balancing data with RUS approach revealed that the performance of all algorithms had slightly increased. Logistic regression yields the best performance with 87.54% accuracy, 57.49% F1-score, 89.97% recall, 42.24% precision, 88.63% ROC_AUC, and 38.95 AP. Followed by RF, DT, KNN, and GNB. Consequently, LR algorithm built with balanced data using RUS approach (RUS-LR) outperformed all the other algorithms (Table 4.4).

4.8 Discussion

The outcome of the present investigation demonstrates that logistic regression classifier applied to the balanced data using RUS approach (RUS-LR) attained the best performance with 87.54% accuracy, 42.24% precision, 89.97% recall, 57.49% F1-score, 88.63% ROC_AUC, and 38.95 AP.

Table 4.4 Algorithms comparison after balancing data with RUS.

Model	Train_score (%)	Test_accuracy (%)	F1-score (%)	Recall (%)	Precision (%)	ROC_AUC (%)	AP (%)
GNB	87.30	85.73	53.92	89.12	38.65	87.25	35.47
DT	93.16	87.06	56.24	88.76	41.16	87.82	37.59
RF	93.15	86.74	56.51	91.96	40.79	89.08	38.26
RUS-LR	88.69	87.54	57.49	89.97	42.24	88.63	38.95
KNN	84.70	89.52	57.21	74.81	46.32	82.92	37.01

4.9 Conclusion

The comparison of these results with those of papers [10–12] exhibits that our best classifier logistic regression combined with RUS approach (RUS-LR) outperforms the results of [11]. Additionally, our result overcomes the best classifier XGBoost found in [12] in terms of recall, ROC_AUC, and AP. Given that a high recall with low precision can increase the risk of false positives, which can generate false alarms in detecting individuals at high risk of casualty and affect the allocation of resources, the AP metric is essential in comparing algorithms in this case, since it takes into account the precision–recall trade-off and prioritizes precision at various recall levels, enabling the achievement of our objective of reducing false alerts. Consequently, our study improves the prediction of COVID-19 mortality compared to the paper in [12]. Furthermore, this comparison reveals that our best model RUS-LR surpasses the results of the best classifier, logistic regression, found by [10], regarding F1-score and recall. However, this algorithm outperformed our results with respect to accuracy and precision (Table 4.5).

Accordingly, our analysis has significantly improved the prediction of COVID-19 risk of mortality among infected people. This can help clinicians and medical industries to be more resilient and make appropriate decisions to face such critical health crisis.

Table 4.5 Results comparison.

Ref.	Model	Accuracy (%)	Precision (%)	Recall (%)	F1-score	ROC_AUC (%)	AP (%)
[11]	LR: Before visiting a medical facility	73%	-	-	-	69%	-
	LR: After visiting a medical facility	**76%**	-	-	-	**74%**	-
[12]	Logistic regression	91.5	32.2	0.9	-	70	18
	XGBoost	**91.9**	**52.1**	**5.1**	-	**77**	**26**
	XGBoost+ SMOTEENN	89.3	30.3	22.8	-	76	24
[10]	**Logistic regression**	**92.272**	**62.169**	**46.516**	**53.215**	-	-
	Decision tree	92.558	80.767	27.88	41.452	-	-
	Boosted random forest classifier	91.06	96.42	5.48	10.37	-	-
Our study	**RUS-LR**	**87.54%**	**42.24%**	**89.97%**	**57.49%**	**88.63%**	**38.95**

4.9 Conclusion

The current study explores an artificial intelligence method for predicting COVID-19-related mortality among infected patients. Since the problem of imbalanced datasets is very common in COVID-19 data, the development of high-performing algorithms for predicting COVID-19 mortality become a challenging issue. To this end, this study investigates the application of different balancing data approaches to tackle this issue and build an accurate classifier. The findings of this research reveal that logistic regression model applied to the balanced data using RUS approach (RUS-LR) achieved the best performance with 87.54% accuracy, 57.49% F1-score, 89.97% recall, 42.24% precision, 88.63% ROC_AUC, and 38.95 AP.

References

[1] A. U. M. Shah *et al.*, "COVID-19 outbreak in Malaysia: Actions taken by the Malaysian government", *Int. J. Infect. Dis.*, vol. 97, p. 108-116, août 2020, doi:10.1016/j.ijid.2020.05.093.

[2] C. Huang *et al.*, "Clinical features of patients infected with 2019 novel coronavirus in Wuhan, China", *The Lancet*, vol. 395, no 10223, p. 497-506, févr. 2020, doi:10.1016/S0140-6736(20)30183-5.

[3] Q. Li *et al.*, "Early Transmission Dynamics in Wuhan, China, of Novel Coronavirus–Infected Pneumonia", *N. Engl. J. Med.*, p. 9, 2020.

[4] D. Wolff, S. Nee, N. S. Hickey, et M. Marschollek, "Risk factors for Covid-19 severity and fatality: a structured literature review", *Infection*, vol. 49, no 1, p. 15-28, févr. 2021, doi:10.1007/s15010-020-01509-1.

[5] M. J. Hashim, A. R. Alsuwaidi, et G. Khan, "Population Risk Factors for COVID-19 Mortality in 93 Countries", *J. Epidemiol. Glob. Health*, vol. 10, no 3, p. 204-208, sept. 2020, doi:10.2991/jegh.k.200721.001.

[6] S. El Khamlichi, A. Maurady, et A. Sedqui, "Comparative study of COVID-19 situation between lower-middle-income countries in the eastern Mediterranean region", *J. Oral Biol. Craniofacial Res.*, vol. 12, no 1, p. 165-176, janv. 2022, doi:10.1016/j.jobcr.2021.10.004.

[7] N. Salari *et al.*, "The prevalence of sleep disturbances among physicians and nurses facing the COVID-19 patients: a systematic review and meta-analysis", *Glob. Health*, vol. 16, no 1, Art. no 1, déc. 2020, doi:10.1186/s12992-020-00620-0.

[8] N. Salari *et al.*, "The prevalence of stress, anxiety and depression within front-line healthcare workers caring for COVID-19 patients: a

systematic review and meta-regression", *Hum. Resour. Health*, vol. 18, no 1, p. 100, déc. 2020, doi:10.1186/s12960-020-00544-1.

[9] J.-L. Vincent et J. Creteur, "Ethical aspects of the COVID-19 crisis: How to deal with an overwhelming shortage of acute beds", *Eur. Heart J. Acute Cardiovasc. Care*, vol. 9, no 3, p. 248-252, avr. 2020, doi:10.1177/2048872620922788.

[10] C. Iwendi, C. G. Y. Huescas, C. Chakraborty, et S. Mohan, "COVID-19 health analysis and prediction using machine learning algorithms for Mexico and Brazil patients", *J. Exp. Theor. Artif. Intell.*, vol. 0, no 0, p. 1-21, avr. 2022, doi:10.1080/0952813X.2022.2058097.

[11] S. Wollenstein-Betech, C. G. Cassandras, et I. Ch. Paschalidis, "Personalized Predictive Models for Symptomatic COVID-19 Patients Using Basic Preconditions", *medRxiv*, p. 2020.05.03.20089813, mai 2020, doi:10.1101/2020.05.03.20089813.

[12] S. Bolourani *et al.*, "A Machine Learning Prediction Model of Respiratory Failure Within 48 Hours of Patient Admission for COVID-19: Model Development and Validation", *J. Med. Internet Res.*, vol. 23, no 2, p. e24246, févr. 2021, doi: 10.2196/24246.

[13] R. Mohammedqasem, H. Mohammedqasim, et O. Ata, "Real-time data of COVID-19 detection with IoT sensor tracking using artificial neural network", *Comput. Electr. Eng. Int. J.*, vol. 100, p. 107971, mai 2022, doi:10.1016/j.compeleceng.2022.107971.

[14] J. Wu, J. Shen, M. Xu, et M. Shao, "A novel combined dynamic ensemble selection model for imbalanced data to detect COVID-19 from complete blood count", *Comput. Methods Programs Biomed.*, vol. 211, p. 106444, nov. 2021, doi:10.1016/j.cmpb.2021.106444.

[15] M. AlJame, I. Ahmad, A. Imtiaz, et A. Mohammed, "Ensemble learning model for diagnosing COVID-19 from routine blood tests", *Inform. Med. Unlocked*, vol. 21, p. 100449, janv. 2020, doi:10.1016/j.imu.2020.100449.

[16] R. Mohammed, J. Rawashdeh, et M. Abdullah, "Machine Learning with Oversampling and Undersampling Techniques: Overview Study and Experimental Results", *in 2020 11th International Conference on Information and Communication Systems (ICICS)*, Irbid, Jordan: IEEE, avr. 2020, p. 243-248. doi:10.1109/ICICS49469.2020.239556.

[17] Y. Kamei, A. Monden, S. Matsumoto, T. Kakimoto, et K. Matsumoto, "The Effects of Over and Under Sampling on Fault-prone Module Detection", *in First International Symposium on Empirical Software*

Engineering and Measurement (ESEM 2007), sept. 2007, p. 196-204. doi:10.1109/ESEM.2007.28.

[18] K. Fujiwara *et al.*, "Over- and Under-sampling Approach for Extremely Imbalanced and Small Minority Data Problem in Health Record Analysis", *Front. Public Health*, vol. 8, 2020, Consulté le: 31 décembre 2023. [En ligne]. Disponible sur: https://www.frontiersin.org/articles/10.3389/fpubh.2020.00178

[19] R. Blagus et L. Lusa, "Joint use of over- and under-sampling techniques and cross-validation for the development and assessment of prediction models", *BMC Bioinformatics*, vol. 16, no 1, p. 363, nov. 2015, doi: 10.1186/s12859-015-0784-9.

[20] N. V. Chawla, K. W. Bowyer, L. O. Hall, et W. P. Kegelmeyer, "SMOTE: Synthetic Minority Over-sampling Technique", *J. Artif. Intell. Res.*, vol. 16, p. 321-357, juin 2002, doi:10.1613/jair.953.

[21] "A Review on Imbalanced Data Handling Using Undersampling and Oversampling Technique", *Int. J. Recent Trends Eng. Res.*, vol. 3, no 4, p. 444-449, mai 2017, doi:10.23883/IJRTER.2017.3168.0UWXM.

[22] B. Das, N. C. Krishnan, et D. J. Cook, "RACOG and wRACOG: Two Probabilistic Oversampling Techniques", *IEEE Trans. Knowl. Data Eng.*, vol. 27, no 1, p. 222-234, janv. 2015, doi: 10.1109/TKDE.2014.2324567.

[23] T. Zhu, Y. Lin, et Y. Liu, "Synthetic minority oversampling technique for multiclass imbalance problems", *Pattern Recognit.*, vol. 72, p. 327-340, déc. 2017, doi:10.1016/j.patcog.2017.07.024.

[24] "Enhancing Imbalanced Dataset by Utilizing (K-NN Based SMOTE_3D Algorithm)". Consulté le: 31 décembre 2023. [En ligne]. Disponible sur: https://www.peertechzpublications.org/articles/ARA-4-102.php

[25] "Comparing Oversampling Techniques to Handle the Class Imbalance Problem: A Customer Churn Prediction Case Study | IEEE Journals & Magazine | IEEE Xplore". Consulté le: 31 décembre 2023. [En ligne]. Disponible sur: https://ieeexplore.ieee.org/document/7707454

[26] G. Ahmed *et al.*, "DAD-Net: Classification of Alzheimer's Disease Using ADASYN Oversampling Technique and Optimized Neural Network", *Molecules*, vol. 27, no 20, Art. no 20, janv. 2022, doi:10.3390/molecules27207085.

[27] X.-Y. Liu, J. Wu, et Z.-H. Zhou, "Exploratory Undersampling for Class-Imbalance Learning", *IEEE Trans. Syst. Man Cybern. Part B Cybern.*, vol. 39, no 2, p. 539-550, avr. 2009, doi:10.1109/TSMCB.2008.2007853.

[28] H. He et E. A. Garcia, "Learning from Imbalanced Data", *IEEE Trans. Knowl. Data Eng.*, vol. 21, no 9, p. 1263-1284, sept. 2009, doi:10.1109/TKDE.2008.239.

[29] M. Bach, A. Werner, et M. Palt, "The Proposal of Undersampling Method for Learning from Imbalanced Datasets", *Procedia Comput. Sci.*, vol. 159, p. 125-134, janv. 2019, doi:10.1016/j.procs.2019.09.167.

[30] M. Saripuddin, A. Suliman, S. Syarmila Bt Sameon, et B. N. Jørgensen, "Random Undersampling on Imbalance Time Series Data for Anomaly Detection: The 4th International Conference on Machine Learning and Machine Intelligence. Virtual", *MLMI21 2021 4th Int. Conf. Mach. Learn. Mach. Intell.*, p. 151-156, sept. 2021, doi:10.1145/3490725.3490748.

[31] A. Farshidvard, F. Hooshmand, et S. A. MirHassani, "A novel two-phase clustering-based under-sampling method for imbalanced classification problems", *Expert Syst. Appl.*, vol. 213, p. 119003, mars 2023, doi:10.1016/j.eswa.2022.119003.

[32] J. M. Johnson et T. M. Khoshgoftaar, "Survey on deep learning with class imbalance", *J. Big Data*, vol. 6, no 1, p. 27, mars 2019, doi:10.1186/s40537-019-0192-5.

[33] A. El hariri, M. Mouiti, O. Habibi, et M. Lazaar, "Improving Deep Learning Performance Using Sampling Techniques for IoT Imbalanced Data", *Procedia Comput. Sci.*, vol. 224, p. 180-187, janv. 2023, doi:10.1016/j.procs.2023.09.026.

Part II

Cybersecurity Challenges and Resilience in Healthcare and Industrial Domains

5

Penetration Testing in Operations Technology and SCADA Environments

Yassine Maleh[1] and Mounia Zaydi[2]

[1]LaSTI Laboratory, Sultan Moulay Slimane University, Morocco
[2]ICL, Junia, Université catholique Lille, LITL (Lille Interdisciplinary Transitions Laboratory), France
E-mail: y.maleh@usms.ma; mounia.zaydi@junia.com

Abstract

The high expense of the necessary hardware to gain practical expertise with industrial control systems is one of the main obstacles to breaking into the field of industrial cybersecurity, which we discuss in this chapter (ICS). Everything related to penetration testing in an ICS setting, including tools, techniques, procedures, and activities, is what we want to explain in detail. A key contribution is the elucidation of the process of establishing a virtual industrial cybersecurity laboratory, enabling simulation of a complex control system. The main problem revolves around the accessibility barrier to real-world ICS interactions. This chapter navigates through the intricacies of conducting penetration testing in the IoT landscape, shedding light on IoT concepts and the practical aspects of such testing. It addresses the heightened susceptibility of ICS environments to cyber threats and identifies typical risks within these settings. The problem statement emphasizes the critical need for cost-effective solutions to gain practical experience in industrial cybersecurity. The proposed solution lies in the creation of a virtual industrial cybersecurity laboratory, offering a simulated environment for hands-on training. This chapter's main contribution is its practical approach to overcoming the financial barriers associated with obtaining real-world experience in ICS cybersecurity, providing valuable insights for both novices and seasoned professionals in the field.

Keywords: Penetration testing, operational technology (OT), SCADA systems cybersecurity, virtual laboratory, industrial control systems (ICS), vulnerability assessment, network security, cyber threat mitigation.

5.1 Introduction

In the fabric of contemporary society, operational technology (OT) stands as a linchpin, orchestrating a symphony of interconnected devices designed to operate seamlessly within integrated systems [1]. This technological ecosystem pervades diverse sectors, from telecommunications to industrial control processes, propelling the efficiency and sophistication of modern operations. Among the myriad domains under the influence of OT, the industrial control systems (ICS) environment holds a paramount position, shaping the trajectory of industrial processes and critical infrastructures [2].

The significance of ICS within the operational technology framework cannot be overstated. It represents a convergence of hardware and software, meticulously crafted to monitor, operate, and control assets in industrial processes. However, navigating the landscape of industrial control systems poses unique challenges, particularly for those seeking to understand and fortify its security. The intricacies of ICS demand a nuanced exploration, considering the diverse components, communication protocols, and layers that constitute its architecture [3].

Even while OT has made many technical advancements possible, there is still one major obstacle: the high bar to entry for industrial cybersecurity. The exigent cost associated with gaining hands-on experience within the Industrial Internet of Things (IIoT) environment serves as a deterrent for aspiring cybersecurity professionals and researchers [4]. This chapter presents a comprehensive exploration of tools, techniques, methodologies, and activities employed during penetration testing within the ICS landscape.

The crux of this chapter lies in its commitment to providing practical solutions to the financial impediments obstructing genuine engagement with OT technologies. It introduces the concept of a virtual industrial cybersecurity laboratory – an innovative approach that enables the emulation of complex industrial processes. This replicated industrial setting is ideal for doing real-world cybersecurity tests and logic programming in a virtual setting.

As we delve into the specifics of setting up a virtual industrial cybersecurity laboratory, the focus expands to encompass not only the technical intricacies of penetration testing but also the foundational understanding of key OT concepts [5]. Through this holistic approach, we aim not only to empower aspiring professionals with hands-on experience but also to contribute valuable insights to the proactive defense against cyber threats within the intricate landscape of OT environments.

In the following sections, we navigate through the concepts that underpin OT, explore the various layers of industrial control systems, and delve into the security implications and challenges of these intricate networks. The chapter culminates in a pragmatic examination of IoT concepts, penetration testing methodologies, and the potential vulnerabilities within OT environments. Through this exploration, we strive to illuminate the path toward a robust and secure future in the ever-evolving landscape of industrial cybersecurity [6].

5.2 Methodology

The cornerstone of our methodology is the establishment of a virtual industrial cybersecurity laboratory. This simulated environment replicates the complex ecosystem of an ICS, enabling detailed analysis and penetration testing without the high costs associated with physical lab setups. The laboratory includes virtual machines simulating various components of an ICS, including routers, programmable logic controllers (PLCs), and human–machine interfaces (HMIs), all interconnected within a controlled network infrastructure [7].

The penetration testing approach adopted in this study is comprehensive, covering a wide range of tools, techniques, and activities tailored to the unique characteristics of ICS environments [8]. It encompasses:

- Information gathering: Leveraging tools like Shodan and specialized scripts to identify exposed systems and potential entry points.
- Vulnerability assessment: Employing automated tools and manual techniques to discover vulnerabilities in the systems under test.
- Exploitation: Executing controlled attacks to validate identified vulnerabilities and assess their impact on the ICS environment.

A detailed walkthrough of configuring the test environment is provided, including the installation and setup of key components like OpenPLC and ScadaBR. This section also covers the networking configurations necessary for realistic simulation and interaction within the virtual lab. The execution phase focuses on applying the penetration testing framework within the virtual laboratory. It involves:

- Network traffic analysis: Using tools like Wireshark to capture and analyze communication between ICS components [9].
- Modbus TCP packet injection: Demonstrating the injection of malicious packets using Scapy to manipulate the behavior of simulated ICS components [10].

5.3 Implementation and Experiments

Today, industrial systems are more interconnected with the Internet than ever before, thereby exposing them to increased vulnerabilities and cyberattacks. Attackers are launching increasingly sophisticated and targeted cyberattacks that result in the physical destruction of industrial systems. In some instances, companies utilize devices running outdated software to meet compatibility requirements and share sensitive information with third parties for remote equipment maintenance. These factors pose significant threats to business security.

5.3.1 Implementation of the test environment

The hefty price tag of the gear needed to get hands-on expertise with OT (operational technology) systems and procedures is a big deterrent to getting into industrial cybersecurity. Virtualization is a tool that enables you to overcome this initial entry barrier and provides an experience like what one might encounter in a real environment without requiring a significant investment. The objective of this laboratory is to simulate a simple process containing several key elements involved in a control process.

The following components will be used to implement this design:
- A pfSense VM simulates a router (PFSENSE)
- A Ubuntu VM simulates a PLC (OpenPLC), a Ubuntu VM simulates a HMI (ScadaBR) [11]
- A Windows 10 VM simulates our Filling Reservoir (Factory IO) [12]
- A Linux Kali VM representing the attacker's machine

As depicted in the diagram shown in Figure 5.2, the router will require two interfaces: one external for internet access (WAN) and one internal for all our virtual machines to connect to (LAN).

TL; DR: We'll need to configure the WAN interface as NAT and the LAN as Host-Only as shown in Figure 5.1, but if you want to know why, keep reading.

5.3 Implementation and Experiments 129

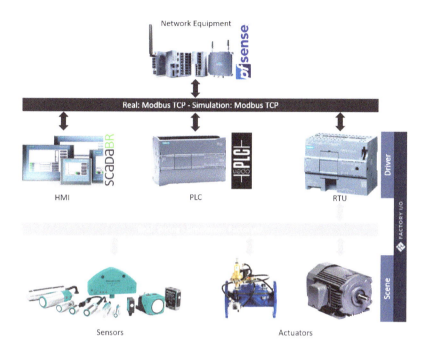

Figure 5.1 Virtual industrial cybersecurity laboratory – physical diagram.

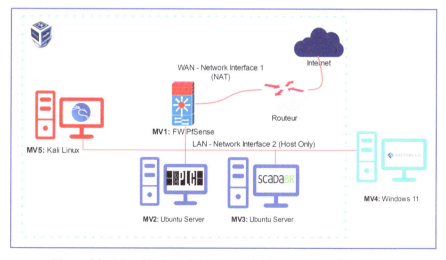

Figure 5.2 Virtual industrial cybersecurity laboratory – logical diagram.

5.3.1.1 Installation of OpenPLC and ScadaBR

To the best of my ability, I'd want to simulate a real-world setup in which a PLC and an HMI are two independent devices that communicate with one another across a network, even if it is theoretically possible to run both programs on the same computer.

- First, we'll need to download Ubuntu Server and install it on two separate virtual machines. Make sure to setup the same adapter on both computers.
- The pfSense router's LAN interface should be the same adapter.
- In order for the freshly spun-up workstations to connect to the Internet and download updates, the pfSense virtual machine has to be turned on.

The two servers should be given a static IP address in pfSense when installation is finished so that the OpenPLC [13] and ScadaBR web apps may be bookmarked for convenient access. Just do as instructed:

1. Access the pfSense web application portal (in our case, https://192.168.10.1).
2. Select "Status > DHCP Lease" after you've logged in. There are two gadgets that are linked (one for each virtual machine).
3. Go into the router's settings and give every connected device an IP address that is static and not in the DHCP range that was established when you first set it up.

Once static IPs are assigned, restart both machines and refresh the pfSense console to ensure they are correctly assigned and online.

It's also recommended to verify that both machines have Internet access and can see each other:

- From VM2: ping www.google.com
- From VM2: ping 192.168.88.202 (ping to VM3)
- From VM3: ping www.google.com
- From VM3: ping 192.168.88.201 (ping to VM2)

5.3.1.2 Installation of OpenPLC in VM2

We start by downloading Ubuntu Server, followed by the installation of a virtual machine. It is essential to configure the same adapter as that used for the LAN interface of the pfSense router. The pfSense virtual machine must be enabled to allow the new machine to access the Internet. Once the server installation is complete, a static IP address is assigned in pfSense to facilitate

5.3 Implementation and Experiments 131

access to the bookmarks tab of the OpenPlC web application Figure 5.3. To do this

- Access the pfSense web application portal https://192.168.88.201:8080.
- Then navigate to "Status > DHCP Lease."
- For each device connected, access the configuration and assign a static IP address outside the DHCP range initially defined for the router.

Now we check that our machine has access to the Internet.

Figure 5.3 OpenPLC interface.

5.3.1.3 Installation of ScadaBR in MV3

We start by downloading Ubuntu Server, followed by the installation of a virtual machine. It is essential to configure the same adapter as that used for the LAN interface of the pfSense router. The pfSense virtual machine must be enabled to allow the new machine to access the Internet. Once the server installation is complete, a static IP address is assigned in pfSense to facilitate access to the bookmarks tab of the ScadaBR web application, as shown in Figure 5.4. To do this

- Access the pfSense web application portal http://192.168.88.202:9090/ScadaBR
- Then navigate to "Status > DHCP Lease."
- For each device connected, access the configuration and assign a static IP address outside the DHCP range initially defined for the router.

Now we check that our machine has access to the Internet.

132 *Penetration Testing in Operations Technology and SCADA Environments*

Figure 5.4 ScadaBR web administration portal.

To manually start ScadaBR when you boot the virtual machine, you'll need to execute this command:

– sudo /opt/tomcat6/apache-tomcat-6.0.53/bin/startup.sh

However, my recommendation is to create a cronjob that starts it automatically. To do this, execute the following command in the command line:

– sudo nano crontab -e

Then, add the following line at the end of the file:

– @reboot /opt/tomcat6/apache-tomcat-6.0.53/bin/startup.sh

Save the changes and exit the editor with CTRL+X. Figure 5.5 shows a screenshot of an automatic startup of ScadaBR.

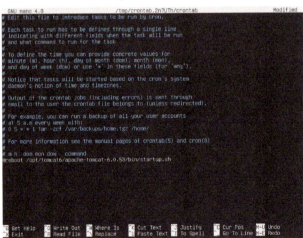

Figure 5.5 Automatic startup of ScadaBR.

5.3 Implementation and Experiments   133

Note: When starting the virtual machines, you may encounter an error message in cloud-init. You can disable it with the following command:

- sudo touch /etc/cloud/cloud-init.z

5.3.1.4 Downloading and installing FactoryIO

FactoryIO was used for this simulation. You can download the software from its website. There are several versions available that include different modules (OPC-UA, Modbus TCP, S7, etc.). However, since we want to control it from OpenPLC, we need a version compatible with ModbusTCP. It's worth noting that the 30-day trial version contains all the modules and is a good option for beginners.

Factory IO serves a dual purpose:

1. Scene-recreates the real-life operation by means of all the necessary sensors and actuators.
2. The driver controls all the scene's sensors and actuators and acts as a remote terminal unit (RTU) by interacting with OpenPLC over Modbus TCP, as shown in Figure 5.6.

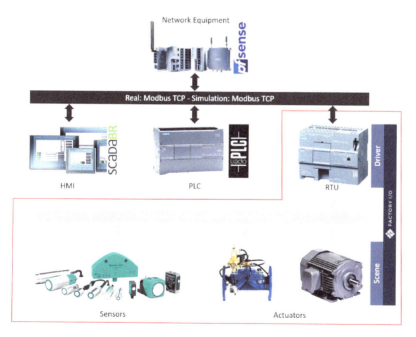

Figure 5.6 Factory IO scene and driver simulating the physical process and RTU respectively.

5.3.1.5 Physical process simulation – scene

Before starting to build the simulation, it is important to have a high-level definition of what we aim to achieve. In this case, the objectives are as follows:

- A conveyor belt moves boxes to a collection point marked by a retroreflective sensor.
- When a box is detected at this point, the conveyor belt stops, and a robot picks up the box and places it on the ground.
- Access to the production line is controlled by a safety door, which triggers an emergency stop if opened while the robot is operating.

We won't delve too much into the use of FactoryIO since it has quite detailed documentation on its website. Once installed, a new scene is created, and all the elements involved in our process are placed:

- Emitter: Element that creates the boxes at the start of the line.
- Start button: Used to activate and deactivate the process. In a real situation, there would also be an emergency stop button, a normal stop button, a reset button, etc. However, for simplicity's sake, only the start button will be used.
- Safety door: It has a pressure sensor that detects if it is open or closed. It limits personnel access to the danger zone presented by the robot's movement. In a real situation, the entire area would be protected by a fence, but for visualization purposes in this case, only the door will be used.
- Conveyor belt: Moves boxes from the emitter to the collection point.
- Light emitter: Emits a continuous beam of light.
- Retroreflective sensor: Detects the light emitted by the emitter to determine if there is a box at the collection point.
- Pick and place robot: Picks up and moves the boxes. Likely the most complex element of the system as it includes multiple sensors and actuators, although for this exercise only the following elements are used:
    - Grab: Activates the suction cup of the head that grabs the boxes
    - Detected: Detects if the head has contacted a box
    - 1Z: Extends/retracts the arm in the Z-axis
    - Moving Z: Detects if the robot is moving in the Z-axis
    - Rotation: Detects if the arm (not the head) is rotating

5.3 Implementation and Experiments 135

○ Rotate CW: Rotates the arm (not the head) clockwise
○ Rotate CCW: Rotates the arm (not the head) counterclockwise
○ Remove: Element that will remove the boxes at the end of the line

Decorations: These objects serve no other purpose than to slightly enhance the appearance of the simulation:

○ Pallet: Where the boxes fall
○ Column + Electrical Panel: Housing for the power button

At this stage, we should have a series of fixed elements placed in the scene, as shown in Figure 5.7.

Figure 5.7 Placement of elements in the FactoryIO scene.

5.3.1.6 Simulation RTU – driver

With all the elements arranged in the environment, we will configure the FactoryIO driver that will communicate with OpenPLC. To do this, from the scene:

– Access the driver's menu by pressing F4.
– Select the Modbus TCP/IP server as the driver (Figure 5.8)

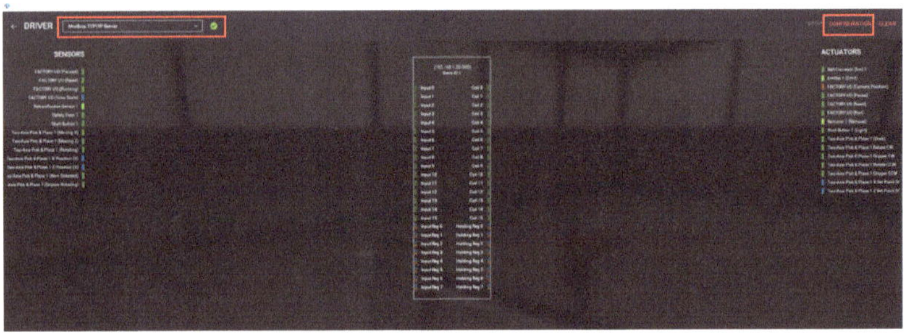

136   *Penetration Testing in Operations Technology and SCADA Environments*

Figure 5.8 Configuration of the driver as Modbus TCP server.

Click on the top right corner (settings).

- **Server:**
    ○ Network adapter: select the host-only virtual network adapter in the lab
    ○ Host: it is automatically configured when choosing the network card
    ○ Port: 502 (default Modbus TCP)
    ○ SlaveID: choose the desired one
    ○ I/O Config: default
    ○ I/O Points: we will only use 6 digital inputs and 5 digital outputs (no registers), so we set the values appropriately (6, 5, 0, 0) and apply Figure 5.9 shows the configuration of Modbus TCP server values in FactoryIO.

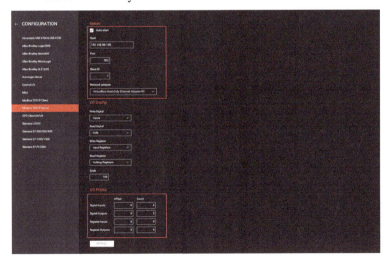

Figure 5.9 Configuration of Modbus TCP server values in FactoryIO.

5.3 Implementation and Experiments   137

Drag each of the inputs and outputs so that they all appear on the controller, as shown in Figure 5.10.

Figure 5.10 Assigning different sensors and actuators from the scene to the inputs and outputs of the driver.

5.3.1.7 Integrating OpenPLC with FactoryIO

To integrate FactoryIO with OpenPLC, we access the OpenPLC Web portal (if we remember, in our case 192.168.88.201:8080) and once inside, we navigate to the "Slave Devices" tab to configure the FactoryIO driver as a slave device (Figure 5.11), taking into account the following considerations:

- Device type: It should be a generic Modbus TCP device.
- Slave ID: Can be any integer greater than 0, but must be the same as the one previously configured in the FactoryIO driver.
- IP addresses: Identical to those previously configured in the FactoryIO driver (host-only adapter VirtualBox).
- IP Port: 502 is the default ModbusTCP port; it is recommended to keep it as default, although it is possible to change it as long as it is correctly set in the FactoryIO driver.
- Discrete inputs: Starting from 0, and ending with the number of required inputs (6 in our case).
- Coils: Starting from 0, and ending with the number of required inputs (5 in our case).
- Input registers: Our example does not have registers (only inputs and outputs), so it can be set to 0,0.
- Holding registers – Read: Our example does not have registers (only inputs and outputs), so it can be set to 0,0.

– Holding Registers – Write: Our example does not have registers (only inputs and outputs), so it can be set to 0,0.

Figure 5.11 Left: driver configured in FactoryIO; Right: configuration of the slave device in OpenPLC.

5.3.1.8 Programming control logic

To program the control logic, we will use the OpenPLC Editor, which is an independent OpenPLC program and can be downloaded and installed on our Windows 10 (host) device. Once downloaded and a new project created, we will define all the variables to be used by the program (Figure 5.12), taking into account the following considerations:

– The variables declared in OpenPLC Editor must be in the same range as those declared in the SlaveDevice configured in the previous point.
– We will use an auxiliary variable "RUN" internally during the program, which will not need to be assigned to any input or output (%IX100.x, %QX100.x).

Once the variables are defined, we can begin developing the control program using the standard industry ladder logic language, implementing the following logic, as shown in Figure 5.13.

– Press the "StartButton" to activate or deactivate the line.
– Open the door for any movement.
– The conveyor belt stops when there is a box waiting.
– If there is a box waiting, the robot descends, activates the suction cup, lifts, rotates, releases the box, and returns to its rest position.

Note that the program presented below does not comply with industry standards or best practices, but it is fully functional and perfectly suited to its purpose of controlling the line without great complexities.

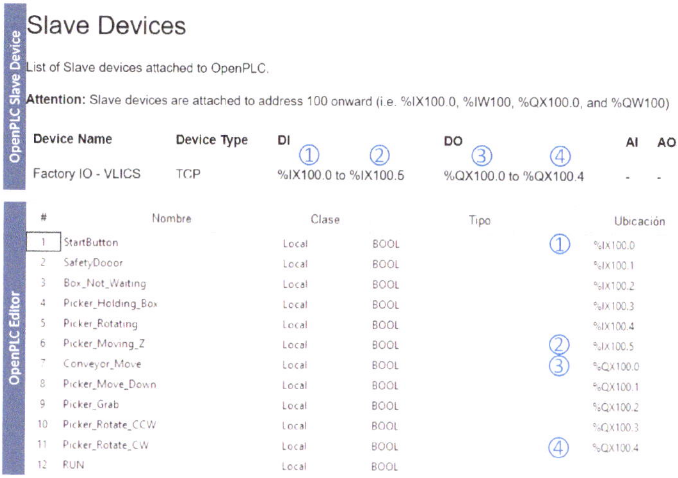

5.3 Implementation and Experiments   139

Figure 5.12   Top: variable range of the slave device in OpenPLC; Bottom: variables declared in the OpenPLC editor within the range of the slave device.

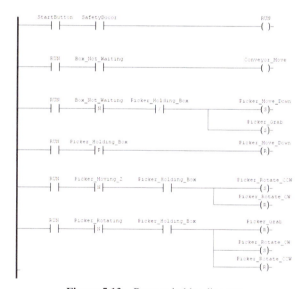

Figure 5.13   Process ladder diagram.

At this stage, the moment of truth is approaching; there are only a few steps left to complete:

- Export the project in OpenPLC as a .ST file.
- Activate the pfSense virtual router.
- Power on the OpenPLC virtual machine.

140 *Penetration Testing in Operations Technology and SCADA Environments*

- Access the OpenPLC administration portal.
- In the "Programs" tab, load the exported .ST file. If everything goes well, you will receive the following message, as shown in Figure 5.14.

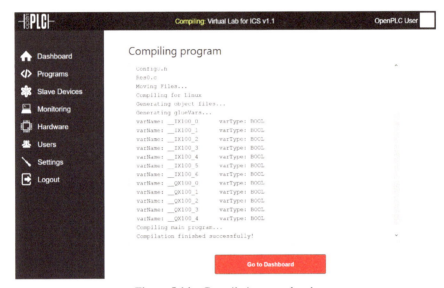

Figure 5.14 Compilation completed.

- Start FactoryIO, load the appropriate scene, and set it to execution mode.
- In the OpenPLC dashboard, click on "StartPLC."
- At this stage, you should be able to see all the states of FactoryIO via the Monitoring tab in OpenPLC, as shown in Figure 5.15.

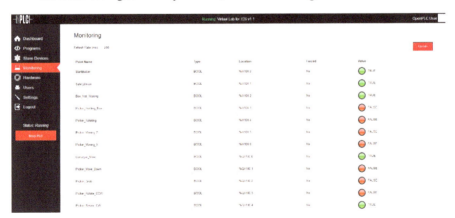

Figure 5.15 OpenPLC monitoring interface.

Set of sensor and actuator states in FactoryIO, as seen from OpenPLC.

- In FactoryIO, press the start button located on the electrical panel, and you will see how your assembly line comes to life, as shown in Figure 5.16.

Figure 5.16 Process in FactoryIO controlled from OpenPLC.

5.4 Pentesting OT

5.4.1 Information gathering

5.4.1.1 Assessment of the Shodan public subnet

To avoid accidentally making an internal system public and all the repercussions that come with it, it is recommended to do a Shodan evaluation on a regular basis. This will provide specifics about your publicly exposed systems [14]. To run a Shodan scan on the range of public IP addresses used by your organization, follow these steps, as shown in Figure 5.17.

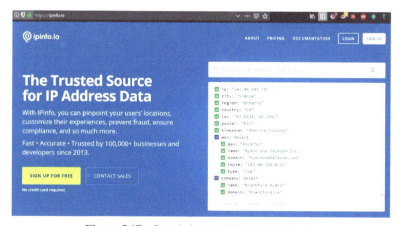

Figure 5.17 Search for a public IP on IPinfo.io.

142 *Penetration Testing in Operations Technology and SCADA Environments*

1. First, we need to find our public IP address range. To do this, simply visit the site:
2. To make sure you aren't unknowingly letting the world in on an internal system and all the repercussions that come with it, you should do a Shodan evaluation that describes your publicly exposed systems on a regular basis. Using Shodan, you may check the public IP address range of your business in the following ways, as shown in Figure 5.18.

```
{} asn: Object
    " asn: "AS19752"
    " name: "Hydro One Telecom Inc."
    " domain: "hydroonetelecom.com"
    " route: "142.46.240.0/21"
    " type: "isp"
{} company: Object
    " name: "Brantford Hydro"
    " domain: "brantford.ca"
    " type: "business"
{} abuse: Object
    " address: "CA, ON, Brantford, 44 King Street Suite 206, N3T 3C7"
    " country: "CA"
    " email: "jnagle@brantford.ca"
    " name: "James Nagle"
```

Figure 5.18 Public IP subnet range.

3. Conducting a Shodan evaluation on a regular basis will uncover information of your publicly exposed systems, helping you avoid accidentally exposing an internal system to the outside world and all the repercussions that come with it. To undertake a Shodan review of your company's public IP address range, follow these steps, as shown in Figure 5.19.
4. The majority of these results pertain to your company's legal online services. In order to identify the compromised ICS systems, we need to begin filtering the data. Searching net:142.46.240.0/21 siemens would be a good example if we knew that our manufacturing facilities used

5.4 Pentesting OT 143

Figure 5.19 Search for an IP address range on Shodan.

Figure 5.20 Search for exposed Siemens Systems.

Siemens hardware. Here, we don't find anything when we search (Figure 5.20).

5. However, if we search for Rockwell with net:142.46.240.0/21 rockwell, we will see that there is a positive result on a system for a 1761-NET-ENI/D module that is directly connected to the Internet, as shown in Figure 5.21.

6. Figure 5.22 shows the details of the result for 142.46.240.78 and see that the device exposes a web server and an ethernet/IP service to the Internet.

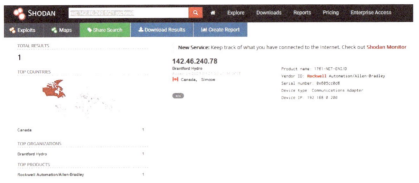

Figure 5.21 Search for exposed Rockwell Systems.

Figure 5.22 Exposed Rockwell System – details.

The only thing left to do is tell RSLogix 500/5000 to connect to the exposed device's public IP address or use a Python package like pylogix (https://github.com/dmroeder/pylogix) to start attacking the system.

The attacker's good fortune in discovering an Internet-enabled system is well-deserved; now they can bypass the corporate network and directly target the most susceptible section of the ICS, eliminating the requirement to pivot to the industrial network.

5.5 Discovering Vulnerabilities

5.5.1 Dissection of OpenPLC communications

The first phase of any attack involves reconnaissance of the environment to identify potential vulnerabilities and available targets. In our case, we begin by examining network traffic with Wireshark.

5.5 Discovering Vulnerabilities   145

5.5.2 Traffic capture

With Wireshark open, it's recommended to add a new filter that facilitates data visualization. For this purpose, only TCP traffic corresponding to port 502 (default Modbus TCP port) will be displayed, as shown in Figure 5.23 [15].

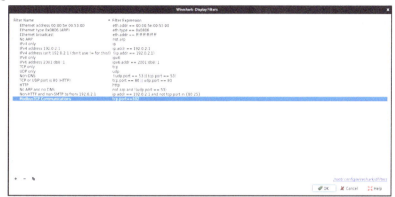

Figure 5.23   Filtering in Wireshark to Observe Only Modbus TCP Traffic.

Once Wireshark is configured and in listening mode, access the OpenPLC web portal and select "Start PLC." From this point on, you will see ModbusTCP traffic on the network. After a few seconds, enough data will have been captured to analyze the OpenPLC communications, as shown in Figure 5.24.

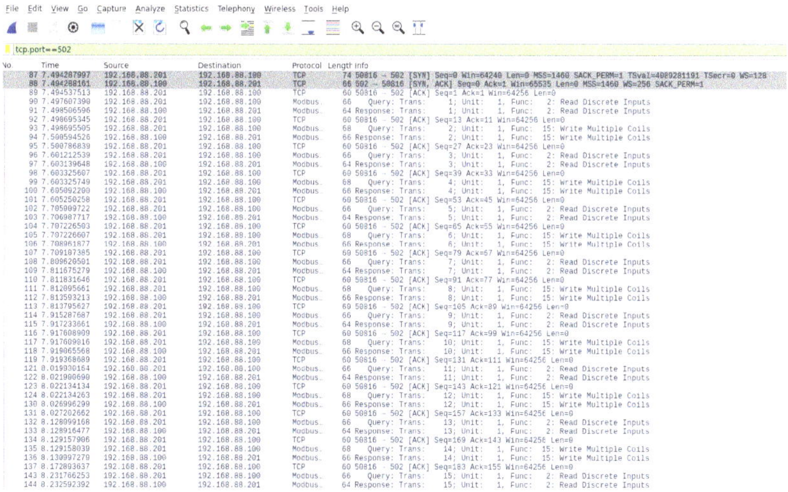

Figure 5.24   Wireshark filtering results.

5.5.3 Network traffic capture with Wireshark

At this point, you should have enough information to analyze how OpenPLC communicates with FactoryIO.

5.5.3.1 Analysis of captures

With the captured traffic data, begin by analyzing both the communication loop and the content of the messages, as shown in Figure 5.25.

5.5.3.2 Communication loop analysis

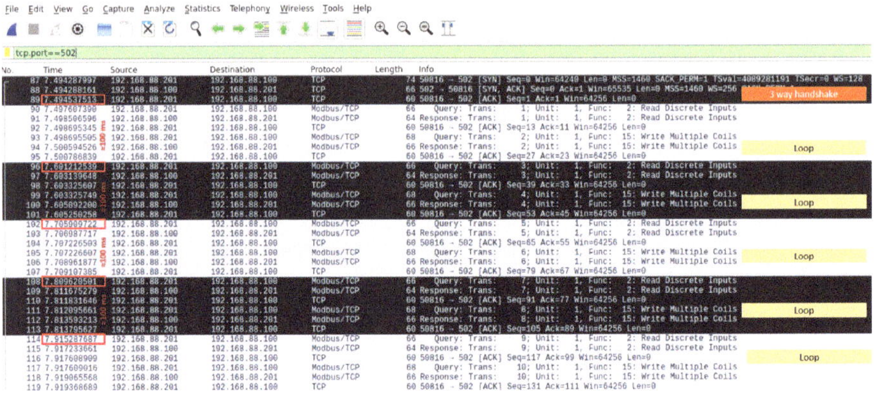

Figure 5.25 Analysis of the OpenPLC communication loop.

We can confirm that a three-way handshake is the starting point of the initial contact between OpenPLC and FactoryIO by observing the traffic capture directly:

– OpenPLC -> FactoryIO: SYN
– FactoryIO -> OpenPLC: SYN/ACK
– OpenPLC -> FactoryIO: ACK

Subsequently, the Modbus TCP request-response structure is repeated periodically while the program is still running:

Reading inputs (Read Discrete Inputs)

– OpenPLC queries FactoryIO: requests sensor states
– FactoryIO responds to OpenPLC: replies with sensor states
– OpenPLC acknowledges to FactoryIO: confirms receipt of the response

Writing outputs (Write Multiple Coils)

– OpenPLC requests FactoryIO: asks to modify actuator states

5.5 *Discovering Vulnerabilities* 147

- FactoryIO responds to OpenPLC: indicates successful actuator state modification
- OpenPLC acknowledges to FactoryIO: confirms receipt of the response

5.5.4 Analysis of Modbus TCP requests and responses

Once the general logic of the communications is understood, it's time to delve into the details of each message to try to gather more information. By double-clicking on each message, it's possible to access the complete view of its content, as shown in Figure 5.26.

5.5.4.1 Reading inputs

Figure 5.26 Request (left) and response (right) of the "Read Inputs" function.

1. By analyzing the TCP layer, the ports used in the communications by both devices can be identified. It's interesting to note that FactoryIO uses the configured port (502), but OpenPLC uses a random one.
2. There is no ACK message between the request and the response; the messages are sequential.
3. Modbus TCP uses a transaction ID that is the same in the question as in the response.
4. The message is directed and replied to the RTU with the identifier number 1 (in this case, the only one that exists; if there were more RTUs, this number would vary).
5. The Modbus function code is 2 (000 0010 in binary), which corresponds to standard codes.

148 *Penetration Testing in Operations Technology and SCADA Environments*

6. You want to read 6 inputs (Bit Count) starting from 0 (Reference Number). Indeed, the FactoryIO driver and the OpenPLC slave device have been defined with a total of 6 inputs. The response indicates the value of each input (1 for on, 0 for off), but it doesn't provide more information about what each value corresponds to (safety door, box detection, etc.), as shown in Figure 5.27.

5.5.4.2 Writing coils

Figure 5.27 Request (left) and response (right) of the "Write Coils" function.

1. By analyzing the TCP layer, the ports used in the communications by both devices can be identified. It's interesting to note that FactoryIO uses the configured port (502), but OpenPLC uses a random one.
2. There is no ACK message between the request and the response; the messages are sequential.
3. Modbus TCP uses a transaction ID that is the same in the question as in the response.
4. The message is directed and replied to the RTU with the identifier number 1 (in this case, the only one that exists; if there were more RTUs, this number would vary).
5. The Modbus function code is 15 (000 111 in binary), which corresponds to standard codes.
6. You want to write 5 outputs (Bit Count) starting from output 0 (Reference Number). Indeed, the FactoryIO driver and the OpenPLC slave device have defined a total of 5 outputs.
7. These 5 outputs will have a value of 00. By examining other messages, you can see values like 14, 16, 0c, 0d, etc. This indicates that the output

5.5 Discovering Vulnerabilities   149

values are transmitted in hexadecimal, and to check which ones are on or off, conversion to binary is necessary. Figure 5.28 shows examples of data in the "Write Coils" requests.

```
▶ Frame 3194: 68 bytes on wire (544 bits), 68 bytes captured (544 bits) on interface eth0, id 0
▶ Ethernet II, Src: PcsCompu_70:45:e8 (08:00:27:70:45:e8), Dst: 0a:00:27:00:00:0c (0a:00:27:00:00:0c)
▶ Internet Protocol Version 4, Src: 192.168.88.201, Dst: 192.168.88.100
▶ Transmission Control Protocol, Src Port: 50816, Dst Port: 502, Seq: 11323, Ack: 9581, Len: 14
▶ Modbus/TCP
▼ Modbus
    .000 1111 = Function Code: Write Multiple Coils (15)
    Reference Number: 0
    Bit Count: 5
    Byte Count: 1
    Data: 0d

▶ Frame 3153: 68 bytes on wire (544 bits), 68 bytes captured (544 bits) on interface eth0, id 0
▶ Ethernet II, Src: PcsCompu_70:45:e8 (08:00:27:70:45:e8), Dst: 0a:00:27:00:00:0c (0a:00:27:00:00:0c)
▶ Internet Protocol Version 4, Src: 192.168.88.201, Dst: 192.168.88.100
▶ Transmission Control Protocol, Src Port: 50816, Dst Port: 502, Seq: 11167, Ack: 9449, Len: 14
▶ Modbus/TCP
▼ Modbus
    .000 1111 = Function Code: Write Multiple Coils (15)
    Reference Number: 0
    Bit Count: 5
    Byte Count: 1
    Data: 14

▶ Frame 3136: 68 bytes on wire (544 bits), 68 bytes captured (544 bits) on interface eth0, id 0
▶ Ethernet II, Src: PcsCompu_70:45:e8 (08:00:27:70:45:e8), Dst: 0a:00:27:00:00:0c (0a:00:27:00:00:0c)
▶ Internet Protocol Version 4, Src: 192.168.88.201, Dst: 192.168.88.100
▶ Transmission Control Protocol, Src Port: 50816, Dst Port: 502, Seq: 11115, Ack: 9405, Len: 14
▶ Modbus/TCP
▼ Modbus
    .000 1111 = Function Code: Write Multiple Coils (15)
    Reference Number: 0
    Bit Count: 5
    Byte Count: 1
    Data: 16
```

Figure 5.28 Examples of data in the "Write Coils" requests.

Table 5.1 shows the correlation between hexadecimal input, binary representation (limited to 5 bits), and the state of five different outputs (QX100.0 to QX100.4).

Table 5.1 Translation of the data in the "Write Coils" request to RTU outputs.

Hex	Bin (5bits)	QX100.0	QX100.1	QX100.2	QX100.3	QX100.4
00	00000	OFF	OFF	OFF	OFF	OFF
14	10100	ON	OFF	ON	OFF	OFF
16	10110	ON	OFF	ON	ON	OFF
0d	01101	OFF	ON	ON	OFF	ON

5.5.4.3 Network mapping of Grassmarlin

Allow Wireshark to collect packets in the background as you scan (such as when using Nmap to do the first network scan). A network mapping tool like Grassmarlin (https://github.com/nsacyber/GRASSMARLIN) may be used with the captured packets to create a visually appealing depiction of the target network, as shown in Figure 5.29 [16]. To create a network. topology, we may use Wireshark to capture data from the interface we're using and the following Nmap scan:

$$nmap--p--A-oAot-scan 192.168.88.0/24$$

This instructs Nmap to scan every port (-p-) of every system on the subnet 192.168.88.0/24 and gather all data (-A), saving the results in the four main formats under the name ot-scan (-oA ot-scan).

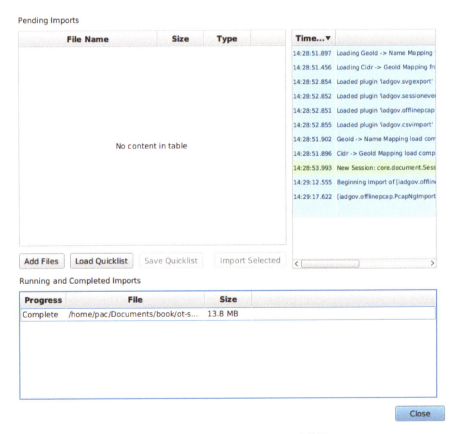

Figure 5.29   Grassmarlin - Import PCAP.

Once we're done, save the Wireshark output into a packet capture (PCAP) file and import it into Grassmarlin:

5.6 Modbus TCP Packet Injection with Scapy

1. Start Grassmarlin and select File Import Files.
   Click Add Files and navigate to the saved PCAP file.
2. Click Import Selection.

Once the import process is completed, close the import screen. Grassmarlin should now display a map of all scanned IP addresses, as shown in Figure 5.30.

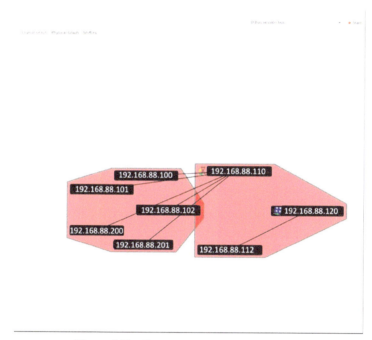

Figure 5.30 Grassmarlin - Logical graph view.

There are numerous other tools, devices, and tricks that can be used to probe network equipment. However, I'd like to move on to exploring Level 3 site operations.

5.6 Modbus TCP Packet Injection with Scapy

In this simulation, we start with a scenario where the attacker already has access to the network, and thus actions on the targets are executed directly without having to go through all the previous phases [17]. The attack aims to stop or disrupt the line to halt production, and the most direct way to achieve this is to try to interact in some way with the unit that controls the sensors and actuators (RTU - FactoryIO). With this in mind, the attack plan is as follows (Figure 5.31):

- Sniff legitimate communications between the RTU (FactoryIO) and the PLC (OpenPLC).
- Use one of the exchanged messages as a seed to predict the values of the TCP sequence (preferably the last message in the communication loop so that you have 100 ms available to generate and inject the packet before OpenPLC communicates again with FactoryIO and invalidates the sequence calculation).
- Generate a fake packet compliant with the TCP sequence and the structure of values expected by FactoryIO, but with malicious Modbus commands.
- Inject the packet.

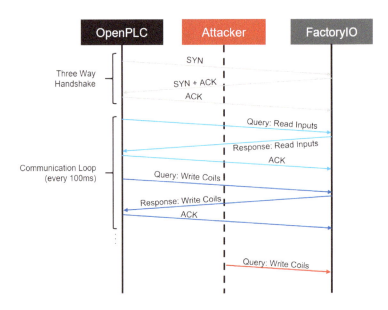

Figure 5.31 Packet injection attack design.

The first step will be to create a Python script and import the Scapy library to be able to access all the classes and functions it offers. From this point on, the objective will be to construct all the layers of the packet to be injected one by one, as shown in Figure 5.32.

5.6 Modbus TCP Packet Injection with Scapy 153

Figure 5.32 Importing from Scapy.

5.6.1 Configuring the IP and TCP layers

During the standard communication loop, messages are exchanged approximately every 0.5 ms, which poses a problem because it takes time to process and inject the new packet. To maximize the chances of success of the attack, the previously acquired knowledge regarding the time between OpenPLC communication cycles with FactoryIO (100 ms) will be utilized, as shown in Figure 5.33.

Figure 5.33 Red: Time between messages during a single iteration of the OpenPLC communication loop; Green: Time between OpenPLC communication loops.

– From the previous analysis, we also know that:

The second-to-last message of all communication loops is a "Query: Write Coils" followed by a final ACK directed from OpenPLC to FactoryIO.

– All "Query: Write Coils" messages have a fixed part in the Modbus layer and a variable part corresponding to the outputs to be modified at any given time, as shown in Figure 5.34.

Green: Fixed part identifying a Modbus TCP packet with the "Write Coils" function // Red: Variable part (desired state of the outputs).

The following logic is used to identify this pattern:

- Using the sniff() function, 4 consecutive messages are captured (it is recommended to capture twice as many messages as needed – in this case, two messages: Query and ACK – to avoid aliasing) with the following filters:
  ○ Has a TCP layer

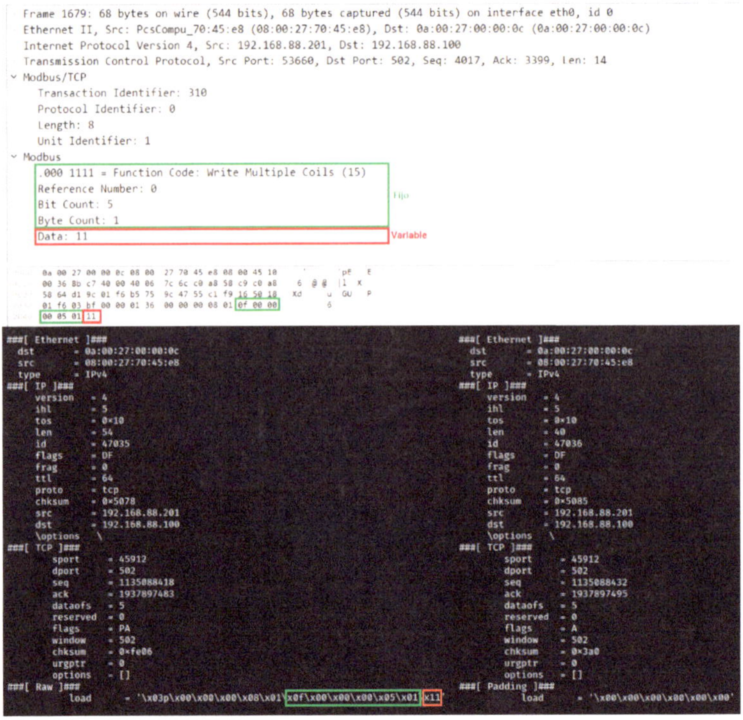

154   *Penetration Testing in Operations Technology and SCADA Environments*

Figure 5.34 Top: ModbusTCP packet captured with Wireshark // Bottom left: ModbusTCP packet sniffed with Scapy // Bottom right: Non-ModbusTCP packet sniffed with Scapy;

- ○ Targeted at the FactoryIO IP
- It checks if the second-to-last of the captured messages:
  - ○ Has a raw layer. Modbus packets have this layer, but ACKs do not (as you can see in the image above). This is done to prevent the next check from failing when attempting to open a layer that does not exist.
  - ○ That this layer contains the string "x0f\x00\x00\x00\x05\x01"
- If both conditions are met, it considers the last captured message to be the end-of-loop message and therefore it will be used as the seed.
- If these conditions are not met, 4 more messages are captured, as shown in Figure 5.35.

Since the seed has a length (len) of 0, there will be no need to increase the values of ACK and SEQ, so with that, you already have all the information

5.6 Modbus TCP Packet Injection with Scapy   155

Figure 5.35 Packet sniffing with Scapy.

you need to create the IP and TCP layers of the new packet, as shown in Figure 5.36:

Figure 5.36 Configuration of TCP and IP layers with Scapy.

5.6.2 Implementation and configuration of Modbus and Modbus TCP layers

While Scapy does have native support for a number of protocols, neither Modbus TCP nor Modbus are among them. But that's not an issue because the library provides the tools to build bespoke protocols from the ground up.

The presence of two distinct layers – the Modbus TCP layer and the Modbus layer – was confirmed in the Wireshark sample. The next two classes are added to the script with the same names as the ones in the screenshot; the third is optional but will make the injected packet look more like a real one, as shown in Figure 5.37:

Scapy provides a variety of data types for use in specifying the fields of a protocol. Click on each field in a comparable packet recorded in Wireshark and see which set of digits is highlighted in the hexadecimal display to determine the type to give to each field. Fields that highlight two sets of two numbers will be of the ShortField type, whereas fields that highlight one set of two numbers will be of the ByteField type, which is a 1-byte integer (2-byte integer), as shown in Figure 5.38:

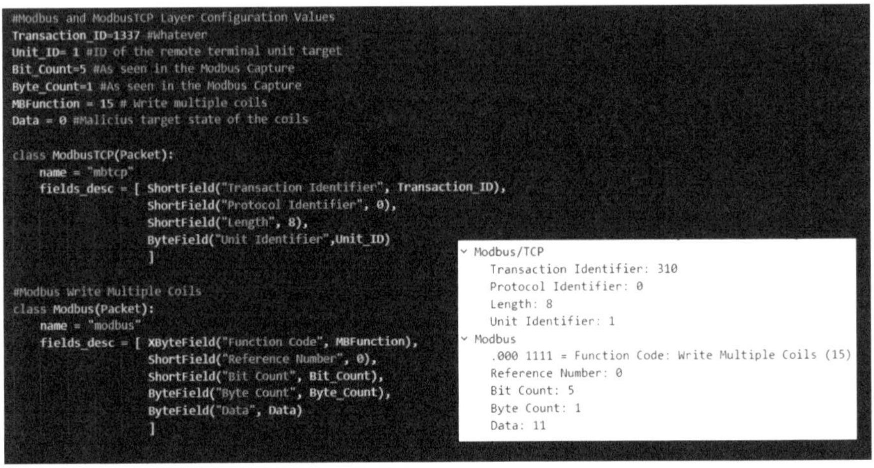

Figure 5.37 Dark background: Implementation of ModbusTCP and Modbus layer with Scapy // Light background: Example Modbus packet extracted from Wireshark.

5.6.3 Packet injection

After the parameters have been computed, the last steps are to use the "/" operator to chain the packet layers and the send() function to program the injection, as shown in Figure 5.39:

5.7 Results

In Figure 5.40, we observe the successful execution of a cybersecurity penetration testing script in action. On the left side of the screen, the terminal window displays a real-time capture of network packets, indicating the detection of a crafted packet during the end of a communication loop within an industrial control system environment. This signifies the penetration tester's ability to intercept and manipulate the Modbus TCP communications between devices, a critical step in identifying system vulnerabilities. On the right, the FactoryIO simulation interface illustrates the industrial process in question – a conveyor belt system with boxes and a robotic arm, representing the physical components of the ICS being tested. The dual view provides a comprehensive look at both the virtual penetration testing process and its potential real-world impact on industrial operations, highlighting the integrated approach necessary for effective cybersecurity analysis in industrial environments.

5.8 Conclusion   157

```
✓ Modbus/TCP
     Transaction Identifier: 310
     Protocol Identifier: 0
     Length: 8
     Unit Identifier: 1
✓ Modbus
     .000 1111 = Function Code: Write Multiple Coils (15)
     Reference Number: 0
     Bit Count: 5
     Byte Count: 1
     Data: 11
```

```
0000  0a 00 27 00 00 0c 08 00  27 70 45 e8 08 00 45 10   ··'·····'pE···E·
0010  00 36 8b c7 40 00 40 06  7c 6c c0 a8 58 c9 c0 a8   ·6··@·@·|l··X···
0020  58 64 d1 9c 01 f6 b5 75  9c 47 55 c1 f9 16 50 18   Xd·····u·GU···P·
0030  01 f6 03 bf 00 00 01 36  00 00 00 08 01 0f 00 00   ·······6········
0040  00 05 01 11
```
                        ShortField

```
✓ Modbus/TCP
     Transaction Identifier: 310
     Protocol Identifier: 0
     Length: 8
     Unit Identifier: 1
✓ Modbus
     .000 1111 = Function Code: Write Multiple Coils (15)
     Reference Number: 0
     Bit Count: 5
     Byte Count: 1
     Data: 11
```

```
0000  0a 00 27 00 00 0c 08 00  27 70 45 e8 08 00 45 10   ··'·····'pE···E·
0010  00 36 8b c7 40 00 40 06  7c 6c c0 a8 58 c9 c0 a8   ·6··@·@·|l··X···
0020  58 64 d1 9c 01 f6 b5 75  9c 47 55 c1 f9 16 50 18   Xd·····u·GU···P·
0030  01 f6 03 bf 00 00 01 36  00 00 00 08 01 0f 00 00   ·······6········
0040  00 05 01 11
```
         ByteField

Figure 5.38 Identification of Short Field (2-byte integer) and Byte Field (1-byte integer) parameters using Wireshark.

```
PAYLOAD = PAYLOAD/ModbusTCP()/Modbus()

print("-------------------------- INJECTING PACKET")
send(PAYLOAD, verbose=0, iface=your_iface)   #Do not confuse with sendp (layer 2)

print("-------------------------- PACKET INJECTED")
PAYLOAD.display()
```

Figure 5.39 Adding Modbus TCP and Modbus layers, and packet injection.

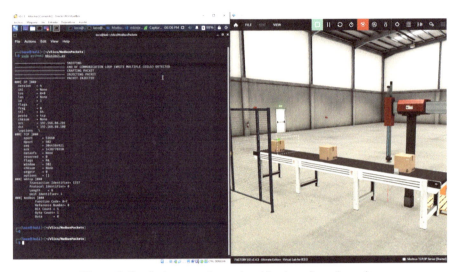

Figure 5.40 Script execution and verification of attack results.

5.8 Conclusion

This chapter has highlighted the multifaceted approach to conducting penetration testing in OT and SCADA environments, culminating in the development and utilization of a virtual industrial cybersecurity laboratory. By exploring the deployment and configuration of this virtual lab, we've demonstrated a safe and effective method for scanning, probing, and attacking within a controlled test bench, mimicking real industrial systems. The processes and techniques detailed herein not only fortify the security of industrial control systems but also serve as an indispensable resource for cybersecurity professionals and researchers. As we navigate the evolving landscape of cyber threats, the necessity for advanced, accessible testing environments becomes increasingly apparent. The insights and methodologies shared in this chapter contribute significantly to a more secure industrial future, effectively reducing the risks associated with cyber threats and advancing the protection of our critical infrastructure.

References

[1] Y. Maleh, "IT/OT convergence and cyber security," *Computer Fraud & Security*, vol. 2021, no. 12, pp. 13–16, Dec. 2021, doi:10.1016/S1361-3723(21)00129-9.

[2] Y. Maleh, S. Lakkineni, L. Tawalbeh, and A. A. AbdEl-Latif, "Blockchain for Cyber-Physical Systems: Challenges and Applications," in *Advances in Blockchain Technology for Cyber Physical Systems*, Y. Maleh, L. Tawalbeh, S. Motahhir, and A. S. Hafid, Eds., Cham: Springer International Publishing, 2022, pp. 11–59. doi:10.1007/978-3-030-93646-4_2.

[3] Yassine MALEH, "Machine Learning Techniques for IoT Intrusions Detection in Aerospace Cyber-Physical Systems," *Machine Learning and Data Mining in Aerospace Technology*, 2020, doi:10.1007/978-3-030-20212-5_11.

[4] M. A. Khan and K. Salah, "IoT security: Review, blockchain solutions, and open challenges," *Future Generation Computer Systems*, vol. 82, pp. 395–411, 2018, doi:https://doi.org/10.1016/j.future.2017.11.022.

[5] Y. Maleh, A. Sahid, A. Ezzati, and M. Belaissaoui, "Building open virtual cloud lab for advanced education in networks and security," in *Proceedings - 2017 International Conference on Wireless Networks and Mobile Communications, WINCOM 2017*, 2017. doi: 10.1109/WINCOM.2017.8238172.

[6] Y. Maleh, A. Sahid, and M. Belaissaoui, "Optimized Machine Learning Techniques for IoT 6LoWPAN Cyber Attacks Detection," in *Proceedings of the 12th International Conference on Soft Computing and Pattern Recognition (SoCPaR 2020)*, A. Abraham, Y. Ohsawa, N. Gandhi, M. A. Jabbar, A. Haqiq, S. McLoone, and B. Issac, Eds., Cham: Springer International Publishing, 2021, pp. 669–677.

[7] A. Staves, A. Gouglidis, and D. Hutchison, "An Analysis of Adversary-Centric Security Testing within Information and Operational Technology Environments," *Digital Threats*, vol. 4, no. 1, Mar. 2023, doi: 10.1145/3569958.

[8] W. Knowles, J. M. Such, A. Gouglidis, G. Misra, and A. Rashid, "Assurance Techniques for Industrial Control Systems (ICS)," in *Proceedings of the First ACM Workshop on Cyber-Physical Systems-Security and/or PrivaCy*, in CPS-SPC '15. New York, NY, USA: Association for Computing Machinery, 2015, pp. 101–112. doi:10.1145/2808705.2808710.

[9] A. P. Mathur and N. O. Tippenhauer, "SWaT: a water treatment testbed for research and training on ICS security," in *2016 International Workshop on Cyber-physical Systems for Smart Water Networks (CySWater)*, 2016, pp. 31–36. doi:10.1109/CySWater.2016.7469060.

[10] R. Rohith, M. Moharir, and G. Shobha, "SCAPY-A powerful interactive packet manipulation program," in *2018 international conference on networking, embedded and wireless systems (ICNEWS)*, IEEE, 2018, pp. 1–5.

[11] T. Alves, R. Das, A. Werth, and T. Morris, "Virtualization of SCADA testbeds for cybersecurity research: A modular approach," *Comput Secur*, vol. 77, pp. 531–546, 2018.

[12] R. J. Mora-Salinas and H. G. G. Hernández, "Virtual labs: 5 ways to connect with Factory IO for mechatronics engineering courses," in *2022 IEEE Global Engineering Education Conference (EDUCON)*, IEEE, 2022, pp. 485–490.

[13] T. R. Alves, M. Buratto, F. M. De Souza, and T. V. Rodrigues, "OpenPLC: An open source alternative to automation," in *IEEE Global Humanitarian Technology Conference (GHTC 2014)*, IEEE, 2014, pp. 585–589.

[14] S. Samtani, S. Yu, H. Zhu, M. Patton, and H. Chen, "Identifying SCADA vulnerabilities using passive and active vulnerability assessment techniques," in *2016 IEEE Conference on Intelligence and Security Informatics (ISI)*, IEEE, 2016, pp. 25–30.

[15] L. Rosa, M. Freitas, S. Mazo, E. Monteiro, T. Cruz, and P. Simões, "A comprehensive security analysis of a SCADA protocol: From OSINT to mitigation," *IEEE Access*, vol. 7, pp. 42156–42168, 2019.

[16] J. E. Efiong, B. O. Akinyemi, E. A. Olajubu, and G. A. Aderounmu, "GRASSMARLIN-based Metadata Extraction of Cyber-Physical Systems Intrusion Detection in CyberSCADA Networks," in *2022 International Conference on Computational Science and Computational Intelligence (CSCI)*, IEEE, 2022, pp. 1122–1128.

[17] S. Figueroa-Lorenzo, J. Añorga, and S. Arrizabalaga, "A role-based access control model in modbus SCADA systems. A centralized model approach," *Sensors*, vol. 19, no. 20, p. 4455, 2019.

6

Cyberattacks in Healthcare: Analyzing Recent Trends and Preventive Measures

Seidi Sanae, Jabari Khawla, Moussaid Hind, and Abdellaoui Abderrahim

Engineering Sciences Lab, ENSA, University Ibn Tofail, Morocc
E-mail: sanae.seidi@uit.ac.ma; khawla.jabari@uit.ac.ma;
hind.moussaid@uit.ac.ma; abderrahim@uit.ac.ma

Abstract

This study examines recent trends in cyberattacks within the healthcare sector and suggests preventive measures to mitigate associated risks. For that purpose, the paper explores common types of cyberattacks, attacker's motivations, and consequences for patients and healthcare organizations. Proposed preventative measures include implementing robust IT security policies, implementing effective security software, and proactive threat monitoring and improving staff training and awareness. In the end, the paper underlines the comparison and the difference between multiple solutions already proposed which makes it possible to guarantee the patient's data security and confidentiality.

Keywords: Cyberattack, security, cybersecurity, cyber threat, ransomware, cybercrime.

6.1 Introduction

Over the past 10 years, there has been an increase in the frequency and seriousness of cyberattacks against healthcare systems. Patients, healthcare professionals, and organizations may suffer severe repercussions as a result of these attacks, which might include ransomware attacks and data breaches [1]. The impact of a cyberattack can be especially severe given the sensitive nature of the data housed in healthcare systems, such as patient health records and financial information. Overall, it is crucial to address cyberattacks in the healthcare industry. The risk of cyberattacks keeps rising as healthcare facilities depend more on technology to store and handle patient data. We may endeavor to preserve patient privacy and security, healthcare providers and organizations, and assure the continuous provision of high-quality healthcare services by taking a close look at the current situation of cyberattacks in healthcare and figuring out effective prevention and mitigation techniques [2]. With an emphasis on their impact, prevalence, and historical patterns, we will explore the current situation of cyberattacks in healthcare in this review paper. We will also go through the things that make healthcare systems susceptible to cyberattacks and the steps that may be taken to stop and lessen them. We seek to provide an in-depth understanding of the nature of healthcare cyberattacks and their consequences for patient safety, data security, and the overall operation of healthcare systems by a thorough analysis of existing research and scientific literature.

6.2 Security Issues in Healthcare

The storage of data from sensors, whether they are implanted in the body, worn on the body, or used externally, plays a critical role in the healthcare system due to the sensitive nature of the information handled and the need for data sharing. As a result, the key challenges to be addressed include enhancing system efficiency, reliability, and data security [3]. The 5G-IoT healthcare system faces security risks and privacy concerns. Attacks can be classified as either passive or active, depending on whether they intend to collect important information but are unable to alter the original material that compromises access or confidentiality. Attacks targeting availability, control, integrity, and authentication such as man-in-the-middle attacks and eavesdropping can compromise the system's confidentiality [4]. The integrity of the system is particularly affected by attacks like replay, data injection, and denial-of-service (DoS) attacks. Meanwhile, attacks such as flooding and jamming are countered through authentication mechanisms. Some malevolent assailants employ drastic measures to pilfer confidential data. Considering all of this, it is clear that protecting patient privacy in healthcare is a critical issue. This indicates that the decision made by the patient to share their data is quite significant. Patient data should be provided in a form that allows it to be accessed by professional staff, other members of the system network, and some sensitive information ought to be kept private. Therefore, personal information is more susceptible to assaults due to increased security dangers while using smart applications or sensitive data in a smart environment. Attacks on access control occasionally compromise data security or result from the application of particular policies. A ciphertext-policy attribute-based encryption (CP-ABE) technique called PASH (Privacy-Aware S-Health access control system) was first developed by the authors in [5]. Where attribute values and access control restrictions are hidden in encrypted Shared Health Records (SHRs) and are only visible The decryption test was conducted using fewer bilinear pairings in order to increase the techniqueŠs efficiency. In comparison to other methods, PASH is safe and efficient both theoretically and experimentally. Medical sensor software solutions are additionally difficult because developers dealing with wireless connectivity will have greater security and privacy issues.

Confidentiality: The main concern is safeguarding private information. Wireless Body Area Network (WBAN) nodes are regarded as significant in healthcare systems because they hold patient private information, which necessitates data protection and protection from illegal access. Vulnerable data is a major overhead during transmission that undermines patient confidence and the network. The utilization of encryption between WBAN and the coordinators is the most effective way to address this [6].

Integrity: Any packet's integrity needs to be upheld in order to safeguard its accuracy and content. Data confidentiality does not provide a solution to the external modification problem since it is simple to make alterations while integrating message fragments, changing data within packets, and even when transmitting message fragments. Changes in a patient's health-related state can be dangerous for the healthcare system and in certain situations could result in death.

Authentication is an essential necessity for any field or application data, including healthcare systems. As a result, nodes that are information-bearing and a part of wireless body area networks need to be aware of which sources to trust and which ones to avoid.

6.3 Types of Cyberattacks in Healthcare
6.3.1 Malware

Malicious software is designed in such a way that if given access to other computer systems it performs harmful operations to obtain personal information. Various types of malware exist, such as viruses, worms, trojan

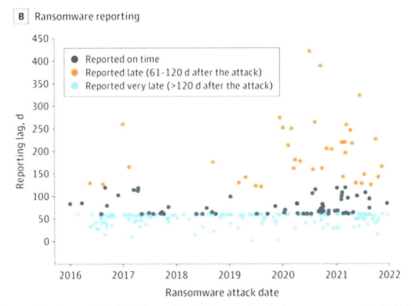

Figure 6.1 Personal health information (PHI) reporting during ransomware attacks [10]

horses, advertising software, spyware, blackmail software, etc., just to obtain personal data, system hijack, identity stealing, and monitoring users are the big threats to operating systems and users.

Malware has 25 families, and is gradually increasing. Therefore, it is very challenging to stop malware attacks, as all the personal data of users as well as industries or companies are at stake [7]. Given the importance of security in the healthcare industry, malware attacks are becoming a bigger threat. It is a more focused sector on a global scale. The growing diversity in the services and gadgets of the next generation of networks presents new challenges for security [8]. Ransomware is one of the most common and popular types of healthcare malware, and the subject of the next section.

6.3.2 Ransomware

A malicious software program known as ransomware is used to lock down computer systems or encrypt data in order to prevent users from accessing it. Once the files have been encrypted or access to the infected systems has been restored, the attackers demand a ransom payment, which is typically made in cryptocurrency [9].

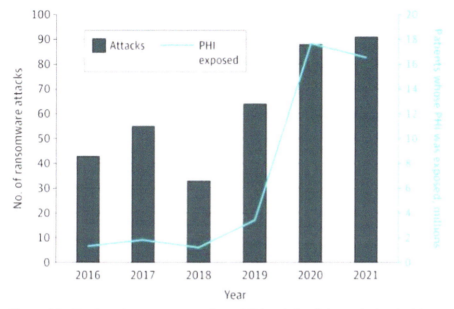

Figure 6.2 Number of ransomware attacks on US hospitals, clinics, and other healthcare service delivery organizations, 2016-2021[12].

6.3.2.1 General ransomware attack operation

An ordinary ransomware attack includes the following steps:

Infection: The ransomware infects the target system using a variety of techniques, including phishing emails, malicious downloads, or taking advantage of software flaws.

File encryption: As soon as the ransomware enters the system, it starts to encrypt files, making them unreadable without the decryption key.

Ransom note: An explanation of the problem and directions for paying the ransom are provided in a ransom note that the attackers post on the hacked system after the encryption process is finished.

Payment and decryption: Should the victim decide to pay the ransom, they typically do so in accordance with the instructions provided. The attackers can hand over the decryption key to unlock the files or regain system access after collecting the cash. But there is no assurance that the assailants will keep their word. [11].

Ransomware is particularly significant in the healthcare sector due to its potential impact on patient care and safety. The threat it poses raises serious concerns within the industry. The ability to quickly access vital patient data and operational systems is crucial to the healthcare industry. The following factors highlight the importance of ransomware in the healthcare sector:

Patient safety: In order to make educated judgments concerning a patient's diagnosis, treatment, and medication, rapid access to patient data is essential. Ransomware disruptions can directly affect patient safety and the standard of treatment provided.

Privacy and confidentiality: Healthcare organizations deal with a great deal of private and sensitive patient data. Data breaches, patient privacy compromises, and the release of private health information to unauthorized parties are all risks associated with ransomware attacks.

Operational disruption: Ransomware attacks that obstruct access to electronic health records (EHRs), medical equipment, and other vital systems can render healthcare institutions paralyzed. This interruption may result in postponed or cancelled procedures, decreased production, and monetary losses.

Financial consequences: For healthcare institutions, recovering from a ransomware assault can be expensive. They might have to pay for incident response, system restoration, legal services, and possible fines from the government.

Healthcare practitioners, IT staff, and policymakers must comprehend the meaning, workings, and effects of ransomware in order to create efficient prevention, detection, and response plans for these attacks [13].

6.3.2.2 Common methods of ransomware infection in the healthcare sector

Phishing emails are a common tactic employed by cybercriminals to initiate assaults within the healthcare industry. Usually, it spreads via shady emails that are skillfully written to look authentic and include attachments like word documents with macros or links to malicious websites. As soon as a user engages with the malicious material, the virus quickly downloads and takes over the computer. The malware searches the impacted machine and any associated drives during this period for files that can be encrypted. Phishing assaults are especially risky for the healthcare industry because they can result in ransomware infections and data breaches, which might seriously jeopardize patient information security and the general operations of healthcare institutions.

6.3 Types of Cyberattacks in Healthcare 167

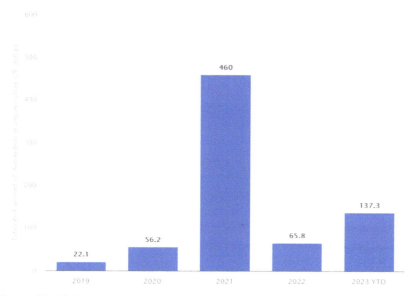

Figure 6.3 Estimated ransom demanded from U.S. healthcare organizations 2019-2023 YTD Statista Published by Ani Petrosyan, Nov 7, 2023.

Healthcare data breaches have increased, according to the Department of Health and Human Services (HHS). From October 1, 2009 to December 31, 2021, 4419 breaches of protected health information affecting over 500 individuals were recorded. Of these breaches, over 800, or around 18%, were linked to email account hacking or healthcare phishing assaults. The most frequent attack vector in U.S. healthcare cyberattacks has been found to be phishing; the 2021 HIMSS Healthcare Cybersecurity Survey found that 57% of participants said that ransomware or phishing assaults were the cause of their most serious security problem.

Using software vulnerabilities for profit: Attackers using ransomware aggressively look for weaknesses in software programs used in the healthcare industry. Operating systems, software, and even medical devices may include these flaws. Once these flaws are discovered, attackers use malware to penetrate computers and launch ransomware attacks to take advantage of them. To reduce the danger of exploitation, healthcare companies must quickly implement security fixes and upgrades.

Compromised connections to the remote desktop protocol (RDP) enables authorized users to log into computers from a distance. However, unsecured RDP connections allow attackers to access systems without authorization by using weak passwords or other security flaws. Once within the system, they can install ransomware and encrypt the data of the company.

Attacks along the supply chain for software, equipment, and services: healthcare organizations rely on a variety of third-party suppliers and vendors. These vendors may be the target of cybercriminals who infect their software or systems with ransomware. Once the infected software or equipment is installed into the architecture of the healthcare business, the ransomware can propagate and do extensive harm. "Although health care is not specifically mentioned in this advisory, it serves as a good reminder that third-party tools, technology and services continue to be a major contributing factor in some of the largest data breaches and ransomware attacks impacting hospitals and health systems," said John Riggi, AHA's national advisor for cybersecurity and risk. Three in four ransomware attacks on hospitals result in operational disruptions (disabled electronic health records, canceled surgeries, extended hospital stays, delays in procedures, ambulance diversion, etc.) Healthcare businesses must comprehend these typical ransomware infection techniques in order to put effective protection measures in place. The danger of ransomware infestations in the healthcare industry can be reduced with proactive employee training, regular software updates, website monitoring, secure remote access procedures, and stringent access controls [13].

6.3.2.3 Case studies of ransomware attacks in the healthcare sector

Examples of recent and well-known ransomware attacks in the healthcare sector have been on the rise, resulting in significant disruptions and financial losses. Several notable incidents highlight the severity of these attacks:

WannaCry: *In May 2017*, various healthcare organizations around the world were impacted by the WannaCry ransomware outbreak. It quickly spread and encrypted data on impacted PCs by taking advantage of a flaw in old versions of the Windows operating system. The disruption of medical care, monetary losses, and need of prompt software patching were all brought home by this attack.

SamSam: *From 2015 to 2018*, the SamSam ransomware targeted a number of industries, notably the healthcare sector. Hackers who had illegal access to networks used a manual attack strategy to manually install the ransomware. SamSam infected a number of healthcare organizations, resulting in extended system outages, patient data breaches, and high ransom demands.

Ryuk: *Since 2018, Ryuk*, a highly advanced ransomware strain, has been attacking healthcare organizations all over the world. It frequently gains access to computers via phishing emails or hacked remote desktop protocols. Ryuk, who then demands hefty ransom payments, encrypts critical files. Financial losses, operational setbacks, and reduced patient care have all been caused by its attacks [14].

In August 2023, a ransomware outbreak hit Prospect Medical Holdings, a California-based healthcare institution. This attack led some locations to close or switch to manual operations, causing disruptions in healthcare services. The exact number of damaged sites remained unknown, but the attack had a major impact on the company's operations. This incident demonstrates the increasing frequency, sophistication, and severity of ransomware assaults on healthcare providers.

The Yuma Regional Medical Center (YRMC) was the target of a ransomware assault in April 2022 that exposed thousands of people's personal information. The hospital had to start implementing downtime protocols following the ransomware deployment. Following an examination, it was discovered that the attacker had been covertly using the network for four days prior to the ransomware's deployment. From April 21 to April 25, the attacker kept access to the network and erased files that included SSNs, patient names, medical records, and details about health insurance [14].

6.3.3 Phishing

Healthcare practitioners are frequently the target of phishing attacks targeting the healthcare sector via email [15]. The employee is required to click on a link in the email [15]. This URL appears reliable most of the time. Hackers used the we11point.com domain name to access Anthem during their attack (Anthem was previously called Wellpoint, Inc.) [16]. Prennera.com served as the gateway for the ensuing Premera attack [17]. Employees are misled into thinking they are accessing a link from within their own system while, in reality, they are being forwarded to a hostile website. Once on the website, users are directed to download malicious software or submit their credentials, which they mistakenly think would log them into their own system but are really captured by the hackers [15]. Phishing relies on its victims' lack of awareness and faith in the emails that arrive in their inbox [18].

Phishing assaults are guided by the digital connections between hospital services and patients, which are facilitated by the notable progress of Healthcare 4.0 and its associated healthcare services. Phishing is a type of cyberattack that targets specific devices and aims to obtain sensitive customer information. Hackers use phishing, a social engineering attack, to get sensitive customer information [19]. Attackers may pose as reliable sources to a user using social media, instant chat, and email in phishing attacks. It has been observed that from 2016 to 2019, 17% of phishing attacks occurred, with malware accounting for 28% of the total [20]. The NHS WannaCry ransomware attack (2017), the Anthem Data Breach (2015), and other real-world phishing attacks all happen in real time.

The COVID-19 vaccine distribution phishing attack (2020–2021) and the Scripps Health ransomware attack (2021) are prime examples of how cybercriminals exploit vulnerabilities in the healthcare sector. An attacker posing as a bank, for example, could send a victim a misleading message stating that their account has been credited.

6.3.3.1 Phishing simulation in healthcare: A case study

As part of its annual training and risk assessment, a large Italian hospital employing over 6000 healthcare professionals conducted a phishing simulation. To compare the response of staff members to a generic phishing email versus one that was tailored to them, three campaigns were issued at around four-month intervals [21]. In the phishing assaults detailed, emails with a first-level national domain (".it") imitating a hospital were sent from a fictitious sender using a ".com" domain. These assaults fall under several campaign categories:

First campaign: March 2019's general phish
-The email purported to be a quarantined Microsoft email pertaining to pay scales.
-To release the email, recipients were asked to click on a link and enter their password.
-The poorly grammatically presented text was displayed as an image.

First campaign: March 2019 customized phish
-Recipients of this email were notified that they have 48 hours to finish the required online training.
-The instruction would begin when you clicked on the provided link.
-The text contained some grammatical flaws and was customized to the hospital's current activities.

Second campaign: Tailored phishing (December 11, 2019)
-A Christmas bonus slated for payment on December 18 was communicated to recipients.
-They were told to click on a link in the email in order to collect the bonus.
-There were no obvious grammatical mistakes in this advertisement.

Campaign 3: Phishing in combination (September 2020)

-This email offered a complimentary dropbox upgrade as a thank you for your assistance during COVID-19.

-In order to take advantage of the offer, recipients were urged to click a link before December.

-As with Campaign 1, the text was not displayed as plain text, but as an image.

The findings indicate that phishing emails with personalization are far more likely to be clicked on. Compared to the 38% of staff members who did not open the personalized phish, 64% of staff members did not open the general phish during the first campaign. The click rate also showed a substantial difference, with a significantly higher number of staff members clicking on the personalized phish. However, because of problems brought up within the organization, the campaigns could not be carried out as planned [21]. For a list of phishing simulation tools used in various studies, see Table 6.1.

Campaign	Unopened emails		Opened emails		% of opened		% of total Emails clicked	
	Standard	Custom	Standard	Custom	Standard	Custom	Standard	Custom
First	64%	38%	36%	62%	18%	88%	7%	55%
Second	-	42%	-	59%	-	87%	-	21%
Third	56%	-	44%	-	7%	-	3%	-

Table 6.1 Phishing simulation tools

NO	Tool name	Type
[22]	GoPhish	OpenSource
[23]	SpearPhisher BETA	OpenSource
[24]	King Phisher	OpenSource
[25]	SpeedPhish Framework (SPF)	OpenSource
[26]	Simple Phishing Toolkit (sptoolkit)	OpenSource
[27]	Phishing Frenzy	OpenSource
[28]	Social Engineer Toolkit (SET)	OpenSource
[29]	Proofpoint	Commercial
[30]	Lucy	Commercial
[31]	InfoSec	Commercial
[32]	Hoxhunt	Commercial
[33]	Cofense	Commercial
[34]	Mimecast	Commercial

6.3.4 Distributed Denial of Service (DDoS)

6.3.4.1 DOS/DDOS attacks

The denial of service (DoS) attack prevents authorized users from accessing network resources. In a DoS attack, the attackers either swiftly send a massive number of regular messages to a single node to exhaust system resources, which causes the system to crash, or they exploit flaws to produce anomalies or cripple network-based systems. Both times, intended users are barred from using network resources or services. Because network traffic is made up of both normal, legitimate traffic and atypical, attack-related traffic, detecting such attacks is extremely challenging [35]. Distributed denial of service (DDoS) is an amplified DoS attack. This attack is any attempt to interfere with a service's normal operation in any way. The term "distributed" (abbreviated as DDoS) refers to an attack when multiple attacking machines (often tens of thousands) are active at the same time.

A DDoS attack targets a particular machine, service, or even the institution's infrastructure. Depending on the system's design, a successful attack prevents a service or network from operating normally and causes quantifiable harm to the owner. A massive number of requests are sent from numerous computers spread out over various places during a DDoS attack.

DDoS attacks pose a serious security risk to IoT-based mobile healthcare platforms. A hacktivist was accused of spreading DDoS attacks against Boston Hospitals in 2018 that disrupted the network for at least two weeks [36–38].

6.3.4.2 Methods of Distributed Denial of Service attacks

We described below some widely known basic denial of service attack methods that are employed by the attack daemons.

SYN flood: The transmission control protocol (TCP) SYN attack, also known as the SYN flood attack, is based on taking advantage of the typical TCP three-way handshake. A three-packet exchange must be completed as part of the TCP three-way handshake before a client can formally use the service. A server responds with a SYN/ACK (synchronize/acknowledge) packet after receiving an initial SYN (synchronize/start) request from a client and waits for the client to send the final ACK (acknowledge). As the server only has a small buffer queue for new connections, SYN flood causes the server to become unable to process other incoming connections as the queue gets full. This is because it is possible to send a large number of initial SYNs without sending the corresponding ACKs. Considering that the server has a limited buffer queue for new connections, a SYN flood results in the server's inability to process further incoming connections as the overloaded queue becomes congested.

Smurf attack: Includes an attacker broadcasting a series of Internet protocol (IP) broadcast addresses with a sizable amount of ICMP echo traffic. The intended victim's source address (a fake address) is included in the ICMP echo packets. When an internet control message protocol (ICMP) echo request is sent, the majority of hosts on an IP network will accept it and respond by sending an echo reply to the source address, in this case, the intended victim. As a result, the traffic is multiplied by the quantity of hosts that react. There could be hundreds of machines responding to each ICMP message on a broadcast network.

UDP flood: The user datagram protocol (UDP) flood attack is based on the character generator and UDP echo services that are offered by the majority of computers on a network. To connect the character generator (chargen) service on one system to the echo service on another, the attacker forges UDP packets. As a result, as the two services exchange characters with one another, they use up all of the network bandwidth between the machines. This technique can also be modified to flood a machine with ICMP packets rather than UDP packets, which is known as ICMP flood [39].

6.3.4.3 DDoS attacks in eHealth concept

"Electronic health," or eHealth, is a crucial component of healthcare in the modern world. With the help of this eHealth system, patients will be able to easily access their medical records, and physicians will be able to diagnose patients accurately by having a clear picture of their condition. There will be one central component in the system (CBC). In addition to medical information systems (MIS), which hospitals and clinics can select from the market and set up, it will be in charge of centralized information processing and storage.

Since eHealth systems rely on public network solutions – such as computer networks, mobile networks, and the Internet – any issues that may develop there will have an impact on how well the system functions as a whole. DDoS attacks are easy to deploy because of this. Denying someone access, however, might result in both trivial financial losses and even fatalities. Thus, one of the most important tasks of the implementation of eHealth systems is security against this kind of attack and early detection of them. A scenario for e-healthcare is shown in Figure 6.4. Health professionals are those who provide medical services, such as doctors, nurses, and associated staff. Patients who wear sensors on their bodies to monitor their health conditions are the consumers of the eHealth system. Patient data confidentiality is extremely important and needs to be protected in order to demonstrate the system's dependability [40, 41].

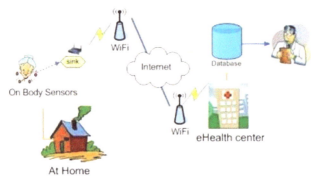

Figure 6.4 eHealthcare system [41].

6.3.4.4 DDoS attack for COVID-19 pandemic

Attackers exploited a large number of compromised PCs during the COVID-19 epidemic to create massive false packets, which brought down the online healthcare website or app. Because a DDoS assault uses up network resources fast, attackers opt to launch them during the COVID-19 time. Even a brief DDoS attack can prevent genuine users from accessing a website or app. DDoS assaults have increased dramatically in COVID-19 compared to 2019, and they have increased by 90% overall in COVID-19 compared to the previous year. Compared to Q1 of 2019, there was an average 24% rise in the duration of DDoS assaults in Q1 of 2020. Figure 6.5 represents the DDoS scenario in this; there are "N" compromised machines which are represented as Attacker 1, Attacker 2, and Attacker N. These compromised machines are generating a large amount of traffic. Due to this, normal users are not benefiting from online services [42].

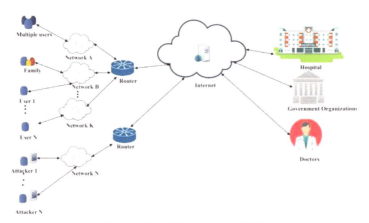

Figure 6.5 DDoS scenario [42].

6.4 Prevention of Cyberattacks in Healthcare

Article	Attacks	Preventions
[43]	Phishing attacks	- Configure and implement the selected methods and tools inside the email infrastructure in accordance with the needs of the company. Test and validate all configuration layers extensively after deployment. Monitoring and incident response: Configure continuous email traffic monitoring and security events including SIEM frameworks, and design alert tools for atypical exercises. -Security layer selection: Choose security layers, such as gateways, filters, and behavioral filters, based on the evaluated data; evaluate, and rank them in order of importance.
[44]	DoS/DDoS attacks	This reference proposed a new approach "WeTrace" by which the privacy of the user is not compromised during sharing health-related data on mobile apps.
[45]	DoS/DDoS attacks	One of the earliest group methods for identifying a DDoS attack was described by the authors of [51]. We refer to this paradigm as the "Pushback technique." In this concept, a router that experiences congestion asks the appropriate upstream router to restrict the amount of traffic it sends downstream. This strategy has the advantage of saving downstream routers' bandwidths since upstream routers screen all fraudulent packets and only allow legal packets to pass through.
[46]	DoS/DDoS attacks	- Reference [52] further suggested the "FireCol" method for DDoS attack detection. Using this method, an artificial perimeter of IDSs (intrusion detection systems) is created around the target, and these IDSs work together to identify any attack activity based on predetermined criteria. Users need to register with their Internet service provider (ISP) in order to utilize these IDSs. Each user receives a unique ID, supported capacity, and TTL (time of subscription) upon registration.

(Continued)

Article	Attacks	Preventions
[47]	Ransomware	- Restore the data and recover from a ransomware attack by making a backup of your crucial practice data and storing it offline. -Secure practice data by encrypting it. All patient data and devices should be encrypted and password-protected, according to providers. -Ensure that fundamental technical safeguards have been put in place. The following technological precautions should be implemented by providers: • Current antivirus programs installed on computers • Developed automated operating system and web browser patches. • Strong passwords • Pop-up blockers

6.5 The Consequences of Cyberattacks in the Healthcare Sector

6.5.1 Loss or alteration of medical data

Ransomware attacks in the healthcare industry raise serious concerns about the loss or manipulation of medical data. Numerous studies have highlighted instances of ransomware in the healthcare industry, highlighting the loss of medical data and the repercussions for healthcare organizations.

Studies have demonstrated that ransomware attacks can result in the loss of vital healthcare data such as test results, patient records, and medical photographs.

Due to the fact that healthcare professionals largely rely on precise and current information to make wise medical decisions, this loss may have very negative effects on patient care. Patient safety may be jeopardized by inaccurate treatment plans, delayed diagnosis, or nonavailability of medical data.

Research has also looked into the unapproved modification of medical data by online criminals. Attacks by ransomware that target healthcare companies have the ability to alter or distort patient records, test findings, prescription information, or other medical data. Such changes run the risk of leading to serious problems like incorrect diagnoses, ineffective therapies, and patient harm. When it comes to ensuring efficient and secure healthcare delivery, the integrity and reliability of medical data are crucial.

The potential for data modification and its potential effects on treatment choices have alarmed the healthcare sector. To defend against ransomware attacks and stop illegal data modifications, healthcare organizations must employ strong cybersecurity measures, such as access limits, data encryption, and data backup systems. Continual staff training and awareness campaigns are also necessary to inform healthcare personnel about the risks.

In conclusion, the healthcare industry faces major hurdles and hazards as a result of the loss or manipulation of medical data caused by ransomware attacks. To protect the integrity of patient data and sustain the caliber of medical choices, healthcare organizations must prioritize cybersecurity measures, make investments in secure systems, and remain attentive against evolving cyber threats.

6.5.2 Consequences of phishing attacks

Misuse of stolen credentials: Once login information has been taken by hackers, it can be used in a number of ways. Hackers frequently check compromised user mailboxes for spreadsheets or documents containing personnel or patient PII. When sensitive identifiers like social security numbers and birth dates are present, this stolen personally identifiable information (PII) is especially valuable. The use of stolen identities for financial fraud, such as the filing of fraudulent tax returns or credit applications, can be done through local criminal networks or black markets.

Network credential fraud: Other fraud schemes can be carried out using stolen network credentials. For instance, in order to access payroll systems and change the direct deposit destinations to bank accounts they control, hackers occasionally use stolen credentials. This gives them the opportunity to steal salaries.

Amplification of phishing attacks: Phishing attempts can seem to come from someone the user knows, which is partially explained by the fact that hackers routinely utilize stolen credentials to start additional phishing assaults. As these users frequently have access to create new accounts, modify account privileges (e.g., granting additional privileges to other users), or directly access databases and file servers, circumventing standard security and monitoring measures, hackers specifically seek credentials with high privileges, such as those belonging to network administrators.

Bridgehead establishment and malware attacks: Once credentials have been stolen and the network has been infiltrated, hackers might create a "bridgehead" to launch further operations, including the malware installation. Hospitals have recently been the subject of ransomware attacks, which prolonged downtime and, in some cases, required ransom payments. Although it appears that attackers used methods other than phishing to carry out these attacks on the Hollywood hospital, phishing credentials continue to be an extremely effective strategy for carrying out more advanced malware attacks.

Reputational damage and additional costs: In addition to the immediate repercussions, firms that fall prey to phishing risk reputational damage and additional expenses, including as regulatory penalties, patient compensation for direct harm, and the cost of identity theft and credit monitoring services. Due to the market's rapid development, insurance plans are available to shield firms against some of these dangers. However, it might be difficult to measure some components of the risk, such as reputational harm [48].

6.5.3 Examination of the different forms of cyberattacks that can disrupt operations and health services

The healthcare sector is highly vulnerable to attacks due to its sensitive and critical nature. Any disruption in its services, even a minor delay or shutdown, can have severe consequences for patient safety. Cyberattacks encompass various threats, including brute force and denial of service attacks, phishing and malware usage, and social engineering techniques to compromise security. Malware known as ransomware is a serious risk to healthcare organizations. Across all industries, there was an average of 4000 ransomware assaults each day in 2016, a 300% rise over 2015. One of the top three global businesses hit hardest by ransomware is healthcare. Hospitals were impacted by an attack on the UK's National Health Service (NHS), which also damaged their radiography and blood product refrigeration systems. In 2017, there was an attack on Grozio Chirurgija, while in 2018 hackers gained access to the system of the Centers for Medicare and Medicaid Services. Due to a zero-day vulnerability in 2019, data from the Health Sciences Authority (Singapore) was exposed. Additionally, Unit Pint Health experienced two data breaches in 2019. In March 2019, hackers infected Life Bridge Healthcare systems with malware in order to steal sensitive data. As a result of these attacks, healthcare professionals no longer have access to crucial virtual records that contain details on comorbidities, allergies, and current medicines, endangering patient safety. Sensitive health information breaches and exposures can also have a negative impact on people's personal and professional lives, leaving them open to blackmail. Additionally, utilizing personally identifiable information about patients, fraudsters can commit a number of crimes, such as identity theft and medical fraud. Overall, the number of computer malware attacks has quadrupled in the past two years, with the healthcare sector becoming one of the most targeted industries worldwide [49–51].

6.5.4 Consequences of Distributed Denial of Service (DDoS) attacks

Distributed denial of service (DDoS) attacks are commonly used by hacktivists and cybercriminals to overwhelm a network, rendering it inoperable. This poses a significant problem for healthcare providers who rely on network access for essential patient care and communication, such as emails, prescriptions, and records. While some DDoS attacks occur by chance, many specifically target victims for social, political, ideological, or financial reasons related to a situation that has provoked the threat actors.

An example of such an attack took place in 2014 at Boston Children's Hospital. Anonymous, a well-known hacktivist group, launched a DDoS attack against the hospital following a contentious case involving the referral of a 14- year-old patient to state custody due to a disagreement between doctors and parents regarding the child's illness. Doctors believed the child's condition was psychological, while the parents sought additional treatments for a disorder they believed the child had. The custody dispute brought Boston Children's Hospital into the spotlight, and some, including members of Anonymous, saw it as a violation of the girl's rights. In response, Anonymous conducted DDoS attacks that not only affected the hospital's network but also caused Internet outages for Harvard University and its affiliated hospitals, which shared the same network. These disruptions lasted for nearly a week, preventing some patients and medical staff from accessing online accounts for appointments, test results, and other vital case information. The Boston Globe reported that the hospital had to spend over $300,000 to respond to and mitigate the damage caused by the attack, as stated in the arrest affidavit of the attacker.

6.5.5 Impacts of cyberattacks in the healthcare sector on reputation and financial costs

Cyberattacks have long-term economic and financial consequences and impact in the health sector. Among its first impacts was the loss of confidence

Articles	Problems	Mitigated	Features				Solutions
			Cfd	Av	Intg	Auth	
[53]	Loss or alteration of medical data	Any attack that targets confidentiality and integrity	✓	✓	✓	X	The system uses IoT devices to continuously monitor processing and updates collected data in a cloud computing environment for easy viewing the result shows an accuracy of 98.88 in identifying threats
[54]	Detecting ransomware	Ransomware	✓	✓	✓	X	The suggested method analyzes the network traffic created during the spreading phase of the ransomware attacks to detect and categorize them in real time in ICE. Additionally, the suggested mechanism automatically mitigates ransomware that has been identified and categorized by using NVF/SDN techniques to isolate and replace compromised devices. And specifically use the SDN paradigm to isolate contaminated medical equipment and replace their software controllers with NFV approaches.
[55]	The scalability and storage issues from patients	Ransomware	✓	✓	✓	X	Ensuring scalability and storage of blockchain-powered healthcare operations that use smart contracts is essential. The network's scalability and efficiency are improved by implementing solutions like sharding, off-chain storage, and sophisticated consensus techniques like proof-of-stake. Large healthcare datasets are effectively managed by off-chain storage, while concurrent transaction processing is made possible by sharding the blockchain into manageable portions. These enhancements optimize patient data gathering, use, and sharing, reducing bandwidth issues and promoting a more streamlined and scalable healthcare environment.
[56]	Collects the client's sensitive data	Phishing	✓	X	X	X	Machine learning, deep learning, recent advancements in DL approaches suggested that the classification of phishing websites using deep NN should outperform the traditional machine learning (ML) algorithms.

Articles	Problems	Mitigated	Features				Solutions
			Cfd	Av	Intg	Auth	
[57]	Intrusions	Attempts to compromise systems	X	✓	✓	X	A stacked autoencoder is used by the scheme to detect intrusions. Stacked autoencoders are used in the intrusion detection framework of the scheme. The three key components of the methodology are feature extraction, intrusion behavior determination, and data preprocessing. The preprocessing stage of the data defines the infiltration behavior accurately. A stacked autoencoder is used in the feature extraction stage to determine parameter weights for different features. Then, at the intrusion behavior determination stage, the XGBoost algorithm is applied to determine if a certain behavior is considered normal or intrusive.

of patients in the ability to talk about their personal data and medical data. They are classified as sensitive data. Another consequence is the significant costs related to the restoration of the information system, that is to say the costs to repair the damage caused by a cyberattack. In the event of personal data theft or any malicious action due to a cyberattack, hospitals may face legal and regulatory action for this alleged reason under data protection laws or other regulations [52].

6.6 Conclusion

In conclusion, various cyberattacks pose an increasing threat to the healthcare industry. Some of the frequent strategies used by hostile actors to target healthcare businesses include supply chain attacks, SQL injection, phishing, DDoS assaults, APTs, insider threats, malware infections, social engineering attacks, insider data theft, and ransomware. Aside from disrupting patient treatment, these attacks have the potential to cause financial losses, patient privacy violations, and compromises of vital healthcare systems. Recognizing the seriousness of these cyber threats and taking proactive steps to strengthen their cybersecurity defenses are essential for healthcare businesses. To effectively mitigate and recover from assaults, this entails putting in place strong security measures, doing frequent risk assessments, educating staff members about online dangers, and creating incident response plans. Healthcare businesses may better protect patient data, guarantee the integrity of healthcare systems, and keep patients' trust by remaining attentive, investing in cybersecurity infrastructure, and establishing a culture of security. In order to defend against cyberattacks and secure the future of healthcare, there must be ongoing research, information exchange, and collaboration in the sector.

References

[1] A Survey of Ransomware Attacks for Healthcare Systems: Risks, Challenges, Solutions and Opportunity of Research

[2] R. Mohammed, R. Alubady, and A. Sherbaz, "Utilizing blockchain Technology for IoT-based Healthcare Systems," Journal of Physics: Conference Series, pp. 1–11, 2021

[3] Gardaševiťc, G.; Katzis, K.; Bajiťc, D.; Berbakov, L. Emerging Wireless Sensor Networks and Internet of Things Technologies— Foundations of Smart Healthcare. Sensors 2020, 20, 3619. [CrossRef] [PubMed]

[4] Zou, Y.; Zhu, J.; Wang, X.; Hanzo, L. A survey on wireless security: Technical challenges, recent advances, and future trends. IEEE 2016, 104, 1727–1765. [CrossRef]

[5] Zhang, Y.; Zheng, D.; Deng, R.H. Security and privacy in smart health: Efficient policy-hiding attribute-based access control. IEEE Internet Things J. 2018, 5, 2130–2145. [CrossRef]

[6] Al-Janabi, S.; Al-Shourbaji, I.; Shojafar, M.; Shamshirband, S. Survey of main challenges (security and privacy) in wireless body area networks for healthcare applications. Egypt. Informatics J. 2017, 18, 113–122. [CrossRef]

[7] Sikder, A.K.; Babun, L.; Aksu, H.; Uluagac, A.S. Aegis: A context-aware security framework for smart home systems. In Proceedings of the 35th Annual Computer Security Applications Conference, San Juan, PR, USA, 9–13 December 2019; pp. 28–41.

[8] An Efficient CNN-Based Deep Learning Model to Detect Malware Attacks (CNN-DMA) in 5G-IoT Healthcare Applications Ankita Anand 1 , Shalli Rani 1,* ,Divya Anand 2 , Hani Moaiteq Aljahdali 3 and Dermot Kerr 4

[9] Paul III, D. P., Spence, N., Bhardwa, N., & PH, C. D. (2018). Healthcare facilities: another target for ransomware attacks. [30] Moran Stritch, M., Winterburn, M., & Houghton, F. (2021). The Conti ransomware attack on healthcare in Ireland: exploring the impacts of a cybersecurity breach from a nursing perspective. Canadian Journal of Nursing Informatics, 16(3-4)

[10] Vogt, P.; Nentwich, F.; Jovanovic, N.; Kirda, E.; Kruegel, C.; Vigna, G. Cross-Site Scripting Prevention with Dynamic Data Tainting and Static Analysis. In Proceedings of the Network and Distributed System Security Symposium (NDSS 2007), San Diego, CA, USA, 28 February–2 March 2007.
[11] Thamer, N., & Alubady, R. (2021, April). A survey of ransomware attacks for healthcare systems: Risks, challenges, solutions and opportunity of research. In 2021 1st Babylon International Conference on Information Technology and Science (BICITS) (pp. 210-216). IEEE.
[12] Trends in Ransomware Attacks on US Hospitals, Clinics, and Other Health Care Delivery Organizations, 2016-2021
[13] Thamer, N., & Alubady, R. (2021, April). A survey of ransomware attacks for healthcare systems: Risks, challenges, solutions and opportunity of research. In 2021 1st Babylon International Conference on Information Technology and Science (BICITS) (pp. 210-216). IEEE.
[14] Paul III, D. P., Spence, N., Bhardwa, N., & PH, C. D. (2018). Healthcare facilities: another target for ransomware attacks. [30] Moran Stritch, M., Winterburn, M., & Houghton, F. (2021). The Conti ransomware attack on healthcare in Ireland: exploring the impacts of a cybersecurity breach from a nursing perspective. Canadian Journal of Nursing Informatics, 16(3-4)
[15] "Protect Healthcare Data from Phishing," HIPAA Journal
[16] B. Krebs, "Anthem Breach May Have Started in April 2014," Krebs on Security, 09-Feb2015
[17] B. Krebs, "Premera Blue Cross Breach Exposes Financial, Medical Records," Krebs on Security, 17-Mar-2015
[18] T. Lam, "PhAttApp: A Phishing Attack Detection Application." 2019 3rd International Conference on Information System and Data Mining, pp. 154–158, 2019
[19] Sharma, P., Dash, B., & Ansari, M. F. (2022). Anti-phishing techniques– a review of Cyber Defense Mechanisms. International Journal of Advanced Research in Computer and Communication Engineering ISO, 3297, 2007
[20] Nisha, T. N., Digant Bakari, and Charmi Shukla. "Business E-mail Compromise—Techniques and Countermeasures." In 2021 International Conference on Advance Computing and Innovative Technologies in Engineering (ICACITE), pp. 217-222. IEEE, 2021

[21] Phishing simulation exercise in a large hospital: A case study Fabio Rizzoni1, Sabina Magalini2, Alessandra Casaroli3, Pasquale Mari2, Matt Dixon4 and Lynne Coventry4 p1-7
[22] Open-Source Phishing Framework. Available online: https://getgophish.com/(accessedon4August2022).
[23] Kennedy, D. Introducing Spearphisher—A Simple Phishing Email Generation Tool. Available online: https://www.faqlogin.com/login/spearphisher-a-simple-phishing-emailgeneration-tool (accessed on 4 August 2022
[24] King-Phisher. Available online: https://www.kali.org/tools/king-phisher/ (accessed on 4 August 2022).
[25] SPF. SPF–Speed Phishing Framework. Available online: https://sectechno.com/spfspeedphishing-framework/ (accessed on 4 August 2022)
[26] sptoolkit. sptoolkit Rebirth–Simple Phishing Toolki. Available online: https://www.darknet.org.uk/2015/04/sptoolkitrebirthsimple-phishing-toolkit/ (accessed on 4 August 2022)
[27] Phishing All the Chings. Available online: https://www.phishingfrenzy.com (accessed on 4 August 2022)
[28] TrustedSec. The Social-Engineer Toolkit (SET). Available online: https://www.trustedsec.com/tools/the-socialengineer-toolkitset/ (accessed on 4 Aug
[29] proofpoint. Attackers Start with People. Your Cybersecurity Strategy Should too. Available online: https://www.proofpoint.com/us (accessed on 4 August 2022)
[30] Lucy. Cyber Security Training Solutions. Available online: https://lucysecurity.com/ (accessed on 4 August 2022).
[31] Infosecinstitute. Prepare Every Employee with Phishing Simulations & Training. Available online:https://www.infosecinstitute.com/iq/phishing-simulations/ (accessed on 4 August 2022).
[32] IronScales. Phishing Simulation & Training: Anti Phishing Simulations and Customized Training Based on Real-Time Data and Real World Situations. Available online:https://ironscales.com/ (accessed on 4 August 2022).
[33] Hoxhunt. Enterprise Security Awareness, ReInvented. Available online: https://www.hoxhunt.com/ (accessed on 4 August 2022). [26] Cofense. Security Solutions Built to Stop Phish. Available online: https://cofense.com/ (accessed on 4 August 2022). [27] Mimecast. Relentless Protection Starts Here. Available online: https://www.mimecast.com/ (accessed on 4 August 2022).

[34] Thamer, N., & Alubady, R. (2021, April). A survey of ransomware attacks for healthcare systems: Risks, challenges, solutions and opportunity of research. In 2021 1st Babylon International Conference on Information Technology and Science (BICITS) (pp. 210-216). IEEE.

[35] Javaid, M., Haleem, A., Singh, R. P., & Suman, R. (2023). Towards insighting cybersecurity for healthcare domains: A comprehensive review of recent practices and trends. Cyber Security and Applications, 100016.

[36] Ray, S., Mishra, K. N., & Dutta, S. (2023). An Innovative Technique for DDoS Attack Recognition and Deterrence on M-Health Sensitive Data. Wireless Personal Communications, 128(3), 1763-1797.

[37] References Gaurav, A. K. S. H. A. T., & Chui, K. T. (2022). Advancement of Cloud Computing and Big Data Analytics in Healthcare Sector Security. Data Science Insights Magazine, Insights2Techinfo, 1, 12- 15.

[38] Weber, M., Hacker, J., Karintaus, L., Pekkola, S., vom Brocke, J., & Ylinen, M. (2023). PREPARING FOR CYBERATTACKS: A CASE STUDY OF RESILIENCE IN THE HEALTH-CARE SECTOR.

[39] Shone, N., Ngoc, T. N., Phai, V. D., & Shi, Q. (2018). A deep learning approach to network intrusion detection. IEEE Transactions on Emerging Topics in Computational Intelligence, 2(1), 41–50.

[40] Zalisky, M., Odarchenko, R., Gnatyuk, S., Petrova, Y., & Chaplits, A. (2018). Method of Traffic Monitoring for DDoS Attacks Detection in e-Health Systems and Networks. In *IDDM* (pp. 193-204).

[41] ul Sami, I., Ahmad, M. B., Asif, M., & Ullah, R. (2018). DoS/DDoS detection for E- Healthcare in internet of things. *International Journal of Advanced Computer Science and Applications*, 9(1).

[42] Zhou, Z., Gaurav, A., Gupta, B. B., Hamdi, H., & Nedjah, N. (2021). A statistical approach to secure health care services from DDoS attacks during COVID-19 pandemic. *Neural Computing and Applications*, 1-14.

[43] Healthcare 4.0: A Review of Phishing Attacks in Cyber Security K S N Sushmaa*, Viji Cb , Rajkumar Nc ,Jayavadivel Ravid ,Stalin Me , Najmusher Hf

[44] De Carli A, Franco M, Gassmann A, Killer C, Rodrigues B, Scheid E, Schoenbaechler D, Stiller B (2020) WeTrace - une approche et une application mobile de traçage du COVID-19 préservant la confidentialité. préimpression arXiv arXiv:2004.08812.

[45] Mahajan R, Bellovin SM, Floyd S, Ioannidis J, Paxson V, Shenker S (2002) Controlling high bandwidth aggregates in the network. ACM SIGCOMM Comput Commun Rev 32(3):62–73

[46] Jérôme Francois RB, Aib I (2012) Firecol: a collaborative protection network for the detection of flooding ddos attacks. IEEE/ACM Trans Netw 20(6):1828. https://doi.org/10.1109/tnet.2012.2194508
[47] Pope, Justin. "Ransomware: Minimizing the risks." Innovations in clinical neuroscience 13.11- 12 (2016): 37
[48] Wright, Adam, Skye Aaron, and David W. Bates. "The big phish: cyberattacks against US healthcare systems." Journal of General Internal Medicine 31 (2016): 1115-1118.
[49] Weber, M., Hacker, J., Karintaus, L., Pekkola, S., vom Brocke, J., & Ylinen, M. (2023). PREPARING FOR CYBERATTACKS: A CASE STUDY OF RESILIENCE IN THE HEALTH-CARE SECTOR
[50] Daniel Mihai, L. E. U., UDROIU, C., RAICU, G. M., GÂRBAN, H. N., & şCHEAU, M. C. (2023). Analysis of some case studies on cyberattacks and proposed methods for preventing them. Revista Română de Informatică şi Automatică, 33(2), 119-134
[51] Mahjabin, Tasnuva, et al. "A survey of distributed denial-of-service attack, prevention, and mitigation techniques." International Journal of Distributed Sensor Networks 13.12 (2017): 1550147717741463
[52] Sanders, A. (2023). Predictive Model for Cyber Attacks to Assess Financial Exposure for IoHT/IoMT (Doctoral dissertation, The George Washington University).
[53] Infosecinstitute. Prepare Every Employee with Phishing Simulations & Training. Available online:https://www.infosecinstitute.com/iq/phishing- simulations/ (accessed on 4 August 2022).
[54] Fernandez Maimo, L., Huertas Celdran, A., Perales Gomez, A. L., Garcia Clemente, F. J., Weimer, J., & Lee, I. (2019). Intelligent and dynamic ransomware spread detection and mitigation in integrated clinical environments. Sensors, 19(5), 1114
[55] Thamer, N., & Alubady, R. (2021, April). A survey of ransomware attacks for healthcare systems: Risks, challenges, solutions and opportunity of research. In 2021 1st Babylon International Conference on Information Technology and Science (BICITS) (pp. 210-216). IEEE.
[56] Basit, A., Zafar, M., Liu, X., Javed, A. R., Jalil, Z., & Kifayat, K. (2021). A comprehensive survey of AI-enabled phishing attacks detection techniques. Telecommunication Systems, 76, 139- 154
[57] Al-Qarni, E. A. (2023). Cybersecurity in Healthcare: a review of recent attacks and mitigation strategies. International Journal of Advanced Computer Science and Applications, 14(5)

7

Enhancing Cyber Resilience: A Study of Red Teaming within Operational Technology Domains

Mounia Zaydi[1] and Yassine Maleh[2]

[1]ICL, Junia, Université Catholique de Lille, LITL (Lille Interdisciplinary Transitions Laboratory), France
[2]LaSTI Laboratory, Sultan Moulay Slimane University, Morocco
E-mail: mounia.zaydi@junia.com; y.maleh@usms.ma

Abstract

This research delves into the strategic utilization of red teaming to enhance the security of digital instrumentation and control (I&C) systems within the operational technology (OT) framework of the industrial construction chain. This study meticulously explores the nuances of red teaming engagement specifically tailored for OT environments. The paper introduces a novel and cost-effective approach to establishing an industrial control system/operational technology (ICS/OT) test environment through virtualization. This innovative setup enables the practical execution of cybersecurity testing and logic programming within a simulated industrial context. The main focus of this research is to contribute valuable insights to the proactive defense against cyber threats within the intricate landscape of OT environments. By addressing the unique challenges posed by the industrial construction chain, the study aims to provide practical solutions and recommendations for fortifying the digital infrastructure of critical systems. This research serves as a significant step forward in advancing the understanding of red teaming strategies within the context of OT security, ultimately contributing to the broader field of cybersecurity in industrial settings.

Keywords: Red teaming, digital instrumentation and control systems, operational technology, industrial construction chain, cybersecurity testing, logic programming.

7.1 Introduction

In the ever-evolving landscape of operational technology (OT), where the convergence of industrial processes and digital frameworks is inevitable, the imperative to fortify against cyber threats becomes increasingly paramount. Analogous to critical infrastructure endeavors, the OT environments within the industrial construction chain confront the formidable challenge of securing digital instrumentation and control (I&C) systems [1].

At the forefront of this discourse lies the strategic adoption of red teaming, a proactive approach pivotal in the identification and mitigation of vulnerabilities. This research paper systematically investigates the application of red teaming within the OT domain, drawing parallels with the cybersecurity concerns prevalent in complex systems. This study orchestrates a parallel exploration within the OT sphere, elevating the prominence of our understanding. Emulating a meticulous methodology, the paper navigates through the intricate landscape of red teaming engagement specifically tailored for operational technology environments. The structural framework mirrors the establishment of a cost-effective industrial control system/operational technology (ICS/OT) test environment through virtualization. This involves the deployment of virtual machines that simulate essential components such as routers, PLCs, and HMI. Network configurations are managed by pfSense, while OpenPLC and ScadaBR find their place on Ubuntu servers. To simulate a physical process, FactoryIO, integrated with OpenPLC, comes into play. This comprehensive setup facilitates practical cybersecurity testing and logic programming within the context of a simulated industrial setting. Our research delves into the strategic utilization of red teaming to enhance the security of digital I&C systems within the OT framework of the industrial construction chain. Through meticulous investigation and parallel exploration within the OT sphere, we've navigated the intricate landscape of red teaming engagement tailored for operational technology environments [2].

The primary findings unfold in two phases. In Phase 1, we establish a cost-effective ICS/OT test environment through virtualization, deploying virtual machines simulating essential components. This setup enables practical cybersecurity testing and logic programming within a simulated industrial context [3].

Advancing into Phase 2, our red team campaign for the ICS/OT environment involves gaining access to the OT network, orchestrating simulated damage to assess defense resilience. This adversarial emulation mirrors real-world threats, offering insights for defense fortification, malware detection, employee training enhancement, and strategic counteraction of advanced persistent threat (APT) tactics.

Guided by the red team kill-chain and integrating the MITRE ATT&CK framework [4], our methodology systematically breaks down attack structures into distinct phases, providing a nuanced understanding of adversaries' tactics. This comprehensive approach contributes valuable insights to the proactive defense against cyber threats in the intricate landscape of OT environments.

This chapter significantly advances the understanding of red teaming strategies within the context of OT security, making noteworthy contributions to the broader field of cybersecurity in industrial settings. The introduction reminds us of the imperative to fortify against cyber threats in the ever-evolving landscape of OT, setting the stage for a comprehensive exploration of red teaming's strategic application tailored for operational technology environments.

7.2 Background and Related Works

In the last decade, there has been a pronounced escalation in the recognition and prioritization of OT cybersecurity. A pivotal event contributing to this shift was the Stuxnet attack in 2010, which targeted the Iranian Nuclear Program, marking one of the earliest instances of a cyberweapon causing industrial damage to a nation-state's activities [5]. The attack specifically aimed at programmable logic controllers (PLCs), inducing centrifuge speed fluctuations in uranium enrichment facilities, resulting in operational shutdowns. Subsequent to Stuxnet, a surge in cyberattacks on industrial control systems (ICS) ensued, particularly targeting critical infrastructure networks. Recent notable incidents include the attack on a Florida town water supply in February 2021 [6] and the DarkSide attack on the US Colonial Pipeline infrastructure in May 2021 [7].

The escalating frequency of cyberattacks on these critical systems prompted significant investments by governments and organizations worldwide to fortify their defenses. For instance, the European Union Agency for Cybersecurity (ENISA) implemented the EU Network and Information Security Directive (NIS Directive) in 2016, emphasizing critical infrastructure cybersecurity across the European Union [8]. Additionally, individual countries, such as the UK and the USA, introduced their strategies to bolster defenses against cyber threats targeting critical infrastructure, exemplified by the UK's Cyber Assessment Framework [9] and the USA's NIST Framework for Improving Critical Infrastructure Cybersecurity [10].

Surveys conducted over the past decade, such as those by the US Government Accountability Office [11] and Westby [12], revealed critical security gaps within the governance of security for critical infrastructure (CI) organizations. These gaps encompassed issues like information sharing mechanisms, cyber awareness, security features in critical infrastructure networks, and metrics for evaluating cybersecurity capabilities. Despite subsequent advances in standards and guidelines, as indicated by a more recent survey [83], the widespread adoption of these measures remained minimal, particularly in ICS and critical national infrastructure (CNI). The surveys underscored the need for comprehensive preparation for incidents, including security assessments such as penetration testing, identified as a crucial phase in enhancing cyber incident response and recovery capabilities.

The challenges in implementing adversary-centric assurance techniques, like penetration testing, were evident due to the skill gap between OT engineering and general penetration testing. The safety-critical nature of ICS posed additional constraints. According to a survey by the SANS Institute [13], OT stakeholders emphasized security assessments and initiatives to bridge the IT/OT gap as top priorities. However, concerns about disrupting operational processes led to limited adoption of comprehensive security testing methods.

Various works have addressed the concerns raised in surveys, proposing solutions to enhance the cybersecurity posture of ICS environments. Conklin [14] highlighted the challenges of applying IT-specific methodologies in an industrial context, suggesting the incorporation of resilience alongside the confidentiality, integrity, and availability (CIA) triad. Song et al. [15] recommended penetration testing in the cyber risk assessment process for I&C systems within nuclear power plants, albeit acknowledging potential disruptions. Murray et al. [16] discussed the cultural differences between IT and OT, emphasizing the need for adjustments in the convergence of the two technologies. Knowles et al. [17] emphasized simulated security assessments, including penetration testing, as a means to generate audit evidence and enhance risk posture in ICS. Dos Santos [18] illustrated the vulnerability of building automation systems (BAS) to straightforward network protocol attacks. Additionally, exploiting both known and undisclosed zero-day vulnerabilities, our study introduces what we believe to be the first BAS-targeted malware. This malware can maintain its presence in the BAS network by using connected OT and IoT devices. Our findings underscore the critical nature of BAS networks, comparable to industrial control systems, and call for increased vigilance from industrial and academic spheres. Demonstrations in a controlled setting showed that these proof-of-concept attacks could be executed with minimal financial and resource investments, suggesting that sophisticated attackers could increasingly target BAS networks, potentially affecting thousands of individuals. Staves et al. [19] assessed the implications by applying such security testing methods to an industrial control system prototype. The outcomes indicate that older OT systems are generally more vulnerable to disruptions from these tests, whereas updated OT systems, equipped with advanced hardware and optimized software, display enhanced resistance to the security testing tools and tactics. This leads to the establishment of defined criteria necessary for conducting adversary-focused security testing in OT environments, ensuring that the risk posed by these methods to the operational continuity is thoroughly assessed and managed.

While existing research underscores the benefits and challenges of adversary-centric security testing, there is limited detail on the technical considerations differentiating IT and OT environments for safe testing. The subsequent sections of this paper delve into a technical analysis of cybersecurity considerations specific to OT environments compared to traditional IT environments. Additionally, the paper analyzes how these distinctions influence the execution of security engagements, such as penetration tests.

7.3 Methodology

In this section, we delve into the methodology employed for executing adversary-centric security testing, specifically focusing on both information technology (IT) and OT environments. The methodology is structured to ensure a comprehensive understanding of defense and response capabilities in the face of potential cyber threats, with a detailed exploration of red teaming methodologies tailored for OT setting.

7.3.1 Adversary-centric security testing preparation

The initial facet of the methodology elucidates the rationale behind conducting adversary-centric testing. This involves highlighting its pivotal role in the cybersecurity lifecycle, emphasizing its critical significance, especially in safeguarding critical infrastructure with high stakes. The section delves into cyberattack implications on critical infrastructure, underscoring the need for robust and effective preparation.

In OT environments, a nuanced examination of red teaming is essential. The methodology addresses the relatively limited adoption of adversary-centric testing in OT and unravels the intricacies surrounding this hesitancy. Specialized expertise emerges as a crucial factor, as the critical nature of OT systems necessitates highly specialized and meticulously vetted teams for effective testing.

7.3.2 Frameworks for adversary-centric security testing

Moving forward, the methodology introduces and dissects two prominent frameworks employed for adversary-centric security testing: the Lockheed Martin cyber kill chain (CKC) and the SANS ICS Cyber Kill Chain. The CKC's seven-step model, elucidated in detail, forms the backbone of understanding adversary tactics, techniques, and procedures (TTPs). Simultaneously, the ICS-specific CKC, with its two-stage approach, hones in on the distinct stages of cyber intrusion preparation and execution and ICS attack development and execution.

Complementing these models, the methodology integrates the MITRE ATT&CK and MITRE ICS ATT&CK frameworks, offering a knowledge base rooted in real-world observations. These frameworks categorize TTPs based on attack types, providing defenders with actionable insights into countering real-world cyber threats.

7.3.3 Technical depth in adversary-centric testing

The third phase of the methodology accentuates the need for technical depth in adversary-centric testing. By leveraging the MITRE frameworks, the analysis extends beyond high-level models, delving into the technical nuances of TTPs. The real-world observations forming the foundation of these frameworks contribute to a nuanced understanding of potential threats, enhancing the actionable intelligence available to defenders.

Customization emerges as a critical consideration, with the methodology acknowledging the necessity for a tailored approach based on the specific goals of each engagement whether it be red team exercises or vulnerability scans, the selection and application of TTPs vary, ensuring a targeted and effective testing process.

7.3.4 Considerations for IT and OT systems

The penultimate segment of the methodology draws attention to the distinct characteristics of industrial control system (ICS) networks. The complexity and sophistication required in ICS attacks prompt integrating a specialized ICS CKC model. The relevance of the MITRE ICS ATT&CK framework is underscored, particularly in addressing the intricacies of cyber–physical attacks within ICS environments.

Operational considerations, characterized by the dependency-based nature of the CKC, are reiterated. This emphasizes the need for a dynamic and flexible approach that allows revisiting previous steps based on the evolving threat landscape. In the context of ICS testing, technical specificity is paramount, and the methodology acknowledges the necessity for frameworks tailored explicitly to industrial control systems.

7.4 Experiments

7.4.1 Setting up the virtual architecture

In the pursuit of comprehensively examining cybersecurity risks within OT infrastructures, a model was meticulously crafted to emulate a genuine construction chain. This deliberate approach facilitated an in-depth analysis of the system's behavior and its defense mechanisms against external threats. In tandem with this investigation, various defense mechanisms, including firewalls, were strategically implemented. Figure 7.1 shows the proposed architecture.

The virtual architecture underwent careful construction, incorporating several components to simulate a router, PLC, and human–machine interface (HMI). The intricate orchestration extended to the expert management of network configurations by pfSense, complemented by the implementation of OpenPLC and ScadaBR on Ubuntu servers. Further enhancing the realism of the simulated environment, FactoryIO was seamlessly integrated with OpenPLC to emulate a tangible physical process. This comprehensive setup not only enabled practical cybersecurity testing but also facilitated logic programming tailored for a simulated industrial context. To contextualize these efforts within the broader architecture:

- **ICS**: Industrial control system. This encompasses the amalgamation of hardware and software designed to oversee and regulate industrial processes.

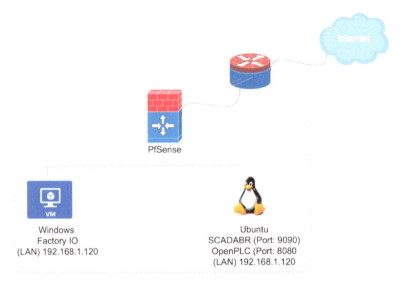

Figure 7.1 The proposed architecture.

- **OT**: Operational technology denotes the application of technology to govern physical processes, focusing on industrial control systems, Scada systems, and other technologies specific to operational processes.
- **PLC**: Programmable logical controller. A vital digital device utilized in industrial automation to control machinery and processes, ensuring efficient operation within manufacturing environments.
- **HMI**: Human–machine interface. An interface facilitating user interaction with machines, presenting data, and enabling control, often through touchscreens or graphical displays.
- **ScadaBR**: An open-source supervisory control and data acquisition (SCADA) system engineered to monitor and control industrial processes, providing a user-friendly interface for managing complex systems.
- **PfSense**: An open-source firewall and routing software platform enhancing network security, commonly employed to safeguard and manage communication in industrial systems.
- **FactoryIO**: A simulation software employed for crafting realistic industrial environments within a virtual setting, enabling the testing and development of control systems within a simulated context.

Our design is intricately woven around the services provided by the machining center, a pivotal station designed for the production of lids

7.4 Experiments   195

Figure 7.2 The formulated design.

and bases from raw materials. The operational sequence unfolds with the articulated robot poised at the entry bay, patiently awaiting the placement of raw materials. Upon detection of new material, a seamless process is initiated as it is loaded into the CNC machine, kickstarting the manufacturing of the intended item. It's worth noting that each item type undergoes a distinct production interval, with lids requiring 6 seconds and bases 3 seconds.

Upon the culmination of this precision manufacturing operation, the robot delicately places the freshly crafted item on the exit bay. This design, rooted in the functionality of the machining center, not only ensures the efficient production of lids and bases but also orchestrates a seamless and automated workflow. The precision and timing intricacies embedded in the design guarantee a streamlined and optimized manufacturing process, aligning with the demands of modern industrial practices, as shown in Figure 7.2.

7.4.1.1 Integration of OpenPLC with FactoryIO

To integrate FactoryIO with OpenPLC, we navigate to the OpenPLC web portal. Once inside, we access the "Slave Devices" tab to configure the FactoryIO driver as a slave device, considering the following considerations:

Device type: Must be a generic Modbus TCP device.

SlaveID: Can be any integer greater than 0 but must match the one previously configured in the FactoryIO driver.

IP addresses: Identical to those previously configured in the FactoryIO driver.

IP port: *502* is the default Modbus TCP port; it is recommended to keep it as default, although it can be changed as long as it is correctly set in the FactoryIO driver.

Discrete inputs: Starting from 0 and ending at the required number of inputs.

Coils: Starting from 0 and ending at the required number of inputs.

Input registers: They are a type of memory location within a PLC or similar system that holds data representing input values.

Holding registers – Read: Locations that store data in a PLC or similar device. The term "Read" indicates that these registers are intended for reading data.

Holding registers – Write: Holding registers for writing are memory locations used for storing data. The term "Write" signifies that these registers are intended for receiving new data values.

7.4.1.2 Programming the control logic

To enable the functionality of the machining center, a code programmed through OpenPLC is essential. The system incorporates a sensor named "I 201BC01Arrivedsens" designed to detect the arrival of parts. Subsequently, these parts are directed to the machining center identified as "Machining-Center201MC01." Within the machining center, a sensor denoted as "T 201BC02EntrySens" serves the purpose of detecting when a part enters the machine, Figure 7.3 shows the coding of the model.

Furthermore, the machining center is equipped with various other sensors, including:

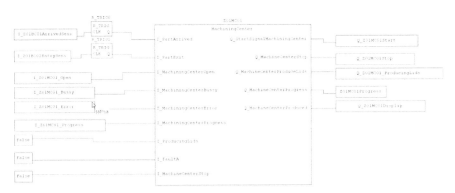

Figure 7.3 The coding of the model.

- **I PartArrived**: Detects the arrival of a part at the machining center.
- **I PartExit**: Identifies when a part exits the machining center.
- **I MachiningCenterOpen**: Determines the status of whether the machining center is open.
- **I MachiningCenterBusy**: Indicates when the machining center is in operation.
- **I 201MC01 Error**: Detects errors within the machining center.

Additionally, the machining center features several outputs, such as:

- **StartsignalMachiningCenter**: Initiates the machining center.
- **MachineCenterStop**: Halts the operation of the machining center.
- **Qz01MC01Start**: Signals the commencement of the machining center.
- **QMachineCenterProduceLids**: Indicates that the machining center is actively producing lids.
- **Q 201MC01 ProducingLids**: Conveys the ongoing lid production status.
- **QMachineCenterProgress**: Communicates the progress of the machining center.
- **Q MachineCenterProduced**: Signals the successful production of a lid by the machining center.
- **Q 201MC01Display**: Transmits information to the display, reflecting the status of the machining center.

7.4.2 Launching a red team campaign for ICS/OIT environment

Embark on a targeted red teaming campaign dedicated to ICS/OT penetration testing, with the overarching goal of evaluating and fortifying the security of our industrial systems. The mission involves gaining access to the OT network with the intent to simulate potential damage to the factory. Red teaming, within this context, entails the emulation of comprehensive attacks on both digital and physical security aspects of a company, mirroring the strategies employed by real adversaries. This strategic approach offers invaluable insights for bolstering defenses, identifying potential malware threats, refining employee training programs, and countering APT tactics. Subsequently, the findings from red team exercises serve as crucial input for blue teams, comprising security professionals who utilize the results for mitigation and verification purposes.

The concept of adversary emulation involves replicating the tactics of a specific adversary to evaluate and enhance an organization's defensive measures. This process focuses keenly on understanding and countering the adversary's tactics, TTPs through a structured methodology.

A pivotal element within the red teaming strategy is the red team kill-chain – a methodological cybersecurity model systematically breaking down the structure of an attack into distinct phases. This model aids cybersecurity teams in comprehending the intricacies of attacks, their structural components, and the tactics employed by adversaries at each stage. In our pursuit of structured adversary emulation, we leverage the MITRE ATT&CK framework. This framework provides a systematically organized kill chain, offering a robust structure for guiding our approach to adversary emulation within the cybersecurity landscape.

7.4.2.1 Essential elements and technologies in red teaming
In the dynamic landscape of cybersecurity, the effective mitigation of threats requires a comprehensive understanding and strategic utilization of key components and technologies. This discussion centers on pivotal elements such as cyber threat intelligence (CTI), tactics, TTPs, advanced persistent threats (APTs), the cyber kill chain, and advanced threat intelligence platforms. Each plays a distinctive role in fortifying defense mechanisms and contributing to a proactive cybersecurity posture.

CTI: CTI serves as a crucial informant for defenders, offering insights into adversary actions. Red teams leverage CTI for the simulation of offensive tactics.

TTPs: TTPs encapsulate the methodologies employed by threat actors. Both red and blue teams analyze TTPs to decipher adversary objectives, strategies, and execution plans.

APT: APTs represent clandestine and persistent threat actors, often nation-states or state-sponsored groups, infiltrating computer networks discreetly and remaining undetected for prolonged periods.

Cyber kill chain: The cyber kill chain outlines the sequential steps an attacker takes, commencing with reconnaissance and culminating in decisive actions on predetermined objectives.

7.4.3 Threat intelligence platforms

Mitre ATT&CK: Mitre ATT&CK serves as a comprehensive global repository of real-world APT tactics, techniques, and procedures.

Cobalt Strike or Caldera: Platforms like Cobalt Strike or Caldera are purpose-built for adversary simulation and red teaming exercises, enhancing overall cybersecurity resilience.

7.4.3.1 Red team engagements

Success in an engagement hinges on meticulous planning and seamless communication among all stakeholders. Campaign planning, a fundamental aspect, involves aligning client objectives and rules of engagement to formulate comprehensive plans and documents for red team activities. Both internal and external red teams adhere to distinct methodologies and documentation for effective planning.

Client objectives, a linchpin in the process, play a pivotal role in shaping planning, documentation, and focus – whether broad or specific. A well-defined set of plans, borrowing from military operations, ensures precise communication and documentation, offering four plans of varying depth and coverage. The red team campaign comprises multiple essential documents, which are described below.

7.4.4 Engagement documentation

CONOPS (Concept of Operations): This initial document provides a high-level overview of the red team engagement process. The CONOPS is crafted to be concise, easily comprehensible for the client, and delineates the approach and conduct of the engagement.

Resource plan: This document furnishes a detailed overview, encompassing dates and allocated resources.

Operation plan: Offering intricate details of the engagement, this plan serves as a comprehensive guide.

Mission plan: Internally focused, the mission plan is tailored specifically for the red team.

Rules of Engagement (RoE): RoE, binding legal guidelines, delineate client objectives, expectations, and responsibilities in engagements. These rules set the parameters for a successful and ethically sound red teaming process.

7.4.5 Operation OT down

The OT down operation involves the compromise of the virtual OT architecture. The primary objective of this operation is to circumvent the defensive mechanisms inherent in the architecture and instigate the disruption of the construction chain within the factory. To achieve this goal, the red team employs a variety of techniques and tactics, which will be elaborated upon in the subsequent sections.

7.4.5.1 Caldera

Caldera stands as an open-source framework meticulously designed to execute autonomous adversary emulation exercises with utmost efficiency. Its primary purpose is to facilitate the emulation of real-world attack scenarios, allowing users to evaluate the efficacy of their security defenses comprehensively. Beyond its emulation capabilities, Caldera provides a modular environment tailored for red team engagements. This environment supports red team operators in the manual execution of tactics, TTPs, while concurrently aiding blue teamers in automating incident response actions. Notably, Caldera is constructed upon the foundation of the MITRE ATT&CK framework and remains an active research project at MITRE, with due credit accorded to MITRE for its creation.

Security analysts can leverage the Caldera framework across various scenarios, with common use cases including:

Autonomous red team engagements: Caldera is originally designed for this purpose, emulating known adversary profiles to identify vulnerabilities across an organization's infrastructure. This use case serves as a means to test defenses and enhance the team's threat detection capabilities.

Manual red team engagements: Caldera offers customization capabilities for red team engagements, allowing the adaptation of adversary profiles based on specific needs. This flexibility enables the replacement or extension of attack capabilities, particularly when the execution of a custom set of TTPs becomes necessary.

Autonomous incident response: Blue teamers can harness Caldera for automated incident response actions through deployed agents. This functionality proves valuable in identifying TTPs that may elude detection or prevention by other security tools.

7.4.5.2 Unpacking Caldera

Prior to delving into the operational aspects of the Caldera interface, it is essential to explore the foundational terminologies that underpin its functionality. This knowledge serves as a prerequisite for a comprehensive understanding of the framework, allowing for tailored adjustments to align with specific engagement requirements. Let's take a brief walkthrough of key elements introduced in this context.

Agents: Programs maintaining continuous connection with the Caldera server, responsible for retrieving and executing instructions.

Abilities: Tactical techniques and procedures (TTP) implementations executed by agents.

Adversaries: Aggregations of abilities associated with a known threat group.

Operations: Instances where abilities are executed on groups of agents.

Plugins: Extensions providing additional functionalities beyond the core utilization of the framework.

1) Agents: In line with their nomenclature, agents within Caldera refer to programs maintaining a continuous connection with the Caldera server, facilitating the retrieval and execution of instructions. The communication between these agents and the Caldera server occurs through a predefined contact method, initially established during the agent's installation process.

During installation, agents can be categorized into specific groups either through command line flags or by editing the agent in the user interface (UI). These groups play a crucial role during the execution of operations, guiding the framework on which agents to target with specific abilities. Furthermore, the assignment to groups determines the categorization of an agent as either a red or a blue agent. Agents belonging to the blue group are exclusively accessible from the blue dashboard, while agents in other groups remain accessible from the red dashboard.

2) Abilities and adversaries: In the Caldera framework, an ability represents a specific implementation of a MITRE ATT&CK technique that agents can execute. These abilities encompass crucial information, including:

– Commands slated for execution
– Compatible platforms and executors (e.g., PowerShell, Windows Command Shell, Bash)
– Payloads to be included
– Reference to a module

Adversary profiles, on the other hand, aggregate various abilities, showcasing tactics, TTPs associated with a specific threat actor. The selection of an adversary profile dictates the abilities that an agent will execute during an operation. For instance, the image below illustrates the abilities listed under the Alice 2.0 adversary profile, with each ability linked to a MITRE ATT&CK tactic and the corresponding techniques slated for execution.

3) Operations: As the nomenclature implies, operations within Caldera involve the execution of abilities on specific agent groups. The definition of adversary profiles dictates the set of abilities to be executed, while agent groups determine which agents will perform these abilities.

During execution, the planner functionality enables the determination of the sequence in which abilities are executed. Notable examples include:

Atomic: Abilities are executed based on the atomic ordering, aligning with the principles of atomic red team.

Batch: All abilities are executed simultaneously.

Buckets: Abilities are grouped and executed according to their ATT&CK tactic.

This planner feature affords users control over the execution order, providing variability during operations.

In addition to the aforementioned terminologies, comprehension of the following concepts is imperative for configuring an operation:

Fact: Identifiable information about the target machine, crucial for the proper execution of certain abilities. Facts are sourced or acquired by previous abilities.

Obfuscators: Configurations specifying the obfuscation of each command before execution by the agent.

Jitter: The frequency at which agents check in with the Caldera server.

4)Plugins: Given its open-source nature, Caldera experiences expansion through various plugins, enhancing the framework's core functionalities. Users have access to several default plugins embedded within Caldera for use in adversary emulation exercises. A few noteworthy examples include – **Sandcat –** One of the agents integrated into Caldera, offering the capability for extension and customization through this functionality.

Training: A gamified certification course designed to facilitate the learning of Caldera.

Response: An autonomous incident response plugin, which will be elaborated on in subsequent tasks.

Human: Allows users to simulate "human" activity, introducing a benign and realistic element to the environment.

Caldera for OT purpose: An extension of the core functionality tailored for integration into the OT environment. Figure 7.4 shows the block diagram.

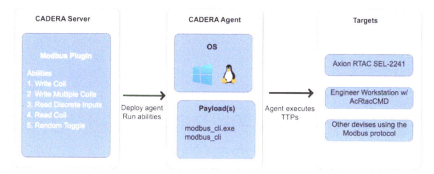

Figure 7.4 Block diagram.

7.4.5.3 Tactics and techniques used in operation OT Down.

In the orchestrated operation OT Down, the strategic focus was directed toward the deliberate deployment of tactics and techniques across various stages of the kill chain. The initiation of the operation involved the first stage access, where a spear phishing attachment was employed, executed through the phishing [T1566] tactic. Subsequently, the command and control stage was marked by the establishment of communication with a C2 server, utilizing the C2 server communication [T1043] technique.

The reconnaissance phase honed in on point & tag identification [T0861], employing specific techniques such as Modbus read coils, Modbus read holding registers, and Modbus read input registers to glean critical information. The weaponization stage, with a focus on the manipulation of control [T0831] tactic, saw the implementation of Modbus write multiple coils and Modbus write multiple registers for impactful actions.

As the operation progressed into the delivery phase, the manipulation of control [T0831] tactic persisted, introducing Modbus fuzz coils and Modbus fuzz registers to augment the attack's effectiveness.

The overarching objectives of this engagement were centered on the identification of system misconfigurations and network vulnerabilities, evaluation of the overall security posture and response mechanisms, and an assessment of the potential impact through data destruction and endpoint denial of service. This comprehensive approach facilitated an in-depth exploration of potential vulnerabilities within the operational technology environment.

7.4.5.4 Initial access

As illustrated in the Figure 7.5, the adversaries identified an external position vis-à-vis the architecture. Following a thorough enumeration process, they

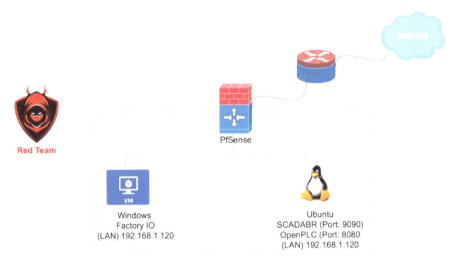

Figure 7.5 The proposed Laboratory Architecture.

determined that the most effective ingress point into the factory involved employing vishing and phishing techniques. This strategy involved contacting an individual employed by the target enterprise, masquerading as an authoritative figure informing them of the need to update the company's software in alignment with new policies. Subsequently, the attackers dispatched an email containing instructions for the software update via command line interface (CLI).

In the subsequent phase, the attackers sent an email to the employee, embedding commands to deploy a Caldera agent on their machine. This agent, once activated, would afford the attackers initial access, enabling the execution of multiple attacks through Caldera on the compromised agent.

7.4.5.5 Command and control establishment

In the subsequent stage, the red team dispatched an email to the targeted employee, incorporating instructions for deploying a Caldera agent on their machine. Upon activation, this agent provided the attackers with initial access, facilitating the execution of a series of attacks through Caldera on the compromised agent.

7.4.5.6 Operation guidelines

Adhering to the outlined methodology covered in the preceding tasks, consider the following guidelines (Figure 7.6):

7.4 Experiments   205

Figure 7.6   Phishing mail.

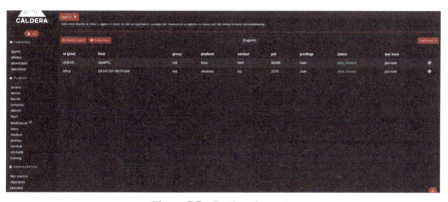

Figure 7.7   Deployed agents.

Initiate the creation of a new threat profile, incorporating all tactics, TTPs mentioned earlier.

Establish a connection to the target machine utilizing an agent, as shown in Figure 7.7.

Commence the emulation of the threat profile and carefully observe the execution of each technique.

Thoroughly document and review the obtained results.

7.4.5.7 Operation guidelines

Our red team engagement concluded with success. Effectively navigating through the network infrastructure (Figure 7.8), we achieved access to the factory premises, resulting in the cessation of the production chain, as shown in Figure 7.9.

Figure 7.8 Adversary Profiles.

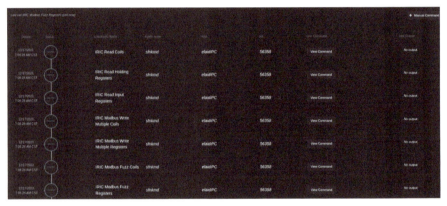

Figure 7.9 Operation results.

7.5 Discussion

In the face of escalating cyber threats targeting OT environments, our red teaming engagement plays a crucial role in strengthening our defenses. Faced with the growing risks to OT systems, our overarching project goal was to simulate attacks, identify vulnerabilities, and bolster the security of our industrial systems.

During Phase 1, we meticulously established an ICS/OT environment, leveraging virtualization technologies and intricately configuring components to create a robust testing ground. This foundational step paved the way for practical cybersecurity testing and logic programming within a simulated industrial setting.

Moving into Phase 2, our red team campaign for the ICS/OT environment unfolded with a specific mission: gaining access to the OT network and assessing the resilience of our defenses by orchestrating simulated damage to the factory. This adversarial emulation mirrored real-world threats, providing invaluable insights for defense fortification, malware detection, employee training enhancement, and strategic counteraction of APT tactics.

Guided by the red team kill-chain, a structured cybersecurity model, our methodology systematically deconstructed attack structures into distinct phases. This approach offered a nuanced understanding of the intricacies of attacks and the tactics employed by adversaries at each stage. The integration of the MITRE ATT&CK framework further enhanced our adversary emulation, delivering a structured kill chain for a comprehensive assessment.

7.6 Conclusion

As we conclude our examination, the insights and knowledge gained from red teaming within operational technology domains are crucial for refining OT security strategies. Our dedication to advancing cybersecurity practices and fostering a culture of perpetual enhancement underpins our commitment to safeguarding vital systems. The intelligence gathered from our research efforts and practical simulations will significantly bolster our defenses, ensuring our infrastructure's integrity amidst the dynamic and complex threats faced by industrial systems. This dedication to security is not just about preventing breaches but about fostering a resilient and responsive environment that can adapt to and repel cyber threats. Future endeavors will delve deeper into refining the red team methodologies and adversary emulation techniques that have been developed. The primary focus will be to enhance the simulated ICS/OT environment to more closely mirror the complexities of real-world industrial networks. The aim is to stress-test and solidify the resilience of our cybersecurity defenses further. Additionally, we will seek to expand our arsenal of tactics, techniques, and procedures within the red team kill-chain to stay ahead of the ever-evolving threat landscape. The incorporation of the latest advancements in the MITRE ATT&CK framework will be pivotal in this effort. By doing so, we will continue to provide critical insights that contribute to the robust fortification of defense mechanisms, the detection of sophisticated malware, and the effective training of cybersecurity personnel to counter APT more efficiently.

References

[1] Y. Maleh, "IT/OT convergenc.e and cyber security," *Computer Fraud & Security*, vol. 2021, no. 12, pp. 13–16, Dec. 2021, doi:10.1016/S1361-3723(21)00129-9.

[2] Y. Maleh, S. Lakkineni, L. Tawalbeh, and A. A. AbdEl-Latif, "Blockchain for Cyber-Physical Systems: Challenges and Applications," in *Advances in Blockchain Technology for Cyber Physical Systems*, Y. Maleh, L. Tawalbeh, S. Motahhir, and A. S. Hafid, Eds., Cham: Springer International Publishing, 2022, pp. 11–59. doi:10.1007/978-3-030-93646-4_2.

[3] A. H. Maleh Yassine, Mohammad Shojaafar, Ashraf Darwish, "Cybersecurity and Privacy in Cyber-Physical Systems," *CRC press*, 2019, [Online]. Available: https://www.crcpress.com/Cybersecurity-and-Privacy-in-Cyber-Physical-Systems/Maleh/p/book/9781138346673

[4] B. E. Strom, A. Applebaum, D. P. Miller, K. C. Nickels, A. G. Pennington, and C. B. Thomas, "Mitre att&ck: Design and philosophy," in *Technical report*, The MITRE Corporation, 2018.

[5] J. P. Farwell and R. Rohozinski, "Stuxnet and the Future of Cyber War," *Survival (Lond)*, vol. 53, no. 1, pp. 23–40, Feb. 2011, doi:10.1080/00396338.2011.555586.

[6] J. Cervini, A. Rubin, and L. Watkins, "Don't drink the cyber: Extrapolating the possibilities of Oldsmar's water treatment cyberattack," in *International Conference on Cyber Warfare and Security*, Academic Conferences International Limited, 2022, pp. 19–25.

[7] T. J. OConnor, "HELO DarkSide: Breaking Free From Katas and Embracing the Adversarial Mindset in Cybersecurity Education," in *Proceedings of the 53rd ACM Technical Symposium on Computer Science Education - Volume 1*, in SIGCSE 2022. New York, NY, USA: Association for Computing Machinery, 2022, pp. 710–716. doi:10.1145/3478431.3499404.

[8] NIST, "Framework for Improving Critical Infrastructure Cybersecurity, Version 1.1," Gaithersburg, MD, Apr. 2018. doi:10.6028/NIST.CSWP.04162018.

[9] D. J. Lonsdale, "Britain's Emerging Cyber-Strategy," *The RUSI Journal*, vol. 161, no. 4, pp. 52–62, Jul. 2016, doi:10.1080/03071847.2016.1232880.

[10] C. I. Cybersecurity, "Framework for improving critical infrastructure cybersecurity," URL:https://nvlpubs.nist.gov/nistpubs/CSWP/NIST.CSWP, vol. 4162018, 2018.

[11] G. A. O. W. D. C, "Critical Infrastructure Protection: Additional Actions Needed to Identify Framework Adoption and Resulting Improvements," 2020.

[12] J. R. Westby, "Governance of cybersecurity: 2015 report," *Report, Georgia Tech Information Security Center, Atlanta*, 2015.

[13] M. Bristow, "A sans 2021 survey: Ot/ics cybersecurity," *eng. In*, 2021.

[14] W. A. Conklin, "IT vs. OT Security: A Time to Consider a Change in CIA to Include Resilienc," in *2016 49th Hawaii International Conference on System Sciences (HICSS)*, 2016, pp. 2642–2647. doi:10.1109/HICSS.2016.331.

[15] J.-G. Song, J.-W. Lee, C.-K. Lee, K.-C. Kwon, and D.-Y. Lee, "A cyber security risk assessment for the design of I&C systems in nuclear power plants," *Nuclear engineering and technology*, vol. 44, no. 8, pp. 919–928, 2012.

[16] G. Murray, M. N. Johnstone, and C. Valli, "The convergence of IT and OT in critical infrastructure," pp. 149–155, 2017, doi:10.4225/75/5a84f7b595b4e.

[17] W. Knowles, J. M. Such, A. Gouglidis, G. Misra, and A. Rashid, "Assurance Techniques for Industrial Control Systems (ICS)," in *Proceedings of the First ACM Workshop on Cyber-Physical Systems-Security and/or PrivaCy*, in CPS-SPC '15. New York, NY, USA: Association for Computing Machinery, 2015, pp. 101–112. doi:10.1145/2808705.2808710.

[18] D. R. dos Santos, M. Dagrada, and E. Costante, "Leveraging operational technology and the Internet of things to attack smart buildings," *Journal of Computer Virology and Hacking Techniques*, vol. 17, no. 1, pp. 1–20, 2021, doi:10.1007/s11416-020-00358-8.

[19] A. Staves, A. Gouglidis, and D. Hutchison, "An Analysis of Adversary-Centric Security Testing within Information and Operational Technology Environments," *Digital Threats*, vol. 4, no. 1, Mar. 2023, doi: 10.1145/3569958.

8

Demystifying the Role of Publicly Available Up-to-Date Benchmark Intrusion Datasets: A Case Study of Web Security

Oumaima Chakir and Yassine Sadqi

Laboratory LIMIATI FPBM, USMS University, Morocco
E-mail: oumaima.chakirfpb@usms.ac.ma; y.sadqi@usms.ma

Abstract

With the proliferation of web application usage, the danger of web-based attacks has also increased. Thus, various machine learning (ML)-based web application firewalls (WAFs) have been proposed to enhance the security of web applications. Although the vast majority of studies focus on investigating algorithms that can improve detection performance, a few studies have been devoted to evaluating the reliability of benchmark datasets in the context of web security. To fill this gap, this article provides valuable information about the publicly available web benchmark datasets to beginner web security researchers by exploring (1) the role of benchmark datasets in developing ML-based WAF, (2) the relation between benchmark datasets and ML-based WAF's performance, (3) the shortcomings of the currently available web-based attack datasets, and (4) the primary factors to consider while assembling appropriate benchmark datasets for ML-based WAF evaluation. The results of this study highlighted the need for up-to-date and representative benchmark datasets for ML-based WAFs evaluation since the currently available datasets are obsolete and do not meet the current-world web security.

Keywords: Benchmark datasets, machine learning, web application firewall (WAF).

8.1 Introduction

With the increased Internet use, many organizations switched to web applications to offer their services, such as e-commerce and education, to get closer to their clients with less effort. Furthermore, this change has dramatically changed people's lives, allowing them to stay online every time and anywhere. Also, the number of attacks targeting web applications has become huge and more complex (Oumaima & et al. 2021) (Chakir O et al. 2023) (Sadqi Y. & Maleh Y., 2022). A WAF is a web security system that aims to detect and protect web apps from attacks by intercepting and analyzing HTTP and HTTPs traffic (Chakir O. et al., 2023a). Over the years, WAFs have evolved from WAF-based signature and anomaly detection approaches to WAF-based ML techniques to protect web apps from continuously growing attacks. To overcome the security issues of WAF-based signature and anomaly approaches (Oumaima Chakir, et al., 2021) (Chakir, O. et al., 2023b) (Sadqi, Y. & Mekkaoui M., 2021), researchers have turned to ML techniques in the hopes of developing efficient WAFs capable of detecting both known and unknown web-based attacks with a low false-positive rate (FPR) and false-negative rate (FNR). However, due to privacy issues, the research community struggles to find up-to-date and representative benchmark datasets to evaluate the quantified quality of their proposed ML-based WAFs (Chakir, O. et al., 2023b). In the web security field, there are very few benchmark datasets for ML-based WAFs evaluation. Two of the most popular datasets with many published works explored in the web security field are the ECML/PKDD 2007 and the CSIC HTTP 2010. In the context of network security, many researchers have investigated the role of benchmark datasets when building network-based attack detection systems. To the best of our knowledge, this is the first study that investigates the reliability of benchmark datasets in the context of web security. The authors of this study emphasize the importance of using up-to-date and representative benchmark datasets while developing effective ML-based WAFs to prevent the ever-increasing number of cyberattacks targeting web applications. Mainly, the authors describe the role of benchmark datasets in developing ML-based WAF and the relationship between ML-based WAF's performance and the dataset's quality. To highlight the need for creating new benchmark datasets for web security, the authors investigated the most used and up-to-date benchmark datasets, such as ECML/PKDD 2007, HTTP CSIC 2010, CIC-IDS 2017, CIC DoS 2017, CSE-CIC-IDS 2018, and CIC-DDoS 2019.

Section 8.2 presents a background of web application security, and Section 8.3 presents the related works. The role of benchmark datasets and the relation between datasets and ML-based WAF's performance are described in Section 8.4. Section 8.5 presents a taxonomy of the most used evaluation metrics. Section 8.6 discusses the advantages and disadvantages of the most widely used and publicly available datasets for the ML-based WAF's evaluation. Section 8.7 discusses the limitations of the current available benchmark datasets for web security. Section 8.8 presents the main challenges that impede the creation of representative benchmark datasets and the primary factors to consider while assembling appropriate datasets for ML-based WAF evaluation. Section 8.9 is dedicated to the conclusion and future work.

8.2 Web Application Security

Web applications have become one of the most popular and commonly used communication and information-sharing platforms. According to (Shahid, W. B. et al., 2022), the number of websites has topped 1.7 billion and continues to increase. Multiple web applications have been developed in various industries to improve people's lives, including e-commerce, online banking, and e-governance. Due to their prevalence, online apps have become an attractive target for the community of attackers who actively exploit their weaknesses to propagate malware, steal sensitive data, insert unauthorized information, conduct fraud, affect the availability of web apps, and so on (Oumaima Chakir, et al., 2021) (Sadqi Y. & Maleh Y., 2022). Web-based attacks are the most common cyberattacks, occurring every 39 seconds (Shahid, W. B. et al., 2022).

A statistical analysis of web application threats and vulnerabilities for 2020–2021 (Technologie s.d.) found that 84% of online apps were vulnerable to unauthorized access. In 5% of cases, the target site was fully controlled. In addition, in 91% of online apps, sensitive data was compromised, and in 98% of web apps, attackers were able to launch attacks against users. These attacks could spread malware, redirect to a harmful site, etc. Seventy-two percent of vulnerabilities are attributable to defects in the coding of web apps, and 15% of vulnerable web apps share vulnerabilities with high severity out of the total number of vulnerabilities discovered. Web applications are vulnerable and valuable targets for attackers because of several important reasons: (1) the open nature of online apps and their widespread use in the delivery of vital services; (2) most developers and administrators of online apps lack security knowledge because they prioritize the delivery of features and the development of a large number of apps ahead of the development of safe web apps; (3) many reports of security vulnerabilities have been exploited successfully, and there are also open-source attack tools like OWASP ZAP, Burp Suit, and Kali Linux that make it easier for attackers to get in; and (4) constraints imposed by both time and finances on web app developers. According to the OWASP Top 10 2021 (OWASP s.d.), web application vulnerabilities are categorized into 10 main categories that present a significant challenge to security professionals.

8.2.1 Broken access control (A01)

Security flaws that result in failed access control have climbed to the top spot from fifth place in the OWASP Top 10 for 2017. 94.5% of web applications have been found to have security flaws that allow attackers to do prohibited actions such as change, disruption, deletion of data, or access to a user's personal information without permission. This kind of vulnerability exists in web apps because they were not designed well, access control and rights were hard coded, and security best practices were not followed during the software development life cycle, and uncontrolled redirection of website pages (Gupta, C. et al., 2022) (Hassan, M. et al., 2018). The following are some solutions to prevent this type of vulnerability: With the exception of public resources, all resources should be denied by default, (2) model access controls should ensure record ownership rather than allowing any user to add, read, modify, or delete any record, and (3) APIs should only accept a limited number of requests within a given time period (OWASP s.d.).

8.2.2 Cryptographic failures (A02)

In the OWASP Top 10 for 2017, this is known as "Sensitive Data Exposure" and refers to the failure of protecting data with reliable cryptography, such as using old cryptographic algorithms and bad server certificates. The following are some solutions to prevent this kind of vulnerability: (1) ensure that all cryptographic algorithms, protocols, and keys are current and of high quality, (2) determine which data, according to privacy regulations, legal standards, or business reasons, is considered sensitive, and avoid storing sensitive data unless it is necessary, and (3) encrypt all sensitive information (OWASP s.d.).

8.2.3 Injection (A03)

The injection vulnerability is now ranked third on the OWASP Top 10 2021 list. It is a type of security hole where harmful code can be inserted into query fields or other similar places. The execution of this code enables an attacker to access the whole database of the web application without the necessary authorization. Web applications are prone to these types of attacks due to insufficient or absent user input data validation. Structured Query Language (SQL), Not Only SQL (NoSQL), Operating System (OS) commands, object-relational mapping (ORM), Lightweight Directory Access Protocol (LDAP), and expression language or object graph navigation library injections are often used. To avoid injection attacks, data must be segregated from queries and actions (OWASP s.d.).

8.2.4 Insecure design (A04)

A new category highlights the risks of design and architectural flaws, advocating for greater use of threat modeling, secure design patterns, and reference architectures. This issue often arises due to insufficient business risk profiling during software or system development, failing to determine the required security level. To address this, take these steps: (1) follow a secure development lifecycle for assessing security and privacy, and (2) utilize threat modeling for critical elements like authentication, access control, and critical flows.

8.2.5 Security misconfiguration (A05)

This vulnerability moved up from sixth place in the previous OWASP Top 10 edition to fifth place in the current edition. According to (OWASP s.d.), 90% of web applications were tested for some form of misconfiguration, which proves the lack of security knowledge of web application developers. Web applications are susceptible to this type of vulnerability if: (1) unneeded features are activated, such as useless ports, services, pages, accounts, or privileges, (2) outdated or vulnerable software is used, (3) default accounts and their passwords remain activated and unchanged, and (4) error handling reveals stack traces or other excessively informative error messages to users, such as the web server's type and version. A secure installation process should be put in place to prevent this flaw (OWASP s.d.).

8.2.6 Vulnerable and outdated components (A06)

This vulnerability moved up from ninth place in the previous OWASP Top 10 edition to fifth place in the current edition. It was known as "Using

Components with Known Vulnerabilities." It refers to the use of obsolete or insecure components, such as operating systems, web/application servers, database management systems (DBMS), libraries, and APIs. The following are some preventative measures for this vulnerability: (1) remove any web app dependencies, features, components, or files that are no longer required; (2) only obtain components from official sources and through secure links; (3) sign up for email notifications about security flaws in used components; and (4) constantly check sources such as common vulnerabilities and exposures (CVEs) and the national vulnerability database (NVD) for used component vulnerabilities (OWASP s.d.).

8.2.7 Identification and authentication failures (A07)

It was known as "Broken Authentication" in the previous version of the OWASP Top 10 list, and it refers to a flaw in the authentication process. According to (OWASP s.d.), web apps are susceptible to this flaw if they allow automated attacks such as credential stuffing or brute force, allow default, weak, or well-known passwords, use ineffective credential recovery and forgot-password processes, store passwords in plain text, encrypted, or weakly hashed, expose session identifiers in the URL, and reuse session identifiers after successful login. The following are some preventative measures for this vulnerability (OWASP s.d.): (1) use a multi-factor authentication process to prevent automated attacks; (2) limit the time between failed login attempts; (3) log all failures and notify administrators when automated attacks are detected; and (4) session IDs should be securely maintained and invalidated after logout and absolute timeouts.

8.2.8 Software and data integrity failures (A08)

It is a new category that focuses on software and data integrity errors that may be traced back to unprotected code and insecure infrastructure. The following are some solutions to prevent this kind of vulnerability: (1) use digital signatures or other similar mechanisms to ensure that the software or data is from the expected source and has not been tampered with; (2) ensure that libraries and dependencies consume trusted repositories; and (3) employ a security tool like OWASP Dependency Check to check for known vulnerabilities in the software's components (OWASP s.d.).

8.2.9 Security logging and monitoring failures (A09)

In the 2017 edition of the OWASP Top 10, this category is recognized as insufficient logging and monitoring, ascending from the tenth to the ninth rank. Its breadth has been extended to encompass diverse types of failures. Nevertheless, deficiencies within this category can notably impact visibility, incident alerting, and forensic procedures. The absence of robust logging and monitoring hinders the timely detection of security breaches. Here are several proactive measures to address this vulnerability: (1) ensure proper encoding of log data to thwart injections or attacks on logging and monitoring systems; (2) confirm logs are formatted for seamless consumption by log management solutions; and (3) guarantee that all instances of login failures, access control issues, and server-side input validation failures are logged with adequate user context for identifying malicious accounts and retain them for a duration conducive to subsequent forensic analysis.

8.2.10 Server-side request forgery (SSRF) (A10)

With the prevalence of convenient features in modern web apps, fetching URLs has become a common occurrence. Consequently, the incidence of SSRF is on the rise, primarily due to the complexity of architectures and the widespread use of cloud services. SSRF vulnerabilities manifest when a web application retrieves a remote resource without adequately validating the user-provided URL. This allows attackers to manipulate the application into sending a crafted request to an unexpected destination. To mitigate such vulnerabilities, it is advisable to thoroughly sanitize and validate all input data from clients and disable HTTP redirections (OWASP s.d.).

8.3 Related Work

The field of intrusion detection constitutes a pivotal and evolving realm of research. In 2020, the authors in Thakkar, A & Lohiya, R., (2020) delved into various benchmark datasets and research advancements employed for evaluation, with a particular emphasis on the CIC-IDS-2017 and CSE-CIC-IDS-2018 datasets. Their primary objective was to elucidate the advantages inherent in utilizing the CIC-IDS-2017 and CSE-CIC-IDS-2018 datasets as opposed to antiquated counterparts. Similarly, in 2022, the authors in Thakkar, A & Lohiya, R., (2022) conducted an extensive survey examining the utility of machine learning and deep learning techniques in the field of intrusion detection. Their study encompassed a variety of research papers published between 2008 and 2020. The authors highlighted challenges associated with 12 benchmark datasets, including DARPA, UNSW-NB15, and KDD CUP 99, compared to the CIC-IDS 2017 dataset. The authors in Yang,

Z. et al., (2022) conducted a systematic literature review of the existing detection and data processing methods, evaluation metrics, and datasets employed in anomaly-based network intrusion detection (ANND). To explore existing datasets in this domain, they examined 52 datasets, considering factors such as year of creation, creation method, data volume, annotation status, as well as the number of tags and download links associated with each dataset. Their findings revealed that despite being outdated, the KDD99 and NSL-KDD datasets were the most frequently utilized in ANND research. Likewise, the authors in Ahmetoglu, H & Das, R., (2022) conducted a thorough review of intrusion detection studies that centered on deep learning and machine learning techniques. They focused primarily on cyberattack types, learning models, and evaluation metrics. While they provided a concise overview of the most readily accessible datasets, they underscored the necessity for an up-to-date dataset due to the obsolescence of existing ones.

Unlike these works, the authors investigated the publicly available web benchmark datasets for beginner web security researchers by exploring: (1) the role of benchmark datasets in developing ML-based WAF, (2) the relation between benchmark datasets and ML-based WAF's performance, (3) the shortcomings of the currently available and most used web-based attack datasets, including ECML/PKDD 2007, HTTP CSIC 2010, CIC-IDS 2017, CIC DoS 2017, CSE-CIC-IDS 2018, CIC-DDoS 2019, and (4) the primary factors to consider while assembling appropriate benchmark datasets for ML-based WAF evaluation.

8.4 Benchmark Datasets and ML-based WAF's Effectiveness

Benchmark dataset is a crucial component in the process of constructing efficient ML-based WAF. As it is a representation of legitimate and malicious traffic targeting web applications (Tama, B. A. et al., 2020). Generally, a dataset is a collection of data used to help the learning model identify the relationships between input features and output classes and construct a generalized classification model that can accurately predict the class of unseen data. According to the learning technique employed (supervised or unsupervised learning), the dataset is categorized into two categories: the labeled dataset, in which the output classes of the input data are known (such as legitimate or malicious classes), and the unlabeled dataset, in which the output classes are unknown. In this study, the authors focus on the labeled

8.4 Benchmark Datasets and ML-based WAF's Effectiveness

datasets. During the construction process of an ML-based WAF, three types of data can be distinguished (see Figure 8.1). (1) The training data is a subset of the dataset used to train the learning model. It contains both input data and the corresponding desired output class. In this phase, the ML-based WAF uses the training data to learn to distinguish between normal and dangerous online traffic patterns and to build a generalized classification model that can accurately classify online traffic as benign or malicious. (2) Validation data is a different subset of the dataset used to tune the model's hyperparameters to improve its generalization performance and avoid overfitting (Viegas, E. K. et al., 2017). Similarly, to the training data, the validation data includes both input and output classes. (3) Testing data is another different subset of the dataset used to test and evaluate the overall performance of the ML-based WAF on unseen data once the training and validation processes are complete (Viegas, E. K. et al., 2017). As a result, the performance of any ML-based WAF (e.g., accuracy, FPR, and FNR) is directly dependent on the quality of

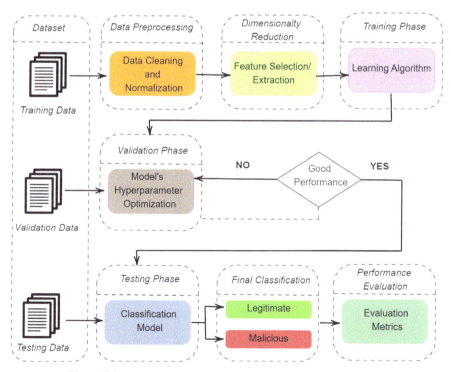

Figure 8.1 Benchmark dataset and ML-based WAF construction.

the used datasets (Viegas, E. K. et al., 2017) (Díaz, V. J. E. et al., 2020). The biases and limits of the datasets used will have a direct impact on the learning model's predictions. Thus, ML-based WAF trained on low-quality data may be severely compromised (Kenyon, A. et al., 2020).

8.5 Evaluation Metrics

After completing the model training, the final step involves evaluating the model on unseen data to assess its effectiveness, utilizing various metrics. Evaluation metrics play a crucial role in assessing the performance of ML-based WAF. They offer a quantitative measure of the WAF's effectiveness, shedding light on its capacity to classify normal and abnormal behavior accurately. Moreover, they play a vital role in assisting cybersecurity professionals by elucidating the trade-off between correctly classified and misclassified instances and facilitating efforts to refine and optimize the WAF's performance. Accuracy, recall, precision, F-value, false-positive rate (FPR), false-negative rate (FNR), specificity, misclassification error (MCE), and the area under the receiver operating characteristic (AUC-ROC) curve are the most known and used evaluation metrics (Chakir O et al., 2023) (Mukhaini, G. A et al., 2023) (Parhizkari, S., 2023) (Salih, A. A. et al., 2021). The computation of these metrics relies on a confusion matrix comprising four primary elements. (1) True negative (TN) represents the count of normal instances correctly classified by the model. (2) False negative (FN) indicates the count of malicious data misclassified as normal by the model. (3) True positive (TP) reflects the count of malicious activity accurately identified as attacks by the model. (4) False positive (FP) represents the count of normal instances misclassified as attacks by the classifier.

In this chapter, the authors categorize these evaluation metrics into three main categories, as follows.

8.5.1 System's overall performance evaluation

This category encompasses evaluation metrics that provide an overview of the overall performance of the ML-based WAF, considering both normal and attack instances:

- Accuracy: One of the most commonly used metrics in the literature represents the ratio of correctly classified instances to the overall number of instances. However, relying solely on accuracy to assess the model's effectiveness is insufficient, especially when dealing with imbalanced

datasets as a model could achieve high accuracy by simply predicting the majority class.
- AUC-ROC curve: Represents the trade-off between True Positive Rate (TPR) and FPR at different threshold settings for the model's predictions. It is particularly useful when using an imbalanced dataset because it evaluates a model's performance across various trade-offs between sensitivity and specificity. A higher value of AUC indicates that the model achieves a high TPR while maintaining a low FPR across all threshold settings, proving the model's ability to distinguish between normal and attack instances.
- MCE: Measure the number of instances that are misclassified by the model, including attack and normal instances. However, it may not be the optimal choice for imbalanced datasets, as it might not adequately represent the model's performance, particularly when the focus is on the minority class (typically the attack class in the majority of cases).

8.5.2 System's detection ability evaluation

This category represents the ML-based WAF's ability to detect both normal and attack instances. It can further be divided into two sub-categories, each focusing on a particular class.

8.5.2.1 Attack detection ability evaluation

This sub-category focuses on evaluating ML-based WAF's ability to correctly classify attack instances:
- Recall: Also referred to as sensitivity, detection rate, or true-positive rate, quantifies the ratio of correctly classified attacks by the model. It reflects the model's proficiency in detecting attacks and avoiding false negatives.
- Precision: Unlike recall, this metrics measures the ratio of correctly classified attacks among all instances classified as attacks by the classifier.
- F1-score: Also known as F-value or F-measure serves as the harmonic mean of precision and recall, offering a balanced metric that accounts for both false positives and false negatives. This metric proves valuable, especially in scenarios with imbalanced datasets, where it ensures the model's proficiency in accurately identifying instances from the minority class is duly considered.
- FNR: Measures the proportion of attack instances that are incorrectly classified as normal by the classifier.

8.5.2.2 Normal detection ability evaluation

This sub-category focuses on evaluating ML-based WAF's ability to correctly classify normal instances:

- Specificity: Also known as the true-negative rate measures the ratio of correctly classified normal instances among all instances classified as normal by the classifier. A high specificity value indicates that the model is effective at correctly identifying negative instances, reducing the rate of false positives.
- FPR: Measures the proportion of legitimate instances that the classifier incorrectly classifies as attacks. It offers insight into the classifier's ability to distinguish between normal and attack instances. A high FPR suggests that the classifier is misclassifying a significant number of legitimate instances as attacks.

8.5.3 System's availability evaluation

- Training time: Represents the duration taken by the model to learn the patterns and features within the training data. In real-time or near-real-time scenarios, it is a crucial factor in developing ML-based WAF. Minimizing training time is essential for swiftly deploying updated models to maintain effective security. Consequently, the choice of a learning model should strike a balance between the requirement for accurate detection and the practical constraints of available time and resources to ensure the web application's availability.
- Prediction time: Also known as detection time refers to the duration takes the trained model to make predictions on unseen data. It is a critical consideration, especially in real-time or near-real-time applications, where quick decision-making based on model predictions is essential.

8.6 Publicly Available Benchmarking Datasets and Web Security

In this section, the authors discuss the advantages and disadvantages of the most used and publicly available benchmark datasets in the context of web security. These datasets are presented in chronological order.

8.6.1 ECML/PKDD 2007

The most known and used benchmark dataset that was generated as a part of the ECML/PKDD discovery challenge. It is developed by monitoring realistic traffic, which is subsequently anonymized by removing sensitive information. This masking procedure involved renaming every URL, parameter name, and value with strings that were produced at random. It contains 35,006 requests classified as legitimate and 15,110 requests classified as seven different types of attacks (Nguyen.TCH et al., 2022). The following are the main shortcomings of this dataset:

- Outdated dataset: It is 16 years old now, which means it doesn't include modern web-based attacks or represent current real-world online app complexity.
- Anomaly dataset: This dataset includes only legitimate data for the training phase, which makes it unsuitable for ML-based WAF. Thus, researchers have to construct malicious data from that reserved for testing.
- Class imbalance: This dataset suffers from a high-class imbalance since over 66% of the records are classified as legitimate. Unbalanced data in the ML field can lead to a bias in favor of the majority class (the benign class in this case) and inaccurately represent the minority class (the malicious class in this case). Thus, researchers have to use sampling techniques such as oversampling or undersampling to mitigate the impact of this imbalance.
- The lack of HTTPs traffic: This dataset only includes HTTP traffic, which means that an ML-based WAF built using this dataset won't be able to identify malicious traffic sent over the encrypted HTTPS protocol.

8.6.2 HTTP CSIC 2010

A benchmark dataset was created to construct and evaluate ML-based WAF. It includes 36,000 valid requests and over 25,000 web-based attacks generated automatically from an e-commerce web shopping app. It is divided into three files (Giménez C. T. et al, 2010): One with legitimate traffic for training, another with legitimate traffic for testing, and a third with malicious traffic for testing. The following are the main shortcomings of this dataset:

- Outdated dataset: It is 13 years old now, which means it is unreliable for the current ML-based WAF performance evaluation.
- Anomaly dataset: This dataset includes only legitimate data for training.
- Only suitable for binary classification: Because the data in this dataset has been labeled as legitimate or malicious, it can only be used to solve problems involving binary classification.

- The lack of HTTPs traffic.
- Raw samples with improper encoding: This dataset includes some raw instances that were not encoded correctly. Thus, a new version of this dataset was created and given the name CSIC-2010v2 (Tama, B. A. et al., 2020) (Tekerek, 2021). However, the first version is still more widely used in literature than the second one.
- Class imbalance: The number of normal instances is higher than the attack instances.

8.6.3 CIC-IDS 2017

A benchmark dataset provided by the Canadian Institute of Cybersecurity (CIC) to evaluate the performance of ML-based intrusion detection systems (IDS). It consists of a five-day normal and attacks data capture distributed over eight files (CIC-IDS 2017 s.d.). In contrast to the ECML/PKDD 2007 and CISC HTTP 2010 datasets, the CIC-IDS 2017 dataset contains both network-based attacks and web-based attacks, which means that it can be used in the context of network and web security. In this chapter, the authors focus on web-based attacks captured on Thursday morning and Wednesday. However, the authors noticed that when researchers (Viegas, E. K. et al., 2017) use this dataset for ML-based WAF evaluation, they only use the web attacks captured on Thursday morning, ignoring the application layer Denial of Service (DoS) and Distributed Denial of Service (DDoS) attacks captured on Wednesday. The main advantages of this dataset are that it contains the most updated attack scenarios compared to the previous datasets and is suitable for both multi-class and binary classification. In addition, it includes real data obtained via emulated interactions in a secure environment. The following are the main shortcoming of this dataset:

- Outdated dataset: It is currently six years old and does not represent the current web-based attacks reality. Compared to the ECML/PKDD 2007 and HTTP CSIC 2010 datasets, the CIC-IDS 2017 is more recent.
- Insufficient web attack instances: The number of detected web-based attacks depends heavily on the quantity of representative malicious samples available in the dataset. This dataset contains only 21 SQL Injection (SQLI) instances, 652 Cross-site scripting (XSS) instances and 1507 brute force instances. It is more suitable for application layer DoS/DDoS attacks due to the large number of these attacks.

- High-class imbalance: Since the number of benign instances is higher than the number of attack instances, it is prone to a high-class imbalance.
- Include NAN and duplicate instances.
- Contains features that have a zero value across all rows: Bwd PSH Flags, Bwd URG Flags, Fwd Avg Bytes/Bulk, Fwd Avg Packets/Bulk, Fwd Avg Bulk/Rate, Bwd Avg Bytes/Bulk, Bwd Avg Packets/Bulk, Bwd Avg Bulk/Rate and Fwd Avg Bytes/Bulk.

8.6.4 CIC DoS 2017

A benchmark dataset provided by CIC to gain insights into the characteristics of HTTP-based application layer DoS attacks, contributing to the ongoing efforts to enhance the resilience of web application against such cyber threats (CIC DoS 2017 s.d.). It consists of 24 hours of network traffic with 114,493 normal and 61,751 attack instances with 80 features within a traditional network setting. It contains various web-based DoS attacks, including HULK, GoldenEye, DDoSSim, Slowloris, RUDY, Slowbody2, Slowheaders, and Slowread. Given that application layer DoS attacks manifest in both high-volume and low-volume forms; this dataset comprehensively addresses a diverse spectrum of application layer DoS attack variations. This includes flooding attacks marked by substantial request volumes and low-volume attacks strategically leveraging timing parameters or exploiting specific vulnerabilities in application-level protocols, with a specific focus on slow-rate attacks. It's essential to note some limitations of this dataset, including its outdated nature, its exclusive focus on web-based DoS/DDoS attacks, and its classification as an imbalanced dataset.

8.6.5 CSE-CIC-IDS 2018

It is a realistic benchmark dataset developed in collaboration between the communications security establishment (CSE) and the CIC. It is the most recent publicly available dataset consisting of 10-day normal and various web-based attacks traffic capture (CSE-CIC-IDS 2018 s.d.). It is an updated version of the CIC-IDS 2017 with an extended network architecture of simulated attacker and client machines on the Amazon Web Services (AWS) platform. It includes the same web-based attacks as the CIC-IDS 2017 dataset, in addition to DDoS LOIC-HTTP and HOIC attacks. Similar to the CIC-IDS 2017, this dataset can be applied to network and web security. Moreover, this dataset has the same shortcomings as CIC-IDS 2017.

8.6.6 CIC-DDoS 2019

Realistic and up-to-date benchmark dataset provided by CIC to facilitate research and development in the field of cybersecurity, enabling the evaluation of DDoS attack detection systems. This application layer DDoS attack dataset comprises 56,863 instances of normal traffic and 50,006,249 instances of attack traffic, with 88 distinct features. It encompasses 13 types of Distributed Denial of Service (DDoS) attacks, including Network Time Protocol (NTP), Domain Name System (DNS), LDAP, Microsoft SQL Server (MSSQL), Network Basic Input/Output System (NetBIOS), Simple Network Management Protocol (SNMP), Simple Service Discovery Protocol (SSDP), User Datagram Protocol (UDP), UDP-Lag, Web-DDoS, Synchronize (SYN) flood, Port Scan, and Trivial File Transfer Protocol (TFTP) attacks. It's noteworthy that the volume of traffic for WebDDoS is significantly lower, totaling 439 instances compared to others (CIC-DDoS 2019 s.d.). Despite being the most up-to-date dataset, it exhibits a tendency toward high data imbalance and is specifically designed for DDoS attack detection purposes. Table 8.1 presents characteristics of the most known and used publically available benchmark datasets.

8.7 Limitations of Current Web-based Attack Datasets

The lack of up-to-date and representative publicly available web-based attacks datasets is one of the significant challenges in web application security using ML techniques (Chakir.O et al, 2023) (Tama, B. A. et al., 2020) (Applebaum S. et al., 2021). Cybercriminals constantly improve themselves and the tools they use to devise new attack strategies that circumvent web-based attack detection and prevention systems and provide them with unauthorized access to web applications (Tama, B. A. et al., 2020)(Bhatnagar M. et al., 2022). Thus, the current benchmark datasets are inadequate to build efficient and secure ML-based WAFs able to detect the current complex web-based attacks because they are obsolete. The quantity and quality of available datasets are both severely limited and do not meet the current-world web security requirements (Tekerek, 2021) (Kilincer, I. F. et al, 2021). The last recently available dataset that contains various types of web-based attacks, CSE-CIC-IDS 2018, was developed in 2018, making it five years old. Consequently, the results achieved from ML-based WAF trained on these datasets are unrealistic for current web-based attacks. Therefore, they are unsuitable for real-world deployment (Viegas, E. K. et al., 2017). In the realm of web application security, the effectiveness of benchmark datasets extends

8.7 Limitations of Current Web-based Attack Datasets

Table 8.1 Characteristics of the most widely used publically available benchmark datasets.

Dataset name	ECML/PKDD 2007	HTTP CSIC 2010	CIC-IDS 2017	CIC DoS 2017	CSECICIDS 2018	CIC-DDoS 2019
Dataset type	Multiclass	Binary	Multiclass	Multiclass	Multiclass	Multiclass
Year of creation	2007	2010	2017	2017	2018	2019
Number of benign instances	35,006	36,000	608217	114,493	11272461	56,863
Number of malicious instances	15,110	25,000	254 852	61751	1919161	50,006,249
Labeled dataset	Yes	Yes	Yes	Yes	Yes	Yes
Separate train-test	Yes	Yes	No	No	No	No
Traffic type	Real	Emulated	Emulated	Emulated	Emulated	Emulated
Balanced	No	No	No	No	No	No
Attack types	SQLI, XSS, LDAP Injection, XPATH Injection, Path traversal, Command Execution, SSI	SQLI, XSS, buffer overflow, CRLF injection	SQLI, Brute Force, XSS, DoS Slow Loris, DoS Slow HTTP Test, DoS GoldenEye, DoS Hulk, and Heartbleed.	HULK, GoldenEye, DDoSSim, Slowloris, RUDY, Slowbody2, Slowheaders, and Slowread	SQLI, Brute Force, XSS, DDoS LOIC-HTTP and HOIC, DoS Slow Loris, DoS Slow HTTP Test, DoS GoldenEye, DoS Hulk	DDoS attacks, including NTP, DNS, LDAP, MSSQL, NetBIOS, SNMP, SSDP, UDP, UDP-Lag, WebDDoS, SYN, PortScan, and TFTP

(Continued)

Table 8.1 Continued.

Dataset name	ECML/PKDD 2007	HTTP CSIC 2010	CIC-IDS 2017	CIC DoS 2017	CSECICIDS 2018	CIC-DDoS 2019
Download's link	(ECML/PKDD 2007, 2007)	(Giménez C. T. et al., 2010)	(CIC-IDS 2017 s.d.)	(CIC DoS 2017 s.d.)	(CSE-CIC-IDS 2018 s.d.)	(CIC-DDoS 2019 s.d.)
Recent publishedworks	(Chakir, O. et al., 2023b) (Moradi, V. A. et al., 2019) (Betarte G. et al., 2018) (Nguyen.TCH et al., 2022)	(Chakir, O. et al., 2023b) (Moradi, V. A. et al., 2019) (Betarte G. et al., 2018) (Nguyen.TCH et al., 2022)	(Tama, B. A. et al., 2020) (Manimurugan, S. et al., 2020) (Surbhi, D. & Deepak, K., 2021) (Chakir, O. & Sadqi, Y., 2023)	((Ilango, H. S. et al., 2022) (Gogoi, B. & Ahmed, T, 2022) (Yungaicela-Naula. N. M. et al., 2021)	((Zuech, R. et al., 2021) (Richard Zuech et al., 2021) (Richard. Z. et al., 2021)	(Yungaicela-Naula. N. M. et al., 2021) (Akgun, D. et al., 2022) (Korium, M. S. et al., 2024)

beyond their age. Considering the diversity, complexity, and scalability of these datasets is imperative to ensure the robustness and adaptability of ML-based WAFs. Emphasizing diversity, benchmark datasets should encompass a wide range of web-based attacks, traffic patterns, and application behaviors, enabling ML models to gain a comprehensive understanding of real-world threats and effectively mitigate diverse security risks (Kenyon, A. et al., 2020) (El Sayed, M. S. et al., 2022). Additionally, dataset complexity is pivotal in preparing ML models to handle evolving attack strategies. Complex datasets equip WAFs with the agility and resilience necessary to counter novel threats. Moreover, the scalability of benchmark datasets is crucial in accommodating a growing volume of data and new types of attacks, supporting the continuous improvement and adaptation of ML-based WAFs to safeguard web applications against evolving security risks (Sharafaldin, 2018).

8.8 Toward Novel Up-to-Date Benchmark Datasets

Creating a suitable and representative benchmark dataset represents a significant challenge in itself (Viegas, E. K. et al., 2017) (Díaz, V. J. E. et al., 2020). The main ongoing challenges that impede the creation of such datasets for web security are as follows. (1) Real-world online traffic generation: the capacity to generate real web user behavior would help create datasets that better reflect realistic user interactions with a web application. To create such a dataset, a web application must be monitored to capture its real web user traffic. However, because of privacy concerns, it is not feasible to share this dataset with the web researcher's community. And this is the real reason behind the lack of realistic and representative benchmark datasets for the ML-based WAF's evaluation. Therefore, the anonymization of these datasets is crucial to safeguard privacy, which largely alters the ML-based WAF's performance (El Sayed, M. S. et al., 2022). (2) Continuous changes and growth of web-based attack scenarios: Every day, new web-based attacks are discovered, and the attackers' strategies change over time. Therefore, it cannot be assumed that the malicious online traffic behavior included in the dataset represent what would occur over time in a production web application. That's why the created dataset should be simple to update with newly discovered attacks and ensure the constructed ML-based WAF is up-to-date. It is essential to note that incorporating the OWASP Top 10, which outlines the critical risks faced by current web applications, into benchmark datasets can further enhance the relevance and effectiveness of ML-based WAFs in addressing contemporary security challenges. By aligning benchmark datasets with the

OWASP Top 10, ML models can be trained to specifically recognize and mitigate the types of threats that are most prevalent and impactful in today's web application landscape. This targeted approach ensures that the WAFs are well-equipped to address the most pressing security concerns faced by modern web applications, ultimately enhancing their ability to provide robust protection against current and emerging security threats. There are seven primary factors to consider while assembling appropriate benchmark datasets for ML-based WAF evaluation (Viegas, E. K. et al., 2017) (Díaz, V. J. E. et al., 2020):

- Realistic traffic: The generated dataset should contain real and specific traffic for the system to be protected, web application in our case, and represent the real traffic observed in real-world web environments. In addition, the dataset should contain both legitimate and malicious online traffic.
- Validity: The dataset should contain well-formed online traffic with all client and server communications.
- Labeled: Using a labeled dataset is of utmost priority in the construction and evaluation of ML-based WAF. Thus, each data instance from the dataset should be clearly labeled as legitimate or malicious to guarantee correct and accurate training.
- Ease to update: Every day, new services and attacks are discovered, which should be easily incorporated into the dataset.
- Excludes confidential data: The dataset should not contain sensitive information to ensure the safety of dataset sharing among researchers and help develop more suitable ML-based WAF for real-world deployment.
- Sufficient data volume: The dataset should contain enough data volume to train, validate, and test the classifier's performance.
- Correct implementation: During malicious data generation, it is necessary to use tools that follow well-known standards, which are auditable and can be evaluated.

8.9 Conclusion

Intelligent web application firewall is one of the most well-liked methods for securing web applications. Many researchers have developed various ML-based techniques for web-based attack detection. However, few studies have been devoted to evaluating the reliability of web benchmark datasets. In this chapter, the authors investigated the primary role of datasets in constructing

ML-based WAFs and describe the shortcomings of the most known and used benchmark datasets, such as ECML/PKDD 2007, HTTP CSIC 2010, CIC-IDS 2017, CIC DoS 2017, CSE-CICIDS 2018, and CIC-DDoS 2019 in the context of web security. The findings underscore a significant gap in the existing publicly available benchmark datasets widely employed in the literature, revealing their inadequacy for constructing efficient ML-based WAFs that align with contemporary web security standards. The critical analysis presented here emphasizes the pressing need for up-to-date and representative benchmark datasets tailored specifically for ML-based WAFs. Beyond age, the diversity, complexity, and scalability of benchmark datasets are crucial for ensuring the robustness and adaptability of ML-based WAFs. Datasets should encompass a wide range of web-based attacks, traffic patterns, and application behaviors to enable comprehensive threat understanding and mitigation. Complexity in datasets prepares WAFs to counter novel threats effectively, while scalability supports continuous improvement and adaptation to evolving security risks. Addressing these factors is essential for developing efficient and secure ML-based WAFs capable of effectively safeguarding web applications against evolving threats. In the future, the authors will propose novel up-to-date and representative benchmark datasets for web security, considering the seven primary dataset criteria presented in this work.

References

[1] Ahmetoglu, H, & Das, R. (2022). A comprehensive review on detection of cyber-attacks: Data sets, methods, challenges, and future research directions. (Elsevier, Éd.) *Internet of Things*, 100615.

[2] Akgun, D et al. (2022). A new DDoS attacks intrusion detection model based on deep learning for cybersecurity. (Elsevier, Éd.) *Computers & Security, 118*, 102748.

[3] Applebaum.S et al. (2021). Signature-based and machine-learning-based web application firewalls: A short survey. (Elsevier, Éd.) *Procedia Computer Science, 189*, 359-367.

[4] Betarte.G et al. (2018). Web Application Attacks Detection Using Machine Learning Techniques. (IEEE, Éd.) *17th IEEE International Conference on Machine Learning and Applications (ICMLA)*, 1065-1072.

[5] Bhatnagar.M et al. (2022). Web Intrusion Classification System using Machine Learning Approaches. *In 2022 International Symposium ELMAR*, 57-60.

[6] Chakir, O et al. (2023a). Evaluation of Open-source Web Application Firewalls for Cyber Threat Intelligence. *Big Data Analytics and Intelligent Systems for Cyber Threat Intelligence*, 9781003373384-3.

[7] Chakir, O, & Sadqi, Y. (2023). Detection of Web-Based Attacks using Tree-Based Learning Models: An Evaluation Study. (Springer, Éd.) *International Conference on Artificial Intelligence and Green Computing*, 163-170.

[8] Chakir.O et al. (2023b). An Empirical Assessment of Ensemble Methods and Traditional Machine Learning Techniques for Web-based Attack Detection in Industry 5.0. (Elsevier, Éd.) *Journal of King Saud University - Computer and Information Sciences*.

[9] *CIC DoS 2017*. (s.d.). Consulté le 1 26, 2024, sur unb: https://www.unb.ca/cic/datasets/dos-dataset.html

[10] *CIC-DDoS 2019*. (s.d.). Consulté le 1 27, 2024, sur unb: https://www.unb.ca/cic/datasets/ddos-2019.html

[11] *CIC-IDS 2017*. (s.d.). Consulté le December 29, 2023, sur UNB: https://www.unb.ca/cic/datasets/ids-2017.html

[12] *CSE-CIC-IDS 2018*. (s.d.). Consulté le December 29, 2023, sur UNB: https://www.unb.ca/cic/datasets/ids-2018.html

[13] Díaz V. J. E. et al. (2020). A methodology for conducting efficient sanitization of http training datasets. (Elsevier, Éd.) *Future Generation Computer Systems, 109*, 67-82.

[14] *ECML/PKDD 2007*. (2007). Consulté le December 29, 2023, sur https://gitlab.fing.edu.uy/gsi/web-application-attacks-datasets/-/tree/master/ecml_pkdd

[15] El Sayed, M. S. et al. (2022). A flow-based anomaly detection approach with feature selection method against ddos attacks in sdns. (IEEEXplore, Éd.) *IEEE Transactions on Cognitive Communications and Networking, 8(4)*, 1862-1880.

[16] Giménez C. T. et al. (2010). ńHTTP data set CSIC 2010.,ż. *Information Security Institute of CSIC (Spanish Research National Council)*.

[17] Gogoi, B., & Ahmed, T. (2022). HTTP Low and Slow DoS Attack Detection using LSTM based deep learning. *IEEE 19th India Council International Conference (INDICON)*, 1-6.

[18] Gupta, C et al. (2022). An Approach for Verification of Secure Access Control Using Security Pattern. (Hindawi, Éd.) *Wireless Communications and Mobile Computing*.

[19] Hassan, M et al. (2018). Quantitative assessment on broken access control vulnerability in web applications. *In International Conference on Cyber Security and Computer Science*.
[20] Ilango, H. S et al. (2022). A FeedForward–Convolutional Neural Network to Detect Low-Rate DoS in. (Elsevier, Éd.) *Engineering Applications of Artificial Intelligence, 114*, 105059.
[21] Kenyon. A et al. (2020). Are public intrusion datasets fit for purpose characterising the state of the art in intrusion event datasets. (Elsevier, Éd.) *Computers & Security, 99*, 102022.
[22] Kilincer.I. F et al. (2021). Machine learning methods for cyber security intrusion detection: Datasets and comparative study. (Elsevier, Éd.) *Computer Networks, 188,*, 107840,.
[23] Korium, M. S et al. (2024). Intrusion detection system for cyberattacks in the Internet of Vehicles environment. (Elsevier, Éd.) *Ad Hoc Networks, 153*, 103330.
[24] Manimurugan.S et al. (2020). Effective attack detection in internet of medical things smart environment using a deep belief neural network. (IEEE, Éd.) *IEEE Access, 8*, 77396-77404.
[25] Moradi.V.A et al. (2019). Leveraging deep neural networks for anomaly-based web application firewall. (W. O. Library, Éd.) *IET Information Security, 13(4)*, 352-361.
[26] Mukhaini, G. A et al. (2023). A Systematic Literature Review of Recent Lightweight Detection Approaches Leveraging Machine and Deep Learning Mechanisms in Internet of Things Networks. (Elsevier, Éd.) *Journal of King Saud University-Computer and Information Sciences*, 101866.
[27] Nguyen.TCH et al. (2022). Improving Web Application Firewalls with Automatic Language Detection. (Springer, Éd.) *SN Computer Science, 3(6)*, 446.
[28] Oumaima Chakir et al. (2021). Experimental study on the effectiveness of machine learning methods in web intrusion detection. (Springer, Éd.) *In Advances in Information, Communication and Cybersecurity: Proceedings of ICI2C'21*, pp. 486-494.
[29] *OWASP*. (s.d.). Consulté le December 29, 2023, sur OWASP Top 10 2021: https://owasp.org/www-project-top-ten/
[30] Parhizkari, S. (2023). Anomaly Detection in Intrusion Detection Systems. *intechopen*.

[31] Richard Z et al. (2021). Feature Popularity Between Different Web Attacks with Supervised Feature Selection Rankers. *20th IEEE International Conference on Machine Learning and Applications (ICMLA)*, 30-37.

[32] Richard Zuech et al,. (2021). Detecting SQL injection web attacks using ensemble learners and data sampling. (IEEE, Éd.) *In 2021 IEEE International Conference on Cyber Security and Resilience (CSR)*, 27-34.

[33] Sadqi. Y , & Maleh. Y. (2022). A systematic review and taxonomy of web applications threats. (T. &. Francis, Éd.) *Information Security Journal: A Global Perspective, vol. 31(1)*, pp. 1-27, 2022.

[34] Sadqi. Y, & Mekkaoui. M. (2021). Design Challenges and Assessment of Modern Web Applications Intrusion Detection and Prevention Systems (IDPS). (Springer, Éd.) *In Innovations in Smart Cities Applications Volume 4: The Proceedings of the 5th International Conference on Smart City Applications*, pp. 1087-1104.

[35] Salih, A. A et al. (2021). Evaluation of classification algorithms for intrusion detection system: A review. *Journal of Soft Computing and Data Mining, 2(1)*, 31-40.

[36] Shahid, W. B et al. (2022). An enhanced deep learning based framework for web attacks detection, mitigation and attacker profiling. *Journal of Network and Computer Applications, 198, .*, 103270.

[37] Sharafaldin, I. e. (2018). Toward generating a new intrusion detection dataset and intrusion traffic characterization. *ICISSp, 1*, 108-116.

[38] Surbhi.D, & Deepak.K. (2021). Analysis of Tree-Based Classifiers for Web Attack Detection. (Springer, Éd.) *In Advances in Signal and Data Processing: Select Proceedings of ICSDP 2019*, 421-428.

[39] Tama. B. A et al. (2020). An enhanced anomaly detection in web traffic using a stack of classifier ensemble. *IEEE Access, 8*, 24120-24134.

[40] Technologie, P. (s.d.). *Threats and vulnerabilities in web applications: Statistics for 2020-2021*. Consulté le Decembre 28, 2023, sur https://www.ptsecurity.com/ww-en/analytics/web-vulnerabilities-2020-2021

[41] Tekerek, A. (2021). A novel architecture for web-based attack detection using convolutional neural network. (Elsevier, Éd.) *Computers & Security, 100*, 102096.

[42] Thakkar, A , & Lohiya, R. (2020). A review of the advancement in intrusion detection datasets. (Elsevier, Éd.) *Procedia Computer Science, 167*, 636-645.

[43] Thakkar, A, & Lohiya, R. (2022). A survey on intrusion detection system: feature selection, model, performance measures, application perspective, challenges, and future research directions. (Springer, Éd.) *Artificial Intelligence Review, 55(1)*, 453-563.
[44] Viegas.E.K et al. (2017). Toward a reliable anomaly-based intrusion detection in real-world environments. (Elsevier, Éd.) *Computer Networks, 127*, 200-216.
[45] Yang, Z et al. (2022). A systematic literature review of methods and datasets for anomaly-based network intrusion detection. (Elsevier, Éd.) *Computers & Security, 116*, 102675.
[46] Yungaicela-Naula, N. M et al. (2021). SDN-based architecture for transport and application layer DDoS attack detection by using machine and deep learning. *IEEE Access, 9*, 108495-108512.
[47] Zuech.R et al. (2021). Detecting web attacks using random undersampling and ensemble learners. *Journal of Big Data*, 1-20.

Part III

Advanced Technologies for Cybersecurity and Privacy

9
Advancing Blockchain Privacy: The Role of Homomorphic Encryption

Yulliwas Ameur, Idriss Taberkane, and Samia Bouzefrane

CEDRIC Lab, Cnam, 292 rue Saint Martin, France

Preface

As a student involved in the field of cybersecurity my academic journey has consistently focused on the relationship, between new technologies and security. The chapter titled "Advancing Blockchain Privacy: The Role of Homomorphic Encryption" represents my research. It highlights the potential these technologies have in shaping our digital future. This chapter is intended to stimulate thought and discussion among students, professionals, and enthusiasts in the cybersecurity field. It is an invitation to explore the possibilities that lie between blockchain and encryption and to contemplate the future of digital privacy. My hope is that this exploration will not only provide insights into the current state of blockchain privacy but also inspire future innovations in this area. Throughout my internship I've had the privilege of engaging with scientific research and industry practices of cybersecurity and blockchain. This chapter reflects what I've learned during this time aiming to clarify the connection between blockchain privacy and encryption. It explores how encryption while initially appearing complex holds promise in addressing privacy concerns, in various applications involving blockchain. I would like to express my gratitude to my mentor whose insights and feedback have shaped this work. The contributions have not enriched the content it also challenged me to think critically about the future of cybersecurity. As you will embark on this journey through these pages I encourage you to contemplate the possibilities, question established norms, and envision a future where privacy and blockchain technology coexist seamlessly.

9.1 Blockchain

Blockchain technology has revolutionized various sectors by introducing transparency, trust, and security. However, its characteristics also pose significant challenges to user privacy. This chapter delves into the relationship between blockchain and homomorphic encryption, exploring how the integration of these technologies can bolster data privacy within blockchain-based systems. Blockchain's distributed ledger mechanism ensures data immutability and trust through cryptographic primitives. Nevertheless, this transparency can inadvertently compromise user privacy, as transactions and data become publicly accessible. To address this conundrum, homomorphic encryption emerges as a potent solution. Homomorphic encryption allows computations to be performed on encrypted data without the need for decryption. This cryptographic technique maintains data confidentiality while enabling various operations, such as addition and multiplication, on the encrypted data. Thus, it aligns with the fundamental principles of blockchain, offering a potential avenue to reconcile transparency and privacy. This chapter explores the nuanced interplay between blockchain and homomorphic encryption, shedding light on the advantages and limitations of their integration. By dissecting the underlying security methods, encompassing encryption types and protocols, we provide a comprehensive understanding of how these technologies synergize to enhance user privacy within blockchain ecosystems.

Keywords: Blockchain, homomorphic encryption, data privacy, decentralized systems, cryptography, smart contracts, symmetric encryption, asymmetric encryption, hash functions, user privacy, security protocols, IoT.

9.1.1 Introduction to blockchain

Since the early 2000s, blockchain technology has become a game-changing innovation. The introduction of Bitcoin by Satoshi Nakamoto in 2008, changed the financial industry worldwide. At the time, there were ongoing economic crises known as the subprimes putting immense pressure on traditional finance systems. Blockchain recognized the weaknesses of these finance systems and became an alternative. It primarily operates through structuring peer-to-peer transactions securely based on transparency, trust. The blockchain is composed of blocks, it's a chain system. The block is fundamental to blockchain technology and operates essentially as a dynamic data storage unit that contains essential information specific to each blockchain type's transactional details. The nodes are another component of the blockchain; they represent machines of the users connected to the peer-to-peer network that hosts and synchronizes a copy of the entire blockchain. In a network, nodes validate transactions, by following sets of rules called consensus protocols. This decentralized method guarantees the authenticity of each transaction eliminating the need for supervision, from any authority. Miners play a role within the network. Their main responsibility is to contribute blocks to the chain, which is crucial for the ongoing stability and integrity of the existing blockchain. Once they have successfully added a block, miners share it with nodes in the network for additional validation. However it isn't easy going about it since miners must solve intricate mathematical problems while attaining irreversibly labeled proof-of-work before attaining privileges assigned in publishing their mined blocks into the chain enabling seamless continuity uninterrupted by anyone. To make that work they use powerful hardware such as gaming GPU to handle the complex mathematical problems. In the process of moving through the network nodes make sure that the added blocks are valid so they can't be changed in their database. This guarantees that they will always stay connected. It's important to mention that including homomorphic encryption could really improve these roles. For example miners could check transactions without having to decode the transaction data, which would add a layer of privacy to the blockchain. Similarly nodes could do their verification tasks, on encrypted data making the network more secure and private. However the utilization of homomorphic encryption can be a problem due to its complexity, as we will see in this chapter. The nodes system ensures that all transactions are fully irreversible preventing any manipulation and deletion attempts. Unlike traditional databases blockchain technology operates on a decentralized model that eliminates the need for middlemen or human intervention. This system fosters trust among global stakeholders and improves transparency in a variety of areas, such as supply chain management, voting systems, healthcare, and legal industries. The potential of blockchain technology extends beyond cryptocurrencies. For example, it can provide greater transparency by enabling appropriate oversight regimes. This makes it possible to quickly identify problems requiring special attention before they become more problematic. In healthcare, it can improve patient data security and consent management while reducing fraudulent acts and errors. In addition, blockchain technologies hold great promise in the digital entertainment industry by facilitating the management of digital rights such as equitable distribution of royalties while bypassing intermediaries an essential feature for decentralized finance (DeFi) empowering global creators through peer-to-peer lending concepts made practical by blockchain technology. Global blockchain technology has had a revolutionary impact on various industries guaranteeing improved transparency and financial accountability while eliminating friction points in financial transactions via decentralized finance (DeFi) protocols such as autonomous decentralized organizations (DAOs). Governments around the world have begun to explore central bank digital currencies (CBDCs) because of their potential for fast and secure transactions. Meanwhile, organizations are focusing on creating innovative applications using blockchain technology with a focus on transparency. Homomorphic encryption could enable private transactions without compromising the transparency and integrity offered by blockchain. Similarly, organizations and governments can benefit from better data protection while continuing to exploit the accountability features offered by the technology. However, I doubt that governments will adopt homomorphic encryption as a solution because of its nature. Indeed, by allowing data to be encrypted and thus hiding information about users, amounts, etc., it could lead to the use of this technology being diverted to criminal activities such as money laundering. Furthermore, we have seen that governments are trying to regulate blockchain more and more, for example by requiring KYC for users, which is contrary to the decentralized and anonymous nature of blockchain and homomorphic encryption. It's an innovative technology that allows the improvement of services and greater security of users. Organizations and governments need to understand the issues and mobilize to use the blockchain and meet growing technological needs and challenges.

9.1.1.1 Blockchain technology and privacy protection

In todays' tech world, it is nothing out of the ordinary for entities run by third parties to acquire large amounts of personal information regularly, raising concerns about individuals' fundamental right to privacy. While such practices provide convenience to users, centralized models managing our data have received criticism due to the potential compromise on private information security emanating from these frameworks. This threat is brought into sharp focus when there are cases involving hackers illegally sharing sensitive data or high profile data breaches occur highlight calling for stronger protections mechanisms be put in place urgently. Data is often compared to a valuable resource, the 'new oil,' making its protection a top priority. However, as technology rapidly advances, some organizations struggle to keep up, relying on outdated systems and approaches. The infamous Equifax data breach of 2017 serves as a stark reminder of this challenge and the potential consequences for public trust. (During September 2017 Equifax,

9.1 *Blockchain* 243

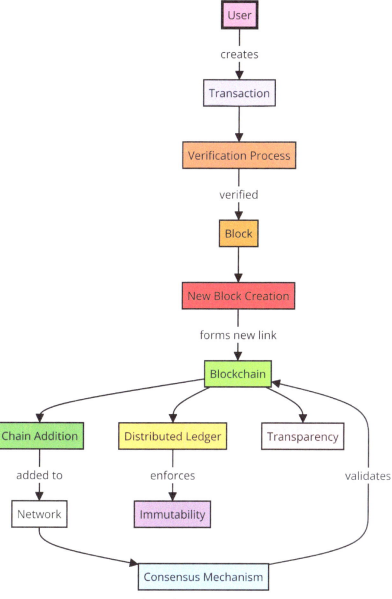

Figure 9.1 Blockchain.

one of the three credit reporting agencies in the United States made a distressing announcement regarding an extensive data breach. This incident exposed details belonging to around 147 million Americans, including their names, social security numbers, birth dates, addresses, and in some instances drivers license numbers. Additionally the credit card details of 209,000 U.S. consumers were compromised.) Originally conceptualized as an underlying foundation facilitating digital currencies like Bitcoin, blockchain technology has metamorphosed into an encouraging response toward increasing user-related security toward private information protection concerns. The restructured model replaces sole control holders of users transactional processes using networks of peers creating a revolutionary redefined information management approach in computing environments. Transactions on the network are auditable and transparent with blockchain technology providing reliable and secure environments for its users. One setback to blockchains privacy benefits is its transparency, which can work against privacy protection by revealing pseudonyms or informations that connect to real-world identities through OSINT or DOX methods. Homomorphic cryptography provides a solution by using encryption methods that allow for computations on encrypted data without the need for decryption interpretation. By merging homomorphic cryptography with blockchain technology user data privacy can be enhanced significantly and this chapter will provide an in-depth understanding of how this integration works. We will explore pertinent issues such as the advantages and limitations of using blockchain technology alongside deep diving in exploring homomorphic cryptography potential to elevate user privacy protections and identifying areas it could fit into current blockchain solutions alongside exploring feasibility and implications emphasizing both benefits and drawbacks. As mentioned earlier, encryption and cryptography are essential in blockchain technology, incorporating key concepts that ensure the integrity and security of information.

Symmetric encryption uses a single cryptographic key for both encrypting plaintext and decrypting ciphertext, which presents challenges in secure key management and distribution.

Asymmetric encryption, also known as public key cryptography, involves two mathematically linked keys: a public key for encryption and a private key kept secret from unauthorized parties. While it offers greater security than symmetric encryption, it is more computationally demanding.

Hash functions are used to ensure distributed ledger security by transforming inputs into predictable yet random byte strings of information known as hash values. This ensures data tampering cannot occur as even slight changes in input values will render different hash values. Digital Signatures provide more straightforward authentication of incoming blockchain

Technology data. Senders prove authenticity by signing documents with their private keys. Anyone with access to the sender's public key can securely verify the authenticity of any signed document transmitted via blockchain technology.

Finally, merkle trees are fundamental to the efficiency of blockchain. They provide a condensed and efficient summary of all the transactions in a block, enabling the verification of a particular transaction without needing to examine every transaction. These concepts intertwine to provide a secure environment for transactions and communications in the blockchain, ensuring data integrity, authentication, and confidentiality. As we go further into the integration of homomorphic encryption in blockchain, the understanding of these foundational elements will provide crucial context and highlight the potential advancements in privacy preservation. In the next section we will dive deeper into the principal concept of encryption and cryptography in blockchain.

9.1.1.2 Assymetric encryption intro

Asymmetric encryption is a secure method that uses two keys: a public key for encryption and a private key for decryption. Although the keys are mathematically related, it is practically impossible to derive the private key from the public key. This method is crucial in blockchain applications, providing both authentication and confidentiality.

When a user wants to send a transaction over the blockchain they sign it using their private key. The signature is then verified by anyone using the users public key. This process proves that only the user could have created such a transaction. As their private key is confidential and required to produce such signature. This ensures that transactions are authentic. Confidentiality is ensured in some blockchain applications by encrypting transaction data with the recipients' public key. Because only the recipient has access to the corresponding private key they are able to decrypt and view this encrypted data while keeping away any unauthorized parties. These cryptographic key pairs are generated through complex mathematical algorithms such as elliptic curve digital signature algorithm (ECDSA) or RSA algorithm in blockchain systems. Such algorithms generate random numbers as private keys and points on elliptic curves or large numbers derived from prime numbers as public keys respectively. The security of asymmetric encryption in blockchain depends on secure storage and handling of ones' confidential private keys. If exposed to unauthorized parties, anyone can sign transactions or decrypt data meant only for them causing potential security breaches within those systems. Asymmetric encryption stands as a vital feature when it comes to the implementation of blockchain technology. Notably, its function enables secure authentication and confidentiality.

9.1.1.3 Symmetric encryption intro

An essential component of blockchain that contributes to its robustness is symmetric encryption. It's a method that uses one key for encrypting and decrypting data processes with fast results. Symmetric encryption plays a vital role in maintaining high levels of security inside blockchain systems by encrypting new incoming data initially with a unique critical key resulting in an output termed "Ciphertext" before undergoing multiple node verification procedures. During individual user access attempts of encrypted sensitive information they must use the original security key obtained via random number generator sources from their ciphertext transformation process to convert back into plaintext by applying decryption protocol steps. Adopting symmetric encryption methods within blockchain systems requires several measures toward effective protection for confidentiality and integrity. Firstly using a cryptographically secure random number generator generates unique keys for encryption purposes that cannot be predicted. Next step involves encrypting plain text message into ciphertext using obtained private keys through an intricate ensemble involving algorithms specific to each system's requirements like AES which mix blocks of information through several rounds based on substituting value placements. The encrypted information is broadcasted across all nodes in the network, with the ciphertext becoming part of new blocks. Each node verifies the block before adding it to its copy of the blockchain, enhancing security. This process establishes higher standards of vigilance to guard against potential security breaches. When access to the originally encrypted content is needed, decryption involves applying reverse algorithms along with the corresponding private keys. This process transforms the ciphertext back into plaintext, ensuring data integrity by verifying it before making the information accessible. Integrity verification checks the hashed values of all the new plain texts generated with already implanted hash strings within blockchain and communication networks; any alterations in value differences implies violated security practices. It is integral to bear in mind that ensuring secure transmission involves keeping encryption keys a guarded secret since infiltrating them poses a high risk of total security breaches. Hence, rigorous key management procedures function as critical components needed to guarantee strong symmetric encryption mechanisms for blockchain operations.

9.1.1.4 Comparison

We have seen that symmetric encryption is known for its speed and efficiency 1.2. It faces challenges when it comes to keys management, which makes it less suitable, for decentralized systems like blockchain. On the other hand asymmetric encryption enhances the security of distribution but it can be computationally demanding, potentially slowing down blockchain transactions. However homomorphic encryption (HE) offers a capability of performing computations on encrypted data thereby enabling privacy preserving transactions and smart contracts on the blockchain. The ability of HE to carry out calculations on encrypted data makes it a great fit for applications that prioritize both transparency and privacy. Although it requires power compared to the other methods mentioned earlier, its advantages in facilitating confidential and decentralized computations make it a very good choice, for blockchain technology.

9.1.2 Hash functions

To ensure data security within blockchain technology, hash functions serve as critical cryptographic tools. When presented with an input or message, these determinative functions generate outputs consisting of fixed size byte strings - referred to as hash values or hash codes. Each unique information set produces its specific hash value since even minute changes to inputs create entirely different outputs due to what cryptographers term "avalanche effect." The chain of hashes within a blockchain acts as a means of verifying the entire systems integrity. Particularly the hashes act as indexes that allow for quick data retrieval within the blockchain. Hash functions themselves require notable properties to be considered secure such as preimage and second preimage resistance, and collision resistance. By complying with these properties, manipulating input data to achieve a desired hash output is made impossible. An extra layer of security is added against malicious actors who might alter transaction data or create fraudulent transactions.

9.1.2.0.1 SHA-256

To explain SHA-256's role in the blockchain: it operates within a Merkle-DamgÃěrd structure, using a one-way compression function based on a

Figure 9.2 Comparaison.

block cipher in Davies–Meyer mode. The algorithm processes data in 512-bit blocks, producing 256-bit digests through a series of bitwise operations, logical functions, and modular arithmetic. These blocks undergo 64 rounds of operations, including logical functions, bitwise rotations and shifts, and addition modulo 2^{32}, among other techniques. This process generates eight 32-bit constants, derived from the fractional parts of the cube roots of the first 64 prime numbers. The result is an extensive mixing of bits, where even the slightest change in input causes a dramatic change in output, known as the avalanche effect.

In blockchain, every transaction is paired with a hash–often generated using algorithms like SHA-256–to ensure authenticity. This allows nodes to verify that the transaction hasn't been altered, preventing fraud or cyberattacks. Not only are the transactions verified, but the blocks containing them are also hashed to guarantee the integrity of all data within the block. Each block is linked to its predecessor by a hash, making the entire blockchain resistant to tampering. As a result, all nodes in the network hold data that is securely protected against any form of tampering. Data retrieval becomes more efficient through hashing, which serves as an index, enabling faster query resolution. SHA-256 enhances security by providing cryptographic hash-function properties such as preimage resistance and second preimage resistance, making it difficult to reverse the original input or generate a different input that produces the same output. Additionally, collision resistance ensures that two unique inputs cannot create identical hashes, further strengthening security.

These robust protections pose significant challenges for malicious actors, preventing fraudulent transactions and data tampering. As a result, SHA-256 plays a crucial role in generating unique identifiers for digital signatures and blockchain addresses.

9.1.2.1 Digital signature

Digital signatures play an essential role in blockchain and are used for verifying transactions' authenticity while ensuring no unauthorized people made modifications during transit. In blockchain, two critical things occurs: signing and verification. The sender of the transaction generates a signature in the process using their private key and transaction data. After adding this signature to the transaction data, the signed message is broadcasted over the blockchain network. Upon reception of this message, other network nodes use this sender's public key to verify its authenticity. If successfully done in this verification, that means it meets all proper criteria for authenticity to be valid on blockchain after which it should carry out subsequent actions. The digital signatures implementation used in blockchains involves complex cryptographic algorithms compared to typical ones; ECDSA (Elliptic Curve Digital Signature Algorithm), in particular, has been used under Bitcoin protocols. Here's a breakdown of how it's used: Every bitcoin user creates a pair of keys consisting of a private key and a public key. The public key is then converted into an address through hashing. When a user wants to send bitcoins they use their key to sign the transaction using ECDSA. This signature serves as proof that the genuine owner of the Bitcoins has initiated the transfer. The miners and nodes within the bitcoin network verify each transactions validity by using the senders key. If the signature is valid the transaction is considered legitimate, added to the blockchain. By employing ECDSA authorized owners of bitcoins can spend their funds. Even if someone knows your key (or your Bitcoin address) they cannot create a forged signature without possessing the corresponding private key.

The adoption of ECDSA by bitcoin has played a role in safeguarding the network against attacks and fraudulent activities. However it's important to note that while ECDSA currently provides security as with any technology it remains crucial to stay updated on advancements in cryptanalysis and consider alternatives if necessary, in the future, such as homomorphic encryption as we will see later. Although proven effective at protecting privacy and ensuring secure transmission when enacted correctly within blockchain structures these digital signatures may present security hazards against related activities primarily linked to fraudulently gaining access or using one's private identification information without consent predictably leading toward theft. To safeguard against unscrupulous transactions, there are multiple ways blockchain-based systems can minimize the risk; including using secure wallets for storing access tokens. Access tokens can be either provided through hardware or software mechanisms which add an extra layer of protection by mandating user verification before allowing access, we can quote Ledger. It's integral for organizations or individuals to guarantee that their transaction's digital signature algorithm remains up-to-date and impervious from hacking attempts because compromised algorithms could allow hackers into forging invalid signatures and authorizing deceitful entries in the distributed ledger systems. Performing routine oversight such as conducting regular security evaluations and updating patches as well as isolation of private key, and other technical can ensure that data integrity involving any blockchain-based transaction remains secure while protecting transaction privacy owing to cryptographic hashing efforts.

9.1.1.2 Merkle tree

The Merkle tree 1.3 plays a role in blockchain technology contributing significantly to its efficiency. Ralph Merkle introduced it in 1979 with the objective of verifying the consistency and integrity of extensive sets of data. In this section we will delve into how Merkle trees function within the context of blockchain technology. A Merkle tree is a binary tree where each non-leaf node holds the cryptographic hash of its child nodes labels. The leaf nodes represent data blocks wiche are labeled using a cryptographic hash. One key characteristic of the Merkle tree lies in its structure, combined with the application of hash functions. By hashing and combining each step from leaf nodes upwards until we reach a hash for all the data, at the root we obtain a unique identifier called the "Merkle Root." The successful functioning of networks heavily relies on efficiently checking large sets of data while adhering to stringent security standards, which can be achieved through Merkle trees. A crucial task performed by a Merkle tree within technology is summarizing transactions contained within blocks. This process follows a linked list approach by constructing these trees from transactions included in each block. The optimal outcome is represented by hash outputs; specifically the root reflects all created transactions resulting in increased storage efficiency without compromising performance. In general, by incorporating Merkle trees into the mechanics of blockchain, technology users are able to provide proof that a particular transaction exists within a block without

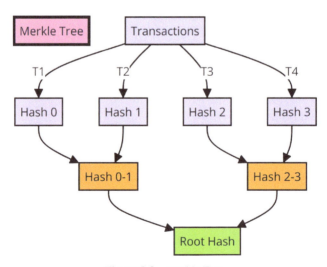

Figure 9.3 Merkle Tree.

having to sift through every piece of data. The use of Merkle trees is crucial in cryptocurrency systems as they offer two important advantages to decentralized networks, like blockchain technology: enhanced operational efficiency and strengthened security.

9.2 Enhancing Privacy

9.2.1 Enhancing privacy protection with homomorphic cryptography

There are three main types of homomorphic encryption: partially homomorphic encryption (PHE), somewhat homomorphic encryption (SHE), and fully homomorphic encryption (FHE). In this section we will talk about the PHE encryption. Partially homomorphic encryption (PHE) serves as an encryption tool executing specific computations on encrypted data resulting in identical outcomes as those expected when carried out on unencrypted data. Its unique capabilities make PHE an integral aspect in securing information privacy while implementing computational commands without requiring access to sensitive data. Partially homomorphic encryption supports restricted arithmetic operations for limitless times; only one type of operation addition or multiplication may be executed repeatedly. Commonly known popularized examples using PHE methods involve RSA or ElGamal cryptographic methods: According to the approach of homomorphism RSA enables the decryption of the multiplied ciphertext components to obtain the plaintext. Specifically if we have plaintexts m1 and m2 with their corresponding ciphertexts c1 and c2 multiplying c1, by c2 and then decrypting it will give us a result to m1 multiplied by m2. This property allows multiplication operations to be performed on encrypted data. On the hand the standard ElGamal encryption system also offers homomorphic encryption. When we multiply two ciphertexts c1 and c2 and then decrypt them we get a result that's equivalent to m1 multiplied by m2. Therefore standard ElGamal also allows for multiplication operations on encrypted data. However it's important to note that there are variants of ElGamal that can exhibit additive homomorphic properties. In these variants certain operations performed on ciphertexts c1, c2 will yield a result to adding m1 and m2 when decrypted. This enables addition operations on encrypted data. It's essential to clarify that this is not a feature of ElGamal but a specialized adaptation, this specificity is very important since its more secure than the original ElGamal Scheme: [15, see abstract]. Partially homomorphic encryption (PHE) which includes both RSA

Year	Contributors	Hom. Operations	ρ
1978	Rivest, Shamir and Adleman [42]	$\langle \cdot \rangle_N$	1
1982	Goldwasser and Micali [23]	$\langle + \rangle_2$ (i.e. XOR)	$O(\log N)$
1984	ElGamal [18]	$\langle \cdot \rangle_p$	2
1985	Cohen and Fischer [9]	$\langle + \rangle_p$ (for small prime p)	$O(\frac{\log N}{\log p})$
1994	Benaloh [2]	$\langle + \rangle_p$ (for small prime p)	$O(\frac{\log N}{\log p})$
1998	Naccache and Stern [35]	$\langle + \rangle_{\prod p_i}$ (for small primes p_i)	$O(\frac{\log N}{\log \prod p_i})$
1998	Okamoto and Uchiyama [37]	$\langle + \rangle_p$	3
1999	Paillier [38]	$\langle + \rangle_N$	2
2001	Damgård and Jurik [14]	$\langle + \rangle_{N^{k-1}}$	$1 + \frac{k-1}{k}$

Figure 9.4 PHE.

and ElGamal has applications, in scenarios where sensitive information needs processing or analysis without compromising privacy. Partially homomorphic encryption (PHE) has extensive applications in various situations where sensitive information has to be processed or analyzed without compromising privacy. However, it comes with limitations related to supported computations types while providing significant potential for enhancing data security and privacy across numerous applications. As research in this field continues, more sophisticated and efficient PHE schemes are expected to improve our ability to protect privacy and security.

9.2.1.0.1 SHE encryption

Somewhat homomorphic encryption (SHE) has progressed from partially homomorphic encryption (PHE), which only supported single arithmetic operation such as either addition or multiplication. The term "somewhat" indicates that SHE operates both addition and multiplication operations to a certain depth based on noise (To prevent attacks on cryptosystems, randomization techniques such as introducing small terms called "noise" into ciphertexts are used. These noises are typically integers or polynomials depending on the selected scheme's type and complexity. Whether these noises qualify as small or not depends on several factors such as security considerations and system correctness properties, the decrpyion function fails if the noise surpasses set thresholds unique for each parameter set used by different schemes hence limiting operations to minimize noise growth.) accumulation during encryption processes; excess beyond that depth may lead to decryption inaccuracies. According to this aspect, it unlocks more advanced computational possibilities than PHE while having some limitations compared with fully homomorphic encryption (FHE). One prominent example of SHE is the Brakerski-Gentry-Vaikuntanathan (BGV) scheme based on ring-learning with error (RLWE). Under this system, each ciphertext has its level or depth assigned; adding two ciphertexts retains the maximum value while multiplying them grows their total levels together. BGV also introduces modulus switching operation to control noise growth in keeping accuracy in decryption computation, the flexibility of the BGV scheme to operate in either SHE or FHE mode (using bootstrapping) is one of the reasons why it is considered a major breakthrough in homomorphic cryptography. For modern cryptography somewhat homomorphic encryption (SHE) is a powerfull tool that supports multiple operations but still has a limit due to noise accumulation, that leads to problems for entity that need to work with a lots of data.

9.2.1.0.2 FHE encryption

Fully homomorphic encryption (FHE) represents a significant advancement from both partially homomorphic encryption (PHE) and somewhat homomorphic encryption (SHE) as it enables an unlimited number of both addition and multiplication operations using methods like bootstraping that can reduce noises. The ability to perform an unlimited number of operations with the encrypted data while maintaining the same result when decrypted makes FHE a powerful tool for data privacy and security. FHE has various technical aspects that make it work: we'll talk about the first-ever proposed fully homomorphic encryption (FHE) system: Craig Gentry introduced his work in 2009, Gentry's scheme is the first-ever proposed fully homomorphic encryption (FHE) system. Before this proposal, the notion of encryption that allows both additions and multiplications on ciphertexts was not very developed, indeed the concept of homomorphic encryption has its roots at the begining in 1978 not after Rivest, Shamir, and Adleman introduced RSA encryption. Rivest Adleman and Dertouzos initially proposed the idea of privacy homomorphisms. Faced opposition from Brickell and Yacobi a decade later. While other researchers like Feigenbaum and Merritt also explored this topic there was progress until Gentry, a graduate student at Stanford University took on the challenge as part of his thesis to develop a homomorphic encryption system. Subsequently other researchers have built upon his work by proposing their variations of encryption schemes in the following years. Fully homomorphic encryption (FHE) is a highly advantageous

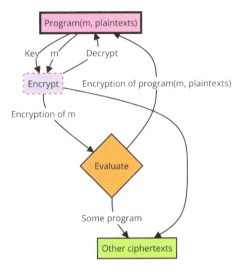

Figure 9.5 FHE.

tool for machine learning processes where privacy is paramount. It permits user data to remain confidential while allowing accurate model training. Fully Homomorphic Encryption (FHE) can be combined with various protocols to enhance user experience and security. For example, secure multiparty computation becomes more robust and flexible when integrated with homomorphic encryption, allowing for safer and more efficient data processing. Despite some challenges with computational efficiency and managing noise, FHE holds potential as a means of enhancing data security and privacy across many applications. The development of even more efficient FHE schemes will continue based on ongoing research efforts leading to even stronger safety and security solutions for our digital world.

9.2.1.0.3 FHE and smart contracts

The emergence of blockchain technology has brought about a revolution in the digital world. Its transparent and decentralized features have had an impact. However there are concerns about privacy particularly when it comes to smart contracts. In this small section we will explore one way to use homomorphic encryption: The implementation of fully homomorphic encryption (FHE) for smart contracts discussing the benefits, challenges, and the process involved. Smart contracts play a role in the seamless operation of blockchain technology. However, because of the networks nature, transaction details are accessible to everyone, which compromises users expectations of privacy. By incorporating homomorphic encryption we can address this issue. Implementing FHE brings advantages that enhance user confidentiality when engaging in secure blockchain transactions. For instance encrypting transaction amounts within blockchains promotes improved confidentiality over time and space among parties involved. With FHE encryption in place account balances can be updated without revealing information to unauthorized parties beyond those directly involved in the transaction. It is worth noting that FHE also provides computation correctness verification, in contracts. Using fully homomorphic encryption (FHE) in platforms allows individuals to transact anonymously safeguarding their information and financial details. Similarly businesses can securely conduct operations without compromising trade secrets or insider trading information. Homomorphic Encryption (HE) can also enhance users' physical security. By encrypting sensitive information such as financial data and wallet details, HE reduces the risk of users being targeted or harmed in real life due to the visibility of their information on the blockchain. While FHE offers benefits like enhanced confidentiality and privacy control across networks or nodes there are challenges to overcome. These include computation procedures that can impact performance and integration difficulties with blockchain systems. Implementing FHE within smart contracts involves selecting encryption schemes that meet specific requirements while considering available computational resources. It's crucial to strike a balance between security and efficiency for results. Over time advancements in cryptography and blockchain technologies may simplify overcoming limitations related to computation demands or integration issues, with existing contracts, for a concrete example we can talk about SmartFHE wich is a framework that allow users to create their own private smart contracts using fully homomorphism encryption [12].

9.2.1.0.4 Limitations and challenges

Despite its potential, homomorphic encryption is not without its challenges, these include: homomorphic encryption is well known for its computational demands. The processes of encrypting, decrypting, and performing operations on encrypted data require resources surpassing the requirements of working with unencrypted data. As a result these intensive tasks lead to slower processing times making homomorphic encryption less suitable for scenarios that necessitate quick responses or efficient data processing. When integrating encryption into blockchain technology, these performance challenges become even more noticeable. Blockchain networks inherently require effective and fast transaction processing. However, incorporating encryption adds an extra layer of computational complexity that can potentially slow down transaction processing times and impact the overall performance of the blockchain network. Furthermore, the decentralized nature of blockchain networks poses another hurdle when it comes to integrating encryption. Each node in the network must have the capability to handle demanding homomorphic encryption operations. This requirement can lead to increased hardware demands escalating both the cost and complexity involved in implementing and maintaining a network with homomorphic encryption. The computational complexity isn't the only problem indeed there is the noise management limitations. The term "noise" in this context refers to the information that gets added during the encryption process. This additional information increases with each operation performed on the encrypted data. If not managed properly as the noise grows it can cause decryption errors. Become a significant challenge for implementing homomorphic encryption (HE) in blockchain technology. In HE, the growth of noise is not linear but exponential. This means that with each operation on the encrypted data, the level of noise increases. Managing this noise becomes particularly difficult in scenarios where multiple operations are performed on encrypted data like smart contracts on a blockchain. One of the strategies for dealing with noise in HE is to carefully select parameters. The choice of parameters, such as degree and coefficient modulus size can have a significant impact on noise growth. By selecting these parameters it's possible to control and minimize noise growth to some extent. However this often involves finding a balance between security, accuracy, and efficiency. Another approach to managing noise in HE is through bootstrapping which reduces the noise level in a ciphertext, to its initial state. When it comes to dealing with noise bootstrapping can be quite effective. However, it's important to note that this process can be computationally intensive which might not be ideal in a blockchain setting where efficiency is crucial. Additionally, there have been advancements in homomorphic encryption (HE) schemes that offer more efficient methods of handling noise. One such scheme is the ring learning with errors (RLWE)-based schemes. These schemes use Gaussian noise (it is added to the encrypted data and helps to ensure security and confidentiality), which has properties that make it easier to manage. However, it's worth mentioning that these schemes are still in their stages and require further research to fully comprehend their potential and limitations within a blockchain context. The term "key" refers to the information used for encryption and decryption. Managing these keys is crucial for maintaining the security and integrity of data especially when implementing homomorphic encryption (HE) in a blockchain environment. One major challenge in management for HE in blockchain is ensuring secure storage and distribution of keys. Since blockchain networks are decentralized it becomes complex to store and distribute keys across all network nodes. Any compromise in security can expose vulnerabilities, including unauthorized access to encrypted data. Another challenge involves managing the lifecycle of keys, which includes their generation, distribution, rotation, and retirement. Each stage presents its unique challenges that require careful management to ensure ongoing system security. For example, regular key rotation is necessary to reduce the risk of compromise. However, this process can be resource intensive and complex in large blockchain networks. Additionally, managing public and private keys, within an HE scheme also poses challenges. In an encryption system there is a public key used for encrypting information and a private key used for decrypting it. Making sure that the right keys are used at the time and by the appropriate parties is crucial to maintain the system's integrity. To sum up, managing keys play a role in implementing homomorphic encryption in blockchain environments. It involves intricate tasks, such as securely storing and distributing keys as well as effectively managing their lifecycle. These examples show how homomorphic encryption is not fully effective in blockchain environnement, but we have several research paths and known problems that will lead research and improve the integration of homomorphic cryptography in the blockchain.

9.2.2 Application of homomorphic encryption in blockchain

As we said before, homomorphic encryption can really enhance privacy in blockchain, in plenty of important fields, such as health, politics, finance, etc. In this section, we will see how homomorphic encryption can be used with blockchain to make it more efficient and enchance privacy and user experiences in a case study. The healthcare industry is increasingly embracing solutions to improve patient care streamline processes and ensure data security. One of these solutions is the use of technology, which offers a secure and decentralized way to store and share health information. However, given the nature of health data it's crucial to have robust privacy measures in place. This is where homomorphic encryption becomes valuable by allowing computations on encrypted data without compromising privacy. In the healthcare field homomorphic encryption can be employed to encrypt health data before storing it on the blockchain. This allows for performing computations on the encrypted data, such as algorithms without jeopardizing patient confidentiality. For example, medical problems information of an important person (politician, pdg, etc.) can be stored securely on the blockchain whitout risking a leak of sensitive data. We can even imagine a cloud-based diagnostics service that can conduct computations using this encrypted data to provide insights, into a person's health status without accessing their actual readings. This ensures that the patient's data remains private while allowing for important health information to be obtained. A study conducted by Thanh Nguyen Van presents a protocol that can be implemented on a blockchain to ensure outcomes that're unpredictable, resistant to tampering, scalable, and publicly verifiable [7]. The key components of their protocol are encryption (HE) and verifiable random functions (VRF). By using encryption mathematical operations can be performed on encrypted data without revealing the outcome beforehand. The protocol involves elliptic curve multiplications and additions with O(n) complexity, as well as signature signing and verification operations with O(n) complexity. This design ensures that the protocol is scalable and can efficiently handle increases in data size or the number of users. In another research paper, Jingjing Chen and Fucheng You discuss the principle of encryption and its practical application in ensuring data security when combined with blockchain technology [2]. The paper examines the used RSA encryption algorithm in blockchain applications to protect the user's private key from being compromised. Another research of HE integration in blockchain: In the field of transportation systems (ITS) there are often issues, with sensor failures or transmission distortions when acquiring data. This can result in the loss or abnormality of traffic flow data that is sent to the edge server. To tackle this problem Ailing Gao, Xiaomei Liu, Ying Miao, and others proposed a method called ASMVPdistr LSH. The ASMVPdistr LSH method relies on distributed locality hashing (LSH) techniques. Its main goal is to address challenges related to user privacy and data sharing efficiency across platforms. This method addresses the challenge by ensuring the privacy of traffic data during sharing and enhancing scalability as new data is introduced. To maintain privacy while still allowing for analysis and prediction of traffic flow the ASMVPdistr LSH method employs an encryption scheme. This scheme allows computations to be performed on encrypted data without decryption maintaining confidentiality. To safeguard the integrity and decentralization of the data, encrypted information is stored on a blockchain that serves as a record. The use of technology ensures that data remains authentic as every transaction on the blockchain is transparent and can be traced back to its original source. The authors shared a real-life example to demonstrate the practicality and effectiveness of the ASMVPdistr LSH approach. The results from their experiments indicated that this proposed method not only improved data storage and supervision efficiency but also proved resilient against common attacks. But it incurred cost and offered a higher level of security compared to other competing algorithms. This particular case study showcases how combining encryption, with blockchain can be applied in real-world scenarios offering solutions to actual problems.

9.2.3 IoT application

In the context of IoT, one way to combine encryption and blockchain is through the implementation of a scheme called privacy preserving IoT data aggregation (PrivDA). This scheme was proposed by F. Loukil and other researchers [5] in their paper titled "Privacy Preserving IoT Data Aggregation Based on Blockchain and Homomorphic Encryption." The PrivDA scheme uses both homomorphic encryption technologies to ensure the security and privacy of data aggregation in IoT. In this system, each data consumer has the ability to create a smart contract that includes terms of service and specifies the requested IoT data. The smart contract then brings together data producers who can fulfill the consumers request selecting an aggregator for computation. The role of this aggregator is to perform computations in order to generate the desired group level result. By employing group level aggregation sensitive information inference from IoT devices becomes more challenging due to the obfuscation of data. As a result, this scheme offers a level of privacy protection for devices contributing data to the aggregation process. To evaluate its performance, PrivDA was implemented on a private Ethereum blockchain. To initiate this process within PrivDA, a data consumer creates a contract, on the blockchain. This smart contract encompasses the terms of service and the specific IoT data that the consumer has requested. It acts as an agreement ensuring transparency and immutability through blockchain technology. Afterward, the smart contract identifies data producers capable of fulfilling the consumer's request. These data producers are IoT devices that have the required data. The smart contract selects one of these data producers to act as an aggregator.

In the PrivDA scheme, the aggregator plays a crucial role. It is responsible for collecting data from the IoT devices within its group and performing computations on this encrypted data to produce the desired results. Instead of handling raw data, the aggregator exclusively works with encrypted information. This is where homomorphic encryption becomes crucial. In the PrivDA scheme, IoT devices encrypt their datasets using homomorphic encryption before transmitting them to the aggregator. The aggregator then carries out computations, on this encrypted information. Due to the properties of homomorphic encryption these calculations produce accurate results even when performed on encrypted data. This procedure ensures that the original data from devices remains concealed throughout the aggregation process. Even the entity responsible for performing computations on the data, known as the aggregator only has access to encrypted data. This offers a high level of privacy protection for IoT devices. Subsequently, the aggregator securely transmits the computed results (in an encrypted format) back to the data consumer via blockchain technology. The consumer can then access the desired information from those results. The PrivDA scheme was tested on a private Ethereum blockchain which was selected due to its support for contracts, which play a crucial role, in facilitating the PrivDA scheme.

9.2.4 Future

Finally, the combination of encryption and blockchain technology is an emerging area of study that holds great potential for game-changing applications in various sectors. We will talk about future research directions in this field with a specific focus on healthcare secure decentralized business models and cell less architecture along with distributed security models. For example, in the healthcare sector, there is a growing adoption of solutions to improve patient care streamline processes and enhance data security. By integrating encryption and blockchain technology, we can significantly enhance the privacy and security of health data. However, there are still challenges that need to be addressed. As we said in a previous section, one such challenge is the scalability of homomorphic encryption algorithms and the efficiency of computations performed on encrypted data. Current techniques for encryption can be computationally intensive and may not scale well when dealing with large datasets commonly found in healthcare applications. Future research could focus on developing efficient algorithms or techniques to reduce the computational complexity associated with operations performed on encrypted data. Furthermore, there are research opportunities through the integration of other emerging technologies like machine learning and artificial intelligence, with homomorphic encryption and blockchain. Consider the development of machine learning algorithms that prioritize privacy when handling encrypted health data. One potential approach is the creation of machine learning models of training and making predictions directly

9.2 Enhancing Privacy 261

on encrypted data. This way data privacy remains intact while valuable insights can still be derived. For example, IBM researchers have successfully used encryption to apply machine learning on fully encrypted banking data. The encryption scheme they employed allowed predictions similar to those made by models based on unencrypted data. Studies indicate that machine learning can make predictions based on a client's underlying data while mitigating data risks. In the case of institutions like banks, homomorphic encryption could prevent both breaches and internal vulnerabilities that arise when employees gain unrestricted access to sensitive information. In the realm of business models, blockchain technology has opened up new possibilities. However, ensuring secure and private transactions within these models poses a challenge. Homomorphic encryption emerges as a solution by enabling computations on encrypted transactions thus preserving privacy. To further explore this concept, future research could focus on developing secure business models using both homomorphic encryption and blockchain technology. For example, one exciting direction is the design of privacy preserving contracts–a type of self-executing contract where agreement terms are directly encoded into code. Another area seeing increasing interest is cell less architecture, in communication networks–where networks aren't divided into cells and each user equipment is served by multiple access points. Integrating encryption and blockchain into cell less architecture can greatly enhance communication security and privacy. In the way models that distribute security across network nodes instead of centralizing it offer intriguing possibilities for research. The combination of encryption and blockchain technology can play a vital role in advancing these models. The convergence of encryption and blockchain technology presents fascinating research avenues, while significant strides have been made there are still challenges to overcome and areas to explore. Future research directions hold promise in developing scalable and efficient homomorphic encryption algorithms integrating encryption, with other emerging technologies and applying these technologies in decentralized business models and distributed security systems. Now we will discuss the potential impact of research on privacy protection in homomorphic encryption and blockchain applications. Many people believe that homomorphic encryption (HE) is not practical for use due to its perceived complexity and high computational demands. As a result, HE is often considered theoretical or specialized than being seen as a useful tool for broader practical applications. However, a recent academic paper titled "Circuit Copyright Blockchain Blockchain Based Homomorphic Encryption for IP Circuit Protection" challenges this prevailing notion by showing the implementation of HE in a real-world context [4]. The study specifically focuses on using HE to protect property (IP) related to circuits. This example shows how HE can be used to address problems beyond theoretical applications. The application of homomorphic encryption (HE) in safeguarding property in the field of digital circuits is groundbreaking. The referenced paper presents an approach to ensure the protection of design and ownership rights, for circuits. By incorporating homomorphic encryption (HE) into this process the system ensures safeguards, against access and duplication safeguarding the intellectual property rights of creators and innovators. This practical implementation of HE does not demonstrates its usefulness. It also emphasizes its potential to revolutionize the protection of intellectual property in todays digital world. The incorporation of technology into transactions, which is an important point in the paper represents a good advancement in sectors such as government administration and financial services. The decentralized nature, transparency, and security features inherent to blockchain make it an ideal framework for managing transactions. In the context of government, blockchain has the ability to enhance efficiency and integrity in services leading to trust and participation. Similarly, within the sector blockchain technology provides an efficient method for handling transactions while reducing risks associated with fraud and speeding up processing times. This combination of blockchain with transactions signifies a shift, in how sensitive data and financial activities are managed and protected in todays digital world. Another example of HE capability in enhancing real problematic is explained in this paper titled "Enhancing Data Transmission Security, in Internet of Things (IoT) Networks A New Approach Using Homomorphic Encryption" [8]. It presents a breakthrough in addressing the challenges related to data transmission within IoT networks. These networks often face issues such as safeguarding against cyber threats protecting data privacy and ensuring the integrity of transmitted information. Additionally, achieving efficient, reliable, scalable, and low latency data transmission is crucial for the functioning of systems. To tackle these challenges head on the paper introduces a method that greatly enhances the security and privacy of data transmission in environments. The core foundation of this method lies in utilizing encryption–a cryptographic technique that maintains data encryption even during processing. This ensures that data remains secure throughout its journey during transmission effectively addressing a vulnerability found in data transmission methods.

Moreover, the research paper incorporates technology into its proposed method. By leveraging blockchain's nature and its ability to create evident

9.2 Enhancing Privacy

records, it becomes an ideal solution, for ensuring both the integrity and traceability of networked data. This integration not only strengthens the security of the data transmission process but also enhances its reliability and transparency. Another important aspect that the method addresses is the preservation of privacy. Given that IoT devices often handle information it is crucial to ensure that this data remains private and secure during transmission, the proposed method effectively safeguards data minimizing the risk of access or exposure. The effectiveness of the method is underscored by its high level of accuracy and reliability, as evidenced by a success rate of 88 out of 100 during setup. This accuracy demonstrates the method's capability to securely transmit data within networks. Additionally, the method is designed to be time-efficient, which is crucial for real-time data processing scenarios commonly encountered in applications. Over time, researchers have made strides in making Homomorphic Encryption (HE) more practical in technical contexts. As highlighted in our paper, while HE can be complex and resource-intensive, future research aims to address these challenges with new methods, such as hardware customization, which require less computational power. One way of responding about HE problem is the development of custom hardware for HE. As we already said the computational complexity of HE poses challenges leading to inefficiencies and slow processing times. Custom hardware designed specifically for homomorphic encryption addresses these challenges by improving performance. This specialized hardware is tailored to meet the requirements of HE algorithms, enabling computation and more efficient processing. It focuses on optimizing operations such as integer multiplication and modular arithmetic reducing the time required for

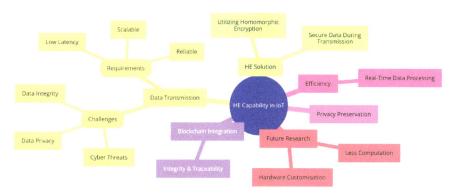

Figure 9.6 Homomorphic encryption enhancing IoT.

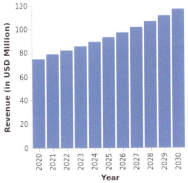

Figure 9.7 Homomorphic encryption market size.

HE operations. In addition to speed improvements custom hardware also enhances processing capabilities. This means multiple data points can be processed simultaneously allowing for handling of calculations compared to traditional computing systems. One important advantage of custom hardware is its energy efficiency. These designs are not optimized for speed. Also prioritize lower power consumption. This is particularly valuable in applications that need sustainability and scalability such as data centers where energy usage has an impact, on costs. Furthermore, when it comes to protecting encrypted data custom hardware can play a role by incorporating advanced security features that guard against attacks and side channel breaches. Integrating custom hardware into applications where homomorphic encryption (HE)'s, in high demand, such as secure cloud services, confidential medical data processing and secure financial transactions can drive the wider adoption of HE in practical scenarios. However, developing custom hardware for HE does come with its share of challenges. It requires investments in research and development. Producing such specialized hardware can be quite costly, its important to do it to make HE practical for daily use. Attempt had already been made as the paper "A Custom Accelerator for Homomorphic Encryption Applications" by Erdinç, *et al.* published in 2017, shows it [3]. They made a custom hardware accelerator optimized for somewhat homomorphic encryption (SHE) schemes, which improved computation time in order to make HE more suitable for real-life application.

As we see the potential impact of future researches is very good and can be used in many fields, the combination of encryption and blockchain applications is an emerging area of study that holds tremendous potential for transformative applications in various industries 2.4. We will see the impact of this research on safeguarding privacy particularly in cloud computing, the Industrial Internet of Things (IIoT), and database applications. In the cloud computing field there is often a conflict between data availability and privacy requirements. However, by using homomorphic encryption and blockchain technology it becomes possible to perform computations on encrypted data stored in the cloud. This means that cloud-based services can offer insights or services without ever accessing the actual data itself [11]. For instance, a health analytics service operating in the cloud could analyze encrypted data to provide valuable health insights while ensuring patient privacy. When it comes to the IoT, integrating blockchain and homomorphic encryption can establish a scheme for preserving data privacy. In this scheme, data from industrial devices can be encrypted and stored in a decentralized manner on the blockchain. Computation, on this encrypted data can then be performed using encryption techniques preserving the confidentiality of the information while enabling valuable insights to be extracted. For example, a manufacturing company could securely analyze its machine-generated data using this approach to optimize its operations without compromising information. Furthermore, exploring the application of encryption in safeguarding database privacy shows great promise. By employing forms of homomorphic encryption technology we can ensure that data remains confidential thereby boosting privacy protection for database applications. To illustrate financial institutions can leverage this technology to perform computations on encrypted customer data offering personalized services without compromising sensitive information.

9.2.4.1 Conclusion

Despite its advantages there are still challenges that need to be addressed, future research in this field could focus on computational demands, noise management rapidity, and efficiency as we already seen in this chapter. Indeed homomorphic encryption is still slower than other encryption methods that are more commonly used than homomorphic encryption and all the limitations and problems that occur for homomorphic encryption, are for the moment a slowdown for its standardization. Another exciting direction could be combining machine learning, artificial intelligence, and Internet of Things (IoT), with encryption and blockchain technology as we have seen. Such interdisciplinary research has the potential for groundbreaking applications like real-time encrypted data analytics in healthcare, finance, or voting systems. In order to promote adoption across sectors, standardization efforts for homomorphic encryption techniques will be crucial. Policy makers also have a role, in shaping this field so future research should aim to provide insights that influence policy decisions. Considering the importance of achieving acceptance it becomes crucial to have an understanding of the user experience, it would be beneficial to conduct research that focuses on enhancing the usability of these technologies ensuring that they can be easily accessed by individuals who do not possess expertise. By addressing these challenges to detail and actively pursuing the suggested research opportunities we can not only overcome the current limitations but also unlock new possibilities. During our research we saw how homomorphic encryption was adapted to blockchain, this will further strengthen the privacy of users and allow many innovations in this area to meet the challenges of our society.

References

[1] Jingjing Chen and Fucheng You. Application of homomorphic encryption in blockchain data security. In *Proceedings of the 2020 4th International Conference on Electronic Information Technology and Computer Engineering*, pages 205–209, 2020.

[2] Jingjing Chen and Fucheng You. Application of homomorphic encryption in blockchain data security. In *Proceedings of the 2020 4th International Conference on Electronic Information Technology and Computer Engineering*, EITCE '20, page 205–209, New York, NY, USA, 2021. Association for Computing Machinery.

[3] Yarkın Doröz, Erdinç Öztürk, and Berk Sunar. Accelerating fully homomorphic encryption in hardware. *IEEE Transactions on Computers*, 64(6):1509–1521, 2015.

[4] Wei Liang, Dafang Zhang, Xia Lei, Mingdong Tang, Kuan-Ching Li, and Albert Y. Zomaya. Circuit copyright blockchain: Blockchain-based homomorphic encryption for ip circuit protection. *IEEE Transactions on Emerging Topics in Computing*, 9(3):1410–1420, 2021.

[5] Faiza Loukil, Chirine Ghedira-Guegan, Khouloud Boukadi, and Aïcha-Nabila Benharkat. Privacy-preserving iot data aggregation based on blockchain and homomorphic encryption. *Sensors*, 21(7), 2021.

[6] Vilma Mattila, Prateek Dwivedi, Pratik Gauri, and MD Ahbab. Homomorphic encryption in 5ire blockchain. *International Journal of Social Sciences and Man-agement Review*, 5, 2022.

[7] Thanh Nguyen-Van, Tuan Nguyen-Anh, Tien-Dat Le, Minh-Phuoc Nguyen-Ho, Tuong Nguyen-Van, Nhat-Quang Le, and Khuong Nguyen-An. Scalable distributed random number generation based on homomorphic encryption. In *2019 IEEE International Conference on Blockchain (Blockchain)*, pages 572–579, 2019.

[8] Sheng Peng, Zhiming Cai, Wenjian Liu, Wennan Wang, Guang Li, Yutin Sun, and Linkai Zhu. Blockchain data secure transmission method based on homomorphic encryption. *Computational Intelligence and Neuroscience*, 2022, 2022.

[9] Zhiniang Peng. Danger of using fully homomorphic encryption: A look at microsoft seal. *arXiv preprint arXiv:1906.07127*, 2019.

[10] Rakesh Shrestha and Shiho Kim. Chapter ten - integration of iot with blockchain and homomorphic encryption: Challenging issues and opportunities. In Shiho Kim, Ganesh Chandra Deka, and Peng Zhang, editors, *Role of Blockchain Technology in IoT Applications*, volume 115 of *Advances in Computers*, pages 293–331. Elsevier, 2019.

[11] Rakesh Shrestha and Shiho Kim. Integration of iot with blockchain and homomorphic encryption: Challenging issues and opportunities. In *Advances in computers*, volume 115, pages 293–331. Elsevier, 2019.

[12] Ravital Solomon, Rick Weber, and Ghada Almashaqbeh. smartfhe: Privacy-preserving smart contracts from fully homomorphic encryption. Cryptology ePrint Archive, Paper 2021/133, 2021. https://eprint.iacr.org/2021/133.

[13] Zhang Wenhua, Faizan Qamar, Taj-Aldeen Naser Abdali, Rosilah Hassan, Syed Talib Abbas Jafri, and Quang Ngoc Nguyen. Blockchain technology: security issues, healthcare applications, challenges and future trends. *Electronics*, 12(3):546, 2023.

[14] Guangxia Xu, Jiajun Zhang, Uchani Gutierrez Omar Cliff, and Chuang Ma. An efficient blockchain-based privacy-preserving scheme with attribute and homomorphic encryption. *International Journal of Intelligent Systems*, 37(12):10715–10750, 2022.

[15] Ronghao Zhou and Zijing Lin. An improved exponential elgamal encryption scheme with additive homomorphism. In *2022 International Conference on Blockchain Technology and Information Security (ICBCTIS)*, pages 25–27, July 2022.

10

Developing a Big Data Infrastructure: Integral Modules and Best Procedures for Alleviating Security and Privacy Challenges

Danish Bilal Ansari

Department of Computer Science and Information Technology,
Virtual University of Pakistan
E-mail: danishbilalansari@gmail.com

Abstract

With the growing nature of data in the modern day and age, many organizations tend to use Big Data as a source of storing enormous information and performing significant diagnostics on it. In many areas from social to commercial and economic, Big Data plays an essential role in the progression of any organization. With such a humongous volume of data, it creates various security and privacy concerns that can lead to numerous threats and vulnerabilities. The traditional techniques of manipulating and securing the data are no longer feasible when practiced from the Big Data viewpoint. This paper provides a comprehensive overview of the attributes of Big Data and its empirical features and its integral modules. It also reviews the challenges of security and privacy of Big Data and provides an infrastructure to discuss and alleviate these challenges.

Keywords: Big Data, Security and Privacy Challenges, Big Data Infrastructure, Big Data Empirical Features, Big Data Integral Modules.

10.1 Introduction

Previously, documents were gathered and archived in paper form instead of electronic files. As the volume of data collected increases, it is becoming harder to store and maintain them, which is why it is important to have the latest technology that enables the preservation and accessibility of such information. This can be done through the use of various tools that are designed to sustain and improve the data.

The term "data" refers to the collection of information that is used for study or analysis. In the past few years, the amount of data that has been collected has become a major management issue for various organizations. To address this issue, the Ministry of Defense has coined the term "Big Data." This term refers to a large amount of data that can be used to analyze and improve the operations of an organization. Economic movements, modernization, novelty, and development, like other vital factors such as material assets and human resources, could not occur without the essence of data [1].

Big Data is the term used to describe the vast amount of data that has been obtained from many sources, such as the Internet of Things (IoT), in which every device that is linked to the internet generates, gathers, and stores enormous amounts of data. When traditional methods are unable to handle the vast and heterogeneous volume of data, Big Data becomes relevant. As seen in Figure 10.1, extensive processing, analysis, and storage are needed to extract meaningful information from data gathered from various sources.

The privacy and confidentiality of the information acquired are the primary issues with data collection from many sources. In a big data system, data is gathered at several levels, and each layer has security problems related to data availability, anonymity, and integrity as well as privacy in various stages, including collection, storage, and processing. The paper is structured as follows, with 7 sections to address these. The Big Data Literature Review is presented in Section 2. Section 3 concentrates on the Attributes of Big Data, which are divided into 8 Vs. The difficulties with security and privacy with big data are discussed in Section 4. After a detailed proposal for an

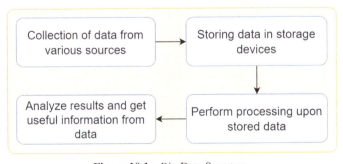

Figure 10.1 Big Data Structure.

infrastructure in Section 5 to address security and privacy concerns, the article is concluded in Section 7 with a presentation of Research Methodology in Section 6.

10.2 Literature Review

Most firms have used big data in the past for analytics and data management, with a strong focus on analysis. Big data analytics has enormous potential, but to fully capitalize on its growing capabilities, businesses must make changes to their infrastructure and business practices [24]. Because cloud computing offers higher storage capacity for large data combined with cost-effectiveness, flexibility, resource management, and data handling qualities, academics choose to concentrate on this other term [25, 26]. But cloud computing also comes with a lot of privacy and security risks [27, 28].

In the last few years, a lot of surveys and research have been done on data integrity and anonymity in cloud-based and Internet of Things systems [29]. However, because big data systems are distributed and have a variety of characteristics, research is now focusing more on security and privacy issues in these systems [30]. Due to big data's pervasiveness in the health sector, research studies on the subject have been carried out as e-health systems advance [31, 32]. However, due to the widespread use of social media and Internet of Things (IoT) devices in various organizations and by many individuals, personal information and user behaviors have been gradually collected online. This has resulted in a number of security and privacy issues, making the solutions currently available insufficient to meet the needs of different consumers [33, 34]. Recent years have seen a large number of literature reviews, surveys, and studies in the field of big data, with a focus on security and privacy. The findings highlight the importance of security and privacy in large data in terms of computational characteristics. These literature reviews and surveys tend to concentrate on well-known study fields, such as privacy and security. Only a few have presented an indication of large data and recommended a replacement for study in this field [35, 36]. However, none of them address the issue of big data security.

As a result, this analysis of the literature shows that there are differences in the study on big data security and privacy concerns at various layers and stages of the big data life cycle. In addition, the development and expansion of new technologies have given rise to extraordinary problems and worries regarding big data security and privacy. Nevertheless, there is a lack of comprehensive research to tackle the main problems with big data.

It is critical to recognize the impending big data issues from the outset. Initially, there are a lot of characteristics and qualities of big data that need to be discovered that are developing along with the development of new technologies. Furthermore, the expanding characteristics of big data highlight particular, compelling factors that influence the security and privacy aspect of big data. These implications call for a thorough investigation since they may give rise to different big data security and privacy risks that must be identified and addressed. To the best of our knowledge, these problems and worries have not been adequately addressed from the start. Our primary incentive to resolve the discrepancies in the literature with this paper's first step is the dearth of research on the security and privacy aspects of big data.

10.3 Attributes Of Big Data

To better understand the terminology of Big Data, it can be characterized into 8 V's as follows:

10.3.1 Volume

The storage component of big data also referred to as "Volume" or the first V of big data, emerged as a result of the massive amount of data that has been generated recently in the form of photographs, videos, text, graphics, etc. Terabytes, zettabytes, and yottabytes are some of the different sizes of data [2]. This [3] states that over 1.1 trillion pictures were taken in 2016, and the figure increased to 9% in 2017. Sensitive material from social media is spied into databases every day by more than 500 terabytes [17].

10.3.2 Velocity

"Velocity," another V in big data, refers to the speed at which data is created, accessed, and processed. Huge amounts of data are being generated by website clicks alone as a result of increased internet usage [2]. These statistics show that Google processes about 40,000 requests a day, or 3.5 billion searches per year and 1.2 trillion per day [4].

10.3.3 Variety

There are three different types of data: unstructured, semi-structured, and structured. Because it is structured, the structured format is simple to understand. Analysis and processing are made simple since it can be easily managed as a repository, which is usually a database. However, because unstructured data lacks a set of defined guidelines, it can be challenging to manage formats like audio, video, and image files. In addition to the data mentioned above, log files and sensor and machine data are examples of many data formats. It is more difficult to process and interpret data that is so diverse.

10.3.4 Veracity

The veracity of big data is related to the correctness and reliability of the data being used. Many websites, social media platforms, and other sources are used to gather and store data, which is then processed and analyzed to produce various statistics. Inaccurate data frequently yields false information in the shape of facts. When it comes to measuring the validity of data and how it is used in analysis, veracity is important.

10.3.5 Variability

Variability is another essential component of big data, and it's frequently compared to veracity. On the other hand, the variability of data is changing quickly with respect to meaning and context. For example, a word on Facebook may signify completely different in two posts that are exactly the same. The variability algorithm should be able to decipher the true meaning of a term in the context of the data and comprehend the data context better in order to produce an accurate and correct analysis [5].

10.3.6 Visualization

In order to make information and knowledge easier to utilize, data can be represented graphically in a technique known as visualization. An e-commerce site such as Amazon, for instance, generates a lot of data by selling millions of things each month to its millions of registered users who use it to purchase goods and services. Representing such data in a spreadsheet format is insufficient to improve its interpretability. In this case, visualization is useful. In every corporate sector, the ability to make decisions with a visual representation, such as graphs or charts, is crucial. Amazon's Revenue at the end of the first quarter of 2021 is $108.518 billion [6]. Based on a graph, Figure 10.2 displays Amazon's revenue in billions during the previous five years.

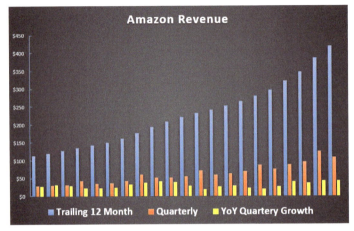

Figure 10.2 Amazon Revenue.

10.3.7 Value

While data on its own is meaningless, when processed and analyzed, it can provide value by helping an organization make the right decisions. Because big data contains important information, value is seen by researchers as a crucial and necessary component [7]. When properly evaluated, big data can give a corporation a considerable advantage.

10.3.8 Validity

The validity of the data becomes a crucial factor in the evaluation of the information [37]. The completeness and correctness of information derived from collected data is referred to as validity in big data [38]. For example, in a medical system, a doctor cannot treat a patient without first validating any clinical trials. The 8 V's of big data are displayed in Figure 10.3.

10.4 Security and Privacy Challenges in Big Data

The ubiquity of big data analytics has ushered in transformative opportunities but has also brought forth significant security and privacy challenges. A prominent case study involves the Yahoo data breaches in 2013 and 2014, where billions of user accounts were compromised, exposing sensitive personal information. This breach underscored the vulnerabilities of massive datasets and highlighted the pressing need for robust security measures, including encryption and access controls [16].

10.4 Security and Privacy Challenges in Big Data

Figure 10.3 V's of Big Data.

Another breach was the Equifax data breach in 2017, one of the largest credit reporting agencies, affecting nearly 145 million consumers, exemplifies the security challenges in handling extensive financial data. The breach included names, Social Security numbers, birth dates, and in some cases, driver's license numbers. Beyond financial implications, the incident emphasized the imperative of safeguarding personal information and the potential consequences of inadequate security measures [8].

In 2018, it was revealed that the political consulting firm Cambridge Analytica had improperly harvested data from tens of millions of Facebook users for targeted political advertising. The scandal also serves as a compelling case study highlighting privacy challenges associated with extensive data collection for targeted advertising. This incident prompted a reevaluation of data-sharing practices and the importance of user consent in big data analytics [9].

The Uber data breach in 2016 stands as a compelling example of the complex security and privacy challenges associated with big data. In this incident, personal information of 57 million users was compromised, including names, email addresses, and driver's license numbers. What exacerbated the situation was Uber's attempt to cover up the breach by paying the hackers to delete the stolen data [10]. This case underscores the importance of transparency and prompt disclosure in handling security incidents related to big data. It also sheds light on the ethical considerations surrounding data breaches, emphasizing the need for organizations to prioritize both security and user trust.

The healthcare industry has been a recurrent target for data breaches, showcasing the intricate security and privacy challenges associated with the vast amounts of sensitive patient information. Notable cases include the Anthem Inc. breach in 2015, where nearly 78.8 million patient records were exposed. Such breaches underscore the critical need for robust security measures to safeguard highly sensitive healthcare data. In the healthcare sector, the privacy implications are particularly severe, as compromised data can include not only personal information but also sensitive medical history and treatment records [11]. These incidents highlight the ongoing challenge of balancing the digitization of health records for improved patient care with the imperative to fortify security and privacy safeguards.

Big Data has garnered tremendous interest due to its potential applications in a wide range of areas, including industry, finance, healthcare, telecommunications, science, and more. However, security and privacy was a crucial issue that had to be resolved before Big Data could be implemented in large-scale applications.

10.4.1 Big Data Security

Big data security and the security of different information systems that contain structured data are rather comparable. But big data security demands a number of workable strategies, appropriate techniques, and advanced data analytics abilities. For the management of data gathered from both internal and external sources, a robust security strategy is also necessary. Regarding these points, a few inquiries come up:

a) How can heterogeneous and unstructured data be maintained securely?
b) How can distributed systems be made more functional while utilizing security measures?
c) How can big data be analyzed without compromising data security and privacy?

Finding vulnerabilities, security threats, and unusual activity is typically the goal of big data security. It also aims to provide role-based access control, robust secret data preservation, and security operation indications. It also helps with quick decision-making in the event of a security incident. Significant reasons led to the emergence of numerous large data security issues:

10.4.1.1 Inadequate Standard Solutions

A large number of encryption methods for data security, data exchange, and storage, and data reliability concerning hardware are offered in [12]. The following methods are used to preserve data security [13]:

- In most cases, data is kept in an unencrypted format.

- Plaintext data is used for authentication when it comes to data access.
- When data is stored, it is encrypted; when it is needed, it is decrypted.

Standard techniques, such as data encryption, take a long time to process large amounts of data and perform slowly. Besides, they are ineffective. Only a small portion of data is processed for security reasons, which leads to a disastrous incident because most security intrusions are discovered after the occurrence. Big Data systems are utilized for parallel processing and multiple product management. Performance is therefore a crucial component of data protection and data assessment in these kinds of platforms.

10.4.1.2 Primitive Security Applications

A big data system may face a number of hazards if several technical applications are combined and not properly evaluated. These security applications are also rudimentary and underdeveloped. As a result, big data applications may present risks to security and lead to data integrity negotiations, which safeguard against any unauthorized user alteration of data. Additionally, a lot of security risks come from coworkers, subordinates, and end users. Therefore, having improved security technologies is crucial for safeguarding big data platforms.

10.4.1.3 Data Secrecy

Anonymity or data secrecy is seen to be crucial to large data security. Achieving data privacy shouldn't interfere with the usefulness and real-time analysis of the data. On the other hand, the traditional method of data anonymization involves multiple iterations as well as computationally slow and wasteful processes. Conventional data anonymization may have an impact on system performance and data consistency with different repetitions when dealing with large data heterogeneity groups. Big data makes handling and evaluating anonymity difficult as well.

10.4.1.4 Data Reliability

Data reliability is the capacity to protect data from being altered by unauthorized users. As demonstrated in [13], a large number of data reliability problems are the result of user error, device malfunction, and software flaws. Some of the most well-known attacks against data reliability are salami attacks, data diddling attacks, trust relationship attacks, man-in-the-middle attacks, and session hijacking assaults [15]. The following methods can be used to ensure the dependability of data:

- Data Provenance
- Data Trustworthiness
- Prevention of Data Loss
- Data Deduplication

Data storage protection, digital signatures, improved hardware integration, and big data query security are just a few of the strategies that can be used to ensure data reliability and security [12].

10.4.1.5 Data Accessibility

The availability of data to authorized users is referred to as data accessibility. Highly Available (HA) systems can be used to guarantee data accessibility [13]. In order to construct a highly accessible system, backup servers, replacement communication lines, and reproductions are needed. Improved solutions are needed for some of the security vulnerabilities pertaining to big data availability, such as Distributed Denial of Service (DDoS) attacks, SYN flood attacks, Internet Control Message Protocol (ICMP) attacks, Server Room attacks, Denial of Service (DoS) attacks, and Electricity Power attacks [14].

10.4.2 Big Data Privacy

Big data, as we all know, is simply the accumulation of enormous amounts of valuable information. As a result of technological advancements, massive amounts of data are constantly being collected from various sources, including social media, IoT devices, and organizations. Managing this enormous amount of data is also the biggest challenge; many problems have been addressed and their solutions have also been considered in parallel. However, the security and privacy of the data are the most crucial of these issues. Security and privacy with big data are not the same. Protecting sensitive user information, such as name, address, social security number, login passwords, and account information, is known as big data privacy. On the other hand, security safeguards any kind of data and information that a company gathers from any source. Big data needs privacy because various administration jobs have been operating at various levels in the field of analytics. Privacy is also necessary at various stages of the data's life cycle, including during its creation, storage, and processing phases.

10.4.2.1 Data Acquisition/Generation Phase

When data is generated, it can be transferred to a third party in two ways: in the first, the data owner is fully aware that the information is shared between two people without the involvement of a third party; in the second, the user's information is collected by an unauthorized party without the owner's knowledge. Therefore, hackers have the ability to access a user's personal information at any moment when they are engaged in any online activity. To prevent this kind of privacy problem, users should refrain from sending sensitive information over the internet or to websites with fewer security measures. If necessary, users should use intermediary tools like firewalls, anti-virus software, anti-malware software, and anti-spam software when sending information over the internet. For instance, when sending credit card information to an online retailer, the information should be encrypted using any tool that helps to protect the privacy of data at the time of generation.

10.4.2.2 Data Sharing/Storage Phase

When it comes to big data technology, traditional storage methods fall short because big data requires a lot of storage capacity. Large businesses store and process big data using distributed file systems like Hadoop Distributed File System (HDFS) or Google File System (GFS) [23], but small and medium-sized businesses find it difficult to use these systems because of financial difficulties. To address this issue, cloud computing can be used. Although the organization used several security and privacy mechanisms to protect its information, there are still many security and privacy risks. Small and medium-sized businesses find great benefits from the processing and storage of big data on the cloud, but it also presents many security and privacy challenges. To guarantee these qualities, many encryption methods and algorithms have been put forth.

- Identity-based encryption:
  A sort of public key encryption known as ID-Base encryption uses a user's unique information, such as their phone number, email address, or CNIC (Computerized National Identity Card), to represent their unique identity [19]. The sender encrypts a message using the recipient's unique identity as a key, and the recipient decrypts it using the key. However, this method's drawback is that it takes a lot of time.
- Attribute-based encryption:
  Another kind of public-key encryption strategy is this one, in which all users' private keys and ciphertexts are tied to a specific user's set of attributes, rather than the ciphertext being encrypted for a single user as in previous encryption techniques [22]. If the encrypted text and the user's private key match, the user can only decipher the ciphertext.

- Fully Homomorphic Encryption:
  This is another method of data encryption that protects privacy when moving or storing data on the cloud. [19] When the ciphertext and the decrypted data are computed using the Fully Homomorphic Encryption approach and the results match, the computation's output is kept encrypted or secure. Thus, some algebraic operations are carried out and the encrypted and decrypted text are treated equally.

10.4.2.3 Data Processing Phase

Data processing is the process of applying certain procedures to data in order to derive some valuable information. Therefore, while processing the data, take care to ensure that neither privacy nor unintentional data leakage affects the information that is safely put back into the cloud.

10.4.3 Security and Privacy Comparison in Big Data

Security and privacy challenges in the context of big data are multifaceted, involving various technical, organizational, and regulatory considerations. Table shows a deep comparison and analysis of some key aspects of these challenges.

10.5 Infrastructure for alleviating Security and Privacy in Big Data

An infrastructure for resolving concerns with privacy and security in large data was suggested in this section. The framework's five main layer portions are as follows:

- Data Management
- IAM (Identity & Access Management)
- Data Safety and Privacy
- Network and Transport Security
- Structural Security

These sections are further divided into various sub-sections where each section ensures security and privacy in big data with respect to the vulnerabilities, security risks & threats and, anomalous activities. The infrastructure for alleviating security and privacy challenges in big data is shown in Figure 10.4.

10.5 Infrastructure for alleviating Security and Privacy in Big Data

Table 10.1 Comparison of Security Challenges and Privacy Concerns in Big Data.

Aspects	Security Challenges	Privacy Concerns
Volume and Scale	The sheer volume of data generated and processed in big data environments poses a challenge for traditional security measures. Large datasets make it harder to monitor, analyze, and protect every piece of information effectively.	The extensive data collection may include sensitive personal information. Preserving privacy becomes challenging when dealing with massive datasets, as anonymization techniques might be insufficient to prevent re-identification.
Data Variety	Big data often involves diverse data types, including structured, semi-structured, and unstructured data. Securing this varied data requires flexible security solutions capable of handling different formats.	Protecting privacy becomes complex when dealing with diverse data sources. The integration of disparate datasets might lead to unintentional privacy violations if not carefully managed.
Velocity of Data Processing	Real-time or near-real-time data processing requires security mechanisms that can keep pace with the speed of data ingestion and analysis. Traditional security tools may struggle to handle the velocity of big data streams.	Rapid data processing can raise privacy concerns, especially when it comes to real-time tracking or monitoring of individuals. Balancing the need for quick insights with privacy safeguards is crucial.
Data Life Cycle Management	The lifecycle of big data, from creation to archival, requires consistent security measures. Ensuring data integrity, confidentiality, and availability at every stage is essential.	Managing the lifecycle of data involves understanding and implementing privacy-preserving practices throughout, especially during data sharing, storage, and eventual disposal.
Distributed Computing and Storage	Big data frameworks often involve distributed computing and storage across multiple nodes. Ensuring secure communication and data transfer between nodes is critical.	Distributing data across multiple locations increases the risk of unauthorized access. Implementing strong encryption and access controls becomes imperative to protect privacy.
Regulatory Compliance	Adhering to data protection regulations becomes more complex as data volumes grow. Ensuring compliance with various regional and industry-specific regulations is a considerable challenge.	Violating data protection regulations can lead to severe legal consequences. Ensuring that big data practices align with privacy laws and regulations is crucial for organizations.

(Continued)

Table 10.1 Continued.

Aspects	Security Challenges	Privacy Concerns
Data Ownership and Sharing	Determining ownership and managing data sharing agreements in big data ecosystems is a complex task. Establishing clear policies for data access and sharing is essential.	Sharing data for collaborative analytics introduces privacy risks. Striking a balance between data sharing for innovation and protecting individual privacy rights is a significant challenge.
Machine Learning and Analytics	Integrating security into machine learning models and analytics processes is crucial to prevent adversarial attacks and ensure the reliability of insights derived from big data.	The use of machine learning on large datasets may unveil sensitive patterns. Implementing privacy-preserving machine learning techniques becomes essential to prevent unauthorized disclosure.
Granularity of Access Controls	Managing access controls at a granular level in big data environments can be challenging due to the diverse nature of data and the need for different users to access specific subsets of information.	Granular access controls are crucial for protecting privacy, ensuring that only authorized individuals have access to sensitive data. However, defining and enforcing fine-grained access policies can be complex.
Intrusion Detection and Prevention	Detecting and preventing intrusions in real-time is vital for protecting big data systems. The dynamic nature of these environments requires adaptive security measures capable of identifying evolving threats.	Intrusion detection mechanisms need to operate without compromising user privacy. Balancing the need for effective security monitoring with privacy protection is a challenge.
Supply Chain and Third-Party Risks	Big data systems often involve complex supply chains with multiple vendors and third-party services. Ensuring the security of each component in the supply chain is challenging.	Third-party data processors can pose privacy risks. Organizations must vet and manage these external entities carefully to prevent unauthorized access or mishandling of sensitive information.
Cross-Border Data Transfers	Transferring big data across borders introduces legal and security challenges, particularly concerning compliance with different data protection regulations.	Cross-border data transfers can raise privacy concerns, as data might be subject to different legal frameworks. Organizations need to navigate international data protection laws effectively.

10.5 *Infrastructure for alleviating Security and Privacy in Big Data* 283

Table 10.1 Continued.

Aspects	Security Challenges	Privacy Concerns
User Consent and Transparency	Ensuring that users are aware of and consent to the collection and processing of their data is a security challenge. Lack of transparency can lead to distrust.	Transparency is crucial for privacy, and organizations must communicate clearly about data practices. Obtaining informed consent while maintaining user trust is essential.
Incident Response and Data Breach Management	Rapid and effective incident response is critical in the event of a security breach. Organizations need robust plans to identify, contain, and mitigate breaches promptly.	Timely response to data breaches is equally critical for privacy, as delays can exacerbate the impact on individuals. Organizations must prioritize both security and privacy considerations in incident response.
Ethical Considerations	Ethical considerations in big data security involve issues such as responsible disclosure and avoiding the use of security measures for malicious purposes.	Ethical considerations in privacy involve respecting user rights, avoiding unjust surveillance, and ensuring fair and transparent data practices.

10.5.1 Data Management

Data management, which includes both structured and unstructured data, is the process of arranging, managing, and overseeing a vast quantity of data. Assuring excellent data quality and availability for analytical applications is referred to as data management in big data. The four parts of data management are as follows:

10.5.1.1 Data Classification

Big data management strategies are implemented by organizations, governmental bodies, and well-established businesses to deal with the growing volume of data, which can contain many terabytes or even petabytes of information. Effective data classification is regarded as one of the most important factors in any Big Data environment that leads to the implementation of effective security laws. Different businesses handle big data by making sure that the security protocols on such a platform are followed by clearly defining the reasons for the importance of the data, the data that must be cryptographed, and the data that must be organized before the others for security. Here are some basic ideas that can help with any big data environment's data classification matrix.

284 *Developing a Big Data Infrastructure: Integral Modules and Best Procedures*

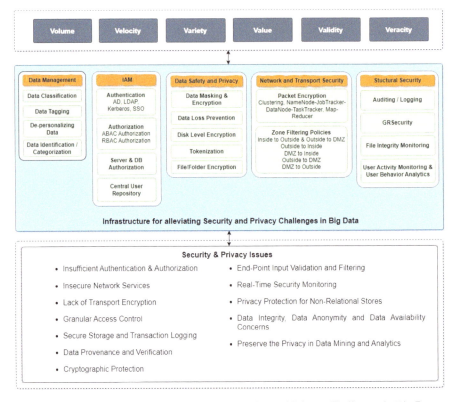

Figure 10.4 Infrastructure for Alleviating Security and Privacy Challenges in Big Data.

- Perform a risk assessment on classified information
  It is possible to do a risk assessment on classified material in a Big Data setting by speaking with compliance members, business executives, and stakeholders. This can result in the accomplishment of the classified goals and guarantee a thorough comprehension of the monitoring and classified criteria.
- Define an official classification policy
  The official classification of policies ought to be easily accessible. It is recommended to establish no more than three to five classification categories, as this will assist in reducing uncertainty and ambiguity and make the process more manageable. Sort and arrange employee roles and tasks.
- Define types of data categorization

Data can be classified based on how sensitive they are. There are difficulties in addition to the available classified material. Assessing the level of sensitivity in data can be a laborious task best left to the business processes and process owners. The following are some crucial inquiries that need to be taken into account when discussing data privacy and protection:

- What type of data about clients is collected by your firm?
- What proprietary data is collected?
- What type of transactional information is used?
- Is all the collected information classified and sensitive?

- Determine data location
  After your company has identified the different categories of data, it is critical to categorize the electronic data storage methods. What is the process for both internal and external data flow, and how is the data stored? Are services like Dropbox and OneDrive, among others, also utilized? Regardless of the data format, a plethora of data detection programs assist in locating the data storage.
- Maintenance and monitoring of data
  Firms are required to structure their systems after classification, which makes updates crucial. When it comes to classification, dynamic policies and processes should be adhered to.

10.5.1.2 Data Tagging

Understanding the flow in a Big Data environment with all of the intake and outflow processes is essential. Some of the crucial phases in data tagging are as follows:

1. The initial step is to identify every inflow mechanism, including manual and automated processes as well as those that operate on a meta-layer.
2. Determining the data inflow is also essential since data may enter the system through any API or a CLI (Command Line Interface).
3. Finding every outflow technique in the Big Data environment is the second stage.
4. Since it will define the application's limits and trust zones, identifying the data outflows is also a crucial stage.
5. These might be reporting jobs that use PIG, JDBC/ODBC connections, or some kind of Restful API for distribution.

10.5.1.3 De-personalization Data

To secure sensitive data in databases, depersonalization is the act of changing private information. Effective data depersonalization is necessary to preserve referential integrity and the distinctive qualities of the data. Character mixing, hashing, and salting are commonly used techniques for data change in data depersonalization.

Due to security and privacy issues, depersonalizing data is becoming essential in any Big Data context. When dealing with large amounts of both structured and unstructured data, it is crucial to separate personally identifiable information from datasets or make sure that data anonymity is maintained.

For data privacy, another method that can be employed is pseudonymization. One or more mock identifiers can be used to replace known fields in data in order to accomplish this. Pseudonyms are the names given to these identities. When replacing numerous fields at once or just one field, a single pseudonym can also be used. Furthermore, data re-identification is possible with pseudonyms.

10.5.1.4 Data Identification/Categorization

If sufficient understanding is lacking, confidential information may be exposed to various dangers and vulnerabilities. Finding out whether or not confidential data is available, where it is, and implementing the necessary data security precautions are the most important aspects. Some methods for protecting both structured and unstructured data in a big data environment are listed below.

- Structured data in Hadoop is stored in CSV, JSON, or relational databases. Confidential data is identified, located, and categorized in a known manner in the structured data format. By identifying the engine that grants view level security to these columns and fields, columns and fields can be secured for data security.
- The location, identification, and classification of private data become difficult when dealing with unstructured data. In this situation, the first step in protecting the big data environment is determining the existence and placement of the data.

Following are the steps for data identification/categorization Big Data environment:

1. The data's schema and structure need to be established and verified.
2. There ought to be conditions-based search algorithms available.

10.5 Infrastructure for alleviating Security and Privacy in Big Data

3. Data redundancy should be eliminated by computing the data count. Only one count will be taken into account for multiple records.
4. An analysis of these findings is necessary to develop an improved threat prevention model.

10.5.2 IAM

Entities can have access to the appropriate resources at the appropriate time thanks to identity and access management, or IAM [18]. In the Big Data environment, IAM gives users the ability to restrict who has access to sensitive data. IAM is made up of the following components in every given application:

- Individual identification and verification within a system.
- Assigning/de-assigning of roles to users.
- User management includes adding, updating and removing a user, and their roles.
- Access level mapping for a single user or a group consists of multiple users.
- Security of confidential information and the system itself.

Organizations can increase accessibility to their sensitive data in a big data environment while maintaining security and privacy thanks to identity and access management (IAM). IAM is composed of the following elements:

10.5.2.1 Authentication

The process of verifying a user against their ID and password is known as authentication. Verifying an individual's identity in a Big Data context involves comparing it to the profile they have built on the platform. The authentication system uses the collected data to verify user profiles in response to any request for system access. Unauthorized access will arise from every incorrect effort. In the context of big data, authentication can be implemented by any of the following methods:

- AD (Active Directory)
  For domain networks, Active Directory is a user identification directory service. AD can be used to control user access to Hadoop cluster nodes as well as additional operational costs.
- LDAP (Lightweight Directory Access Protocol)
  Distributed directory services, such as AD, are managed via LDAP. It is predicated on protocols for open standards. LDAP authentication is beneficial in Hadoop clusters as well.

- Kerberos
  As an authentication protocol, Kerberos works by granting tickets to various nodes (Hadoop nodes) so that they can communicate with one another over an unsecured network. Using this method, the tickets are utilized for identity verification after being issued by the Kerberos server to the requested users.
- SSO (Single-Sign-On)
  SSO is another authentication protocol that is used for simplifying the complexity of saving and preserving identifications for various applications. One important advantage of a big data environment is that platform access usually requires a single sign-in from users. Users can access all platform-related technologies after logging in successfully and don't need to reenter their credentials.

10.5.2.2 Authorization

The process of figuring out a user's access privileges for a certain resource is called authorization. Usually, it comes first, following user authentication. Authorization in the Hadoop cluster determines a user's scope of permissions upon authentication. In most cases, HDFS file permissions control this. In the context of big data, authorization can be obtained using any of the following methods:

- ABAC (Attribute Based Access Control)
  Another name for it is policy-based access control, where a user's access permissions are determined by policies that have been established. These rules can be established against resources, objects, and users, among other things. These regulations typically rest on Boolean logic principles, such as IF, THEN. Hadoop employs ABAC as well, applying it to the data layer for data retrieval.
- RBAC (Role Based Access Control)
  Similar to ABAC, role-based access control (RBAC) is based on user-assigned privileges and roles [20]. RBAC serves as a fine-grained authorization control in a big data system. Sensitive and private data is handled by the roles rather than the users when using RBAC. Role-related rules are applied to all data access pathways through LDAP or AD controlling groups.

10.5.2.3 Server and DB Authorization

ACLs (Access Control Lists) are typically used in Big Data implementations to enable server and database authorization. These are employed to

10.5 Infrastructure for alleviating Security and Privacy in Big Data

link specific authorization to specific user IDs. HDFS supports permission methods such as limiting granular access to HDFS files, limiting access to service APIs, and limiting task execution on servers.

When distributing queries from the server to HDFS, integrated security between different modules allows the user's identity to be shared across the Hadoop clusters. In the context of big data, traditional SQL Server permissions can also be utilized for authorization. AD/LDAP integration with big data clusters is achieved through automated deployment. User groups and pre-defined identities can be managed across all endpoints once they are configured.

10.5.2.4 Central User Repository

A Central User Repository is useful in a Big Data context because it allows credential verification and stores and distributes user identity information to several services. The Central User Repository presents various organizations with a rational perspective.

The LDAP standard is used by directory services in big data and has grown to be a key component of central user repositories. For this, meta-directory and virtual-directory are both utilized. To combine multiple user sets with user identity information from different databases into a single LDAP view, a virtual directory is utilized. A meta-directory, on the other hand, offers a logical representation of identity information and is used to combine several identity sources into a meta-set.

10.5.3 Data Safety and Privacy

Privacy and data protection constitute yet another crucial component of a big data system. Many Hadoop vendors and distributors employ different methods to protect the confidentiality and security of data. Some of the fundamental components for safety and privacy in a big data environment are as follows:

10.5.3.1 Data Masking and Encryption

The security and privacy of their client data is the most crucial factor for every Big Data company; a breach might destroy their reputation, cause financial loss, and erode customer trust. Data masking and encryption are therefore becoming necessities in the Big Data context. When vital and critical data is gathered from customers, exact identification is required for all sensitive data, including personally identifiable information (PII), health information, and other sensitive data.

The following factors need to be taken into account while using data masking and encryption:

- Information that has been encrypted and masked should be irretrievable.
- Sensitive data was the only data that required encryption and masking.
- The ultimate result must exhibit the same input or source data and be able to be replicated.
- It is important to preserve referential integrity in data.

Many masking and encryption techniques are employed, however in a Big Data context, preserving the format of sensitive data is crucial. As a result, some of the masking techniques that are applicable are as follows:

- **Substitution**: This method involves replacing the sensitive data with a meaningful but random value.
- **Masking and spacing**: This method involves replacing relevant data with a random piece of information. One such would be the CNIC (Computerized National Identity Card) numbers, which are transaction-specific and can be substituted for XXXXX-XXXXXXX-X.
- **Dates and Numeric Data**: This technique modifies data that contains dates or numbers by adding or subtracting arbitrary percentages from the initial value. Adding or removing 20% of an individual's income from their starting compensation is one example.
- **Encryption**: This method transforms confidential data from an unencrypted format into a ciphertext or encoded format. Another name for the plaintext format is the decoded format. Once data has been encrypted, it cannot be processed until it has been decrypted, which can be accomplished with a decryption key. There are many different encryption techniques, and which one to choose relies on the security and privacy regulations of the Big Data environment. The following encryption methods have the potential to be very beneficial:
    - Triple DES 24-Byte Key
    - Advanced Encryption Standard (AES) 128-bit Key
    - Secure Hash Algorithm 256 Byte (SHA256)
    - RSA – Public/Private Key

10.5.3.2 Data Loss Prevention

Procedures that are helpful in preventing data breaches or the erasure of private information from unwanted sources are included in data loss prevention (DLP). Preventive techniques are used by several organizations to

10.5 Infrastructure for alleviating Security and Privacy in Big Data

protect their sensitive data. The following justifies the adoption of DLP by the organization:

- Protect personal identifiable information
- Accomplish information prominence
- Secure sensitive data and information in Big Data systems

The three categories of data loss are typically motion, at rest, and in use. Data loss in a big data system typically results from internal risks, attacker extrusion, or accidentally disclosed information.

By establishing proper monitoring procedures and policies, it is possible to prevent the leakage of confidential data. In a big data context, these DLP procedures might be carried out either at the host or on the network side. Furthermore, data loss blocking processes can be implemented and utilized on the network for traffic classification, network traffic analysis, network traffic maintenance, detection of illicit data storage, and application of appropriate blocking control.

However, the suggestions that are helpful in DLP at the host are as follows:

- Securing sensitive information and data that are in motion.
- Securing sensitive information and data that are at rest.
- Securing sensitive information and data that are in use.
- Secure endpoints used for data communication with external agents.
- Use the right data leak detection application like IDS, IPS or SIEM, etc.

10.5.3.3 Disk Level Encryption

Using a technique called disk level encryption, important data stored on disks can be shielded from unwanted access by being converted into unintelligible, scribbled code in big data systems. The following are a few benefits of disk level encryption:

- It provides transparent encryption.
- It helps in processing-based access control.
- It is used to secure metadata, log files and configuration files.
- It uses an external key manager to access data in Disk Level Encryption.

Operating system files and other files kept on hard drives can also be encrypted with a different name called Full Disk Encryption (FDE). Sectors are typically used for the FDE. When employing FDE encryption, a key is needed to decrypt the data; in the event that the drive is replaced, this authentication key is still needed because without it, the drives cannot be accessed.

10.5.3.4 File/Folder Encryption

Another helpful method for protecting data in a big data setting is file/folder encryption, which encrypts individual files as well as directories or folders. A different name for it is FileBased Encryption (FBE). In order to identify the encryption or decrypt data, a variety of software agents are utilized in conjunction with read and write activities to disks. After that, the relevant policies are applied. Any data kept in folders can be encrypted, just like FDE. Figure 10.5 shows the encryption of files and folders. File/folder encryption comes in a variety of forms.

- General purpose file system
- Cryptographic file system

10.5.3.5 Tokenization

Tokenization is the technique of maintaining all required information while substituting unique classified data for sensitive and crucial information without compromising security.

While they are somewhat similar, encryption and tokenization are distinct methods for obfuscating data. Tokenization, in contrast to encryption, does not call for a mathematical process to transform sensitive data into tokens. Tokenization eliminates the need for an algorithm or key in order to retrieve the original data against a token. A database is utilized in this procedure

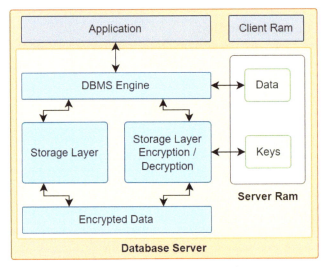

Figure 10.5 File/Folder Encryption.

to hold the association between the token and the data. We refer to this as the token vault. Subsequently, the original data in the vault is secured via encryption. In many applications, the token value serves as a substitute value for the original data. The token is given to the vault in order to recover the original value if the original data is needed.

Tokenization is used in Big Data applications to store sensitive data, such as Protected Health Information (PHI) and Personally Identifiable Information (PII). Big Data firms can safeguard and protect sensitive information from various vulnerabilities and dangers by making it opaque through the use of tokenization in PII and PHI. Additionally, this helps the enterprises comply with industry mandates and governmental standards.

10.5.4 Network and Transport Security

Network security is the process of making sure data is protected during transmission. Numerous protocols have been developed for network and transport layer security in big data. IPSec, SSH, and SSL/TLS are a few examples of them. It can be separated into the subsequent parts:

10.5.4.1 Packet Encryption

In networking, a secure connection is necessary for the delivery of large data packets. Because of the various risks and vulnerabilities that exist, it is imperative that Transport Layer Security (TLS) be used instead of Secure Socket Layer (SSL) in order to guarantee the privacy and authentication of packets between TaskTracker, Applications, DataNodes, and NameNodes. The following are a few potential threats:

- An attacker could be able to change Hadoop consoles and get unauthorized access to data.
- The information obtained could enable the attacker to obtain user credentials.
- Users are given authentication tokens, which can be used on the NameNode to mimic them through Kerberos authentication.

Some of the techniques ensure the protection of data as follows:

- TLS can be used to perform packet level encryption from clients to the Hadoop cluster.
- You can use HTTPS within the NameNode-JobTracker-DataNode-TaskTracker clustering.
- Another application for Map-Reducer is packet level encryption.

- When accessing to common business indexes, LDAP with SSL, or LDAPS, should be utilized to prevent sniffer attacks.

10.5.4.2 Zone Filtering Policies

Implementing a firewall that upholds the access control policy is part of network security. It also shows the traffic that is permitted to flow between NameNode, DataNode, TaskTracker, and other nodes. Furthermore, end users were limited to connecting to NameNodes rather than individual DataNodes. Some of the suggested network zone filtering settings among these are as follows:

- Inside-to-Outside/DMZ
  Traffic that originates inside may head toward the demilitarized zone (DMZ) or outside. Inspection of this data flow is necessary, as is the imposition of any necessary traffic limitations.
- DMZ/Outside-to-Inside
  If the request is coming from the outside or the DMZ, it should be fully restricted until it is a request and response from an internal process.
- Outside-to-DMZ
  Data may enter the DMZ from the outside. In this scenario, a firewall must be used to inspect the data flow and determine whether to give or deny authorization. Certain types of data transmission, such as DNS, HTTP, HTTPS, etc., should be permitted to flow.
- DMZ-to-Outside
  Data transmission from the DMZ may go outside. In this situation, according to the firewall and provision criteria, particular permission ought to be granted. If data traffic is coming from the DMZ to the outside, the firewall will also open the port.

10.5.5 Structural Security

Big Data systems also require various levels of security and privacy in addition to structural security. Four additional components can be identified while dissecting infrastructure security:

10.5.5.1 Auditing/Logging

The practice of recording and keeping track of system transactions is known as auditing. Rules aid in the analysis of user access in relation to specific data, and logging is helpful in many situations when it comes to spotting any unusual activity involving stored data. Every change made to the Hadoop clusters and nodes should be audited for Big Data. Among the instances are:

- Adding and deleting nodes
- Changes made within nodes including NameNode, JobTracker, DataNode or TaskTracker.

Most of the main Hadoop components involve data transfer, which contributes significantly to fragmentations. As a result, all fragments provide a massive audit trail of metadata and logs.

In addition, MapR is used to store any data accesses as well as operations on different objects and implementations, such as commands for changing MapR clusters. The audit logs stored in MapR can be evaluated using the following methods:

- Security Information and Event Management
- Apache Drill
- Third party tools

10.5.5.2 GRSecurity

Big Data apps based on Linux and UNIX can choose from a variety of secured operating systems with customizable access permissions. Users now have the ability to function as administrator users. Many protected operating systems, such as AppArmor, SELinux, and GRSecurity, are available to accommodate access control rights.

GRSecurity is a collection of patches designed to enhance Linux kernel security. It is published under the General Public License (GPL) and is used for identifying and mitigating threats and vulnerabilities on multi-layer models. Mandatory Access Control is the foundation of the GRSecurity framework (MAC). Among GRSecurity's fundamental characteristics are:

- It is used to handle RBAC, which can be used to maintain minimal privileged policies, without utilizing no or low configuration.
- Change root, commonly referred to as chroot, undergoes hardening. Moreover, GRSecurity stays away from /tmp racing, which helps shield against command injection attacks.
- A comprehensive auditing system is accessible.
- The kernel stack serves as the basis for randomization in GRSecurity, enabling additional randomization of the heap, library, and stack.
- It is not possible for any arbitrary code to execute on the kernel base, regardless of the mechanism employed, such as heap, library, or stack.

- The kernel provides security against any exploitable flaws pertaining to the null-pointer.
- The user can set limitations to view only their tasks.
- Any alerts initiated by the user are stored in audit logs along with their IP.

10.5.5.3 File Integrity Monitoring

The process of determining whether or not operating systems, databases, and files have been tampered with is known as file integrity monitoring, or FIM. The process used by FIM involves comparing these files to a reliable baseline. Should any changes be made to the files, databases, or operating systems, FIM will send out a notice for further investigation, and if necessary, an appropriate fix will be produced.

FIM is utilized in many Big Data enterprises for process compliance, security, and optimization. The trustworthy or good baselines in the Hadoop filesystem are regarded as a standard for file monitoring, which typically operates on the basis of the file's version, creation date, modification date, and so on. This ensures the authenticity of the file. Many tools like Trustwave, Tripwire, LogRythm, and Splunk, etc. [21] are available for file integrity monitoring. The benefits of using FIM in Big Data platforms are:

- Identifying illegal activity
- Locating unintended alterations
- Validate update position and also observe system health
- Sustain compliance mandates including PCI DSS and HIPAA etc.

10.5.5.4 User Activity Monitoring and User Behavior Analytics

The system may also experience several anomalies as a result of users engaging in strange behavior. Applications used in Big Data businesses use User Activity Monitoring to track and log actions taken by users. System commands, typing or editing text, visiting URLs, opening dialog boxes, and all on-screen activities are typically included in this category. The majority of the breach occurred as a result of user credentials that were weak, which allows for data exploitation.

Another term created in conjunction with user activity monitoring is user behavior analytics (UBA). The technique of identifying abnormalities, including dangerous threats and vulnerabilities, through statistical analysis and detection algorithms is known as UBA. It is used by Hadoop to identify long-term and insider threats. Some of the features that Big Data systems for behavior analytics should have are as follows:

- Account negotiation, account hijacking and account information sharing
- Data exfiltration
- Personal auditing
- Detection of insider threats
- Stateful session trailing
- Anomalous user behavior
- Risk analysis
- Alert generation in real-time

10.6 Research Methodology

The research methodology provided here is on the basis of data classification which results in categorizing sensitive information to be protected effectively. The technique is based on homomorphic encryption implementation where encrypting sensitive information and storing it on one cloud server for effective usage while non-sensitive information is stored on another cloud server. The objective of the proposed work is to give better outcomes by enhancing the privacy and integrity of data on the cloud server. Research methodology is shown in Figure 10.6. Different parameters used for the advised system are:

- Classified data precision
- Time for data classification
- Positivity Rate
- Encryption/Decryption Time

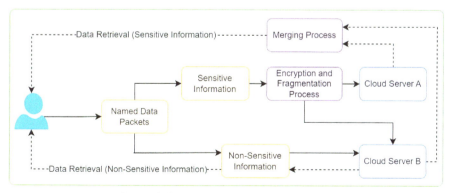

Figure 10.6 Big Data Research Methodology.

298 *Developing a Big Data Infrastructure: Integral Modules and Best Procedures*

The proposed works aims to enhance the privacy and integrity of data on a cloud server using Homomorphic Encryption.

10.6.1 Methodology
10.6.1.1 Homomorphic Encryption Implementation
- Sensitive information is encrypted using a homomorphic encryption scheme before being stored on the cloud server.
- This allows computations to be performed on the encrypted data directly without the need for decryption, maintaining the confidentiality of the sensitive information.

10.6.1.2 Data Storage Separation
- Sensitive encrypted data is stored on one cloud server.
- Non-sensitive information, which doesn't require encryption, is stored on another cloud server.

10.6.1.3 Performance Metrics
Table 10.2 shows the performance metrics in Hadoop in a distributed storage system with a storage capacity of 5 terabyte.

Table 10.2 Performance Metrics.

Aspects	Description
Homomorphic Encryption Overhead in MapReduce Framework	The 10% increase in MapReduce task execution time results in approximately 1.1X minutes for encrypted data where as it was X minutes for regular job.
Data Retrieval Time in Hadoop Distributed File System (HDFS)	The 5% increase in HDFS block retrieval time results in 1.05X seconds for retrieving the block with encrypted data where as it was X seconds for unencrypted data.
Communication Overhead in Hadoop	The 3% increase in network transfer time results in 1.03X seconds for encrypted data where as it was X seconds for unencrypted data.
Storage Efficiency in HDFS	The 5% increase in storage space utilization results in 1.15X petabytes for encrypted data where as it was X petabytes for unencrypted data of HDFS storage if 5 TB of space was utilized.
Computational Complexity in Hadoop	The 12% increase in MapReduce job execution time results in 1.12X minutes with encrypted data where as it was X minutes for unencrypted data.

In future research, the investigation into the impact of homomorphic encryption on MapReduce tasks in Hadoop environments can take various directions. One avenue is the exploration of advanced optimization strategies to minimize computational overhead, enhancing the efficiency of encrypted data processing. Algorithmic enhancements, including the development of tailored encryption algorithms and hybrid schemes, offer opportunities for innovation. Research on parallel processing, distributed encryption, and dynamic key management aims to further improve the security and performance of homomorphic encryption in dynamic, distributed environments. Integration with other advanced security mechanisms, exploration of real-world applications, scalability studies, and user-centric research contribute to a holistic understanding of the trade-offs between data security and computational efficiency. Additionally, investigating energy efficiency and contributing to standardization efforts can shape the development of best practices for implementing homomorphic encryption in Hadoop clusters. This multifaceted research agenda aims to advance the theoretical foundations and practical applications of secure data processing in large-scale distributed environments.

10.7 Conclusion

Big Data's features in data analysis, management, and storage have made it a prominent topic in contemporary technology. This essay gives some background information on big data's historical development and current applications in businesses. Big Data analytics is a common tool used by many businesses and organizations to improve customer retention and satisfaction. Following a concise introduction, we go over the literature review and define the framework and parameters of a big data system in order to classify security and privacy-related issues. Subsequently, we move on to discuss some important big data system features and group them into eight categories: volume, velocity, variety, veracity, variability, visualization, validity and value. Next, we discuss the various security and privacy issues that Big Data presents and how it may jeopardize sensitive data. Because many security applications are unavailable and conventional solutions are insufficient, we address several security concerns and how they affect data availability, anonymity, and integrity. This study delves into the topic of privacy in a big data environment, highlighting the need for diverse administrative responsibilities to function at multiple levels in big data analytics. Additionally, privacy is necessary at several stages of the data lifecycle, including acquisition/generation, sharing/storage, and processing. Next the paper also discuss the comparison and analysis of some key aspects of these challenges. Subsequently, the article suggested an architecture of five components within the core layer to safeguard Big Data applications from various dangers and abnormalities. It also established the foundation for evaluating Big Data systems' security and privacy risks. A variety of Vs were linked to different levels, including as data management, identity and access management, network and transport security, safety and privacy, and infrastructure for enhancing security and privacy. The research methodology done on encrypting Big Data across cloud servers was also presented in the publication. This paper gives the reader an understanding of big data applications. It also discusses the issues that big data presents, including security and privacy concerns, as well as possible solutions. Additionally, the research society will benefit from this paper's intellectual support for research and development.

References

[1] Rusi, https://www.rusi.org/downloads/assets/rusi bigdata report 2013.pdf.

[2] Elisa Bertino, "Big Data – Security and Privacy", 2015 IEEE International Congress on Big Data

[3] http://mylio.com/true-stories/next/how-many-digital-photos-will-be-taken-2017-repost

[4] http://www.internetlivestats.com/google-search-statistics/

[5] Xu, J. S., Zhang, E., Huang, C. -H., Chen, L. H. L., & Celik, N. (2014). Efficient multi-fidelity simulation optimization. Proceedings of 2014 winter simulation conference. GA: Savanna

[6] https://www.macrotrends.net/stocks/charts/AMZN/amazon/revenue

[7] Uthayasankar Sivarajah, Muhammad Mustafa Kamal, Zahir Irani, Vishanth Weerakkody, "Critical analysis of Big Data challenges and analytical methods", Journal of Business Research 70 (2017) 263–286

[8] Dongre, S., Mishra, S., Romanowski, C., Buddhadev, M. (2019). Quantifying the Costs of Data Breaches. In: Staggs, J., Shenoi, S. (eds) Critical Infrastructure Protection XIII. ICCIP 2019. IFIP Advances in Information and Communication Technology, vol 570. Springer, Cham. https://doi.org/10.1007/978-3-030-34647-8_1

[9] Vashishtha, S., Rhinard, M. (2021). Big Data as a Creeping Crisis. In: Boin, A., Ekengren, M., Rhinard, M. (eds) Understanding the Creeping

Crisis. Palgrave Macmillan, Cham. https://doi.org/10.1007/978-3-030-70692-0_5
[10] https://www.reuters.com/business/autos-transportation/uber-enters-non-prosecution-agreement-admits-covering-up-2016-data-breach-2022-07-22/
[11] Shankar, N. & Mohammed, Z. (2020). "Surviving Data Breaches: A Multiple Case Study Analysis". Journal of Comparative International Management, 23(1), 35–54. https://doi.org/10.7202/1071508ar
[12] L. Xu and W. Shi, "Security Theories and Practices for Big Data", Big Data Concepts, Theories, and Applications, 2016, pp. 157-192.
[13] S. Sudarsan, R. Jetley and S. Ramaswamy, "Security and Privacy of Big Data", Studies in Big Data, 2015, pp. 121-136.
[14] "Types of Network Attacks against Confidentiality, Integrity and Availability", Omnisecu.com, 2019. [Online]. Available: http://www.omnisecu.com/ccna-security/types-of-network-attacks.php. Accessed on 19-Dec-2019.
[15] Apache Cassandra Project, http://cassandra.apache.org/.
[16] Daswani, N., Elbayadi, M. (2021). The Yahoo Breaches of 2013 and 2014. In: Big Breaches. Apress, Berkeley, CA. https://doi.org/10.1007/978-1-4842-6655-7_7
[17] https://www.guru99.com/what-is-big-data.html
[18] https://www.gartner.com/en/information-technology/glossary/identity-and-access-management-iam
[19] V. Reena Catherine, A. Shajin Nargunam, Encryption Techniques to Ensure Data Confidentiality in Cloud, International Journal of Innovative Technology and Exploring Engineering (IJITEE), Vol 8, no. 11, 2019.
[20] https://en.wikipedia.org/wiki/Role-based_access_control
[21] https://en.wikipedia.org/wiki/File_integrity_monitoring
[22] Lewko, A., Okamoto, T., Sahai, A., Takashima, K., Waters, B.: Fully Secure Functional Encryption: Attribute-Based Encryption and (Hierarchical) Inner Product Encryption. In: Gilbert, H. (ed.) EUROCRYPT 2010. LNCS, vol. 6110, pp. 62–91. Springer, Heidelberg (2010)
[23] Siddiqa, A., Karim, A. & Gani, A. Big data storage technologies: a survey, Frontiers of Information Technology & Electronic Engineering, vol 18, pp. 1040–1070(2017)
[24] W. Xindong, Z. Xingquan, W. Gong-Qing, et al. *Data Mining with Big Data*, IEEE T. Knowl.Data En., **26** (2014), 97–107.

[25] Stergiou C.L., Plageras A.P., Psannis K.E., Gupta B.B. (2020) Secure Machine Learning Scenario from Big Data in Cloud Computing via Internet of Things Network. In: Gupta B., Perez G., Agrawal D., Gupta D. (eds) Handbook of Computer Networks and Cyber Security. Springer, Cham

[26] Rajabion, Lila & Shaltooki, Abdusalam & Taghikhah, Masoud & Ghasemi, Amirhossein & Badfar, Arshad. (2019). Healthcare big data processing mechanisms: The role of cloud computing. International Journal of Information Management. 49. 271-289.

[27] S. Bahulikar, "Security measures for the big data, virtualization and the cloud infrastructure," *2016 1st India International Conference on Information Processing (IICIP)*, Delhi, 2016, pp. 1-4.

[28] N. Chitransh, C. Mehrotra and A. S. Singh, "Risk for big data in the cloud," *2017 International Conference on Computing, Communication and Automation (ICCCA)*, Greater Noida, 2017, pp. 277-282

[29] C. Liu, C. Yang, X. Zhang, et al. External integrity verification for outsourced big data in cloudand IoT: a big picture, Future Gener. Comp. Sy., 49 (2015), 58–67.

[30] S. Arora, M. Kumar, P. Johri and S. Das, "Big heterogeneous data and its security: A survey," 2016 International Conference on Computing, Communication and Automation (ICCCA), Noida, 2016, pp. 37-40.

[31] I. de la Torre-Díez, B. Garcia-Zapirain, M. Lopez-Coronado, et al. Proposing telecardiologyservices on cloud for different medical institutions: a model of reference, Telemedicine ande-Health, 23 (2017), 654–661.

[32] Mishra K.N., Chakraborty C. (2020) A Novel Approach Towards Using Big Data and IoT for Improving the Efficiency of m-Health Systems. In: Gupta D., Hassanien A., Khanna A. (eds) Advanced Computational Intelligence Techniques for Virtual Reality in Healthcare. Studies in Computational Intelligence, vol 875. Springer, Cham

[33] S. Agarwal, M. Gupta and A. Sharma, "Big Data Privacy Issues & Solutions," *2019 Fifth International Conference on Image Information Processing (ICIIP)*, Shimla, India, 2019, pp. 225-228.

[34] K. R. Sollins, "IoT Big Data Security and Privacy Versus Innovation," in *IEEE Internet of Things Journal*, vol. 6, no. 2, pp. 1628-1635, April 2019.

[35] J. Moreno, E. B. Fernandez, M. A. Serrano and E. Fernández-Medina, "Secure Development of Big Data Ecosystems," in *IEEE Access*, vol. 7, pp. 96604-96619, 2019.

[36] J. Andrew, J. Karthikeyan and J. Jebastin, "Privacy Preserving Big Data Publication On Cloud Using Mondrian Anonymization Techniques and Deep Neural Networks," *2019 5th International Conference on Advanced Computing & Communication Systems (ICACCS)*, Coimbatore, India, 2019, pp. 722-727
[37] N. Zhou, G. Huang, S. Zhong, "Big Data Validity Evaluation Based on MMTD", Mathematical Problems in Engineering, vol. 2018, Article ID 8058670, 6 pages.
[38] S, Arockia, "The 17 V's of Big Data". International Research Journal of Engineering and Technology, 2017, 4. 329-333.

11

Evaluation of the Performance of Pattern Search and Genetic Algorithms for Enhancing the Lifetime of WSNs

Ibtissam Larhlimi, Maryem Lachgar, Hicham Ouchitachen, Anouar Darif, and Hicham Mouncif

Laboratory of Innovation in Mathematics, Applications and Information Technology, Polydisciplinary Faculty, Sultan Moulay Slimane University, Morocco
E-mail: ibtissam.larhlimifpb@usms.ac.ma; maryem.lachgarfbp@usms.ma; a.darif@usms.ma; h.mouncif@usms.ma

Abstract

The limitation of energy resources poses a significant obstacle for wireless sensor networks, given that the sensor nodes rely on batteries with finite energy capacity, typically non-rechargeable or non-replaceable. Prior research has operated under the assumption that inactive sensors exhibit minimal energy consumption. The conventional methodologies, grounded on this assumption, involve selecting a specific group of nodes that systematically encompass all desired objectives through iterative processes. The subsets, referred to as coverage sets, are activated while the remaining subsets are in a state of energy conservation or dormancy. The issue is classified as NP-hard and is technically called the maximum coverage set scheduling problem (MCSS).

This study presents a comparative analysis of two proposed methodologies, namely the pattern search algorithm and the genetic algorithm, to enhance the longevity of wireless sensor networks (WSNs). These methods ensure the discovery of a feasible coverage set collection schedule to maximize network lifetime performance, taking into account each sensor's active time. The simulation results demonstrate that the proposed algorithms effectively enhance network lifetime compared to the greedy algorithm. The reason for this might be attributed to the favourable characteristics of the method when it comes to addressing limited optimization situations.

Keywords: Wireless sensor network, pattern search algorithm, genetic algorithm, maximization, lifetime, coverage, cover set scheduling.

11.1 Introduction

In today's era of rapid technological advancement, sensors have transcended their initial role of merely measuring and monitoring physical values at a basic level. The integration of wireless technologies and the Internet has propelled these sensors into wireless sensor networks (WSNs). As we embrace the Internet of Things (IoT) as the next evolutionary step, the ability of interconnected objects to communicate and share information over the Internet becomes paramount. WSNs play a pivotal role in this IoT landscape by facilitating the collection, analysis, and deployment of vast data, transforming it into meaningful information and knowledge.

This paper focuses on an energy optimization approach based on the inactivity/activity mode. Specifically, we propose a method to create subsets of sensor nodes sequentially activated for defined durations. In contrast, the remaining nodes remain on standby, maximizing the network's operational duration. Addressing the NP-hard maximum lifetime coverage problem (MLCP), our research delves into a critical aspect often overlooked in the literature, the energy consumption of sensors in standby mode.

The coverage problem is dissected into two integral steps: first, identifying numerous coverage sets for the network's sensors, and second, scheduling these sets to maximize the network's lifetime. The maximum coverage set scheduling (MCSS) problem addresses all coverage concerns. For a coverage set $C = \{C1, C2, ..., Cm\}$, where each subset $Cj \in C$ comprises sensors with ample battery power capable of fully covering targets or the entire area, the MCSS problem involves determining the optimal scheduling strategy for coverage sets to maximize network lifetime. Our research is dedicated to crafting schedules for coverage sets acquired from autonomously monitoring sensors, employing two approaches: the pattern search algorithm (PSA) and the genetic algorithm. The objective is to maximize network lifetime by considering sensor energy and active time. The constraint ensures that the total active time in the schedule does not exceed the first time slot.

The rest of this chapter is organized as follows. Section 11.2 presents WSN and it is problematic. surveys the related work in Section 11.3. Section 11.4 presents the formulation of the MCSS problem. Section 11.5 introduces the proposed algorithms approach and its novelties. The simulation results arc illustrated in Section 11.6. Finally, Section 11.7 concludes this work.

11.2 Wireless Sensor Network

Wireless sensor networks (WSNs) are systems of numerous wireless sensors deployed in a specific environment to monitor, collect, and transmit data on physical or environmental phenomena [1]. These networks are versatile technologies used in various fields, including agriculture, environment, industrial monitoring, health, and logistics. They have several distinctive features, such as wireless communication, energy autonomy, limited processing capabilities, mass deployment, heterogeneous capabilities, adaptability to the environment, ability to form self-organizing networks, real-time data collection, and low cost [4–7].

The architecture of WSNs can vary depending on the application and network's specific needs. Essential elements include sensors, relay nodes, base stations, and communication infrastructure. Sensors collect data from the environment, relay nodes transfer data to a base station or central node, and base stations are connected to monitoring, processing, or warning systems. Communication infrastructure covers the communication protocols and technologies used to transmit data between nodes.

However, the deployment of WSNs poses several challenges and issues that need to be considered for efficient and reliable operation. Energy consumption is essential as batteries power sensors, and developing energy management mechanisms is essential to extend the network's life. The network topology can change frequently due to the dynamic environment in which they are deployed, and routing mechanisms must be adapted to these dynamics. Security is crucial as data collected by sensors can be sensitive and requires adequate protection against attacks and intrusions. Reliability is essential as wireless communication is subject to interference and disruption, and scalability is essential as WSNs can become large. Figure 11.1 presents the architecture of a WSN.

To address these issues, ongoing research in wireless sensor networks is needed to develop innovative and robust solutions to meet the diverse needs of applications deployed in real environments. By understanding the challenges

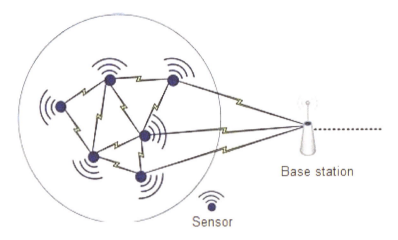

Figure 11.1 WSN architecture.

and opportunities presented by WSNs, researchers can develop innovative and robust solutions that meet the diverse needs of applications deployed in real environments.

11.3 Related Work

Various methodologies have been employed to tackle the sensor deployment challenge in wireless sensor networks (WSNs). This section introduces several techniques that specifically align with our research objectives.

In the study in [8], a proposed algorithm prioritizes sensors with minimal energy levels and uses a blacklist to limit the number of sensors covering critical targets. They discuss situations in which sensors must remain active during specific time slots to monitor specific locations within a given area. In addition, an upper limit is set for the maximum potential lifetime of this unique situation. A genetic technique is proposed to achieve an almost perfect node activity plan [9].

The work in [10] introduces a mathematical model that aims to optimize the density of active sensor nodes in a WSN from a geometric perspective. This optimization is accomplished by utilizing concentric hexagonal tessellations and coverage contribution areas for nodes that are randomly placed within the designated area. An algorithm is proposed to generate a high number of separate and independent subsets of sensor nodes, providing an optimized solution to the k-coverage problem.

In [11], the authors present a recursive neighborhood-based estimation of distribution algorithm (NEDA) to tackle this challenge. Every person in NEDA embodies a coverage strategy in which sensors are selectively activated to monitor all targets. In order to maximize the network's longevity among the current population, a team of experts has developed a linear programming (LP) model to efficiently distribute activation times to the various schemes.

The work in [12] discusses an incoming routing strategy for WSNs that utilizes a hybrid energy-efficient distributing (HEED) algorithm and a fuzzy approach. Their proposal algorithm involves clustering WSNs using the stable election procedure HEED method and considering metrics such as residual energy, minimal hops, and node traffic counts using fuzzy inference and the low-energy adaptive clustering hierarchy (LEACH) method.

In [13], a model called efficient topology-driven cooperative self-scheduling (TDCSS) is proposed. This model utilizes a hybrid strategy instead of centrally scheduling network nodes. This technique allows for bidirectional scheduling based on the specific circumstances. Node statistics are periodically shared to minimize control packet transmission overhead.

Their research in [14] centers around the maximum α-lifetime problem, with the goal of developing a heuristic solution that maximizes network lifetime while satisfying coverage criteria. They achieve extended network lifespan by selectively activating and deactivating various groups of sensors while ensuring the necessary minimum coverage rate is maintained.

11.4 Modeling and Problem Formulation

11.4.1 Energy consumption in wireless sensor networks (WSNs)

Analyze the energy consumption characteristics of a wireless sensor node to begin constructing the energy system for the sensor system. An exhaustive examination of a sensor node's energy is crucial for detecting any problems within the energy system in order to facilitate efficient optimization. The primary contributors to energy consumption in a sensor are detection, processing, and communication activities [18].

11.4.1.1 Sensing energy

The energy consumption sources for nodes during sensing or capture processes include sampling, analog-to-digital conversion, signal processing, and capture probe activation [19].

11.4.1.2 Energy processing

Processing energy encompasses two distinct forms of energy: switching energy and leakage energy. The act of switching energy is influenced by the voltage of the power supply and the combined capacitance that is being switched during the execution of software. Leakage energy refers to the energy that is used by the computer unit while it is not doing any processing. In general, the amount of energy needed for processing is lower than the amount needed for communication.

11.4.1.3 Communication energy

The energy required for communication may be divided into three components: energy for receiving, energy for transmitting, and energy for idle state. The energy required is contingent upon the quantity of data to be sent, the distance of transmission, and the physical characteristics of the radio module. Signal transmission is determined by its power. A higher transmission power leads to a greater signal range, but also increases energy consumption. It is important to mention that communication energy accounts for the majority of energy used by a sensor node.

The primary energy consumption of sensor nodes can be linked to three fundamental processes: sensing, communication, and processing. These activities are essential to the operation of WSNs, but they also contribute to one of the main issues facing these networks: efficient energy management. Effectively regulating the energy consumption of sensor nodes is a significant challenge if they are to have a long life and sufficient autonomy. Energy-saving techniques such as energy-efficient routing protocols, selective node sleep, operating mode management, and processing optimization are used to improve energy efficiency in wireless sensor networks.

11.4.2 Mathematical model

Consider a scenario where S represents a set of m sensors, denoted as $S = \{s_1, ..., s_m\}$. Similarly, Tg denotes a set of p targets, represented as $Tg = \{t_1, ..., t_p\}$ [2]. Additionally, there exists a collection C, denoted as $C = \{C_1, C_2, - - - -, C_n\}$, comprising n coverage sets. Each set $Cj \in C$ comprises sensors capable of fully covering all targets, along with their active time denoted as T_j. It's crucial to note that j ranges from 1 to n. The scheduling approach $(T_1, T_2, - - -, T_n)$ refers to the strategy used for scheduling the cover sets C. Each sensor, denoted as s_i, has a specific battery lifetime, b_i, and a sensing range that dictates the extent of monitored targets by that sensor s_i.

The problem of maximum coverage set scheduling can be represented as an integer linear programming (ILP) formulation [20].

$$\max \sum_{j=1}^{n} T_j (f). \quad (11.1)$$

Subject to:

$$\sum_{j=1}^{n} (\delta_{i,j} T_j) \leq b_i \ \forall s_i \in S, \quad (11.2)$$

where $\delta_{i,j} = \{1, \text{ if } s_i \in C_j \ 0, \text{ otherwise}\}$.

The objective function (f) is to optimize the overall active time for the collecting of cover sets. Constraint (C) guarantees that the cumulative duration of active time intervals in the scheduling method for each sensor does not exceed the duration of the first active time intervals.

11.5 Proposed Approaches

This section contains our proposed genetic algorithm for the MCSS problem. Finding a scheduling method for the cover sets in C that ensures just one cover set is active at each time slot and maximizes their combined active time will improve the network lifetime.

11.5.1 Genetic algorithm approach

11.5.1.1 Initialization

Within a genetic algorithm (GA), a chromosome serves as a representation of a potential solution to an optimization issue. Thus, a chromosome within the proposed genetic algorithm should include a timetable for gathering cover sets [3].

Assume that C finishes collecting cover sets, where each gene represents a specific set of covers denoted as C_j. The chromosome C may be denoted as $C = \{C_1, C_2, - - - -, C_n\}$, where n represents the population size. Furthermore, the representation technique has the capability to include the whole solution space, ensuring that each chromosome accurately represents a distinct schedule.

11.5.1.2 Fitness

The fitness assessment ensures that the candidate solution adheres to the energy constraints. The total energy consumption across all schedule covers must not surpass any sensor's initial energy. Candidate schedules failing to meet this criterion will be excluded from future genetic algorithm (GA) processes using the fitness function.

11.5.1.3 Selection

From the adapted population, the two best candidate programs with the maximum lifetime are selected as parents.

11.5.1.4 Crossover

A suitable crossover method, specifically the double-point crossover, is applied to generate offspring for the subsequent generation and update the population. The crossover points are randomly chosen, following the typical GA approach.

11.5.1.5 Mutation

Applying appropriate mutation is crucial to refine the offspring and prevent them from getting trapped in local optimal solutions. One or more genes are randomly selected and altered. Enhancement involves increasing the value of the genes and, consequently, the chromosome. Mutation genes are selected randomly to maintain diversity.

11.5.1.6 Fitness assessment of offspring

For the "new chromosome" children, the fitness function is recalculated concerning the active time in constraint (C) to ensure no sensor exceeds its initial energy. Parents are updated if the improved children demonstrate a better gene pool or enhanced lifespan.

11.5.2 Pattern search algorithm approach

The pattern search algorithm (PSA) is a derivation-free approach that falls within the category of direct search methods.

A pattern search algorithm seeks a set of locations near the current position where the objective function value is superior to the current point's value. This contrasts with traditional optimization techniques that rely on a gradient or higher derivative information to locate an optimum place [16].

11.5 Proposed Approaches

Below is a concise explanation of the pattern search algorithm. It identifies a sequence of positions that gradually approach the ideal point [17].

The method iteratively explores a mesh, a collection of points, to find a spot that yields a superior objective function value compared to the present position. In the subsequent phase of the algorithm, the new point assumes the position of the current point. The "Pattern Vector" refers to a predetermined collection of vectors. To create the mesh, multiply these vectors by a scalar

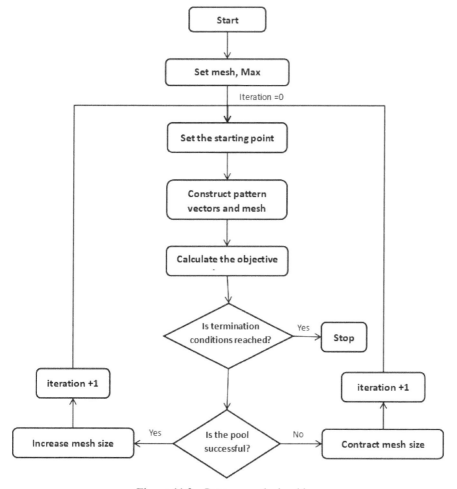

Figure 11.2 Pattern search algorithm.

value and then add them to the current point. Figure 11.2 depicts the flowchart of the PS algorithm. The primary stages of this algorithm are:

Phase 1: Establishing precise and concise explanations: The current phase is divided into the following steps:

- The solution space encompasses the objective function, the optimization variables, and their respective lower and upper limits. In discussing an optimization problem, it is crucial to establish the optimization variables and an objective function. These elements serve as a connection between the physical problem and the optimization approach.
- Working parameter definition: This step entails establishing the expansion and contraction factors for the N-dimensional pattern vector to generate a mesh around the active working point.
- Starting point definition: The algorithm must have predetermined a starting point within the solution space before execution. Various stochastic or deterministic methods may be used to get the initialization set. This procedure might also be referred to as a startup.

Phase 2: The process of conducting a poll: The following protocols are executed:

- Assess the goal at the grid locations.
- Assess the mesh points' values relative to the objective function at the current position.
- Confirm that the specified criteria are met if the current point is more precise than the mesh points. The solution point and its objective value are outputted when they are fulfilled. Alternatively, go to the subsequent stage.

Phase 3: The pattern search method may be halted by several conditions. The criteria include the mesh size, iteration duration, time limit, and termination tolerance for the objective function value.

11.6 Simulation and Results

The simulations conducted in this study involve deploying a network with N sensors randomly distributed across a defined geographical area. The main goal of these simulations is to evaluate the efficiency and effectiveness of the proposed pattern search and genetic algorithms in optimizing sensor coverage and maximizing network performance. To conduct a comprehensive

11.6 Simulation and Results

evaluation, a comparative analysis is conducted, comparing the performance of the genetic algorithm and the pattern search algorithm to that of the greedy algorithm, a commonly used heuristic approach in sensor network optimization. The results are obtained through averaging 150 iterations, conducted using MATLAB R2020 for all simulation procedures. In our simulation, we consider the following parameters as given in Table 11.1:

Table 11.1 Parameters of simulations.

Parameters	value
Length of chromosome	The scheduling strategy of the collection of cover sets C
Crossover rate	0.5
Mutation rate	0.2
Iteration	150
R (Sensing range of each sensor node)	6
M (Number of coverages sets)	100

Figure 11.3 presents a comprehensive comparative analysis, elucidating the lifetimes achieved through our proposed approach compared to the other two algorithms across various active time slots for the sensors. The

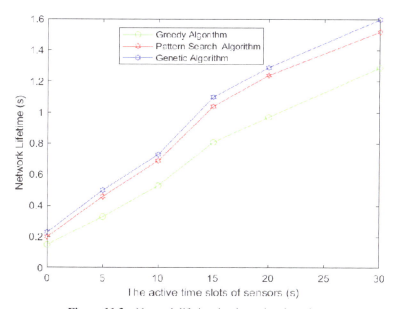

Figure 11.3 Network lifetime by the active time slots.

experimental setup involves the deployment of 100 sensors, with the active time slots incrementing systematically from 0 to 30.

The results consistently show a discernible trend, indicating the superior performance of both the genetic algorithm (GA) and the pattern search algorithm (PSA) in terms of calculated lifetimes, in comparison to the greedy algorithm. This recurring observation underscores the effectiveness and practicality of the genetic and pattern search methods in enhancing the activation of sensors and ultimately prolonging the network's lifespan.

The comparative analysis presented in Figure 11.4 provides compelling evidence that our proposed algorithms are capable of addressing the challenges associated with wireless sensor networks. The genetic and pattern search approaches show their adaptive ability to optimize network resources by surpassing the performance of the greedy algorithm across different active time slots. This translates into increased longevity and improved efficiency of the system.

These findings not only emphasize the practical applicability of advanced optimization techniques, but also highlight the potential for significant advancements in the field of wireless sensor network management and deployment strategies. Consequently, they offer valuable insights for the

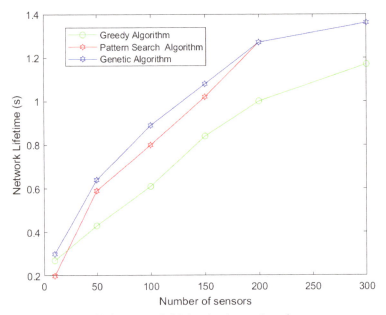

Figure 11.4 Network lifetime by the number of sensors.

design and implementation of future-generation sensor networks, with a focus on enhancing performance and extending operational lifespans.

In this experiment, we conducted a comprehensive analysis using 100 coverage sets and varying sensor counts ranging from 10 to 300. Each sensor was assigned a time slot of 10. The results clearly show that the proposed algorithms are highly efficient in maximizing network lifetime compared to the greedy algorithm.

The graph clearly illustrates that increasing the number of sensors used positively impacted the network's lifetime. This indicates that the proposed algorithms are effective in improving the overall network lifetime.

A key aspect of the genetic algorithm (GA) lies in its fitness and selection phase, where the two best-performing solutions are carefully chosen as parents. This strategic selection greatly increases the chances of producing offspring with favorable genetic traits, thereby enhancing the algorithm's ability to prolong the network's lifespan.

Furthermore, the steps involved in the pattern search (PS) algorithm play a crucial role in achieving these impressive results. The PS algorithm's iterative nature and systematic exploration of solution spaces synergistically contribute to optimizing network performance and enhancing its overall longevity.

11.7 Conclusion

This paper presents a mathematical model aimed at solving the challenging problem of maximum coverage set scheduling (MCSS) in wireless sensor networks (WSNs). Leveraging genetic algorithm (GA), pattern search algorithm (PSA), and integer linear programming (ILP), the model operates in a dual approach: it initially establishes coverage sets and subsequently determines the most optimal scheduling strategy. Experimental results demonstrate the superiority of the pattern search algorithm (PSA) and genetic algorithm (GA) over existing techniques such as the greedy algorithm, particularly in optimizing sensor lifetime. Their effectiveness stems from their simplicity, minimal computational requirements, and ease of implementation.

The type of WSN addressed in this article holds potential for various critical situations in different medical and environmental domains. In future work, we aim to enhance this study by considering the mobility of both sensors and targets.

References

[1] Lachgar, and al. Performances Evaluation of LRP Protocol in Wireless Sensor Network. ICAIGC (2023). Lecture Notes in Networks and Systems, vol 806. Springer.

[2] LARHLIMI, and al. A Genetic Algorithm Approach Applied to the Cover Set Scheduling Problem for Maximizing Wireless Sensor Networks Lifetime. AICV (2023). Lecture Notes on Data Engineering and Communications Technologies, vol 164. Springer.

[3] LARHLIMI, and al. Contribution to Solving the Cover Set Scheduling Problem and Maximizing Wireless Sensor Networks Lifetime Using an Adapted Genetic Algorithm. A2IA 2023. Lecture Notes in Networks and Systems, vol 772. Springer.

[4] M.T. Thai, al.: Coverage problems in wireless sensor networks: designs and analysis. In International Journal of Sensor Networks, vol. 3, no 3, p. 191. (2008)

[5] G. Fan, al.: Coverage Problem in Wireless Sensor Network: A Survey. In Journal of Networks, vol. 5, no 9, p. 1033 1040. (2010)

[6] M.M.T. Cardei, al.: Energy-efficient target coverage in wireless sensor networks. In Proceedings IEEE 24th Annual Joint Conference of the IEEE Computer and Communications Societies, Miami, FL, USA, p. 1976–1984. (2005)

[7] Mitigeur, A., & Trojanowski, K. (2019). Maximization of The Sensor Network Lifetime by Activity Schedule Heuristic Optimization. Ad Hoc Networks, 101994.

[8] Tchuani Tchakonté, D., Simeu, E., & Tchuente, M. (2018). Lifetime optimization of wireless sensor networks with sleep mode energy consumption of sensor nodes. Wireless Networks. doi:10.1007/s11276-018-1783-3

[9] D'Ambrosio, C., Iossa, A., Laureana, F., & Palmieri, F. (2020). A genetic approach for the maximum network lifetime problem with additional operating time slot constraints. Soft Computing. doi:10.1007/s00500-020-04821-y

[10] Chauhan, N., & Chauhan, S. (2021). A Novel Area Coverage Technique for Maximizing the Wireless Sensor Network Lifetime. Arabian Journal for Science and Engineering, 46(4), 3329–3343. doi:10.1007/s13369-020-05182-2

[11] Chen, Zong-Gan; Lin, Ying; Gong, Yue-Jiao; Zhan, Zhi-Hui; Zhang, Jun (2020). Maximizing Lifetime of Range-Adjustable Wireless Sensor Networks: A Neighborhood-Based Estimation of Distribution Algorithm. IEEE Transactions on Cybernetics, (), 1–12. doi:10.1109/tcyb.2020.2977858

[12] Jabbar, M.S., Issa, S.S., Ali, A.H., Improving WSNs execution using energy-efficient clustering algorithms with consumed energy and lifetime maximization, (2023) Indonesian Journal of Electrical Engineering and Computer Science 29(2), pp. 1122-1131

[13] Brindha, G., Ezhilarasi, P., Topology Driven Cooperative Self Scheduling for Improved Lifetime Maximization in WSN, (2023) Computer Systems Science and Engineering 45(1), pp. 445-458

[14] Dua, A., Jastrząb, T., Czech, Z.J., Krömer, P., A Randomized Algorithm for Wireless Sensor Network Lifetime Optimization, Q2SWinet 2022 - Proceedings of the 18th ACM International Symposium on QoS and Security for Wireless and Mobile Networks pp. 87-93

[15] A. Rossi, A. Singh, and M. Sevaux, "An exact approach for maximizing the lifetime of sensor networks with adjustable sensing ranges," Comput. Oper. Res., vol. 39, no. 12, pp. 3166–3176, 2012

[16] I. Larhlimi, al.. Maximization of Lifetime in Wireless Sensor Networks Using Pattern Search Algorithm. ICAIGC 2023. Lecture Notes in Networks and Systems, vol 806. Springer, Cham. https://doi.org/10.1007/978-3-031-46584-0_11.

[17] Güneş, F., & Tokan, F. (2010). Pattern Search optimization with applications on synthesis of linear antenna arrays. Expert Systems with Applications, 37(6), 4698–4705. doi:10.1016/j.eswa.2009.11.012

[18] Anouar Darif, Hicham Ouchitachen, "Performance Improvement of a New MAC Protocol For Ultra Wide Band Wireless Sensor Networks", Journal of Theoretical and Applied Information Technology, Vol.100. No 4, pp.1015-1026, 2022.

[19] H. Ouchitachen, A. Hair , N. Idrissi, "Improved multi-objective weighted clustering algorithm in Wireless Sensor Network ", In: Egyptian Informatics Journal-Elsevier, Volume 18, Issue 1, pp. 45–54, 2017.

[20] Chuanwen Luo, Yi Hong, Deying Li, Yongcai Wang, Wenping Chen, Qian Hu, Maximizing Network Lifetime Using Coverage Sets Scheduling in Wireless Sensor Networks, Ad Hoc Networks (2019)

Index

A

ADASYN 103, 108, 115
Access control 160, 163, 168, 182, 214, 217, 274, 281, 288
Anomaly detection 7, 17, 21, 212
Artificial intelligence (AI) 1, 47, 63
Asymmetric encryption 244, 245, 246

B

Benchmark datasets 211, 212, 213, 218, 227, 229
Benchmark intrusion datasets 2, 211
Big data 2, 14, 62, 121, 185, 232, 269, 272, 274, 276, 280
Big data empirical features 269
Big data infrastructure 2, 269
Big data integral modules 269
Blockchain 1, 69, 180, 239, 242, 243, 257
Blockchain privacy 2, 239

C

Cover set scheduling 318
Coverage 41, 73, 199, 305, 308, 311, 315, 317
COVID-19 1, 46, 103, 114, 117, 118, 174
Critical infrastructures 1, 33, 35, 126
Cryptography 1, 214, 244, 251

Cyber resilience 2, 53, 187
Cyber risk management 1, 33, 35, 39, 48, 58
cyber threat 1, 17, 49, 125, 158, 177, 181, 187, 206, 262
cyber threat mitigation 126
cyberattack 7, 14, 15, 44, 58, 128, 161, 175, 176, 179, 213
Cybercrime 41, 66, 74
Cyber-physical systems 44, 45, 159, 208
Cybersecurity 1, 33, 39, 125, 188, 193, 224, 326
Cybersecurity testing 187, 188, 193, 206
Cyber-threat intelligence 62

D

Data analytics 2, 185, 232, 265, 271
Data collection 78, 270, 275, 281, 307
Data privacy 240, 253, 277, 278, 286
Data protection 13, 163, 181, 277, 281
Decentralized autonomous organization (DAO) 69, 70, 78, 96
Decentralized systems 247
Definition 36, 37, 134, 201, 314
Digital instrumentation and control systems 188

E

Epidemiology 110
Ethereum 69, 73, 259, 260
Extreme gradient boosting 82, 84, 106
Encryption algorithms 260, 299

F

Fraud detection 1, 69, 71, 74, 80, 86

G

Genetic algorithm 77, 305, 306, 311, 316

H

Hash functions 244, 247, 250
Healthcare systems 1, 7, 15, 18, 103, 161
Homomorphic encryption 2, 239, 240, 247, 251, 257, 264, 299

I

Imbalanced dataset 1, 79, 106, 111, 221
Incident response 34, 166, 175, 181, 190, 200, 202
Industrial construction chain 187, 188
Industrial control systems (ICS) 1, 44, 45, 125, 127, 189, 191
Intelligent systems 232, 267
Internet of Things (IoT) 1, 7, 45, 126, 262, 265, 270, 306
Intrusion detection 16, 17, 35, 46, 175, 217, 282
IoT security 16, 31, 159

L

Lifetime 305, 306, 309, 315, 316, 318

Logic programming 126, 187, 188, 193, 206
Logistic regression 55, 69, 70, 76, 82, 92, 94, 110

M

Machine learning 1, 47, 55, 69, 103, 109, 260, 282
Malware analysis 33
Maximization 318, 319

N

Network security 47, 194, 212, 293, 294

O

Operational technology (OT) 48, 128, 187, 188, 194, 203

P

Pattern search algorithm 305, 306, 312, 313, 316, 317
Penetration testing 2, 125, 126, 156, 190
Privacy 2, 166, 239, 242, 251, 257, 269, 274, 278, 281
Privacy challenges 2, 15, 269, 274, 284
Privacy preservation 245

R

Random forest 48, 55, 69, 82, 83, 84, 93, 103, 110
Ransomware 19, 25, 164, 165, 166, 168, 176
Red teaming 2, 187, 189, 198, 207
Review 16, 33, 53, 142, 162, 205, 269, 271
Risk management 1, 33, 35, 50, 53, 54, 55, 57

RUS 103, 115, 116, 117, 118, 208,

S

Sampling techniques 2, 75, 103, 107, 119, 223
SCADA environments 158
SCADA systems cybersecurity 126
Secure communication 281
Security 13, 61, 162, 175, 189, 211, 213, 215, 222, 269, 274, 276
Security and privacy challenges 2, 269, 274, 284
Security challenges 2, 36, 44, 123, 275, 281
Security policies 161
Security protocols 16, 283
Smart contracts 69, 70, 180, 247, 254
SMOTE 75, 103, 107, 116
Symmetric encryption 244, 246, 247

T

Threat management 7, 103, 104, 105, 113

U

User privacy 240, 244, 258, 282

V

Virtual laboratory 127
Vulnerability assessment 127, 160

W

web application firewall (WAF) 211, 230, 233
Web security 2, 211, 222
Wireless sensor network 305, 306, 307, 308, 309, 317, 319

About the Editors

Prof. Mounia Zaydi is an associate professor of cybersecurity at the Engineering School JUNIA ISEN in France. She is a member of IEEE and also a member of the International Association of Engineers (IAENG). Dr. Zaydi has made significant contributions in the fields of information security and privacy, IT governance, risk management, and the application of artificial intelligence to IT changes, IT incidents, and IT agility. Her research interests include information security and privacy, the Internet of Things, network security, information systems, IT governance, and intrusion detection. She has published over 20 papers, including book chapters, international journals, and conferences/workshops.

Dr. Zaydi has also served and continues to serve on executive and technical program committees, and as a reviewer for numerous international conferences and journals.

Prof. Yassine Maleh (http://orcid.org/0000-0003-4704-5364) is an associate professor of cybersecurity and IT governance at Sultan Moulay Slimane University, Morocco. He received the PhD in computer sciences in 2017. He is the founding chair of IEEE Consultant Network Morocco and founding president of the African Research Center of Information Technology & Cybersecurity. He is a senior member of IEEE and a member of the International Association of Engineers (IAENG) and the Machine Intelligence Research Labs. Dr. Maleh has made contributions in the fields of information security and privacy, Internet of Things security, wireless and constrained networks security. His research interests include information security and privacy, Internet of Things, networks security, information system, and IT governance. He has published more than 100 papers (book chapters, international journals, and conferences/workshops), 17 edited books, and 3 authored books. He is the editor-in-chief of the International Journal of Information Security and Privacy, and the International Journal of Smart Security Technologies (IJSST). He serves as an associate editor for IEEE Access (2019 Impact Factor 4.098), the International Journal of Digital Crime and Forensics (IJDCF), and the International Journal of Information Security and

Privacy (IJISP). Dr. Maleh is a series editor of Advances in Cybersecurity Management, by CRC Taylor & Francis. He was also a guest editor of a special issue on Recent Advances on Cyber Security and Privacy for Cloud-of-Things of the International Journal of Digital Crime and Forensics (IJDCF), Volume 10, Issue 3, July–September 2019. He has served and continues to serve on executive and technical program committees and as a reviewer of numerous international conferences and journals such as Elsevier Ad Hoc Networks, IEEE Network Magazine, IEEE Sensor Journal, ICT Express, and Springer Cluster Computing. He was the Publicity chair of BCCA 2019 and the General Chair of the MLBDACP 19 symposium and ICI2C'21 Conference. He received Publons Top 1% reviewer award for the years 2018 and 2019.

Prof. Gabriel Chênevert is the Head of the Computer Science & Mathematics Department at JUNIA, and an associate professor of mathematics and computer science in charge of the Cybersecurity track at JUNIA ISEN. He specializes in subjects such as information theory, Fourier analysis, quantum computing and cybersecurity, with a particular focus on cryptography. With a strong background in arithmetical geometry and computational algebra, he has worked on error-correcting codes, elliptic curve cryptography, homomorphic encryption, and post-quantum cryptography.

Prof. Hayat Zaydi is a professor of computer science at the National Superior School of Mines in Rabat (ENSMR), Morocco. She is a Cisco Academy instructor and a member of the International Association of Engineers (IAENG). Her academic contributions cover various aspects of the Internet of Things (IoT), with a specialized focus on its implications in healthcare. She has also conducted extensive research in artificial intelligence (AI) and architectural concepts, including edge computing, fog computing, and cloud computing. A significant area of her research centres on cybersecurity mechanisms within these data-driven hybrid architectures, particularly when implementing machine learning and deep learning algorithms. Other aspects of her work involve big data, as well as optimization and load balancing in IoMT (Internet of Medical Things) architectures.

Prof. Zaydi has published numerous papers, including book chapters, international journals, and conferences. She has actively participated in organizing and serving on technical program committees and has contributed as a reviewer for numerous international conferences and journals.

Prof. Amina EL Yaagoubi is a lecturer-researcher of Mathematics and Computer Sciences at Engineering School JUNIA ISEN, France. She has expertise in combinatorial and multi-objective optimization, mathematical programming, and operations research. She is a member of the European Working Group "Multiple Criteria Decision Aiding." She completed her PhD degree in Mathematics and Computer Sciences and subsequently pursued a postdoctoral research position for three years at Le Havre Normandy University in France. She is the author of numerous scientific publications, including journal papers, conference papers, and book chapters. Dr. El Yaagoubi's research focuses on the application of optimization techniques in logistics and transportation, encompassing both inland and maritime transportation domains. She is actively engaged in the research community and serves as a reviewer for various international journals and participates in the organizing and scientific committees of different conferences.